REPUBLIC OF TEXAS: POLL LISTS FOR 1846

Compiled by

MARION DAY MULLINS

Baltimore

GENEALOGICAL PUBLISHING CO., INC.

1982

Library of Congress Cataloging in Publication Data

Mullins, Marion Day, 1893-
    Republic of Texas poll lists for 1846.

      1. Texas—Genealogy. 2 Poll-tax—Texas.
I. Title.
F385.M84   929'.3764   73-17065
ISBN 0-8063-0598-3

FOREWORD

In 1836, at great cost in lives and property, the province of Texas gained its independence from Mexico and immediately proclaimed itself The Republic of Texas. It set up a form of government similar to that of its neighbor, the United States. About four-fifths of the citizens of this new Republic had migrated into the province from the United States. As early as 1820-1821 people from the various states began emigrating into the northern territory of Mexico. Moses Austin, recently from Missouri, petitioned the Mexican government for empresario rights to settle immigrants in this vast empty land. The father's mantle soon fell upon the son, Stephen F. Austin, who explored an area both fertile and rich in natural resources and set about bringing in his settlers. Other ambitious citizen-adventurers followed the Austin example and applied for empresario contracts. In the years prior to 1836, with the exception of a period when the door was closed to Anglo-Americans, more than twenty such grants were confirmed by the Mexican government. However, of that number only seven were even partially fulfilled.

When Mexico surrendered control of the province the newly proclaimed Republic found itself with a small population which was spread mainly along its Louisiana boundary and along the rivers that flowed into the Gulf and along the Gulf of Mexico itself. Yet it possessed millions of acres of land known only to wandering and hostile Indians. As a means of support the legislature established a system of taxation—an experience new to the inhabitants, for Mexico had previously granted them land free of taxation in return for settlement and development. Even with this income the Republic found itself deeper in debt each year.

The citizens of the Republic resolutely objected to the return to the empresario system, fearing an influx of the wrong kind of settlers. When Sam Houston was elected president for the second time, in 1841, he convinced the people that only lands beyond their frontiers would be open to newcomers. These emigrants would serve a dual purpose; not only would they develop new land but they would also provide a buffer against the Indians. In 1841 Houston made the first contract for the Republic with the Texas Agricultural, Commercial and Manufacturing Company, familiarly known as Peter's Colony. Through a series of grants during the next five years the Peters brothers and their associates settled at least 1,800 families on open land in the northern part of the country. One of the earliest settlements was Dallas. The Peter's Colony contract was the largest ever undertaken for the settlement of emigrants, and one more nearly fulfilled than any other. In the opinion of Attorney-General Caleb Cushing, by the time the contractors' agreement expired Peter's Colony had settled 8,145 persons (one-twelfth of the population of the Republic at that time).

At about the same time Peter's Colony was being developed another, much smaller enterprise known as Mercer's Colony, with land located south-east of the Peter's territory, was getting underway. In 1843 the German Emigration Company acquired the Fisher-Miller grant and in 1844 a ship from Bremen arrived at Galveston with 700 settlers. By slow degrees the settlers moved toward their land in the interior of the country, their destination New Braunfels. 4,304 settlers came to this settlement from Germany in 1845, and 2,376 in 1846. In 1842 Henri Castro petitioned the Republic for a colonization contract. One tract assigned to him was along the Rio Grande River, the other west of San Antonio. The next year 114 emigrants arrived from LeHavre. Castro ultimately brought in a total of 2,134 new citizens. Castroville, D'Hanis and Quihi are among the existing towns founded by them. Simultaneously, other streams of emigrants were entering the country without empresario sponsorship. The last six years of the Republic saw much growth and development, with a great deal of new territory opened for settlement. By 1846, when Texas became the thirty-sixth state, there were sixty-seven county governments already organized as functioning units of the state.

James M. Day, Director of Texas Archives at the time this present poll list was researched, writes about the manuscript documents as follows: "Housed in the Archives Division of the Texas State Library, the manuscript tax rolls consist of 5,718 bulky volumes. They cover the years 1836-1901, beginning in each county with that unit's organization. . . . The books were compiled in the office of the State Comptroller, shifted to the Records Division of the Texas State Library in 1957-1958, and transferred to the Archives in 1962. Some are in a deplorable state of repair."

This 1846 poll list is the nearest thing we have to a complete census of the period. A "Poll" tax of one dollar was applied to every white male resident over the age of twenty-one and to women who were heads of households (usually widows). In making the tax rolls the assessor was required to prepare at least two alphabetical copies from his original lists. One copy went to the State Treasurer and one to the Sheriff who made the collections. Spelling of names was rendered according to sound, so the researcher is advised to try all possible variants of a name.

NAME	COUNTY	NAME	COUNTY
Abott, W. C.	Liberty	Adams, H.	Travis
Abby, James W.	Polk	Adams, H. H.	Cherokee
Abell, James C.	Colorado	Adams, Harvey	Austin
Abell, Thomas G.	Travis	Adams, J. W.	Harrison
Abels, G. B.	Red River	Adams, Jesse	Red River
Abercrombie,		Adams, John	Goliad
Seriney	Lavaca	Adams, John	Nacogdoches
Ables, Andrew	Nacogdoches	Adams, Mrs. L. G.	Harrison
Ables, E.	Henderson	Adams, Margaret	Fannin
Ables, Ezekiel	Henderson	Adams, Mary Jane	Panola
Ables, Ezekiel,		Adams, Richard	Red River
Sr.	Nacogdoches	Adams, S. E.	Lamar
Ables, Ezekiel,		Adams, Spencer	Cherokee
Jr.	Nacogdoches	Adams, Thomas J.	Wharton
Ables, H.	Henderson	Adams, W. H.	Houston
Ables, Harrison	Rusk	Adams, Warren	Galveston
Ables, J.	Henderson	Adams, William	Anderson
Ables, John	Nacogdoches	Adams, William	Fayette
Ables, Joseph E.	Henderson	Adams, William	Rusk
Ables, Joseph S.	Cherokee	Adams, William H.	Harrison
Ables, Joseph S.	Henderson	Adams, William L.	Walker
Absher, Asa	Galveston	Addison, G. S.	Burleson
Absher, Benjamin,		Addison, Isaac,	
Jr.	Liberty	Jr.	Burleson
Absher, Benjamin,		Addison, Isaac S.,	
Sr.	Liberty	Sr.	Burleson
Absher, Edward	Nacogdoches	Addison, James M.	Burleson
Absher, Jacob	Rusk	Addison, Joseph J.	Burleson
Ackerman, V. P.	Washington	Addison, Nathaniel	Jasper
Ackinson, Henry	Denton	Addison, O. M.	Burleson
Acock, Winifred	Anderson	Addison, W. F.	Brazoria
Acosta, Juan	Bexar	Adeste, Dolores	Bexar
Acosta, Maria	Nacogdoches	Adeste, Jesus	Bexar
Acosta, Nocolos	Nacogdoches	Adkeson, John	Austin
Acosta, San Hidro	Nacogdoches	Adkeson, John T.	Austin
Acres, Henry	Hopkins	Adkins, H. C.	Harrison
Acres, Smith	Hopkins	Adkins, J. W.	Houston
Adams, Alexander	Victoria	Adkins, Peter	Harrison
Adams, Ard.	Sabine	Adkins, William L.	Fayette
Adams, B. F.	Shelby	Adkinson, A. J.	Fayette
Adams, B. H.	Houston	Adkinson, Agrippa	Nacogdoches
Adams, Benjamin	Lamar	Adkinson, Henry	Anderson
Adams, C. B.	Galveston	Adler & Cohen	Sabine
Adams, C. W.	Galveston	Adriance, C. G.	Colorado
Adams, Christian	Titus	Adriance, John	Brazoria
Adams, D. H.	Harrison	Adriance, John	Goliad
Adams, Daniel	Henderson	Agassio, Jose	Henderson
Adams, David	Galveston	Agry, Edward H.	Gonzales
Adams, Dorothy	Houston	Ahlers, George	Brazoria

NAME	COUNTY	NAME	COUNTY
Ahuns, Henry	Brazoria	Alfred, G. G.	Houston
Aikin, James	Newton	Alfred, Hatch	Austin
Ainsworth, A. S.	Polk	Alfred, Isaac	Austin
Ainsworth, J. P.	Polk	Alfred, James	Shelby
Akin, Colin M.	Bowie	Alfred, James P.	Bowie
Akin, James	Bowie	Alfred, John	Austin
Akin, William	Bowie	Alfred, Kemp	Austin
Akis, Jacob	Cass	Alfred, L. P.	Henderson
Akridge, E.	Guadalupe	Alfred, M. A. E.	Henderson
Alameda, Jose	Bexar	Alfred, Mary M.	Austin
Alamis, Gertrudus	Bexar	Alfred, Nedom	San Augustine
Albrecht, Blasius	Comal	Alfred, Right	Austin
Alby, Abraham	Colorado	Algier, R. N.	Liberty
Alby, William	Colorado	Allbright, A. F.	Newton
Alcantosa, Rafael	Bexar	Allbright, Edward	Houston
Alcantro, Pedro	Victoria	Allbright, George	Houston
Alderette, Miguel	Victoria	Allbright, Jacob	Houston
Alders, Thomas	Nacogdoches	Allbright, Solomon	Houston
Aldrette, Dolores	Goliad	Allbright, T.	Houston
Aldrich, Elizabeth	Houston	Allbright, W. L.	Austin
Aldrich, George	Houston	Allbright, Wm.	Houston
Aldridge, Joel W.	Angelina	Allcorn, G. J.	Brazos
Aldridge, John A.	Angelina	Allcorn, J. D.	Brazos
Aldridge, William B.	Brazoria	Allcorn, James D.	Washington
Aldridge & Davis	Brazoria	Allcorn, John H.	Washington
Alexander, A.	Cass	Allcorn, Thomas J.	Washington
Alexander, C. C.	Smith	Allcorn, Wm. E.	Washington
Alexander, C. H.	Shelby	Allen, A.	Harrison
Alexander, C. P.	San Augustine	Allen, Alfred	Red River
Alexander, Daniel	Burleson	Allen, B.	Henderson
Alexander, E.	Lamar	Allen, B. C.	Milam
Alexander, F. A.	San Augustine	Allen, Benjamin	Austin
Alexander, H. N.	Henderson	Allen, Brazeal	Bowie
Alexander, J. L.	San Augustine	Allen, Burtis	Cherokee
Alexander, J. M.	Henderson	Allen, Caroline	Austin
Alexander, John M.	Polk	Allen, Clement	Austin
Alexander, John R.	Fayette	Allen, D. Y.	Fannin
Alexander, L. W.	Colorado	Allen, Daniel	Goliad
Alexander, M. F.	Washington	Allen, David	Red River
Alexander, Moses	Colorado	Allen, Dixon	Hunt
Alexander, R.	Galveston	Allen, E. H.	Grimes
Alexander, S. G.	Harrison	Allen, E. J.	Fannin
Alexander, Samuel	Fayette	Allen, Elijah	Jasper
Alexander, T. D.	Bastrop	Allen, Elijah	Jefferson
Alexander, W. R.	Harrison	Allen, Elijah	Nacogdoches
Alexander, William	Goliad	Allen, Elisha	Jefferson
Alfero, Guadalupe	Smith	Allen, Ferrill	San Augustine
Alford, Winifred	Austin	Allen, George	Anderson
Alfred, B. D.	Bowie	Allen, George	Bexar
		Allen, George	Jefferson

NAME	COUNTY	NAME	COUNTY
Allen, George	Leon	Allen, William	Jasper
Allen, George E.	Brazoria	Allen, William	Lavaca
Allen, H.	Bexar	Allen, William A.	Fannin
Allen, H. H.	Harris	Allen, William K.	Cass
Allen, H. R.	Harris	Alley, Daniel N.	Cass
Allen, H. S.	Fannin	Alley, James	Cass
Allen, Harriet E.	Brazoria	Alley, John	Jackson
Allen, Hugh	Guadalupe	Alley, William	Jackson
Allen, Hugh	Titus	Allinson, J.	Henderson
Allen, J. E.	Henderson	Allison, Elihu	Houston
Allen, J. J.	Fayette	Allison, Elijah	Lamar
Allen, J. J.	San Augustine	Allison, James	Henderson
Allen, J. T.	Austin	Allison, James	Houston
Allen, James L.	Jackson	Allison, John	Harrison
Allen, James R.	Austin	Allison, John	Panola
Allen, Jared	Nacogdoches	Allison, Thomas	Panola
Allen, John	Austin	Allison, W. F. A.	Houston
Allen, John	Cherokee	Allison, William	
Allen, John	Fannin	E.	Houston
Allen, John	Jasper	Allred, Alford	Panola
Allen, John A.	Cass	Allred, Elijah	Panola
Allen, John M.	Jasper	Allred, Panola	Panola
Allen, John W.	Sabine	Allred, Stephen	Rusk
Allen, Joseph	Jackson	Allston, Henry	Montgomery
Allen, M.	Henderson	Allston, James	Bastrop
Allen, M. H.	Henderson	Allston, N. K.	Montgomery
Allen, Margaret	Cherokee	Allston, S. F.	Harrison
Allen, Mary	Fannin	Almaguer, Eucebia	Goliad
Allen, Moses	Fannin	Almance, Ygancia	Bexar
Allen, Moses	Jefferson	Almey, William	Grimes
Allen, Nathaniel	Jasper	Alsabrook, William	
Allen, P. A.	Jackson	H.	Limestone
Allen, Phebe	Jackson	Alsberry, Young T.	Brazoria
Allen, R. E.	Cass	Alsup, N. G.	Bastrop
Allen, R. J.	Henderson	Alvice, William	Shelby
Allen, R. J.	Montgomery	Amacker, William	Guadalupe
Allen, Reuben	Grayson	Amadar, J.	Bexar
Allen, Richard	Cass	Amason, Jesse	Shelby
Allen, Richard	Refugie	Ambrose, Armstrong	Rusk
Allen, Robert B.	Rusk	Ames, Charles	Cass
Allen, Samuel	Cass	Ames, Joseph	Fannin
Allen, Samuel	Fayette	Amminecker, Joseph	Victoria
Allen, T. J.	Bastrop	Ammons, Jesse	Grimes
Allen, T. J.	San Augustine	Amory, Nathaniel	Nacogdoches
Allen, Thomas D.	Goliad	Ampana, Ma de	Bexar
Allen, Thomas M.	Fannin	Amsley, Charles C.	Austin
Allen, Thompson	Sabine	Amsley, Mark	Austin
Allen, W.	Henderson	Anders, James	Montgomery
Allen, W. B.	Fannin	Anders, John	Montgomery
Allen, W. S.	San Augustine	Anderson, Mrs.	Grimes

NAME	COUNTY	NAME	COUNTY
Anderson, A. F.	Bastrop	Anderson, Maxfield	Harrison
Anderson, A. P.	Nacogdoches	Anderson, O. H.	Panola
Anderson, B.	Nacogdoches	Anderson, Perry	Shelby
Anderson, B. W.	Henderson	Anderson, Quinton	Navarro
Anderson, Bailey	Harrison	Anderson, R. G.	Nacogdoches
Anderson, Bailey,		Anderson, S. R.	Henderson
Jr.	Harrison	Anderson, T. H.	Nacogdoches
Anderson, Baley H.	Panola	Anderson, T. K.	Jasper
Anderson, Ben W.	Nacogdoches	Anderson, T. W.	Henderson
Anderson, C.	Lamar	Anderson, Thomas	Harrison
Anderson, C. T.	Nacogdoches	Anderson, Thomas	Travis
Anderson, Calvin	Harrison	Anderson, Thomas	
Anderson,		K.	Dallas
Christian	Brazoria	Anderson, U. H.	Bastrop
Anderson, Elijah	Nacogdoches	Anderson, W. C.	Jasper
Anderson, F. A. E.	Shelby	Anderson, Walter	Montgomery
Anderson, H. G.	Washington	Anderson,	
Anderson, Hampton	Harrison	Washington	Travis
Anderson, Holland		Anderson, William	Harrison
L.	Panola	Anderson, William	Rusk
Anderson, Hugh	Limestone	Anderson, William	
Anderson, J.	Collin	B.	Fayette
Anderson, J.	Henderson	Anderson, William	
Anderson, J.	Rusk	G.	San Augustine
Anderson, J. B.	Lamar	Anderson, William	
Anderson, J. C.	Galveston	J.	Fayette
Anderson, J. C.	San Augustine	Anderson, William	
Anderson, Jacob	Robertson	N.	Navarro
Anderson, James	Dallas	Anderson, Wyatt	Montgomery
Anderson, James	Fannin	Anding, Abram	Houston
Anderson, James	Harrison	Andre, Nicholas	Bexar
Anderson, James H.	Panola	Andrews, C. K.	Harrison
Anderson, James W.	Dallas	Andrews, Isabella	Brazoria
Anderson, Jesse	Hunt	Andrews, James	Polk
Anderson, Joel	Milam	Andrews, Jesse	Shelby
Anderson, John	Anderson	Andrews, John	Jackson
Anderson, John	Hunt	Andrews, John D.	Harris
Anderson, John	Milam	Andrews, Lewis	Liberty
Anderson, John	Red River	Andrews, Mary	Fayette
Anderson, John D.	DeWitt	Andrews, Pamela	Fort Bend
Anderson, John D.	Gonzales	Andrews, R. H.	Galveston
Anderson, John E.	Panola	Andrews, Reddin	Fayette
Anderson, John H.	Panola	Andrews, Samuel	DeWitt
Anderson, Jonathan	Panola	Andrews, Susan A.	Fort Bend
Anderson, Jonathan	Shelby	Andrews, William	DeWitt
Anderson, Joseph	Wharton	Andrews, William	Red River
Anderson, M. B.	Nacogdoches	Angier, St., Jr.	Brazoria
Anderson, Margaret	Bastrop	Anglin, Abram	Limestone
Anderson, Matthew	Robertson	Anglin, Adron	Anderson
Anderson, Matthew	Travis	Anglin, Elisha	Limestone

NAME	COUNTY	NAME	COUNTY
Anglin, John	Anderson	H.	Sabine
Anglin, John	Henderson	Armstrong, John	Galveston
Anglin, John	Limestone	Armstrong, L. M.	Fort Bend
Anglin, John, Jr.	Limestone	Armstrong, Martha	Fort Bend
Anglin, M.	Limestone	Armstrong, Thomas	Brazoria
Anglin, Orpha	Limestone	Armstrong, William	Jefferson
Anglin, V. S.	Anderson	Armstrong, William	
Anglin, William	Limestone	T.	Washington
Anglin, William J.	Henderson	Arnett, Granville	Robertson
Anthony, A. B.	Leon	Arnett, J. C.	Tyler
Anthony, G. J.	Henderson	Arnett, J. H.	Limestone
Anthony, John	Henderson	Arnett, James	Tyler
Anthony, Jonathan	Henderson	Arnett, T. C.	Tyler
Anthony, L. B.	Henderson	Arnold, Abraham	Houston
Anthony, R.	San Augustine	Arnold, Catherine	Bexar
Antwell, J. R.	Titus	Arnold, D.	Grimes
Apperson, James	Henderson	Arnold, Daniel	Bexar
Applewhite, Isaac	Harris	Arnold, E.	Titus
Aquilar, F.	Bexar	Arnold, E. J.	Grimes
Aracha, S.	Nacogdoches	Arnold, E. J.	Montgomery
Arbuckle, Samuel	Polk	Arnold, E. L.	Grimes
Archer, Branch T.	Brazoria	Arnold, E. L.	Montgomery
Archer, Powhattan	Brazoria	Arnold, H.	Bexar
Archibald, Thomas	Robertson	Arnold, H. S.	Montgomery
Ardrey, J. M.	San Augustine	Arnold, Hayden	Nacogdoches
Ardrey, John N.	San Augustine	Arnold, James R.	Nacogdoches
Ariola, Gabriel	Bexar	Arnold, John	Comal
Armelong, Otho	Travis	Arnold, John	Lavaca
Armitage, H. K.	Lamar	Arnold, Levi	Harrison
Armour, James	Shelby	Arnold, Nelson	Galveston
Armour, Robert	Grimes	Arnold, Peter	Comal
Armstead, Robert		Arnold, Samuel	Harris
S.	Washington	Arnold, W. K.	Harrison
Armstrong, A.	Fort Bend	Arnspiger, David	Grayson
Armstrong, Aaron	Galveston	Arocha, Antonio	Bexar
Armstrong, Andrew	Jefferson	Arocha, B.	Bexar
Armstrong, Cavett	Robertson	Arocha, L.	Bexar
Armstrong, Edward	Goliad	Arocha, Ma Ygna	Bexar
Armstrong, George	Brazoria	Arocha, Maudonia	Bexar
Armstrong,		Arocha, Neporn	Bexar
Harriette	Harrison	Arrington,	
Armstrong, Irwin	Goliad	Claiborn	Cherokee
Armstrong, J.	Henderson	Arrington, Edmund	Cherokee
Armstrong, J. K.	Upshur	Arrington, Eli	Travis
Armstrong, James	Dallas	Arrington, G.	Henderson
Armstrong, James	Jefferson	Arrington, Joel	Titus
Armstrong, James	Liberty	Arrington, John S.	Cherokee
Armstrong, James		Arrington, N. B.	Red River
C.	Washington	Arrington, Thomas	
Armstrong, James		C.	Cherokee

5

NAME	COUNTY	NAME	COUNTY
Arrington, W. F.	Cass	Ashworth, William,	
Arrington, William	Grimes	Jr.	Jefferson
Arriola, Dolores	Grimes	Ashworth, William,	
Arriola, Eli	Grimes	Sr.	Jefferson
Arriola, Joseph	Grimes	Askew, Harrison	Gonzales
Arriola, Massimore	Grimes	Askew, Henry	Polk
Arthur, F.	Travis	Askew, John	Bowie
Arthur, Francis	Bexar	Askew, Levi H.	Nacogdoches
Arthur, William	Jefferson	Askew, S. A.	Brazoria
Arvill, Timothy S.	Burleson	Askew, W. S.	Burleson
Asbury, Robert	Cass	Askew, William	Polk
Asbury, S.	Leon	Askins, Charles	Henderson
Ash, Jacob E.	Houston	Askins, Charles	Lamar
Ash, Robert	Hopkins	Askins, Charles	Shelby
Ashby, Jeremiah S.	Hopkins	Askins, James W.	Shelby
Ashcraft, L. H.	Shelby	Askins, Thomas	Lamar
Asher, James	DeWitt	Askins, Wesley	Lamar
Asher, Pleasant	DeWitt	Asocha, Jose	Henderson
Asher, Thomas	DeWitt	Atkins, Daniel	Nacogdoches
Asher, William J.	DeWitt	Atkins, Joseph	Galveston
Asherbraner,		Atkins, William	Montgomery
George G.	Panola	Atkinson, Alfred	Cherokee
Asherbraner, Henry	Shelby	Atkinson, Bossey	Victoria
Ashley, A. N.	Lamar	Atkinson, J. B.	Washington
Ashley, James	Lamar	Atkinson, Mary	Travis
Ashley, James	Milam	Atkisson, Arthur	Rusk
Ashley, John A.	Lamar	Atkisson, John S.	Rusk
Ashley, Josiah	Lamar	Atterberry, Jesse	Dallas
Ashley, Nancy	Lamar	Atterberry, Nathan	Dallas
Ashley, William	Lamar	Atwell, James	Matagorda
Ashley, Willis	Nacogdoches	Atwell, P. M.	Titus
Ashlock, M. M.	Collin	Atwood, James B.	Henderson
Ashmore, Baily	Hopkins	Augustine, H. W.	San Augustine
Ashmore, J. E.	Hopkins	Aulanier, Alphonso	Galveston
Ashmore, N.	San Augustine	Austin, David	Fort Bend
Ashmore, Spencer	Sabine	Austin, David	Goliad
Ashton, C. D.	Nacogdoches	Austin, Edward T.	Brazoria
Ashworth, Aaron	Jefferson	Austin, Ephraim	Anderson
Ashworth, Aaron,		Austin, G. J.	Harrison
Jr.	Jefferson	Austin, Henry	Galveston
Ashworth, Abner	Jefferson	for Mrs. Holley	
Ashworth, David	Jefferson	Austin, Henry	Grimes
Ashworth,		Austin, J.	Brazos
Henderson	Jefferson	Austin, Norris	Sabine
Ashworth, Hetta	Jefferson	Austin, Richard H.	Harrison
Ashworth, Jesse	Jefferson	Austin, S. F.	Brazos
Ashworth, Joshua	Jefferson	Austin, William	Colorado
Ashworth, LeeRe	Jefferson	Austin, William D.	Fort Bend
Ashworth, Louisa	Jefferson	Austin, William	
Ashworth, Mary	Jefferson	Henry	Brazoria

NAME	COUNTY	NAME	COUNTY
Austin, William T.	Brazoria	Bahliman, J.	Galveston
Auston, J. L.	Henderson	Bahling, Charles	Galveston
Auton, R.	Anderson	Bailes, Alfred	Polk
Avant, D.	Anderson	Bailey, A.	Wharton
Avant, William	Houston	Bailey, Alexander	Austin
Avery, Charles	Austin	Bailey, C. C.	Cass
Avery, Ingram	Harrison	Bailey, Celia	Burleson
Avery, Polly Ann	Harrison	Bailey, Elijah	Burleson
Avery, Warren	Galveston	Bailey, I. J.	Cass
Avery, William	Harrison	Bailey, J. B.	Galveston
Awalt, Henry	Rusk	Bailey, J. C.	Red River
Awocha, Mary	Henderson	Bailey, James	Harris
Aycock, R. M.	Brazoria	Bailey, John H.	Fannin
Ayguar, Ulyses	Red River	Bailey, Lucinda	Brazoria
Aylott, William	Galveston	Bailey, Marcus	Galveston
Ayres, Alfred	Austin	Bailey, Nathaniel	Polk
Ayres, B. P.	Shelby	Bailey, O. P.	Victoria
Ayres, David	Galveston	Bailey, W.	Cass
Ayres, Edward	Refugio	Bailey, Winford	Milam
Ayres, John	Austin	Bain, N. M.	Austin
Ayres, Raymond	Fayette	Bainbroot, Charley	Henderson
Ayres, Thomas	Jackson	Bains, J.	Henderson
		Bains, William C.	Panola
		Baird, A.	Liberty
Babbitt, R. R.	San Augustine	Baird, A. J.	Polk
Babbitt, Sarah	Austin	Baird, Andrew	Polk
Baccus, Enoch	Lamar	Baird, David	Lamar
Baccus, G. S.	Collin	Baird, J. M.	Fannin
Baccus, J.	Collin	Baird, James	Fort Bend
Baccus, P.	Collin	Baird, Joseph	Polk
Bachelder, L. G.	Galveston	Baird, S. M.	Montgomery
Backburns, A. J.	Fayette	Baird, S. M.	Nacogdoches
Bacon, Elizabeth	San Augustine	Baird, William W.	Grimes
Bacon, John B.	Travis	Baker, A. E.	San Augustine
Bacon, Thomas H.	Travis	Baker, A. P.	Brazoria
Baden, Marmaduke	Burleson	Baker, A. P.	Goliad
Bader, Englebert	Grimes	Baker, Abram	Jackson
Bader, Joseph	Bexar	Baker, Basil	Montgomery
Badger, James	Harris	Baker, Benjamin	Cass
Badgley, David A.	Dallas	Baker, C. C.	Lamar
Badgley, Job	Dallas	Baker, Charles	Colorado
Bagatt, James	Tyler	Baker, Charles	Dallas
Bagby, B. C.	Red River	Baker, Charles	Goliad
Bagby, G. H.	Red River	Baker, Daniel	Fayette
Bagby, Henry	Washington	Baker, Daniel	Henderson
Bagby, John A.	Red River	Baker, Daniel	Panola
Bagby, Thomas M.	Harris	Baker, Edward	Polk
Bagley, Henry H.	Panola	Baker, Eli R.	Jasper
Bags, H. L.	Montgomery	Baker, G. W.	Anderson
Bagwell, Milor	Red River	Baker, George E.	Cass

7

NAME	COUNTY	NAME	COUNTY
Baker, H.	Red River	Baldwin, William	
Baker, H. N.	Travis	J.	Grimes
Baker, Henry	Grayson	Baleman, Micajah	Limestone
Baker, Henry	Lamar	Baley, Henry	Nacogdoches
Baker, Isaac	Grimes	Baley, J. H.	Titus
Baker, J.	Cass	Baley, Jeremiah	Nacogdoches
Baker, J. H. L.	San Augustine	Baley, John	Nacogdoches
Baker, J. L.	Walker	Baley, Reuben	Nacogdoches
Baker, J. M.	Cass	Ball, Albert	Galveston
Baker, James	Fannin	Ball, E.	Red River
Baker, James	Travis	Ball, George	Galveston
Baker, James M.	DeWitt	Ball, S. D.	San Augustine
Baker, John	Gonzales	Ball, William McK.	Leon
Baker, John	Grimes	Ballance, R. C.	Newton
Baker, John	Guadalupe	Ballansweller, R.	Houston
Baker, John	Henderson	Ballard, B. M.	Red River
Baker, John	Limestone	Ballard,	
Baker, John W.	Panola	Callotrines	Lavaca
Baker, Joseph	Lamar	Ballard, John	Red River
Baker, Joseph L.	DeWitt	Ballard, Robert	Harrison
Baker, L. D.	Grimes	Ballard, Ryland C.	Goliad
Baker, Moseley	Harris	Ballard, V. Volla	
Baker, N. N.	Red River	Fernes	Lavaca
Baker, Thomas C.	Fannin	Ballou, S. T.	Grimes
Baker, W.	Henderson	Bamon, C.	Brazoria
Baker, W. C.	Fannin	Bane, ----	Henderson
Baker, W. H.	Montgomery	Banes, Moses	Washington
Baker, W. W.	Nacogdoches	Bankhead, George	Navarro
Baker, Walter E.	Grimes	Banks, Joel	Angelina
Baker, Walter E.	Limestone	Banks, John B.	Washington
Baker, William	Dallas	Banks, R. J.	Cherokee
Baker, William	Guadalupe	Bankston, James	Red River
Baker, William R.	Fannin	Banner, Nathan	Jefferson
Baker, William R.	Galveston	Banta, Henry	Hunt
Baker, William R.	Harris	Banta, Isaac	Hunt
Baker, WIlliam W.	Cass	Banta, William	Lamar
Baker, Y.	Grimes	Banton, G. W.	Walker
Balch, John	Nacogdoches	Barbee,	
Balden, ---	Henderson	Christopher	Panola
Baldinger, A.	Galveston	Barbee, James G.	Shelby
Baldridge, H. B.	Lavaca	Barbee, Joseph	Fannin
Baldridge, James	Jefferson	Barbee, M. E.	Harrison
Baldridge, James		Barbee, Marshall	San Augustine
W.	Washington	Barbee, Mrs. Susan	
Baldridge, W. H.	Lavaca	P.	Harrison
Baldus, Charles J.	Comal	Barbee, T. S.	Harrison
Baldwin, H.	Galveston	Barber, Adison	Liberty
Baldwin, John	Cherokee	Barber, Amos	Liberty
Baldwin, William		Barber, Benjamin	Liberty
F.	Harrison	Barber, George	Shelby

NAME	COUNTY	NAME	COUNTY
Barber, John	Liberty	Barksdale, Callier	Nacogdoches
Barber, P. W.	Shelby	Barksdale, Lewis	Fayette
Barber, Reuben	Liberty	Barksdale, P. C.	Rusk
Barber, William	Bastrop	Barksdale, R. H.	Dallas
Barbo, Anthony Y.	Henderson	Barlow, John H.	Dallas
Barcelo, Juan	Bexar	Barnard, Abram	Dallas
Barckney, John	Red River	Barnard, Stephen	Fort Bend
Barclay, A.	Tyler	Barnes, Benjamin	Cass
Barclay, David	Limestone	Barnes, C. A.	Grimes
Barclay, David	Tyler	Barnes, Harrison	Newton
Barclay, James	Tyler	Barnes, J. M.	Rusk
Barclay, Sarah	Tyler	Barnes, James	Tyler
Barclay, Walter	Tyler	Barnes, James	Wharton
Barden, Jesse	Fayette	Barnes, James W.	Grimes
Barden, Thomas	Fayette	Barnes, John M.	Cass
Barden, W.	Fayette	Barnes, John S.	Cass
Barecroft, Daniel	Cass	Barnes, Moses	San Augustine
Barecroft, Daniel,		Barnes, Samuel	Milam
Jr.	Cass	Barnes, Talton G.	Titus
Barecroft, E. H.	Cass	Barnes, W. M.	Tyler
Barecroft, E. H.	Cass	Barnes, William	Cass
Barefield, J.C.	Leon	Barnes, William	Wharton
Barefield, J. H.	Leon	Barnes, William A.	Limestone
Barefield, J. L.	Leon	Barnes, William D.	Dallas
Barefield, T. J.	Leon	Barnet(t), D. C.	Goliad
Barefield, W. C.	Leon	Barnet, E.	Lamar
Barefoot, Bareing	Titus	Barnet, E. D.	Red River
Barens, W. H.	Dallas	Barnet, Eli	Lamar
Barention, Joseph	Harrison	Barnet, G. W.	Lamar
Barker, B.	Cass	Barnet, George	Red River
Barker, Calvin	Bastrop	Barnet, James	Fort Bend
Barker, D.	Hunt	Barnet, James	Lamar
Barker, James A.	Grimes	Barnet, Len	Gonzales
Barker, James S.	Dallas	Barnet, P. S.	Gonzales
Barker, Jesse		Barnet, Richard T.	Gonzales
(decd)	Bastrop	Barnet, Sally	Harris
Barker, Leman	Bastrop	Barnet, W. H.	Rusk
Barker, Robert	Grimes	Barney, R.	Bastrop
Barker, William	Hopkins	Barney, S. A.	Guadalupe
Barker, William	Walker	Barnhill, William	Henderson
Barker, William,		Barnoba, J. T.	Rusk
Jr.	Hopkins	Barr, John	Grayson
Barkley, A. G.	Rusk	Barret, A. G.	Houston
Barkley, N.	Harris	Barret, John	Brazoria
Barkley, N.	Walker	Barret, John, Jr.	Nacogdoches
Barkley, Richard	Fayette	Barret, Martin H.	Titus
Barkman, James D.	Bowie	Barret, Sarah	San Augustine
Barkman, James W.	Bowie	Barret, Sidney	Grimes
Barkman, John	Bowie	Barret, Thomas C.	Nacogdoches
Barkman, John, Jr.	Bowie	Barret(t), William	Brazoria

9

NAME	COUNTY	NAME	COUNTY
Barret, William W.	Walker	G.	Panola
Barrickman, Joshua	Anderson	Barziza, Francis	
Barrier, A.	Fayette	L.	Limestone
Barrier, Micajah	Fayette	Basey, Jonas	Nacogdoches
Barritte, J. W.	Harrison	Bass, A.	Victoria
Barritte, J. W.	Montgomery	Bass, Cintha M.	Polk
Barron, David	Angelina	Bass, Joseph	Newton
Barron, G. M.	Brazos	Bass, Robert	Newton
Barron, H. P.	Nacogdoches	Bass, T. R.	Gonzales
Barron, H. R.	Henderson	Bass, William A.	Polk
Barron, J. M.	Milam	Bass, William P.	Lavaca
Barron, Samuel	Harris	Bass, Willis	Sabine
Barron, Thomas	Milam	Basset, C. N.	Harris
Barrow, A. L.	Liberty	Basset, John	Bowie
Barrow, Benj., Jr.	Liberty	Bassford, E. S.	Fayette
Barrow, Benj., Sr.	Liberty	Bassford, W. P.	Fayette
Barrow, Levi	Liberty	Basson, Fielding	Grayson
Barrow, Reuben,		Basson, H.	Galveston
Jr.	Liberty	Batae, Adam	Navarro
Barrow, Reuben,		Batae, Rachel	Navarro
Sr.	Liberty	Bateman, Ekisar	Red River
Barrow, Samuel	Gonzales	Bateman, Evan	Red River
Barrow, Samuel C.	Jasper	Bateman, Isaac	Bowie
Barrow, Solomon	Liberty	Bateman, Isaac	Red River
Barrow, Z. A.	Jasper	Bateman, James	Red River
Barry, D. N.	Red River	Bateman, Jonathan	Red River
Barry, J. W.	Lavaca	Bates, A. T.	Nacogdoches
Barry, L. D.	Red River	Bates, David E.	Nacogdoches
Barry, Samuel	Lavaca	Bates, E.	Galveston
Barry, William	Fannin	Bates, John C.	Lamar
Barry, William G.	Panola	Bates, Seth H.	Limestone
Bartlett, Charity	San Augustine	Bates, Silas H.	Limestone
Bartlett, George	San Augustine	Batey, Edward	Jackson
Bartlis, William	Austin	Batson, Daniel	Liberty
Barton, Albert	Limestone	Batson, Eli	Liberty
Barton, David	Limestone	Batson, F.	Liberty
Barton, David, Sr.	Limestone	Batson, Mary	Liberty
Barton, George M.	Anderson	Batson, Seth	Liberty
Barton, Irie	Titus	Batson, Thomas	Liberty
Barton, John	Limestone	Batte, W. C.	Titus
Barton, Kimber	DeWitt	Battin, Samuel	Nacogdoches
Barton, Robert	Limestone	Battle, J. R.	Bowie
Barton, S.	Bastrop	Battle, James W.	Bowie
Barton, Samuel	Goliad	Battle, M. M.	Fort Bend
Barton, Samuel	Limestone	Battle, O. D.	Bowie
Barton, W. F.	Bastrop	Battle, R. J.	Bowie
Barton, Wayne	Bastrop	Battle, William H.	Fort Bend
Barton, Zilpha	Rusk	Baty, Isiah	Anderson
Bartz, Adam	Bexar	Bauer, Charles	Grayson
Barxdall, Nathan		Baugh, Robert G.	Shelby

NAME	COUNTY	NAME	COUNTY
Baum, Jose de la	Bexar	Bean, William	Grayson
Baxter, B. B.	Washington	Bear, Brassillai	Grimes
Baxter, Charles	Galveston	Beard, A. S.	Cass
Baxter, Deborah	Galveston	Beard, William	Guadalupe
Baxter, E.	Bowie	Beard, William C.	Jefferson
Baxter, Henry	Matagorda	Bearton, John	Milam
Baxter, Joseph W.	Nacogdoches	Beasley, Charles	Limestone
Baxter, T. S.	Austin	Beasley, R. E.	Fannin
Baxter, William	Matagorda	Beasley, William	Grimes
Bayless, Hezekiah	Bowie	Beason, H. W.	Houston
Bayless, William		Beaty, A. B.	Victoria
C.	Brazos	Beaty, E.	Cass
Baylor, J. R. E.	Fayette	Beaty, G. W.	Walker
Baylor, R. E. B.	Fayette	Beaty, James	Harrison
Baylor, W. H.	Fayette	Beaty, John	Cass
Baylor, William M.	Fayette	Beaty, John	Harrison
Baylor, William R.	Fayette	Beaty, M. H.	Gonzales
Bayne, E. W.	Montgomery	Beaty, Thomas	Jasper
Bayne, G. H.	San Augustine	Beauchamp, A. G.	Lamar
Bayne, Griffin	Brazos	Beauchamp, James	Fayette
Bayne, William G.	Brazos	Beauchamp, N. H.	Lamar
Bayon, Michael	Angelina	Beavers, J.	Upshur
Bays, Peter	Walker	Beavers, W. H.	Cass
Bays, William B.	Brazoria	Beazle, Joseph	Fayette
Baysinger, Martin	Rusk	Beazley, E. C.	Harrison
Bayton, J. A.	Fayette	Bebe, Elnathan	Jackson
Beach, Vlark	Liberty	Beck, B.	Henderson
Beachamp, J. R.	Shelby	Beck, Charles	Sabine
Beachamp, John	Leon	Beck, J.	Henderson
Beagle, Thomas	Grayson	Beck, James	Leon
Beal, A. L.	Rusk	Beck, John	Shelby
Beal, John S.	Liberty	Beck, John	Travis
Beal, P. C.	Fayette	Beck, Samuel	Tyler
Beal, R. R.	Fannin	Beck, Sandford	Fannin
Beall, Elizabeth		Beck, T. B.	Travis
A.	Galveston	Beck, William	Shelby
Beall, John	Milam	Beckam, Samuel	Shelby
Beall, R. H.	Fort Bend	Becker, Jacob	Newton
Beams, Ezekiel	Shelby	Becknell, John	Titus
Bean, David M.	Cherokee	Becknell, William	Red River
Bean, E. M.	Cherokee	Becton, J. M.	Rusk
Bean, Isaac Y.	Cherokee	Becton, John	Victoria
Bean, Jane	Tyler	Bedsil, Matho	Tyler
Bean, Jesse E.	Cherokee	Bedsil, Orlando	Tyler
Bean, John R.	Grayson	Beede, M.	Henderson
Bean, John T.	Tyler	Beeks, William	Wharton
Bean, Peter E.	Henderson	Beeman, J. S.	Dallas
Bean, Robert	Grayson	Beeman, William H.	Fannin
Bean, T. C.	Fannin	Beemen, James J.	Dallas
Bean, Thomas C.	Grayson	Beene, Franklin H.	Smith

11

NAME	COUNTY	NAME	COUNTY
Beene, James K.	Smith	Bell, W. W.	Fannin
Beesley, James	Brazoria	Bell, W. W.	Henderson
Beesley, Michael	Brazoria	Bell, William	Nacogdoches
Beeson, Abell	Colorado	Bell, William G.	Austin
Beeson, James	Cherokee	Bell, Willis C.	Brazoria
Beeson, Leander	Colorado	Bell, Zulida	Brazoria
Beissner, C. L.	Galveston	Belliman, William	Austin
Bejina, A.	Bexar	Bellmer, Charles	Comal
Belcher, J. G.	Washington	Bellow, ------	Brazoria
Belcher, John	Rusk	Bellow, Elija	Navarro
Belcher, N. Edward	Rusk	Benedict, J. W.	Galveston
Belcher, Woody	Sabine	Benevides, E.	Calhoun
Belden & Parr	Calhoun	Benfer, George	Comal
Belknap, J. T.	Matagorda	Benge, A.	Houston
Bell, A. Jackson	Austin	Benge, T. O.	Red River
Bell, Alexander	Austin	Benge, W. B.	Red River
Bell, Andrew	Nacogdoches	Benites, Antonio	Bexar
Bell, Andrew H.	Bexar	Benjamin, B.	Rusk
Bell, Bluford	Nacogdoches	Benjamin, J. B.	Galveston
Bell, Charles N.	Nacogdoches	Benner, Adolphus	Comal
Bell, Christopher	Brazoria	Bennett, A.	Houston
Bell, Columbus	Shelby	Bennett, A. J.	Sabine
Bell, David	Victoria	Bennett, C.	Bowie
Bell, E.	Fannin	Bennett, C. M.	Lavaca
Bell, Emily A.	Brazoria	Bennett, Charles H.	Brazoria
Bell, Enoch	Grimes	Bennett, E.	Victoria
Bell, Hanibal	Shelby	Bennett, Elijah	Cass
Bell, J. J.	Leon	Bennett, Hiram	Dallas
Bell, James	Austin	Bennett, J. L.	Walker
Bell, James	Nacogdoches	Bennett, J. M.	Dallas
Bell, James H.	Austin	Bennett, Jacob	Rusk
Bell, James M.	DeWitt	Bennett, James	Grimes
Bell, John	Galveston	Bennett, James R.	Grimes
Bell, John	Rusk	Bennett, John	Jasper
Bell, John	Titus	Bennett, John H.	Galveston
Bell, John P.	Fayette	Bennett, Leroy	Panola
Bell, John S.	Grimes	Bennett, Marshall B.	Gonzales
Bell, John S.	Shelby	Bennett, Miles	Anderson
Bell, Johnston	Fannin	Bennett, Miles S.	DeWitt
Bell, Joseph T.	Austin	Bennett, Nancy	Grimes
Bell, Nancy M.	Brazoria	Bennett, Reuben W.	Grimes
Bell, Robert	Rusk	Bennett, S. C.	Bastrop
Bell, Robert A.	Fort Bend	Bennett, S. J.	Walker
Bell, Samuel	Nacogdoches	Bennett, Silas	Washington
Bell, Stephen	Fannin	Bennett, Steven	Anderson
Bell, Thadeus	Brazoria	Bennett, Steven	Lavaca
Bell, Thadeus	Goliad	Bennett, T. K.	Harrison
Bell, Thomas	Austin	Bennett, Theodore	Brazoria
Bell, Thomas	Shelby		
Bell, Thomas H.	Austin		

NAME	COUNTY	NAME	COUNTY
Bennett, W. H.	Dallas	Best, C. W.	Lavaca
Benningfield,		Best, E. W.	Lavaca
Posey	Red River	Best, Steven	Lavaca
Bennington, Reuben	Newton	Bethurum, Robert	Dallas
Benshorn, Henry	Comal	Betts, E.	Colorado
Benson, Herman	Galveston	Betts, J. S.	Montgomery
Benson, J.	Leon	Betts, Samuel S.	Austin
Bentick, H. W.	Galveston	Betts, Thomas	Montgomery
Bentley, Whitmill	Nacogdoches	Beuns, Manuel	Bexar
Benton, Charles	Austin	Bevenroth, Henry	Comal
Benton, B. F.	San Augustine	Bevil, A. M.	Jasper
Benton, Jesse	Cass	Bevil, Jehu	Jasper
Benton, W. H. L.	Houston	Bevil, John	Jasper
Benton, W. W.	Henderson	Bibb, Dandridge J.	Washington
Beokel, Christian	Comal	Bickerstaff, Henry	Titus
Berencky, Henry	Austin	Bickerstaff, J. M.	Titus
Bergais, J. S.	Bexar	Bickford, P.	Victoria
Bergstrom, Ivan	Brazoria	Biddle, Joshua	Bastrop
Berthelet, Heald &		Biddle, Lemuel M.	Brazoria
Co.	Fannin	Biddlecore, A.	Cass
Berry, Alfred	DeWitt	Biddy, Edward	Cass
Berry, Alfred	Goliad	Biers, W. H.	Rusk
Berry, Batson	Fort Bend	Bigger, Richard T.	Shelby
Berry, Dencalion		Bigger, Robert	Shelby
A.	Goliad	Biggs, Asa	Shelby
Berry, Francis	Gonzales	Biggs, David	Cherokee
Berry, J. W.	Guadalupe	Biggs, H. H.	Shelby
Berry, Jackson	Burleson	Biggs, J. H.	Bastrop
Berry, James	Colorado	Biggs, John	Galveston
Berry, James	Gonzales	Biggs, William J.	Limestone
Berry, James	Hopkins	Biggs, William T.	Shelby
Berry, John	Angelina	Biggs, Wilson	Shelby
Berry, John	Burleson	Biglow, William	Anderson
Berry, John	Colorado	Bigner, Fred	Houston
Berry, M.	Bexar	Bilderback, R. T.	Galveston
Berry, Morgan	Anderson	Biler, Abraham	Fayette
Berry, Thomas	Anderson	Biley, T. F.	Titus
Berry, Thos.	Anderson	Billhantz, Joseph	Bexar
Berry, Tilman	Gonzales	Billingsley,	
Berry, William	Anderson	Francis	Wharton
Berryhill, Thomas	Rusk	Billingsley, James	Navarro
Berryhill, W. M.	Henderson	Billingsley, Jesse	Bastrop
Berryhill, W. W.	Henderson	Billingsley, John	Navarro
Berryman, Westly	Grimes	Billingsley,	
Berryman, William	Grimes	Nathaniel	Navarro
Bert, L. P.	Fayette	Billingsley,	
Bertram, Jose	Henderson	Robert	Navarro
Bertrand, Gustavus	Brazoria	Billingsley,	
Bertrand, Thomas	Brazoria	Samuel	Navarro
Bessor, J. S.	Walker	Billingsley,	

13

NAME	COUNTY	NAME	COUNTY
Samuel C.	Wharton	Birmingham, C.	Houston
Billingsley,		Birmingham, Z.	Houston
William	Navarro	Birney, R. A.	Fannin
Billops, George R.	Jackson	Bisbee, Ira	Calhoun
Bines, Henry	Goliad	Bischer, Henry	Colorado
Bines, William H.	Fort Bend	Bishop, E. P.	Upshur
Bingham, Benton	Bowie	Bishop, Oliver	Hopkins
Bingham, Burton	Cass	Bishop, Thos.	Bowie
Bingham, Elisha	Bowie	Bishop, William N.	Cass
Bingham, Elisha	Cass	Bissel, Alfred	Panola
Bingham, Frank	Brazoria	Bissel, Theodore	Victoria
Bingham, Henry	Lamar	Bissell, Robert	San Augustine
Bingham, J. G.	Leon	Bittock, Jonathan	Panola
Bingham, James P.	Brazoria	Bivens, James	Hopkins
Bingham, M.	Anderson	Black, A. J.	Jefferson
Bingham, Mary	Nacogdoches	Black, Charles	Galveston
Bingham, Moses M.	Nacogdoches	Black, Edward	Panola
Binmant, John	Hopkins	Black, G. B.	Grimes
Binnion, Martin	Titus	Black, Henry M.	Newton
Binum, James	Houston	Black, J. W.	Victoria
Binum, Stephen	Houston	Black, James E.	Brazoria
Birch, James	Polk	Black, James P.	Washington
Birch, Montgomery	Fannin	Black, John	Bastrop
Birch, Samuel	Polk	Black, John	Fayette
Birch, Valentine	Polk	Black, John	Gonzales
Birchel, Lucas	Colorado	Black, John D.	Fannin
Bird, G. W.	Travis	Black, John R.	Bexar
Bird, T. B.	Travis	Black, John S.	Grimes
Bird, T. J.	Austin	Black, T. E.	Walker
Bird, William	Austin	Black, T. S.	Walker
Birdsall, M. L.	Harris	Black, William M.	Grimes
Birdsong,		Blackburn, A. J.	Fort Bend
Alexander	Panola	Blackburn, A. S.	Sabine
Birdsong, Jesse M.	Panola	Blackburn, Byres	Fannin
Birdsong, Morian	Panola	Blackburn, Eli	Rusk
Birdsong, William		Blackburn, Gabriel	Sabine
A.	Panola	Blackburn, Gideon	Lavaca
Birdwell, Allen	Rusk	Blackburn, J. L.	
Birdwell, Andrew	Rusk	D.	Fayette
Birdwell, E. M.	Bowie	Blackburn, James	Nacogdoches
Birdwell, Garner	Hopkins	Blackburn, Jesse	Bastrop
Birdwell, George	Hopkins	Blackburn, John	Nacogdoches
Birdwell, George	Rusk	Blackburn, Josiah	Liberty
Birdwell, Matthew	Rusk	Blackburn, Sarah	Shelby
Birdwell, T. G.	Walker	Blackburn, William	Shelby
Birdwell, W.	Henderson	Blackmon, David	Sabine
Birdwell, William	Hopkins	Blackmon, G. J.	Titus
Birdwell, William	Walker	Blackmon, J. G.	Titus
Birdwell, Zack	Lamar	Blackmore, Hermon	Hopkins
Birks, S. B.	Rusk	Blacksher, James	

NAME	COUNTY	NAME	COUNTY
Blackstock, John H.	Sabine	Blanton, Lemuel	Fannin
		Blanton, R. G.	Austin
Blackwell, Clayton	DeWitt	Blase, John	Rusk
Blackwell, J., Jr.	Walker	Bledsoe, Anthony	Dallas
Blackwell, J., Sr.	Walker	Bledsoe, James	Lamar
Blackwell, Thomas	Brazoria	Bledsoe, Levi	Fannin
Blackwell, William	Walker	Bledsoe, S. T.	Fannin
Blagg, James	Grayson	Bledsoe, William	Hopkins
Blagg, Samuel	Grayson	Blessing, Henry	Comal
Blagg, Sarah	Grayson	Blevins, ---	Fannin
Blagler, Phillip	Colorado	Blevins, John	Milam
Blain, B. A.	Limestone	Blevins, L. A. J.	Milam
Blair, A. J.	Titus	Blish, T. R.	Travis
Blair, Clarkey P.	Fayette	Blocker, William J.	Harrison
Blair, J. R.	Titus		
Blair, James	DeWitt	Blondeau, T. F.	Galveston
Blair, James	Fayette	Bloodgood, William	Grimes
Blair, John	Henderson	Bloodgood, William	Harris
Blair, John	Houston	Bloodworth, J. C.	Leon
Blair, Monro F.	DeWitt	Bloodworth, William J.	Limestone
Blair, Rosa	Galveston		
Blair, Sarah	DeWitt	Blossman, R. D.	Galveston
Blair, Thomas C.	Bastrop	Blount, S. W.	San Augustine
Blair, William	DeWitt	Blount, S. W. H.	San Augustine
Blair, William H.	Fayette	Blow, Hammond	Austin
Blake, Briant	Nacogdoches	Blume, Henry	Guadalupe
Blake, George W.	San Augustine	Blundell, Frank	Red River
Blake, Isaac	Nacogdoches	Blundell, Solomon	Titus
Blake, John T.	Travis	Blundell, William	Titus
Blakey, E. C.	Bastrop	Blythe, A. J.	Harrison
Blakey, J. W.	Bastrop	Blythe, A. W.	Harrison
Blakey, James	Fort Bend	Blythe, Samuel	Wharton
Blakey, Nancy	Bastrop	Blythe, Samuel K.	Bowie
Blakey, T. W.	Washington	Blythe, William S.	Cass
Blalock, Charles	Harrison	Boals, Calvin	Milam
Blanchard, Alexis	Jefferson	Board, N. V.	Harrison
Blanchard, C. K.	Jasper	Boatright, Friend	Grimes
Blanchard, S. C.	Jasper	Boatright, Friend	Lavaca
Blanchett, Priam	Liberty	Boatright, Leuy	Lavaca
Bland, James S.	Harrison	Boatright, Willoby	Washington
Bland, John	Jefferson	Bobo, F.	Walker
Bland, Peyton	Jefferson	Bobo, Lewis	Bowie
Blandgo, Peter	DeWitt	Bobo, Samuel	Bowie
Blandin, E.	Galveston	Bocetta, Miguel	Goliad
Blankenship, David	Panola	Bocke, D.	Austin
Blankenship, David	Shelby	Bodan, K.	Henderson
Blankenship, J. J.	Milam	Bodan, T. L.	Henderson
Blankenship, T.	Milam	Bodin, Nancy	San Augustine
Blanton, Elijah	Bastrop	Bodin, William	San Augustine
Blanton, James R.	Cherokee	Bodine, Juan	Henderson

15

NAME	COUNTY	NAME	COUNTY
Bodine, Juan B.	Henderson	Boon, G. E.	Fayette
Bogart, Cornelius	Shelby	Boone, Benjamin Z.	Wharton
Bogart, E.	Fannin	Boone, J. H.	Harrison
Bogart, R.	Fannin	Boone, J. R.	Fannin
Bogart, S.	Collin	Boone, James H.	Fort Bend
Boggs, Henry	Grayson	Boone, John C.	Fort Bend
Boggs, J. C.	Leon	Boone, Thadeus	Brazoria
Boggus, H. M.	Grimes	Boothby, R. R.	Navarro
Boggus, Joel	Brazos	Booth, A. J.	Bowie
Boggus, Leroy	Fayette	Boothe, C. A.	Liberty
Bohanan, Jeremiah	Austin	Boothe, John S.	Liberty
Bohanan, William	Tyler	Boothe, John T.	Shelby
Boice, J. P.	Cass	Boothe, R.	Liberty
Boile, Joseph	Bexar	Boothe, Robert	Liberty
Boland, J. M.	Cass	Boothe, Robert E.	Jefferson
Bolen, W.	Navarro	Boothe, S. S.	Bowie
Boles, M. L.	Henderson	Boothe, Sarah	Liberty
Boles, Rolen	Henderson	Boots, William	Red River
Boles, W. B.	Henderson	Borden, Gail	Brazoria
Bolinger, Hiram	Austin	Borden, John P.	Fort Bend
Bolinger, John	Austin	Borden, John P.	Goliad
Bolinger, Lewis	Austin	Borden, T. P.	Fort Bend
Bolinger, Peter	Austin	Border, J. T.	San Augustine
Bolinger, Susan	Austin	Boren, B. W.	Sabine
Bolton, William	Limestone	Boren, Israel	Lamar
Boman, J. B.	Cass	Boren, John	Lamar
Bomont, James A.	Jefferson	Boren, Joseph	Burleson
Bond, A. J.	Grimes	Boren, Mathew	Washington
Bond, G. W. L.	Galveston	Boren, Michael	Burleson
Bond, Joshua	Rusk	Boren, Nancy	Burleson
Bond, Lemuel	Rusk	Boren, Rhody	Burleson
Bondies, George	Nacogdoches	Boren, Samuel H.	Nacogdoches
Bonds, J. A.	Wharton	Boren, W. W.	Sabine
Bonds, Robert	Smith	Boren, William	Lamar
Bonds, Thomas M.	Grayson	Borgas, F.	Bexar
Bonds, William H.	Panola	Borin, Thomas	Fannin
Bone, A.	Fannin	Bormin, M.	Grayson
Bone, J.	Galveston	Bose, Isaac	Henderson
Bone, James F.	Nacogdoches	Boslyne, James	Henderson
Bone, Marcus L.	Fannin	Boss, G. H.	Henderson
Bonner, George S.	Lamar	Bosten, H. B.	Montgomery
Bonner, John W.	Refugio	Bosten, Joel	Titus
Bonnet, John	Galveston	Bostic, James M.	Austin
Booker, Abraham	Panola	Bostick, Absolom	Fayette
Booker, Enoch	Panola	Bostick, Sion R.	Colorado
Booker, James A.	Panola	Bostick, Susan	Colorado
Booker, Jason H.	Panola	Boston, H. B.	Grimes
Booker, Larkin R.	Panola	Bostwick, John L.	Brazoria
Booker, William G.	Panola	Boswell, Ronsom	
Bookman, Jesse	Grimes	P., Jr.	Burleson

NAME	COUNTY	NAME	COUNTY
Boswell, U. W.	Burleson	Box, B.	Navarro
Bosy, Judy	Guadalupe	Box, Benjamin	Rusk
Bottmer, H.	Comal	Box, James F.	Titus
Bottom, Charles T.	Hopkins	Box, James J.	Titus
Bottom, Michael L.	Fayette	Box, John	Houston
Bottom, S. A.	Nacogdoches	Box, John A.	Cherokee
Bottom, Zachariah	Cherokee	Box, John M.	Cherokee
Botts, G. H.	Fannin	Box, Joshua	Anderson
Boulett, Lewis	Liberty	Box, M.	Victoria
Boulter, James	Cherokee	Box, Nelson	Houston
Boulware, O. T.	Harrison	Box, R. W.	Anderson
Bounds, I. B.	Fannin	Box, Samuel C.	Cherokee
Bounds, J. M.	Fannin	Box, Selina	Rusk
Bounell, William		Box, Stephen	Houston
B.	Burleson	Box, Stilwell	Houston
Bourland, A.	Galveston	Box, Thomas	Henderson
Bourland, B. F.	Fannin	Box, Thomas G.	Houston
Bourland, J. M.	Lamar	Box, William S.	Cherokee
Bourland, James	Lamar	Box, Young	Titus
Boutwell, Alex.	Fannin	Boyce, Isaac	Travis
Boutwell, John	Fannin	Boyce, J. J.	Bowie
Bowden, Bennett H.	Shelby	Boyce, James	Travis
Bowden, James	Navarro	Boyce, Mahala	Bastrop
Bowden, Nancy	Shelby	Boyce, N.	Bastrop
Bowen, A. R.	Grimes	Boyce, Robert P.	Harris
Bowen, Eli A.	Anderson	Boyce, William H.	Bowie
Bowen, G. B.	Milam	Boyd, D. S.	Montgomery
Bowen, John	Lamar	Boyd, Eliza A.	Bowie
Bowen, M. B.	Lamar	Boyd, F. M.	San Augustine
Bowen, Wiley N.	Anderson	Boyd, Goerge	Brazoria
Bowen, William F.	Polk	Boyd, J. A. M.	Guadalupe
Bowen, WIlliam R.	Grimes	Boyd, James	Shelby
Bowers, Harris	Leon	Boyd, John	Limestone
Bowers, John A.	Nacogdoches	Boyd, John	Sabine
Bowers, William	Navarro	Boyd, Robert	Bowie
Bowie, D. M.	Bastrop	Boyd, William A.	Bowie
Bowles, H.	Dallas	Boyles, Alex	Fayette
Bowles, J. P.	Harris	Boyles, B.	Navarro
Bowlin, J.	Henderson	Boyles, William	Milam
Bowlin, James	Shelby	Bozeman, Freeman	Fayette
Bowman, C. B.	Anderson	Bozeman, H. W.	Leon
Bowman, James J.	Brazos	Bozeman, T. R.	Leon
Bowman, James N.	Panola	Bozwell, C.	Titus
Bowman, Jesse B.	Bowie	Braches, Charles	Gonzales
Bowman, John J.	Angelina	Bracht, Victor	Comal
Bowman, Joseph	Bowie	Bracken, J. R.	Houston
Bowman, Sam	Grimes	Bracken, James	Lamar
Bowman, Thomas	Brazos	Bracken, T. H.	Lamar
Bows, Manson	Jefferson	Bracken, Thomas	Panola
Bowton, Nathan	Jefferson	Bracken, W. G.	Lamar

NAME	COUNTY	NAME	COUNTY
Bracken, William	Jackson	Branom, Meril	Hopkins
Bracken, William	Lamar	Brantley, Blake	Grimes
Brackett, Emily	Bexar	Brantley, Henry	Red River
Brackett, Oscar B.	Bexar	Brantley, J. J.	Grimes
Bracy, Maclin	Austin	Brashear, E. P.	Nacogdoches
Bradberry, James	Goliad	Brashear, G. W.	Leon
Bradberry, T. C.	Grimes	Brashear, Isaac W.	Harris
Bradbury, D.	Galveston	Brashear, J. H.	Fayette
Bradbury, Daniel	Fort Bend	Brashear, James W.	Harris
Bradbury, D.	Collin	Braton, David	Cass
Bradbury, Edward	Fort Bend	Bratton, George	Travis
Bradbury, James	Burleson	Bratton, John	Milam
Bradbury, James	Goliad	Bratton, R.	Travis
Bradbury, John	Fort Bend	Bratton, William	Travis
Bradbury, T.	Collin	Brawley, Hugh	Fannin
Bradbury, William	Austin	Bray, Gilbert	Liberty
Bradley, Mrs. Ann		Bray, John	Wharton
M.	Bexar	Brazelton, H. W.	Polk
Bradley, E. H.	Grimes	Brazile, George	Fayette
Bradley, John	Goliad	Brazile, Henry B.	Harrison
Bradley, John	Bexar	Bream, J. T.	Liberty
Bradley, John W.	Brazoria	Brechen, Lemuel	Bexar
Bradley, L.	Rusk	Breeding, Benjamin	Colorado
Bradley, Seymour	Grayson	Breeding, David	Fayette
Bradley, Thomas	Grayson	Breeding, E. J.	Fayette
Bradshaw, David	Dallas	Breeding, G. W.	Fayette
Bradshaw, J. A.	Nacogdoches	Breeding, James	Fayette
Bradshaw, James N.	Nacogdoches	Breeding, John	Fayette
Bradshaw, Rebecca	Dallas	Breeding, N. B.	Fayette
Bradshaw, William	Nacogdoches	Breeding, R. L.	Fayette
Brady, Charles	San Augustine	Bremer, H. C.	Comal
Bragdon, A. G.	Leon	Bremond, Paul	Harris
Bragg, L. D.	Washington	Brenan, Thomas H.	Newton
Brake, Joseph	Polk	Brent, C. B.	Houston
Branard, G. A.	Galveston	Brent, James	Houston
Branard, J. S.	Grimes	Brent, Peter E.	Houston
Branch, Ashur	Rusk	Brent Sarah	Houston
Branch, E. T.	Liberty	Breoher, Jakob	Comal
Branch, G. W.	Rusk	Bresana, Jose	Bexar
Branch, J. W.	Rusk	Brested, Christoph	Bexar
Branch, Nicholas	Milam	Brewer, Balam H.	Harrison
Brandon, James	Cherokee	Brewer, C. C.	Harrison
Brandon, L. H.	Titus	Brewer, Erasmus	Rusk
Brandon, William		Brewer, F. W.	Harrison
M.	Shelby	Brewer, Henry G.	Henderson
Brane, G.	Comal	Brewer, J.	Henderson
Branford, Henry	Liberty	Brewer, J. H.	Grayson
Branham, James M.	Galveston	Brewer, John	Nacogdoches
Brann, J.	Henderson	Brewer, Sackfield	Austin
Brannar, John	Colorado	Brewer, William	Cherokee

18

NAME	COUNTY	NAME	COUNTY
Brewer, William	Washington	Brill, E. W.	Guadalupe
Brewer, William G.	Cherokee	Brimberry, John N.	Nacogdoches
Brewer, William T.	Henderson	Brimberry, Mary	Nacogdoches
Brewster, Mrs.	Galveston	Brimberry, Mary	Walker
Brewster, E.	Galveston	Brimberry, William	
Brewster, O. S.	Galveston	A.	Nacogdoches
Brewster, Robert	Harris	Brindler, Joseph	Fayette
Brian, Calton	Austin	Brinley, George	Bowie
Brian, Charles	Austin	Brinley, Jacob	Cherokee
Briant, John S.	Lamar	Brinton, William	Hopkins
Briant, Stephen	San Augustine	Brisco, A.	Harris
Bridge, Benjamin	Colorado	Brisco, William	Lamar
Bridge, William	Colorado	Briscoe, Elisha	Rusk
Bridgeman, J. C.	Harrison	Briscoe, J.	Henderson
Bridger, Henry	Lavaca	Briscoe, James M.	Fort Bend
Bridger, John	Bexar	Briscoe, R. B.	Henderson
Bridges, A.	Henderson	Briscoe, Thomas	Henderson
Bridges, James	Angelina	Brisham, James	Fannin
Bridges, James S.	Lamar	Brister, Daniel	Liberty
Bridges, John	San Augustine	Brister, William	Liberty
Bridges, W.	Cass	Brittain, Alfred	Liberty
Bridges, William		Brittain, G.	Cass
E.	Fayette	Brittain, John W.	Shelby
Bridges,		Brittain, M. J.	Titus
Williamson	Titus	Brittain, W. B.	Harrison
Bridsly, Nemiah	Henderson	Broadbeck, A.	Fayette
Brigance, A. L.	Grimes	Broadus, Franklin	
Brigance, C. N.	Grimes	C.	Panola
Brigance, F.	Grimes	Broadwell, George	
Brigance, Foster	Grimes	M.	Robertson
Brigance, Franklin	Grimes	Brock, A.	Galveston
Brigance, Harvey	Grimes	Brock, Isaac	Rusk
Brigance, J. M.	Red River	Brock, James	Anderson
Brigance, Phagan	Grimes	Brock, John G.	Galveston
Briggs, J.	Henderson	Brock, Jonathan	Galveston
Briggs, J. L.	Galveston	Brockenbrough, J.	
Briggs, James	Cass	F.	Calhoun
Brigham, S. B.	Matagorda	Brockman, Thomas	
Brigham, W. B.	Cass	P.	Angelina
Bright, Henry	Bastrop	Brockson, C. J.	Houston
Bright, John	Bastrop	Brod, A.	Colorado
Bright, Steve	Bastrop	Brod, John, Sr.	Colorado
Brightling, F.	Austin	Brod, Jr.	Colorado
Brigsman, James C.	Goliad	Brodden, John	Colorado
Brilay, James	Nacogdoches	Brogdon, William	
Briley, A. D. M.	Nacogdoches	H.	Grayson
Briley, Andrew	Nacogdoches	Broils, K.	Henderson
Briley, Green	Nacogdoches	Bromley, William	Smith
Briley, John	Nacogdoches	Bromley, Lieut.	
Briley, Shedrack	Nacogdoches	Wm.	Goliad

19

NAME	COUNTY	NAME	COUNTY
Brondey, Samuel	Hopkins	Brown, D. F.	Bastrop
Bronson, Zeno	Jackson	Brown, D. M.	Leon
Brooke, J. C.	San Augustine	Brown, Daniel	Sabine
Brooke, T. D.	Upshur	Brown, David	Rusk
Brookfield, C. C.	Houston	Brown, David	San Augustine
Brookfield,		Brown, E. E.	Galveston
William	Fayette	Brown, Edward	Bexar
Brooks, A. M.	Bastrop	Brown, Edward	Goliad
Brooks, Bluford	Jasper	Brown, Elizabeth	Galveston
Brooks, Clark	Houston	Brown, Emily C.	Brazoria
Brooks, F. N.	San Augustine	Brown, F.	Henderson
Brooks, F. T.	Angelina	Brown, Francis B.	Nacogdoches
Brooks, G. W.	Montgomery	Brown, G. L.	Grimes
Brooks, George W.	Henderson	Brown, G. W.	Henderson
Brooks, George W.	Washington	Brown, George A.	Brazoria
Brooks, Henry	San Augustine	Brown, George W.	Colorado
Brooks, John W.	Brazoria	Brown, Guyon	Angelina
Brooks, Sam	Henderson	Brown, H. H.	Galveston
Brooks, Samuel	San Augustine	Brown, Henry	Grayson
Brooks, Samuel	Washington	Brown, Henry	Nacogdoches
Brooks, T. G.	San Augustine	Brown, Henry	Navarro
Brooks, William	Henderson	Brown, J. A.	Cass
Brooks, Wilson	Liberty	Brown, J. B.	Goliad
Brookshire, James	Travis	Brown, J. B.	Victoria
Brookshire, Joseph	Fort Bend	Brown, J. D.	Collin
Brookshire, Samuel	Fort Bend	Brown, J. J.	Cass
Broom, George	San Augustine	Brown, J. M.	Cass
Broomfield, -----	Navarro	Brown, J. M.	Leon
Brothers, Jesse	Harrison	Brown, J. M.	Rusk
Brotherton, John	Fannin	Brown, J. S.	Liberty
Brotherton, W. W.	Fannin	Brown, James	Cass
Broughton, Charles	Jackson	Brown, James	Goliad
Brour, Reubin	Fannin	Brown, James	Grayson
Browen, Anthony	Lavaca	Brown, James	Lamar
Browen, Barnard	Lavaca	Brown James	Washington
Browen, James	Lavaca	Brown, James H.	Bexar
Browen, Margaret	Lavaca	Brown, James K.	Harris
Browen, Rufus	Lavaca	Brown, James M.	Jackson
Browen, Thomas	Lavaca	Brown, James S.	Goliad
Brower, H. H.	Galveston	Brown, James W.	Brazoria
Brower J.	Upshur	Brown, James W.	Nacogdoches
Brown, A. E.	Travis	Brown, Jefferson	
Brown, Allen W.	Fannin	P.	Henderson
Brown, B. W.	Henderson	Brown, Jeremiah	Brazoria
Brown, B. W.	Nacogdoches	Brown, John	Bexar
Brown, Bryant	Fannin	Brown, John	Brazoria
Brown, C. S.	Goliad	Brown, John	Galveston
Brown, Charlotte		Brown, John	Henderson
E.	Brazoria	Brown, John	Jasper
Brown, D. B.	Henderson	Brown, John	Lamar

NAME	COUNTY	NAME	COUNTY
Brown, John	Navarro	Browning, Andrew	Leon
Brown, John	Titus	Browning, C. t.	Travis
Brown, John G.	Harrison	Browning, G. W.	Anderson
Brown, John H.	Harris	Browning, Isaac E.	Harrison
Brown, John M.	Washington	Browning, J. C.	Navarro
Brown, John R.	Nacogdoches	Browning, J. P.	Travis
Brown, John S.	Polk	Browning, James E.	
Brown, Jonathan S.	Nacogdoches	est	Cass
Brown, Joseph	Lamar	Browning, L.	Henderson
Brown, Joseph M.	Brazoria	Browning, William	Navarrc
Brown, Joshua	Goliad	Browning, William	
Brown, Leonard	Hopkins	A.	Washington
Brown, M. O.	Henderson	Brownlee, Joseph	Hunt
Brown, Margaret	Brazoria	Brownrigg, G. B.	San Augustine
Brown, Owen	Grimes	Brownrigg, J.	San Augustine
Brown, P. R.	Walker	Brucke, Allen	Lavaca
Brown, R. O.	San Augustine	Brum, George	Colorado
Brown, Reuben	Houston	Brum, Lewis	Colorado
Brown, Reubin R.	Brazoria	Brumet, A. J.	Lamar
Brown, Richard	Rusk	Brumet, Lengston	Lamar
Brown, Robert T.	Harrison	Brumley, William	Henderson
Brown, S.	Henderson	Brundridge, J. W.	Lavaca
Brown, S. B.	Titus	Brune, Edward	Austin
Brown, S. H.	Collin	Brusard, Levan	Jefferson
Brown, S. P.	Henderson	Brush, Ellison	Fort Bend
Brown, Samuel T.	Galveston	Bruster, B. F.	Red River
Brown, Sarah	Fayette	Bruton, Benjamin	Henderson
Brown, Simpson	Jasper	Bruton, Elisha	Titus
Brown, Squire	Brazoria	Bruton, Isaac	Red River
Brown, T. P.	Travis	Bruton, Joab	Limestone
Brown, T. R.	Austin	Bruton, John	Titus
Brown, Taylor	Rusk	Bruton, Richard	Dallas
Brown, Thomas	Colorado	Bruton, William	Dallas
Brown, Thomas	Washington	Bryan, George	Galveston
Brown, W. A.	Grimes	Bryan, J. N.	Dallas
Brown, W. A.	Henderson	Bryan, James B.	Dallas
Brown, W. J.	Lamar	Bryan, John L.	Harris
Brown, Wesley	Titus	Bryan, Kindallis	Liberty
Brown, William	Bexar	Bryan, Moses	
Brown, William	DeWitt	Austin	Brazoria
Brown, William	Galveston	Bryan, Nancy	Liberty
Brown, William	Lamar	Bryan, Pryor	Galveston
Brown, William	Red River	Bryan, Thomas B.	Galveston
Brown, William	Rusk	Bryan, William	Fort Bend
Brown, William	Washington	Bryan, William	Galveston
Brown, William A.	Washington	Bryan, William	
Brown, William C.	Jasper	Joel	Brazoria
Brown, William M.	Brazoria	Bryant, Ben	Milam
Brown, Wilson N.	Cherokee	Bryant, Henry	Galveston
Brown, Young E.	Dallas	Bryant, Jesse	Milam

NAME	COUNTY	NAME	COUNTY
Bryant, John	Shelby	Bumstid, M. W.	Jefferson
Bryant, John J.	Polk	Bunch, David	Rusk
Bryant, L. D.	Cass	Bunch, J. P.	Sabine
Bryant, O.	Galveston	Bundren, Isaac	Red River
Bryant, Solomon	Red River	Bunn, Joseph	Jefferson
Bryant, T. or P.	Polk	Bunner, Nathaniel	Bexar
Bryant, William	Bastrop	Bunton, Desha	Bastrop
Buck, John	Navarro	Bunton, J. W.	Bastrop
Buckhannan, A.	Fannin	Burch, Christopher	Newton
Buckhannan, G. M.	Washington	Burch, Henry	Brazoria
Buckhannan, James		Burch, Nelson	Bastrop
B.	Fannin	Burch, Sarah	Newton
Buckhannan, S.	Titus	Burcher, Michael	Smith
Buckhannan, T. E.	Walker	Burdett, Giles	San Augustine
Buckhannon, Delila	Fannin	Burdett, N. W.	San Augustine
Buckhannon,		Burdit, Jesse	Travis
Francis M.	DeWitt	Burdit, Minos	Travis
Buckholder, N. S.	Harris	Burdit, Wm. B.	Travis
Buckley, C. W.	Harris	Burdon, J. G.	Walker
Buckley, Daniel	Goliad	Burdon, J. W.	Montgomery
Buckley, John	Shelby	Burford, William	Navarro
Buckley, Tyree	Shelby	Burgher, Young	Lamar
Buckner, B. P.	Harris	Burgin, C. H.	Dallas
Buckner, Samuel	Shelby	Burk, Ben G.	Sabine
Buddington, H. J.	Galveston	Burk, James	Brazoria
Buentillo, Thomas	Goliad	Burk, John R.	Newton
Buff, Jacob	Grimes	Burk, John S.	Titus
Buff, Samson	Grimes	Burke, Benjamin	Tyler
Buffington, A.	Grimes	Burke, J. H.	Red River
Bufford, W. R.	Henderson	Burke, James	Tyler
Bufford, William	Rusk	Burke, James	Tyler
Buford, L.	Henderson	Burke, John M.	Grimes
Buford, T. J.	Henderson	Burke, N.	Bastrop
Buford, William R.	Nacogdoches	Burke, William	Titus
Bugnor, P. L.	Bexar	Burket, Nathaniel	
Buillar, Michael	Galveston	B.	DeWitt
Bullard, C. K.	Matagorda	Burkham, A. H.	Red River
Bullard, H. D.	Harrison	Burkham, B. F.	Red River
Bullock, A. C.	Leon	Burkham, James	Red River
Bullock, C. W.	San Augustine	Burkhardt, Henry	Comal
Bullock, Charles		Burleson, Aaron	Fayette
W.	Sabine	Burleson, Aaron	Travis
Bullock, David	San Augustine	Burleson, Jacob	Travis
Bullock, Elizabeth	Nacogdoches	Burleson, Hopson	Leon
Bullock, H. M.	Grimes	Burleson, James	Fort Bend
Bullock, J. Y.	San Augustine	Burleson, James	Gonzales
Bullock, James M.	Bowie	Burleson, James	San Augustine
Bullock, S. N.	Nacogdoches	Burleson, John	Austin
Bullock, W. C.	San Augustine	Burleson, John	Gonzales
Bullock, William	Rusk	Burleson, John,	

NAME	COUNTY	NAME	COUNTY
Sr.	Bastrop	Burns, Samuel	Tyler
Burleson, Jonathan	Bastrop	Burns, Squire	Goliad
Burleson, Jonathan	Fayette	Burns, Thomas L.	Titus
Burleson, Joseph	San Augustine	Burns, W. P.	Grayson
Burleson, Joseph,		Burny, David	Brazoria
Jr.	Bastrop	Burny, L. L.	Henderson
Burleson, Joseph,		Burr, Augustine	Brazoria
Sr.	Bastrop	Burrell, David	Jefferson
Burleson, Mary	Bastrop	Burrell, Elias A.	Burleson
Burleson, R.	Grimes	Burrell, George	Jefferson
Burmingham, R. W.	Cass	Burrell, James	Jefferson
Burmon, Samuel	Navarro	Burrell, Robert	Jefferson
Burmon, William	Houston	Burrios, A. D.	Harrison
Burnet, D. D.	Bastrop	Burrios, Eveline	Harrison
Burnet, D. G.	Harris	Burris, J. C.	Milam
Burnet, David G.	Travis	Burris, J. M.	Milam
Burnet, Isham	Red River	Burris, Mary	Lamar
Burnet, J. P.	Houston	Burris, William M.	Lamar
Burnet, James A.	Red River	Burroughs, James	Fayette
Burnet, Joseph	Walker	Burroughs, James	
Burnet, M.	Red River	M.	Sabine
Burnet, Sally G.	Harris	Burrow, B. M. D.	Nacogdoches
Burnett, Edward	Cass	Burrow, E. W.	Rusk
Burnett, Mrs. Mary	Cass	Burrow, M.	Cass
Burnett, Thomas J.	Cass	Burrow, Philip	Navarro
Burnett, William		Burrow, William	Navarro
H.	Panola	Burrus, Samuel	Angelina
Burnham, J. A.	Fayette	Burt, Israel N.	Panola
Burnham, J. G.	Galveston	Burton, Charles	Houston
Burnham, William		Burton, J. W.	Houston
O.	Gonzales	Burton, John	Jefferson
Burnheart, Joseph	Travis	Burton, John J.	Houston
Burns, A. A.	San Augustine	Burton, John M.	Washington
Burns, Aaron	Galveston	Burton, Robert	Galveston
Burns, Arthur	DeWitt	Burton, Robert	Houston
Burns, Benjamin	Galveston	Burton, Samuel	Brazos
Burns, Daniel	Limestone	Burton, Thomas	Brazoria
Burns, Isaac	Titus	Burton, W. H. est.	Cass
Burns, J. W.	Lamar	Burton, William	Cherokee
Burns, James	Grimes	Burtrong, Thomas	Burleson
Burns, John	Matagorda	Burwick, Thomas,	
Burns, John A.	Grayson	Jr.	Jefferson
Burns, John W.	Shelby	Burwick, Thomas,	
Burns, Joseph	Shelby	Sr.	Jefferson
Burns, Josiah	Grayson	Busby, William	Polk
Burns, Leander	Washington	Bush, H. B.	Fannin
Burns, Leon	Leon	Bush, J. H.	Titus
Burns, Milton	Sabine	Bush, M. H.	Burleson
Burns, R. C.	Walker	Bush, Nathaniel	Austin
Burns, S. T.	San Augustine	Buster, W. W.	Washington

NAME	COUNTY	NAME	COUNTY
Bustillo, Domingo	Bexar	Byfield, Holmes	Shelby
Bustillo, Francois	Bexar	Bynum, N. G.	Walker
Butchta, Aug.	San Augustine	Byrd, Daniel	Walker
Butler, A. G.	Grimes	Byrd, James	Dallas
Butler, A. E.	Red River	Byrd, Thomas	Polk
Butler, A. W.	Henderson	Byrd, W. P.	Montgomery
Butler, Ahera	Shelby	Byrne, Anthony	Grimes
Butler, Anthony	Washington	Byren, James	Goliad
Butler, C. W.	Harrison	Byrne, James	Victoria
Butler, Charles	Polk	Byrne, James W.	Refugio
Butler, George	Henderson	Byrne, William C.	Galveston
Butler, J.	Collin	Byrnside, James P.	Bowie
Butler, James	Fannin	Byrum, John S. D.	Goliad
Butler, James M.	Lavaca		
Butler, Joaseph	Navarro		
Butler, John	Galveston	Cabban, Elizabeth	Galveston
Butler, John	Red River	Cabble, D.	Tyler
Butler, John P.	Polk	Cabble, John	Tyler
Butler, Jonas	Galveston	Cabble, Peter	Tyler
Butler, Jonas	Galveston	Cabburn, William	Refugio
Butler, Mary	Bastrop	Cabiness, John	Harris
Butler, N. C.	Comal	Cabler, E. S.	Washington
Butler, Reese	Fannin	Cabreno, Pedro	Bexar
Butler, Thomas H.	Polk	Cacilla, Juan	Goliad
Butler, W.	Collin	Cacilla, Maria G.	Goliad
Butler, William	Lavaca	Caddenhead, F.	
Butler, William	Polk	John	Rusk
Butridge, R. E.	Bowie	Caddenhead, James	
Butt, G. N.	Cass	T.	Nacogdoches
Butt, Jackson	Cass	Caddel, Andrew B.	Nacogdoches
Button, R. S.	San Augustine	Caddel, Andrew	Nacogdoches
Button, R. T. D.	Shelby	Caddel, J. D.	Nacogdoches
Button, William J.	Shelby	Caddel, J. T. C.	Nacogdoches
Button, Williams		Caddel, M.	Fannin
M.	Shelby	Cadena, Francois	Bexar
Buttrell, William	Brazos	Cadena, Jesus	Goliad
Buxton, A.	Liberty	Cadena, Jose	Bexar
Buxton, J. V.	Liberty	Cadena, Manuel	Bexar
Buxton, P.	Liberty	Cadwell, John	Navarro
Byars, Noe T.	Navarro	Cadwell, Samuel	Navarro
Byas, William	Lavaca	Cady, Moses	Washington
Byerly, Adam	Jasper	Cage, James	Wharton
Byerly, George	Jasper	Cage, John	Wharton
Byerly, Thomas	Newton	Cage, Rufus K.	Nacogdoches
Byerly, William	Jasper	Cagle, M. G.	Lamar
Byers, J. C.	Bowie	Cahier, Mathew G.	Goliad
Byers, J. M.	Walker	Cahill, M.	Galveston
Byers, John	Cass	Cain, J. J.	Harris
Byers, Ross	Cass	Cain, John H.	Harrison
Byers, William W.	Grimes	Cain, Priscilla	Harrison

NAME	COUNTY	NAME	COUNTY
Caison, John	Nacogdoches	Calvo, Miguel	Bexar
Caison, Seth	Nacogdoches	Calwell, James	Anderson
Caiton, J. G.	Wharton	Cambell, E. S.	Henderson
Calahan, H. T.	Austin	Camburr, James B.	Shelby
Calahan, James H.	Guadalupe	Cameron, D.	Galveston
Callahan, Thomas		Cameron, D. R.	Shelby
S.	Brazoria	Cameron, David R.	Dallas
Calaway, A. J. D.	Lavaca	Cameron, John	Cass
Calaway, Joshua	Red River	Cameron, John	Goliad
Calaway, W. F.	Rusk	Cameron, L. R.	Jasper
Calchom, H.	Goliad	Cameron, T. M.	Austin
Calder, Robert J.	Brazoria	Cammel, Gordon G.	Anderson
Calder, Thomas	Galveston	Cammel, W. J.	Anderson
Calderon, Josias	Bexar	Cammel, William	Houston
Caldwell, Alfred	Travis	Camp, John B.	Grimes
Caldwell, E.	Angelina	Camp, Joseph	Titus
Caldwell, James A.	Travis	Campbell, A. C.	Galveston
Caldwell, James R.	Brazoria	Campbell, A. G.	Nacogdoches
Caldwell, John	Bastrop	Campbell,	
Caldwell, Robert	Matagorda	Alexander	Lamar
Calfee, John, Sr.	Shelby	Campbell, Crocket	Titus
Calfield, Thomas	Henderson	Campbell, Cyrus	Austin
Calhoun, J. C.	Bastrop	Campbell, Cyrus	Grimes
Calhoun, W. M.	Harrison	Campbell, D. W.	Leon
Calhoun, William	Walker	Campbell, E.	Wharton
Calicut, James	Austin	Campbell, E. H.	Bowie
Callaghan, Henry	Goliad	Campbell, F. L.	Upshur
Callaghan, Joseph	Goliad	Campbell, F. S.	Harrison
Callahan, B.	Bexar	Campbell, H. E.	Limestone
Callahan, John	Lavaca	Campbell, H. O.	Austin
Callahan, John H.	Harris	Campbell, Isaac	Gonzales
Caller, James M.	Colorado	Campbell, J.	Upshur
Callison, James	Fayette	Campbell, J. G.	Colorado
Callison, John G.	Houston	Campbell, J. K.	Walker
Callison, S. C.	Houston	Campbell, James	Bexar
Callow, J. M.	Fayette	Campbell, James	Galveston
Calseny, J. W.	Rusk	Campbell, James	Lamar
Caltharp, E. S.	Rusk	Campbell, James C.	Cherokee
Caltharp, James	Rusk	Campbell, John	Austin
Calvert, E.	San Augustine	Campbell, John	Guadalupe
Calvert, F. J.	Austin	Campbell, John	Washington
Calvert, H. H.	Washington	Campbell, John P.	Cass
Calvert, J. S.	Bexar	Campbell, John T.	Goliad
Calvert, James	Washington	Campbell, Joseph	Austin
Calvert, Jeremiah		Campbell, Joseph	Nacogdoches
S.	Guadalupe	Campbell, Lewis	Walker
Calvin, Margaret	Burleson	Campbell, M.	Leon
Calvit, Isaac S.	Brazoria	Campbell, Nathan	Milam
Calvit, T. J.	Brazoria	Campbell, P. A.	Harrison
Calvitt, B. M.	Brazoria	Campbell, R.	Victoria

NAME	COUNTY	NAME	COUNTY
Campbell, R. C.	Harris	Carley, William	Grimes
Campbell, R. E.	Austin	Carlile, R.	Victoria
Campbell, Stewart	Lamar	Carlin, Daniel	Jackson
Campbell, Teresa	Bexar	Carlos, Catherine	Harris
Campbell, Thomas		Carlos, John	Harris
Y.	Dallas	Carlton, J. C.	Cherokee
Campbell, W.	Burleson	Carlyle, Alfred	Henderson
Campbell, W. S.	Henderson	Carlyle, Reese V.	Navarro
Campbell, William	Titus	Carmine, John	Washington
Campbell, William		Carmon, John	Jasper
S.	Goliad	Carmon, O. L.	Brazoria
Campbell, Zerilar	Leon	Carnes, Elizabeth	Fayette
Cane, Cornelius	Leon	Carnes, William R.	Nacogdoches
Canfield, E. A.	San Augustine	Caro, H.	Nacogdoches
Cannon, Carter	Cass	Caro, Thomas	Henderson
Cannon, D. C.	Sabine	Carothers, George	Austin
Cannon, W. R.	Bastrop	Carothers, John R.	Harris
Cannon, William	Bastrop	Carothers, R. C.	Victoria
Cannon, William J.	Brazoria	Carothers, Thomas	Victoria
Cantebery, G. W.	Titus	Carpenter,	
Cantrell, James	Anderson	Claiburn	Shelby
Cantu, Jesus	Bexar	Carpenter,	
Cantu, Josus	Bexar	Dangerfield	Goliad
Cantu, Meguil	Bexar	Carpenter,	
Canty, Thomas	Travis	Dangerfield	Panola
Caple, Jabez B.	Brazoria	Carpenter, S. S.	Austin
Caplin, Charles	Galveston	Carpenter, Thomas	Liberty
Capps, Dimon	Limestone	Carpenter, Timothy	Dallas
Capps, F. W.	Limestone	Carper, John	Grayson
Capps, Henry	Limestone	Carper, Wm. M	Galveston
Cappy, Robert	Bexar	Carr, Anthony	Shelby
Capron, G. W.	Harris	Carr, B. F.	Houston
Carasos, S.	Bexar	Carr, B. F.	Liberty
Carbajal, Luis	Bexar	Carr, B. M.	Limestone
Carbajal,		Carr, Ben F.	Henderson
Nichalous	Goliad	Carr, John	Navarro
Carbazoz, Manuel	Bexar	Carr, John F.	Polk
Carbow, H. B.	Bowie	Carr, Joshua	Fannin
Carbowage, G.	Anderson	Carr, Levi	Jefferson
Card, James	Fayette	Carr, Robert	Fayette
Cardemus, H. M.	Guadalupe	Carr, Volney	Goliad
Cardenas,		Carr, William	Jefferson
Francisco	Nacogdoches	Carr, William S.,	
Carder, William P.	Dallas	Jr.	Fannin
Cardett, A. A.	Liberty	Carr, William S.	
Cardry, Easly	Rusk	S., Sr.	Fannin
Cardwell, Crocket	DeWitt	Carradine, Robert	Sabine
Carether, James	Walker	Carragan, John	Refugio
Carether, Thomas	Walker	Carraher, Bernard	Harris
Carey, Seth	Harris	Carrara, Francisco	Goliad

26

NAME	COUNTY	NAME	COUNTY
Carraway, Elisa R.	Sabine	Carter, Sarah	Galveston
Carraway, P. H.	Liberty	Carter, T.	Fayette
Carraway, Thomas	Liberty	Carter, W. H.	Henderson
Carrell, A. J.	Shelby	Carter, W. J. S.	Bastrop
Carrell, Joseph O.	Shelby	Carter, W. J. S.	Cass
Carreona, Manuel	Goliad	Carter, Wiley	Brazos
Carriger, David N.	Washington	Carter, William	Grayson
Carrington, A.	Grimes	Cartmell, Thomas	
Carrington,		P.	Travis
Duncan	Grimes	Cartwright, A. W.	Fort Bend
Carrington, O. P.	Washington	Cartwright, Anna	Houston
Carrington, Sam W.	Cherokee	Cartwright, George	
Carrington, Mrs.		W.	Sabine
Sarah	Washington	Cartwright, J. C.	San Augustine
Carrion, Luis	Goliad	Cartwright, J. H.	Fort Bend
Carrithers, John		Cartwright, J. M.	Titus
L.	Rusk	Cartwright, J. S.	Houston
Carroll, Edward	Bowie	Cartwright, James	
Carroll, Nathaniel		M.	Limestone
H.	Harris	Cartwright, M. W.	Montgomery
Carroll, Revd.	Wharton	Cartwright,	
Carroll, Rufus J.	Colorado	Matthew	San Augustine
Carson, Charles	Bowie	Cartwright, R. G.	Henderson
Carson, H.	Nacogdoches	Cartwright, Robert	
Carson, James	Tyler	G.	Shelby
Carson, John	Harris	Cartwright,	
Carson, John	Tyler	Thomas	Houston
Carson, Lary	Rusk	Cartwright,	
Carson, Mirand H.	Goliad	William	Montgomery
Carson, Sam B.	Goliad	Cartwright,	
Carson, Thomas	Walker	Williford	Montgomery
Carson, William	Brazoria	Caruthers, ---	Brazos
Carstarphen, Eliza		Caruthers, Allan	Fayette
M.	Harrison	Caruthers, G. C.	Grayson
Carter, Allen	Lamar	Caruthers, John	Limestone
Carter, Armstead	Colorado	Caruthers, Martha	Grayson
Carter, Armstead	Goliad	Caruthers, W. R.	Grayson
Carter, C. C.	Panola	Caruthers, William	Fayette
Carter, Mrs. C. E.	Matagorda	Carver, Abraham	Dallas
Carter, Devastus	Cherokee	Carver, Solomon	Dallas
Carter, E. H.	Burleson	Casas, M. Y.	Bexar
Carter, G. J.	Cherokee	Casborn, William	Henderson
Carter, James	Fannin	Casbow, Nathan	Rusk
Carter, John	DeWitt	Case, George W.	Lamar
Carter, John	Walker	Case, Joseph	Anderson
Carter, John H.	Fayette	Case, Nathaniel	Dallas
Carter, John R.	Panola	Case, Uriah F.	Grimes
Carter, Peter A.	Henderson	Case, William	Titus
Carter, R. W. T.	Goliad	Casebeer, James	Lamar
Carter, Richard	Brazos	Caselius, John	Lamar

NAME	COUNTY	NAME	COUNTY
Casew, Elder	Henderson	Caudle, Mark	Titus
Casey, Isaac	Nacogdoches	Caudle, Mary	Titus
Casey, Joel	Smith	Caulder, Alex	Jefferson
Casey, John	Dallas	Causet, Green B.	Sabine
Cash, J. D.	Tyler	Causey, Col.	Sabine
Casiano, Jose	Bexar	Cavanaugh, Alfred	Tyler
Casias, F.	Bexar	Cavanaugh, M.	Harris
Casias, Filippa	Bexar	Cavens, Thomas	Limestone
Casias, Juan	Bexar	Caverion, Orton	Bexar
Casias, Manuel	Bexar	Cavillo, Maria	Bexar
Casias, Manuello	Bexar	Cavillo, Martias	Bexar
Casias, Mateo	Bexar	Cavinas, J. A.	Walker
Casner, Isaac	Travis	Cavitt, Jesse	Cherokee
Casner, Jacob	Fort Bend	Cavitt, Moses	Fannin
Casner, James	Travis	Cavitt, Volney	Robertson
Casner, Martin	Travis	Cawdle, J. A.	Red River
Cassady, John	Panola	Cawley, James C.	Bowie
Cassanobie, C.	Bexar	Cawthon, E. W.	Montgomery
Cassanobie, Juan	Bexar	Cawthon, R. O.	Cass
Cassanobie, Simeon	Bexar	Cayse, John M.	Brazoria
Cassiano, Joseph	Galveston	Cayse, Thomas	Brazoria
Cassillas, Yrrico	Boliad	Caywood, William	Leon
Casson, John P.	Brazoria	Cazanova, Maria	Henderson
Castanise, James	Harris	Cazy, John	Robertson
Castanise, Justin	Harris	Cementt, L.	Collin
Castertine, James		Cervantes, Agajo	Bexar
A.	Refugio	Cervantes, C.	Bexar
Castia, Y.	Bexar	Cervantes, J. M.	Henderson
Castillo, Jose Y.	Bexar	Cgery, Mary	Galveston
Castillo, Juaquin	Bexar	Chaddick, William	Newton
Castillo, Santiago	Bexar	Chadwick, H. A.	Burleson
Castlebury, Jason	Shelby	Chaffin, James	Hopkins
Castlebury,		Chaffin, James A.	San Augustine
Stephen H.	Shelby	Chaffin, Lavina	Anderson
Castleman, ----	Bastrop	Chaine, John	Bexar
Castleman, Jacob	Fayette	Chaine, John	Refugio
Castleman, James	Fayette	Chairs, Elijah	Houston
Castleman, John	Grimes	Chairs, John	Houston
Castleman, M. D.	Limestone	Chairs, Samuel	Houston
Castro, Henry	Bexar	Chalmess, A.	Grayson
Cate, James	Dallas	Chamberlain, Carol	Harris
Cater, Mrs. C. H.	Harrison	Chamberlain, J. T.	Nacogdoches
Cater, Edwin	Harrison	Chamberland, Q. W.	Goliad
Cates, Hiram	Smith	Chambers, James	Fannin
Catlin, J. H.	Austin	Chambers, James	Wharton
Cato, John H.	Lamar	Chambers, James S.	Limestone
Caton, Benjamin	Galveston	Chambers, T. J.	Liberty
Caton, Cynthia	Bowie	Chambers, T. W.	Bastrop
Caton, O. S.	Bowie	Chambers, Thomas	Montgomery
Caton, W. R.	Bowie	Chambers, William	Liberty

NAME	COUNTY	NAME	COUNTY
Chambers, William	Wharton	Chatfield, Norman	Navarro
Chamblee, John	Robertson	Chatfield, William	
Chambliss,		C.	Shelby
Nathaniel	Harris	Chatham, Thomas	Montgomery
Champin, Richard	Brazoria	Chaudoin, Thomas	Lavaca
Chance, Coleman	Burleson	Chauli, Concepsion	Bexar
Chance, E. James	Burleson	Chauncey, John	Smith
Chance, Jacob	Burleson	Chauncey, Mary	Smith
Chance, James	Burleson	Chauncey, Stephen	Smith
Chance, M. A.	Burleson	Chavano, M.	Liberty
Chance, Samuel	Burleson	Chavano, S.	Henderson
Chance, William	Burleson	Chavaria, S.	Bexar
Chancelor, A. H.	Rusk	Chaves, Augustin	Bexar
Chancelor, Abraham	Rusk	Chaves, Ignacio	Bexar
Chancelor, William	Rusk	Chaves, Jose	Bexar
Chandler, David	Travis	Chaves, Y.	Bexar
Chandler, Early M.	Fayette	Cheatham, Edward	Titus
Chandler, Hugh	Grimes	Cheatham, J. B.	Lamar
Chandler, Hugh	Montgomery	Cheatham, James	Titus
Chandler, Lewis	Milam	Cheatham, Joseph	Lamar
Chandler, R. T.	Travis	Cheek, Benjamin	Austin
Chaney, F. R.	Lavaca	Cheek, John	Harris
Chanler, Lewis	Jefferson	Cheek, Noah	Washington
Chapa, Jose	Bexar	Cheek, W. A.	Bastrop
Chapman, D.	Houston	Chemer, John	Fayette
Chapman, G. W.	Milam	Chenault, Felix	Gonzales
Chapman, H. L.	Nacogdoches	Chenault, Wesley	Dallas
Chapman, J. H. F.	Galveston	Cheney, Ebenezer	Fort Bend
Chapman, Matilda		Cheney, Edward	Gonzales
A.	Nacogdoches	Cheney, F. M.	Victoria
Chapman, Silas	Newton	Cheney, F. S.	Grimes
Chapman, W. D.	Nacogdoches	Chenowith, John	Washington
Chapman, William	Washington	Chenowith, Thomas	Dallas
Chappell, F. G.	Washington	Cherino, Antonio	Bexar
Chappell, George		Cherino, Batisto	Nacogdoches
Y.	Washington	Cherino, Jose	
Chappell, N. A.	Washington	Maria	Nacogdoches
Chappell, N. J.	Washington	Cherino, Lucus	Nacogdoches
Chappell, R. W.	Washington	Cherry, Aaron, Jr.	Liberty
Chappell, William	Washington	Cherry, Aaron, Sr.	Liberty
Chares, Pedre R.	Goliad	Cherry, David	Henderson
Charino, L.	Henderson	Cherry, David	San Augustine
Charles, James	Fayette	Cherry, J. V.	Titus
Charles, William		Cherry, Joel	Milam
T.	Washington	Cherry, John	Liberty
Charlton, James M.	Nacogdoches	Cherry, Jesse	Titus
Charlton, N. B.	Tyler	Cherry, S. R.	Titus
Chason, Carlos	Bexar	Cherry, William	Liberty
Chason, R.	Henderson	Cheshire, J. B.	Montgomery
Chassaigm, J. E.	Liberty	Cheshire, James	Jefferson

29

NAME	COUNTY	NAME	COUNTY
Chesire, Thomas	Dallas	Choate, Richard C.	Shelby
Chesser, Daniel	Henderson	Choate, Stinkley	Leon
Chesson, Joseph	Jefferson	Choate, Moses L.	Polk
Chesson, Maguire	Jefferson	Cholwell, Gustavus	Matagorda
Chesson, William	Henderson	Chorcon, Antonio	Bexar
Chevalier, C.	Henderson	Chowning, James	Dallas
Chevalier, Ch.	Nacogdoches	Chowning, Richard	Dallas
Chevis, P.	Goliad	Chowning, Robert	Dallas
Chew, D. S.	Fayette	Chrisman, Horatio	Burleson
Chilcoate, C. C.	Harrison	Chrisman, Horatio	Grimes
Childers,		Chrismas, J.	Walker
Elizabeth	Anderson	Christian, C.	Houston
Childers, G. C.	Goliad	Christian, George	Bexar
Childers, G. W.	Bexar	Christian, George	
Childers, Goldsby	Milam	A.	Nacogdoches
Childers, H. M.	Bastrop	Christian, J.	Henderson
Childers, J. T.	Henderson	Christian, J. C.	Cass
Childers, John	Jasper	Christian, J. M.	Bastrop
Childers, John C.	Nacogdoches	Christian, James	
Childers, John C.	Polk	A.	Nacogdoches
Childers, Prior	Milam	Christian, John	Bowie
Childers, Robert	Milam	Christian, L. J.	Titus
Childress,		Christian, M.	Goliad
Benjamin	Rusk	Christian, R.	Henderson
Childress,		Christian, W. H.	Titus
Elizabeth	Anderson	Chubb, John	Austin
Childress, Jackson	Anderson	Chubb, Thomas	Austin
Childress, L. G.	Red River	Chumley, Bird	San Augustine
Childress, W. H.	Cass	Chumley, Thomas P.	Goliad
Childress, William	Leon	Chumney, A.	Angelina
Chiles, L. L.	Burleson	Chumney, Alexander	San Augustine
Chiles, W. H.	Cass	Chumney, John	San Augustine
Chisholm, William	Jefferson	Chumney, Thomas	San Augustine
Chism, Isham	Rusk	Chunn, Lancelot	Lamar
Chism, John	Rusk	Church, John	Harris
Chism, Larkin	Rusk	Church, M. E.	Grimes
Chism, Thomas	Rusk	Church, T. J.	Henderson
Chism, William	Rusk	Churchill, Andrew	Brazoria
Chism, William,		Cimble, Prudence	Guadalupe
Jr.	Rusk	Cincade, Charles	Fayette
Chissum, Claborn	Lamar	Cirvil, Bateast	Liberty
Chissum, H.	Nacogdoches	Cissna, Joseph M.	Nacogdoches
Chissum, Isham R.	Nacogdoches	Clabo, Charles	Walker
Chissum, V. R.	Lamar	Clanton, L. H.	Walker
Chisum, Elijah	Cherokee	Clap, David	Red River
Chisum, John J.	Hopkins	Clap, Eli	Colorado
Chisum, M.	Liberty	Clap, Elisha	Houston
Choate, C. C.	Shelby	Clap, William	Red River
Choate, D. B.	Tyler	Clapp, G. W.	Rusk
Choate, John	Harris	Clapp, George L.	Sabine

NAME	COUNTY	NAME	COUNTY
Clapp, Joel	Houston	Jr.	Sabine
Clapp, Lucy	Houston	Clark, William	
Clapp, William	Houston	Sr.	Sabine
Clare, A. M.	Jackson	Clark, William H.	Gonzales
Clark, A. T.	Red River	Clarke, Amos	San Augustine
Clark, Alexander	Rusk	Clarke, Benjamin	Liberty
Clark, B. S.	Red River	Clarke, Charles	Goliad
Clark, Barton	Houston	Clarke, D. W. C.	San Augustine
Clark, C. A.	Lavaca	Clarke, Daniel	Walker
Clark, Dan	Houston	Clarke, Daniel,	
Clark, E. A.	Montgomery	Jr.	Cherokee
Clark, Edward	Harrison	Clarke, Dread	Shelby
Clark, Edward N.	Austin	Clarke, Henry	Goliad
Clark, Elijah	Sabine	Clarke, John	Harris
Clark, Erastus	Fayette	Clarke, L. N.	Brazos
Clark, Esther	Gonzales	Clarke, Mary	Brozos
Clark, Frankling	Lavaca	Clarke, William	Guadalupe
Clark, George	Jefferson	Clarke, William	Harris
Clark, H. B.	Cass	Clarke, William	Lamar
Clark, Henry	Sabine	Clarke, William	Shelby
Clark, Henry W.	Cass	Clarkson, H. B.	Nacogdoches
Clark, J.	Titus	Clary, David	Grimes
Clark, J. C.	Montgomery	Clary, F. M.	Grimes
Clark, J. C.	Wharton	Clary, George W.	Grimes
Clark, J. M.	Leon	Clary, Jesse	Grimes
Clark, James	Cass	Clary, Meshac	Austin
Clark, James	Grayson	Clary, T.	Jackson
Clark, James	Sabine	Claude, Mary	Galveston
Clark, John	Gonzales	Claunch, William	
Clark, John	Lavaca	M.	Harrison
Clark, John	Polk	Clawson, L. G.	Cass
Clark, John	Sabine	Clawson, M.	Cass
Clark, John	San Patricio	Clay, J.	Collin
Clark, John W.	Grimes	Clay, Marcus L.	Lamar
Clark, Joseph M.	Nacogdoches	Clay, T. J.	Liberty
Clark, L.	Collin	Clay, Tacitus	Washington
Clark, M. M.	Panola	Claypool, J. S.	Limestone
Clark, Martin	Leon	Claypool, John H.	Limestone
Clark, Micajah	Fayette	Claypool, S. J.	Limestone
Clark, Minerva	Hunt	Clayton, Ann	Liberty
Clark, Mrs.		Clayton, Daniel	Liberty
Saryanne M.	Harrison	Clayton, Henry R.	Liberty
Clark, Rebecca	Montgomery	Clayton, J. B.	Liberty
Clark, Thomas B.	Grimes	Clayton, J. G. W.	Nacogdoches
Clark, Thomas W.	Harrison	Clayton, J. W.	Liberty
Clark, W. L.	Montgomery	Clayton, James	Liberty
Clark, William	Galveston	Clayton, James M.	Liberty
Clark, William	Jefferson	Clayton, Josephus	Liberty
Clark, William	San Patricio	Clear, John D.	Lavaca
Clark, William,		Cleaveland, Ezra	Austin

NAME	COUNTY	NAME	COUNTY
Cleaveland, James M.	Washington	Cline, Jacob	Cass
Cleaveland, Solomon	Austin	Cline, Peter	Henderson
Cleek, Henry	Sabine	Clingman, A. A.	Liberty
Clegg, Edward	Calhoun	Clinton, James	Harrison
Clements, A. G.	Matagorda	Clinton, R.	Brazoria
Clements, E.	Limestone	Clinton, William	Fayette
Clements, Egbert	Red River	Clipper, L. G.	Grimes
Clements, Robert F.	Brazoria	Clipper, Lem G.	Montgomery
Clements, S. C.	Red River	Clopper, A. M.	Harris
Clements, Dr. S. E.	Red River	Clopton, B. M.	Bastrop
Clemmons, Ira	Washington	Close, Hiram	Galveston
Clemmons, J. A.	Washington	Cloud, J. C.	Washington
Clemmons, James	Cass	Cloud, James M.	Austin
Clemmons, James	Washington	Cloud, Jeremiah	Austin
Clemmons, Lewis	Washington	Cloud, S. J.	DeWitt
Clendenen, David F.	Hopkins	Clow, John J.	Grimes
Clendenen, Mathew B.	Hopkins	Clow, R. J.	Lavaca
Clendenen, R. T.	Hopkins	Clower, John	Angelina
Cleveland, Alfred	Brazos	Cloys, Albert	Milam
Cleveland, Charles L.	Brazoria	Clubb, Thomas B.	Jefferson
Cleveland, H. J.	Colorado	Clump, William	Austin
Cleveland, Henry	Fayette	Clute, J. R.	Nacogdoches
Cleveland, J. A. H.	Galveston	Clutter, Grant	Fannin
Cleveland, W. H.	Washington	Clyne, Jacob	------
Clevenger, George	Nacogdoches	Coal, Wesley	Brazoria
Clevenger, Thomas	Hunt	Coale, William	Rusk
Click, A. J.	Houston	Coalter, James	Harris
Click, A. J.	Lamar	Coats, A.	Titus
Click, Calvin M.	Lamar	Coats, Alexander	Rusk
Click, George	Houston	Coats, George	Titus
Click, Malekech	Houston	Coats, James	Rusk
Click, Matthias	Lamar	Coats, Robert	Lamar
Click, Nathaniel	Houston	Cobb, Clark	Robertson
Clifford, Joseph	Goliad	Cobb, Clay	Leon
Clift, Jesse	Fayette	Cobb, David	Leon
Clifton, Ely	Titus	Cobb, Francis R.	Galveston
Clifton, Josiah	Bastrop	Cobb, H. A.	Galveston
Clifton, Reace	Titus	Cobb, J. F.	Liberty
Clifton, V.	Cass	Cobb, Pinckney	Limestone
Clifton, W. S.	Upshur	Cobb, Stancil	Robertson
Clifton, Wilson	Hopkins	Cobb, W. H.	Harrison
Cline, Isaac	Navarro	Cobb, William	Grimes
		Cobern, Hansel	Houston
		Cobern, Isom	Navarro
		Cobern, Shelby	Shelby
		Coble, Adam	Lavaca
		Cochran, A. F.	Galveston
		Cochran, E. S.	Burleson
		Cochran, Henry	Newton
		Cochran, J.	Fannin

NAME	COUNTY	NAME	COUNTY
Cochran, J. S.	Newton	Cole, Alfred A.	Fort Bend
Cochran, James	Austin	Cole, Calvin	Dallas
Cochran, L. M.	Fannin	Cole, David	Harris
Cochran, O.	Harris	Cole, David	Jefferson
Cochran, O. J.	Harris	Cole, Elia	Fort Bend
Cochran, P. J.	Rusk	Cole, Garnett G.	Nacogdoches
Cochran, Robert	Titus	Cole, Garrett P.	Henderson
Cochran, William	Angelina	Cole, H. B.	Henderson
Cochran, William	Newton	Cole, Mrs. J. A.	Harrison
Cochran, WIlliam	Polk	Cole, James	Cass
Cochran, William		Cole, James	Fort Bend
M.	Fannin	Cole, James	Harris
Cockburn, William	Travis	Cole, James	Harrison
Cocke, Ann	Fayette	Cole, James M.	Dallas
Cocke, Benjamin W.	Cass	Cole, James P.	Galveston
Cocke, James H.	Galveston	Cole, Jesse	Houston
Cocke, John A.	Grimes	Cole, John	Dallas
Cocke, S. H.	Grimes	Cole, John	Harris
Cockran, J. B.	Nacogdoches	Cole, John	Jefferson
Cockran, Thomas	Washington	Cole, John H.	Cass
Cockrell, John R.	Milam	Cole, Joseph	Harrison
Cockrell, Simon	Gonzales	Cole, Reuben	Harrison
Cockrell, Wesley	Dallas	Cole, Richard	Fort Bend
Cockrum, C.	Fannin	Cole, T. J.	Harrison
Coe, Phillip H.	Washington	Cole, William	Red River
Coffee, Cleveland	Colorado	Cole, William	Washington
Coffee, Cyrus	Titus	Cole, William A.	Washington
Coffee, Holland	Grayson	Coleman, A.	Bexar
Coffee, James	Colorado	Coleman, A. M.	Harrison
Coffee, Joel	Titus	Coleman, Mrs. Anne	Harrison
Coffee, Logan	Colorado	Coleman, Charles	Jackson
Coffee, M. S.	Titus	Coleman, D. H.	Bastrop
Coffee, Sophia	Grayson	Coleman, John	Cass
Coffee, Thomas J.	Brazoria	Coleman, John	Harris
Coffee, W. J.	Titus	Coleman, John	Harrison
Coffee, William	Colorado	Coleman, Samuel P.	Harrison
Coffee, William	Titus	Coleman, Stephen	Harrison
Coffee, Woodson	Colorado	Coleman, Wiat C.	Brazos
Coffman, J.	Collin	Coleman, Young	Jackson
Coffman, James	Red River	Coles, Benjamin L.	Galveston
Coffman, Lovel	Red River	Coles, John P.	Washington
Coit, D. P.	Liberty	Coles, W. T. F.	Lamar
Coke, Charles	Henderson	Coley, Canah C.	Gonzales
Coker, John	Austin	Collard, E., Jr.	Montgomery
Colambio, Julian	Bexar	Collard, Elija	Walker
Colby, Anthony	Red River	Collard, Eren	Walker
Colderon, James	Henderson	Collard, Honathan	Walker
Colderon, James	Hunt	Collard, James	Walker
Colderson, S.	Henderson	Collard, Job S.	Walker
Colderson, A.	Henderson	Collard, L. M.	Walker

33

NAME	COUNTY	NAME	COUNTY
Colley, J. G.	Robertson	Colvin, John	Polk
Collier, C.	Liberty	Colwell, A.	Collin
Collier, E. G.	Montgomery	Colwell, A. J.	Angelina
Collier, James Y.	Harrison	Colwell, Elizabeth	Angelina
Collier, Patrick	Shelby	Colwell, H.	Collin
Collier, Thomas	Shelby	Colwell, J. M.	Houston
Collins, Allen	Cass	Colwell, James	Rusk
Collins, C.	Cass	Colwell, R. W.	Houston
Collins, David	Rusk	Colwell, T.	Collin
Collins, E. M.	Leon	Colwell, W.	Collin
Collins, G. W.	Angelina	Colwell, William	Angelina
Collins, J. J.	San Augustine	Colwell, William	Rusk
Collins, James	Cass	Colwell, Wyley	Angelina
Collins, James T.	Polk	Colyer, John	Jefferson
Collins, John	Houston	Combs, Levi G.	Dallas
Collins, John	Polk	Combs, William	Dallas
Collins, John W.	Austin	Comes, James	Montgomery
Collins, Joseph	Cherokee	Comes, John	Montgomery
Collins, Joseph	Panola	Comical, Richard	Houston
Collins, Lewis P.	DeWitt	Compton, A. G.	Goliad
Collins, Mary	Robertson	Compton, A. G.	Washington
Collins, R. M.	Brazoria	Compton, Alex	Brazoria
Collins, Reuben D.	Titus	Compton, E. L.	Burleson
Collins, S. E.	Liberty	Compton, J. B.	Fannin
Collins, T. C.	Travis	Compton, Joseph	Fannin
Collins, Thomas P.	Houston	Conbilo, Juana	Bexar
Collins, W. J.	Anderson	Conder, Steven	Anderson
Collins, W. R.	Red River	Cone, H. H.	Harris
Collins, W. V.	Sabine	Cone, William	Anderson
Collins, W. W. G.	Red River	Conger, Eliza	Galveston
Collins, Wade	Panola	Conger, James	Harris
Collins, William	Fort Bend	Conger, John P.	Harris
Collins, William		Conklen, M. D.	Harris
B.	Harrison	Conlan, R. S.	Galveston
Collinsworth, Wm.		Conly, Isaac	Austin
C.	Travis	Conly, Preston	Bastrop
Collom, Catherine	Bowie	Conly, S. B.	Gonzales
Collom, Charles	Bowie	Conn, Hugh L.	Gonzales
Collom, G. G.	Bowie	Connally, M.	Grimes
Collom, J. H.	Bowie	Connell, D. C.	Washington
Collom, John	Bowie	Connell, James	Washington
Collom, Jonathan	Bowie	Connell, Sampson	Washington
Collorn, Martha	Grayson	Connell, William	Washington
Collorn, William	Grayson	Connelly, Charles	Gonzales
Colman, Rebecca	Liberty	Connelly, John B.	Brazoria
Colpaper, J.	Jackson	Connelly, Joseph	Burleson
Colquhoun,		Connelly, Mishael	Harris
Ludovici	Bexar	Connelly, William	Burleson
Colton, H.	Cass	Conner, H. C.	Henderson
Colville, J. B.	Newton	Conner, H. L.	Harris

NAME	COUNTY	NAME	COUNTY
Conner, F. B.	Houston	Cook, Milton	Panola
Conner, Henry M.	Panola	Cook, Rebecca	Sabine
Conner, T. J.	Henderson	Cook, Samuel M.	Cherokee
Conner, William	Houston	Cook, William	Nacogdoches
Connor, Elizabeth	Newton	Cook, William H.	Gonzales
Connor, F. J.	Titus	Cooke, Abner, Jr.	Harris
Connor, John	Cherokee	Cooke, H.	Collin
Connor, THomas	Cherokee	Cooke, Mrs. Mary	Limestone
Connor, William	Cherokee	Cooke, W. G.	Montgomery
Connor, Uriah	Cherokee	Cooke, Wildes K.	Limestone
Conover, W. W.	Dallas	Cooksey, Enoch	Montgomery
Conrow, E. M.	Grimes	Cooksey, John C.	Gonzales
Conrow, E. M.	Montgomery	Coon, Ephriam	Nacogdoches
Contes, C.	Bexar	Coonrod, Thomas	Shelby
Contes, Manuel	Bexar	Coonus, F.	Collin
Contreras, Juan	Refugio	Cooper, A.	Collin
Converse, Sayre	Matagorda	Cooper, Benjamin	Cass
Conway, W. H.	San Augustine	Cooper, C. H.	Harrison
Coody, Joseph	Walker	Cooper, Dillard	Colorado
Cook, A. Hamilton	Calhoun	Cooper, Elisha	Harrison
Cook, A. H.	Travis	Cooper, Ennis	Washington
Cook, Mrs. C. A.	Jackson	Cooper, Isaac	Lamar
Cook, C. T. C.	Limestone	Cooper, Hamilton	Harrison
Cook, D. M.	Titus	Cooper, Henry	Fannin
Cook, David	Cherokee	Cooper, J.	Grimes
Cook, Edward	Lamar	Cooper, J. G.	Leon
Cook, Elias T.	Grimes	Cooper, J. M.	Harrison
Cook, Elihu D.	Cherokee	Cooper, James	Harris
Cook, Elizabeth	Henderson	Cooper, James	Washington
Cook, H. C.	Matagorda	Cooper, Job	Shelby
Cook, Franklin	Rusk	Cooper, Lucy A.	Leon
Cook, George	Galveston	Cooper, Mrs.	
Cook, Henry	Navarro	Margarette	Herrison
Cook, Henry	Rusk	Cooper, Nancy	Newton
Cook, J. H. W.	Limestone	Cooper, Nathan	Hopkins
Cook, J. T.	Cherokee	Cooper, R. M.	Red River
Cook, J. W.	Fort Bend	Cooper, Robert B.	Harrison
Cook, James	Cherokee	Cooper, S. A.	Bowie
Cook, James B.	Limestone	Cooper, S. W.	Washington
Cook, Jeff	Titus	Cooper, Thomas	Galveston
Cook, John	Shelby	Cooper, Thomas	Washington
Cook, John C.	Dallas	Cooper, W. T.	San Augustine
Cook, John F.	Jackson	Cooper, William	Austin
Cook, Joseph G.	Cherokee	Cooper, William	Harrison
Cook, L. A.	Cherokee	Cooper, William	Houston
Cook, M. A. D.	Leon	Cooper, William	Liberty
Cook, Maria	Goliad	Cooper, William C.	Newton
Cook, Mary	Cherokee	Cope, Mason W.	Cherokee
Cook, Mary Ann	Goliad	Cope, Thomas	Liberty
Cook, Melinda	Galveston	Copeland,	

NAME	COUNTY	NAME	COUNTY
Elizabeth	Leon	Coster, George	Anderson
Copeland, John	Leon	Coster, William S.	Anderson
Copeland, Joseph	Leon	Costley, Rebecca	Fannin
Copeland, L.	Grimes	Cothran, Wilson W.	Rusk
Copeland, R.	Grimes	Cotter, Stephen	Grayson
Copeland, W.	Grimes	Cotterell, G. W.	Wharton
Copeland, W.	Leon	Cottle, Joseph	Bastrop
Copeland, William	Fannin	Cottle, Sylvanus	Bastrop
Copes, James W.	Harris	Cottle, Z. T.	Bastrop
Corbet, John	Galveston	Cotton, Cullin C.	Gonzales
Corbet, John	Limestone	Cotton, John	Walker
Corbett, Nathaniel	Lamar	Cotton, M. G.	Grayson
Corbin, William P.	Brazoria	Cotton, Thomas	Walker
Corder, R. S.	Henderson	Cotton, W. D.	Jefferson
Corder, Reuben C.	Shelby	Cotton, W. F.	Jefferson
Corder, William A.	Shelby	Cottrell, Jesse H.	Cherokee
Cordier, Alfred	Bexar	Couch, Chaney	Nacogdoches
Cordier, J. B.	Bexar	Couch, Daniel	Walker
Cordova, Damian	Henderson	Couch, Henderson	Dallas
Cordova, Jacob D.	Harris	Coughlin, John	Harris
Cordova, Jean	Goliad	Coulter, C. H.	San Augustine
Cordova, Jose	Bexar	Coun, Joseph	Newton
Cordova, Maria		Coursey, G. M.	Limestone
Antonio	Nacogdoches	Courtney, J.	Leon
Core, Wiley	Cass	Courtney, Jesse	Montgomery
Corlew, A. M.	Fannin	Covington, Charles	Washington
Corley, Samuel	Red River	Covington, John	Limestone
Cornelison, John	Lamar	Cowan, D. C.	Burleson
Cornelius, Abslm	Bowie	Cowan, G. P.	Burleson
Cornelius, Cooper	Rusk	Cowan, James B.	Brazoria
Cornelius,		Cowan, S. B.	Grayson
Margaret	Bowie	Cowan, T. B.	Red River
Cornelius, R. W.	Red River	Cowen, Hugh	Grayson
Cornelius, T. J.	Red River	Cowen, John B.	Brazoria
Cornelius, W. P.	Red River	Cowets, Thomas	Galveston
Corner, David	Travis	Cowett, Thomas	Fannin
Corner, Evan	Montgomery	Cox, Abner	Fannin
Corner, James	Montgomery	Cox, Andrew J.	Smith
Corner, John	Montgomery	Cox, Anne	Limestone
Cornett, James	Matagorda	Cox, Benjamin	Navarro
Cornett, William	Austin	Cox, Burwell	Fannin
Correy, Ezra	Brazoria	Cox, Cornelius	Dallas
Cortez, Est.	Bexar	Cox, E. M.	Burleson
Cortez, Felipe	Henderson	Cox, Edward W.	Harrison
Cortez, Ja. W.	Fannin	Cox, Eli	Lamar
Cortines, Dolores	Bexar	Cox, Gais	Cass
Cortines,		Cox, George	Brazoria
Gertrudus	Goliad	Cox, George	Dallas
Corzine, H.	Henderson	Cox, George	Hopkins
Corzine, Lewis	Harrison	Cox, George W.	Austin

NAME	COUNTY	NAME	COUNTY
Cox, George W.	Limestone	Crain, J. B.	Nacogdoches
Cox, Hugh	Fannin	Crain, Joel	Lamar
Cox, James	Navarro	Crain, John	Titus
Cox, James	Rusk	Crain, John W.	San Augustine
Cox, James	Washington	Crain, R. T.	Henderson
Cox, Jesse	Walker	Crain, T. G.	Henderson
Cox, John	Dallas	Crain, William	Nacogdoches
Cox, John T.	Fayette	Crain, William	Titus
Cox, Louis	Walker	Crain, William D.	Galveston
Cox, May	Fannin	Crain, William J.	Titus
Cox, Nathan	Fannin	Crane, A.	Cass
Cox, Samuel	DeWitt	Crane, A. P. W.	Galveston
Cox, Samuel	Rusk	Crane, Ambrose	Galveston
Cox, T. W.	Fayette	Crane, Casandra	Harrison
Cox, Thomas	Fannin	Crane, G. B.	Harrison
Cox, Thomas	Panola	Crane, John	Lamar
Cox, W. M.	Henderson	Crane, Mary	Walker
Cox, William	Dallas	Crane, R. G.	Travis
Cox, William	Harrison	Crane, R. T.	Harrison
Cox, William, Sr.	Fannin	Crane, W. C.	Shelby
Coy, F.	Bexar	Crane, William	Wharton
Coy, L. Santos	Bexar	Cranshaw, W. H.	Matagorda
Coy, Matthew	Fannin	Craven, David	San Patricio
Coy, Rafael	Bexar	Craven, G.	Fannin
Coyle, Carlton	Wharton	Craven, James J.	Shelby
Crabb, H. M.	Walker	Cravings, Robert	Lamar
Crabb, Jeremiah	Navarro	Crawford, A.	Harris
Crabtree, John	Cherokee	Crawford, A. C.	Galveston
Crabtree, John	Henderson	Crawford, C. W.	Nacogdoches
Craddock, J. N.	Houston	Crawford, D. C.	Rusk
Craddock, J. R.	Lamar	Crawford, E.	Harrison
Craft, J. A.	Bastrop	Crawford, George	
Craft, J. S.	Bastrop	W.	Washington
Craft, James	Robertson	Crawford, H. R.	Gonzales
Craft, Samuel, Jr.	Bastrop	Crawford, J. C.	Liberty
Craft, Samuel, Sr.	Bastrop	Crawford, J. D.	Cass
Crafton, James R.	Henderson	Crawford, J. F.	Lamar
Craig, Henry, Sr.	Tyler	Crawford, J. F.	Lamar
Craig, J. B.	Bowie	Crawford, J. M.	Harrison
Craig, James	Tyler	Crawford, J. W.	Jackson
Craig, James A.	Jasper	Crawford, Jacob	Sabine
Craig, Jonas	Tyler	Crawford, James M.	Washington
Craig, Jonathan	Harrison	Crawford, Jesse	Nacogdoches
Craig, Samuel	Lamar	Crawford, John B.	Goliad
Craig, T. B.	Nacogdoches	Crawford, John W.	DeWitt
Crain, A.	Henderson	Crawford, Joseph	Anderson
Crain, A.	Nacogdoches	Crawford, M. L.	Cass
Crain, A. H.	Nacogdoches	Crawford, Reuben	Nacogdoches
Crain, C. B.	Henderson	Crawford, Samuel	
Crain, Elizabeth	Henderson	M.	Sabine

NAME	COUNTY	NAME	COUNTY
Crawford, Thomas	Angelina	Crockett, Andrew	Jasper
Crawford, William C.	Harrison	Crockett, Glenn	Anderson
		Crockett, Martha	Jasper
Crawford, William H.	Nacogdoches	Crockett, Thomas	Rusk
		Crofford, Marshal	Hopkins
Crayton, James	Travis	Croft, Jacob	Harris
Creager, George	Cherokee	Croft, John W.	Cherokee
Creawgbaur, R.	Travis	Croger, William	Cass
Creed, Charles P.	Newton	Cronican, John	Galveston
Crenshaw, Abraham	Brazoria	Cronican, M.	Travis
Crenshaw, Charles D.	Grimes	Cronkrite, John	Fayette
		Cronkrite, Lyman	Fayette
Crenshaw, Cornelius	Sabine	Crook, A. M.	Red River
		Crook, J. N.	Lamar
Crenshaw, Cornelius L.	Panola	Crook, Lewis J.	Hopkins
Crenshaw, David	Henderson	Crook, Lewis P.	Hopkins
Crenshaw, Elizabeth L.	Panola	Crook, Richard R.	Hopkins
		Cropper, George W.	Harris
Crenshaw, John C.	Washington	Cropper, Nullbarron	Jefferson
Crenshaw, Minervey	Sabine	Crosby, Henry	Tyler
Crenshaw, Nathaniel	Sabine	Crosby, John R.	Harrison
		Crosby, Josiah J.	Washington
Crenshaw, Oliver B.	Colorado	Crosby, Thomas P.	Brazoria
Crenshaw, William	Fannin	Cross, A.	Henderson
Crier, A.	Colorado	Cross, J. L.	Fannin
Crier, John	Colorado	Cross, J. P.	Grayson
Crippen, Perry	Fayette	Cross, Navarro	Navarro
Crisp, A. R.	Titus	Crossby, Stephen	Travis
Crisp, Carril	Titus	Crossby, Thomas P.	Goliad
Crisp, Jesse	Nacogdoches	Crossland, A. M.	Cherokee
Crisp, Rutha	Titus	Crossland, James	Cherokee
Crisp, W. M.	Lamar	Crossland, James L.	Smith
Crissop, Thomas	Walker	Crossman, Rachel	Galveston
Crist, D. M.	Anderson	Crosstaner, H. S.	Cherokee
Crist, Daniel	Anderson	Crothers, William	Burleson
Crist, George	Anderson	Crouch, Charles W.	San Augustine
Crist, John	Anderson	Crouch, Jackson	Walker
Crist, Rezin	Anderson	Crouch, Joseph	Rusk
Crist, Slaven	Anderson	Crouch, William	San Augustine
Criswell, Joseph	Jasper	Crow, Elizabeth	Lamar
Criswell, L. V.	Fayette	Crow, J. W.	Houston
Criswell, Thomas	Polk	Crow, John L.	Rusk
Crittenden, A. P.	Brazoria	Crow, L. M.	San Augustine
Crittenden, Richard H.	DeWitt	Crow, T. M.	San Augustine
		Crow, W. U.	Cass
Crocheron, H.	Bastrop	Crowder, A.	Titus
Crocker, Alfred	Harrison	Crowder, James H.	Hopkins
Crocker, Nathaniel	Harrison	Crowell, John	Nacogdoches

NAME	COUNTY	NAME	COUNTY
Crowley, James	Colorado	Culver, John	Matagorda
Crownover, A.	Grimes	Culwell, J. H.	Cass
Crownover, Arthur	Fayette	Cuming, David M.	Polk
Crownover, Ben	Red River	Cummings, James	Calhoun
Crownover, J.	Grimes	Cummings, James	Colorado
Crownover, John, Jr.	Fayette	Cummings, James	Fannin
		Cummings, Sidney	Grimes
Crowson, W.	Henderson	Cummings, Steven	Travis
Crozier, R. G.	Galveston	Cummings, U. S.	Grimes
Cruger, James F.	Harris	Cummings, William	Grimes
Cruise, William	Travis	Cummins, John	Henderson
Crump, William E.	Austin	Cummins, M.	Austin
Crumpler, D. D.	Washington	Cummins, Susanah	Washington
Crunk, James	Fort Bend	Cuney, Philip W.	Austin
Crunk, John W.	Harrison	Cunget(?), John	Anderson
Crunk, John W.	Rusk	Cunningham, A. S.	Victoria
Crunk, N. S.	Burleson	Cunningham, C. A.	Panola
Crunk, Paschal	Rusk	Cunningham, Edward	Cass
Cruse, John	Tyler	Cunningham, J.	Collin
Cruse, Squire	Tyler	Cunningham, J. C.	Bastrop
Crutcher, W. H.	Fayette	Cunningham, J. M.	Henderson
Crutchfield, David N.	Nacogdoches	Cunningham, James	Fayette
		Cunningham, John	Dallas
Crutchfield, J. T.	Nacogdoches	Cunningham, John P.	DeWitt
Cruz, Antonio	Bexar		
Cruz, Juan	Nacogdoches	Cunningham, Joseph	Goliad
Cruz, Simon	Bexar	Cunningham, L. C.	Bastrop
Cruzus, D. C.	Wharton	Cunningham, M. E.	Colorado
Cryber, C. C.	Upshur	Cunningham, Sarah	DeWitt
Crye, Henry	Colorado	Cunningham, W.	Cass
Cude, J. W.	Henderson	Cunningham, William L.	Washington
Cude, Timothy	Montgomery		
Cude, William	Montgomery	Cupples, George	Bexar
Culberson, T.	Leon	Curd, J.	Brazos
Culberson, T. C.	Anderson	Curl, Henry H.	San Augustine
Culberson, W. A.	Leon	Curl, T. J.	San Augustine
Culbertson, Margaret	Brazoria	Curling, Patrick	Refugio
		Curneal, P. T.	Milam
Cullen, E. W.	San Augustine	Currie, J. N.	Shelby
Cullen, F. T.	San Augustine	Currie, James	Harris
Cullins, A.	Burleson	Currie, Richard	Polk
Cullins, Daniel	Milam	Currie, Thomas	Brozos
Cullum, Luey A.	Red River	Curry, David	Robertson
Cullumber, A.	Upshur	Curry, Mrs. Ellifair	Limestone
Culp, D. D.	Harris		
Culp, James	Cass	Curry, James	Houston
Culp, Josiah	Limestone	Curry, John R.	Galveston
Culpepper, Henry W.	Smith	Curry, T. T.	Limestone
		Curt, T. J.	Henderson
Culton, A. H.	San Augustine	Curtis, Charles	Jefferson

NAME	COUNTY	NAME	COUNTY
Curtis, Edward	Cass	Dameron, John	Henderson
Curtis, Elijah	Bastrop	Dameron, M. W.	Henderson
Curtis, James	Bastrop	Dammon, Delila	Fannin
Curtis, James	Jefferson	Dampkie, E. H.	Colorado
Curtis, John W.	Grayson	Dampkie, George	Colorado
Curtis, Newton	Newton	Dance, H. B.	Rusk
Curtis, William M.	Austin	Dance, J. S.	Brazoria
Cushman, C. C.	Travis	Dance, J. W.	Brazoria
Cushney, William		Dancer, Ashel	Bastrop
H.	Travis	Dancy, John W.	Fayette
Custard, William	Travis	Danely, Andrew	Rusk
Custer, D. M.	Harris	Danforth, Nancy M.	Goliad
Custer, K. S.	Collin	Daniel, Abraham	Rusk
Custer, John	Hunt	Daniel, J. B.	Bowie
Custis, S. S.	Burleson	Daniel, James M.	Colorado
Cuthberson, J. J.	Anderson	Daniel, Jesse	Bowie
Cutter, D. M.	Harris	Daniel, John	Bowie
Cutter, Samuel	Shelby	Daniel, Joseph	Robertson
Cuyger, William	Grayson	Daniel, Joseph T.	Milam
Cyrus, William	Lamar	Daniel, Mary	Harrison
		Daniel, Robert	Cass
		Daniel, S. N.	Harrison
Dabbs, William	Polk	Daniel, W. C.	Bowie
Dabney, Eliza	Colorado	Daniel, William	Jackson
Dabney, John	Navarro	Daniel, William	Limestone
Dacon, E.	Harrison	Daniel, William	San Augustine
Daggett, C. B.	Shelby	Daniel, Williamson	Colorado
Daggett, E.	Shelby	Danigay, Bryant	Liberty
Daggett, E. M.	Shelby	Danks, A. B.	Dallas
Dagley, Thomas A.	Fannin	Darby, D.	Collin
Dagley, W. B.	Fannin	Darby, Willis P.	Washington
Dailey, Michael	Polk	Darden, Stephen S.	Gonzales
Dakan, Jacob	Red River	Dare, George	Burleson
Dakan, Perry	Dallas	Darling, Hugh	Panola
Dalby, Anne	Bowie	Darling, Socrates	Fayette
Dalby, J. C.	Bowie	Darlington, J. W.	Travis
Dalby, P. A.	Bowie	Darnell, J. H.	Red River
Dalby, Thomas D.	Bowie	Darragh, Ann	Galveston
Dalby, W. K.	Bowie	Darragh, J. L.	Galveston
Dalby, W. K.	Cass	Darst, D. S. H.	Gonzales
Dale, Elijah	Goliad	Darst, Henry	Fort Bend
Dale, J. P.	Red River	Darst, John G.	Fort Bend
Dallas, Alexander	Washington	Darst, Patric	Fort Bend
Dallas, James L.	Washington	Darst, Richard	Fort Bend
Dallas, Walter R.	Washington	Datson, J. W.	Colorado
Dallas, William A.	Washington	Daughdrill, Lott	Newton
Dalrymple, W. C.	Bastrop	Daughttry, B. M.	Colorado
Dalton, Morris	Fannin	Daughttry, James	
Dalton, William	Henderson	J. D.	Panola
Dameron, J. S.	Henderson	Daughttry, John	Panola

NAME	COUNTY	NAME	COUNTY
Daum, John	Comal	Davis, Daniel	Gonzales
Dautry, Briant	Austin	Davis, E. B.	Limestone
Dautry, James	Austin	Davis, E. D.	Brazoria
Davenport, Charles	Harrison	Davis, E. W.	Anderson
Davenport, Charles		Davis, Edward	San Augustine
G.	Harrison	Davis, Edward B.	Grimes
Davenport, John	Houston	Davis, Elenore C.	Rusk
Davenport, Philip	Brazoria	Davis, Eli	Limestone
Davenport, Thomas		Davis, Elias K.	San Augustine
G.	Panola	Davis, Elizabeth	Burleson
Davenport, William	Fannin	Davis, F. W.	Grayson
Davenport, William	Harrison	Davis, Fields	Goliad
Davenport & Buck	Brazoria	Davis, Freeton	Bastrop
Daveron, D.	Victoria	Davis, George W.	DeWitt
David, W. K.	Bexar	Davis, George W.	Nacogdoches
David, William	Colorado	Davis, George W.	Travis
Davidson, A.	Titus	Davis, H. B.	Lamar
Davidson, A. M.	Sau Augustine	Davis, H. H.	Grayson
Davidson, G. R.	Polk	Davis, Harrall P.	Burleson
Davidson, George		Davis, Harrison	Shelby
W.	Cass	Davis, Hiram	Harrison
Davidson, H. H.	Grimes	Davis, Hulda	Panola
Davidson, Hopkins	Lamar	Davis, Isaiah	Lamar
Davidson, Isiah	Panola	Davis, Isham	Denton
Davidson, Joseph	Red River	Davis, J.	Cass
Davidson, L. D.	Collin	Davis, J. H.	Calhoun
Davidson, Q.	Victoria	Davis, J. J.	Austin
Davidson, Samuel		Davis, J. L.	Lamar
L.	Henderson	Davis, J. M.	Limestone
Davidson, Sol	Sabine	Davis, J. S.	Lamar
Davidson, T.	Victoria	Davis, Jackson	Goliad
Davidson, W. K.	Fort Bend	Davis, Jacob	Nacogdoches
Davila, J.	Bexar	Davis, Jacob	Titus
Davis, A.	Fannin	Davis, James	Bowie
Davis, A. A.	Shelby	Davis, James	Burleson
Davis, Abner	Lamar	Davis, James, Jr.	Liberty
Davis, Anna	Henderson	Davis, James, Sr.	Liberty
Davis, Arch. B.	Panola	Davis, James L.	Austin
Davis, Arthur L.	Fannin	Davis, James M.	Shelby
Davis, Ashburn	Angelina	Davis, James R.	San Augustine
Davis, B. B.	Lamar	Davis, Jeremiah G.	Rusk
Davis, B. S.	Fannin	Davis, Jesse K.	Grimes
Davis, Benjamin	Houston	Davis, John	Cass
Davis, Benjamin	Lamar	Davis, John	Goliad
Davis, Biddy	Austin	Davis, John	Lamar
Davis, Brinkley	Limestone	Davis, John	Rusk
Davis, Cade, W.	Sabine	Davis, John	Shelby
Davis, Charles	Liberty	Davis, John	Titus
Davis, D. G.	Milam	Davis, John	Walker
Davis, D. M.	Lamar	Davis, John B.	Anderson

NAME	COUNTY	NAME	COUNTY
Davis, John B.	Polk	Davis, Warren	Henderson
Davis, John E.	Houston	Davis, Wiley	Burleson
Davis, John H.	Liberty	Davis, William	Cass
Davis, John T.	Burleson	Davis, William	Cherokee
Davis, John T.	Galveston	Davis, William	Newton
Davis, Johnson	Grayson	Davis, William	Panola
Davis, Jonathan	Bastrop	Davis, William	Shelby
Davis, Joshua H.	Goliad	Davis, William C.	Rusk
Davis, Josiah	Grimes	Davis, William D.	Grayson
Davis, Lee R.	Milam	Davis, William G.	Burleson
Davis, Mrs. Louisa	Jackson	Davis, William J.	Montgomery
Davis, M. C.	Grayson	Davis, William P.	Houston
Davis, Mary Jane	Galveston	Davis, Wilson	Lamar
Davis, N. H.	Grimes	Davis, Zachariah	DeWitt
Davis, N. T.	Harris	Davison, Allen	Cass
Davis, Nathan	Austin	Davlen, Hew	Henderson
Davis, Nathan, Jr.	Shelby	Davlen, Thomas	Montgomery
Davis, Nathan, Sr.	Shelby	Davy, J. P.	Grimes
Davis, Nathaniel		Davy, Samuel	Brazoria
H.	Montgomery	Dawes, Isaac	Jackson
Davis, Patrick	Jackson	Dawson, Britton	Robertson
Davis, Pleasant	Newton	Dawson, David	San Patricio
Davis, Porter M.	Grayson	Dawson, Dread	Robertson
Davis, R. M.	Gonzales	Dawson, G. T.	Fayette
Davis, R. M.	Guadalupe	Dawson, J.	Collin
Davis, Ralph	Lamar	Dawson, W. C.	Fayette
Davis, Reason S.	Angelina	Dawson, W. N.	Red River
Davis, Robert	Fayette	Day, Franklin	Lamar
Davis, S.	Angelina	Day, Henry	Washington
Davis, S.	Bastrop	Day, J. C.	Liberty
Davis, S. H.	Harrison	Day, James M.	Guadalupe
Davis, S. J.	Walker	Day, Jeremiah	Jefferson
Davis, S. S.	San Augustine	Day, John H.	Washington
Davis, Samuel	Leon	Day, Larkin	Montgomery
Davis, Samuel H.	Henderson	Day, Samuel	Lamar
Davis, Sarah	Gonzales	Day, Sarah	Guadalupe
Davis, Sarah	Houston	Dayell, Junius	Bastrop
Davis, Solomon	Grayson	De Aiste, J. L.	Harris
Davis, Stephen L.	Panola	Deal, Anna	Shelby
Davis, T.	Upshur	Deal, N. G.	Shelby
Davis, T. B.	Walker	Deamwood, Henry	Sabine
Davis, T. C.	Walker	Dean, Alexander	Galveston
Davis, Thomas	Polk	Dean, Alfred	Walker
Davis, Thomas K.	Brazoria	Dean, B. W.	Cass
Davis, Turner	Newton	Dean, Domingo	Bexar
Davis, V. A.	Titus	Dean, E.	Montgomery
Davis, Vilet	Leon	Dean, J.	Upshur
Davis, W. H.	Walker	Dean, J. M.	Henderson
Davis, W. M. H.	Upshur	Dean, J. W.	Victoria
Davis, W. W.	Liberty	Dean, Jabez	Washington

NAME	COUNTY	NAME	COUNTY
Dean, James	Walker	de la Gorcia, Ant.	Henderson
Dean, John	Smith	Delaney, ----	Angelina
Dean, Levi	Red River	Delaney, ---	Houston
Dean, M.	Bexar	Delaney, Eliza	Guadalupe
Dean, Philip	Brazoria	Delaney, Isaac	Sabine
Dean, Sarah	Red River	Delaney, James	Jasper
Dean, T. M.	Walker	Delaney, Jeremiah	Jasper
Dean, Willis	Red River	Delaney, William	
Dearing, William	Harrison	M.	Sabine
Dearmon, Taylor	Hunt	Delaney & Dargon	Brazoria
Deas, Canuto	Bexar	Delaplain, Absalom	Goliad
Deas, Domingo	Bexar	Delaplain, A. C.	Washington
Deas, Es.	Bexar	Delbrel, Theresa	Galveston
Deas, Gordain	Bastrop	De Leon, Fernando	Victoria
Deas, Luis	Bexar	Delesdernier, G.	
Deas, Montas	Bexar	H.	Galveston
de Asuna,		Delesdernier, John	Galveston
Beneficio	Henderson	Delgado,	
de Asuna, Boniface	Angelina	Celedecmio	Bexar
Deaton, H. H.	Bowie	Delgado, Josefa	Bexar
Deaton, John	Hopkins	Delgado, Juan	Bexar
Deats, Anthony	Bastrop	Delgado, Juana	Bexar
Deaver, James	Grayson	Delgado, Martin	Bexar
Deaver, William	Washington	Delgado, Nicolas	Bexar
Debard, J. J.	Anderson	Delino, Marirn	Jefferson
De Blamer, V.	Liberty	Delino, Norman	Jefferson
Dechaumer, Michael	Harris	Delk, William	Washington
Dechine, R. M.	Harris	Delmour, William	
Decker, Colet	Hnederson	P.	Bexar
Decker, E.	Upshur	de los Reyes, Ant.	Henderson
Decker, J.	Upshur	Deloss, A. J.	Anderson
Deckman, Henry	Colorado	Deloss, W. I.	Matagorda
De Cordova, J.	Galveston	de los Santos, B.	Henderson
Decrow, E.	Matagorda	Delouche, Eugene	Bexar
Decrow, Mrs. Mary	Matagorda	Delouche, Joseph	Bexar
Decrow, T.	Matagorda	del Rio, M.	Henderson
Deen, Alexander M.	San Augustine	Demer, Eli	Nacogdoches
Deen, Calaway	San Augustine	De Morse, Charles	Red River
Deen, John	San Augustine	Demott, L. M.	Goliad
Deen, Thomas	Henderson	Dempsey, Maria	Harris
Deewees, Isaac	Sabine	Dendy, James M.	Cherokee
Defee, William	San Augustine	Dendy, Larkin M.	Cherokee
De Graffenreid,		Denemoulin, John	Bexar
Wm., Jr.	Fannin	Denman, C.	Austin
Deigler, Adrian	Harris	Denman, C. H.	Walker
Deister, George	Grayson	Denman, James	Jasper
Deister, Henry	Grayson	Denman, James T.	Liberty
Deister, James	Grayson	Denman, Obediah	Jasper
Deister, S.	Grayson	Denne, Dane	Bexar
Deitrick, James	Wharton	Denne, John	Bowie

NAME	COUNTY	NAME	COUNTY
Dennis, Augustus	Brazoria	Devon, Timothy	Henderson
Dennis, Colby	Lamar	Devore, Jesse	Liberty
Dennis, E. B.	Angelina	De Wall, T. W.	Fort Bend
Dennis, James	Lamar	Dewberry, John	Smith
Dennis, John	Lamar	Dewees, W. B.	Colorado
Dennis, Moses	Navarro	Dewers, G.	Henderson
Dennis, T. M.	Matagorda	DeWitt, Benedict	Bowie
Dennis, Thomas	Lamar	DeWitt, Columbus	Gonzales
Dennissin,		DeWitt, Sarah	Gonzales
Elizabeth	Tyler	DeWitt, W. J.	Newton
Denny, James	Galveston	DeYoung, John	Galveston
Denny, James	Titus	DeYoung, S.	Henderson
Denny, W. H.	Liberty	Dial, B. F.	Harrison
Denson, A. J.	Bastrop	Dial, Eli	Brazoria
Denson, Jesse	Cass	Dial, Eli	Goliad
Denson, John	Houston	Dial, Garlington	
Denson, Joseph	Houston	C.	Harrison
Denson, M.	Cass	Dial, Hastings	Harrison
Denson, O'Conner	Houston	Dial, Isabella P.	Harrison
Denson, Shadrack	Houston	Dial, Joseph	Shelby
Denson, Thomas C.	Houston	Dial, M.	Upshur
Denton, A. C.	Cherokee	Dial, Mary J.	Harrison
Denton, J. B.	Cass	Dial & Dysart	Shelby
Denton, Samuel	Hopkins	Diaz, Jose M.	Goliad
Denton, W. J.	Lamar	Dibble, C. C.	Harris
Denton, William C.	Lamar	Dick, John	Fannin
Depue, J. N.	Newton	Dickens, Lewis	Limestone
Depue, J. W.	Newton	Dickerson, James	San Augustine
Derick, Simon	Lamar	Dickerson, Jesse	Newton
Derirn, J. C.	Titus	Dickerson, John	Houston
Derr, Jacob	Fayette	Dickerson, Joseph	Jefferson
Derrick, H. C.	Galveston	Dickerson, Waller	Houston
Derrick, John	Galveston	Dickerson, William	Houston
Derritt, William		Dickerson, William	San Augustine
H.	Nacogdoches	Dickey, Jacob	Bowie
Derrum, Samuel	Guadalupe	Dickey, John C.	Grimes
De Spain, Wm. K.	Hopkins	Dickey, M. D.	San Augustine
De Velbiss, John		Dickinson, Edward	Gonzales
W.	Guadalupe	Dickinson, J. W.	
Devenport, John	Henderson	T.	Brazoria
Devenport, Joseph	Henderson	Dickinson, John	Harris
Devereaux, Alfred	Grimes	Dickinson, Joseph	Goliad
Devereaux, J. S.	Rusk	Dickinson, Samuel	
Devereaux, Samuel	Grimes	B.	Harrison
Devern, Dennis	Bexar	Dickson, A. R.	Red River
Devers, C.	Liberty	Dickson, Abby	Red River
Devers, Catherine	Liberty	Dickson, David C.	Grimes
Devers, Francis J.	Jackson	Dickson, J. C.	Leon
Devers, James	Jackson	Dickson, J. L.	Grimes
Devers, Thomas	Liberty	Dickson, James	Colorado

NAME	COUNTY	NAME	COUNTY
Dickson, James J.	Smith	C.	Hopkins
Dickson, Joel	Cass	Dillingham, John	
Dickson, R.	Anderson	L.	Lamar
Dickson, Robert	Cass	Dillingham, Joseph	
Dickson, S. A.	Titus	C.	Lamar
Dickson, Samuel	Leon	Dillingham, W. T.	Lamar
Dickson, W. P.	Red River	Dillon, J. T.	Victoria
Dickson, William	Polk	Dillon, John T.	Goliad
Dickson, William		Dillon, W. D.	Liberty
W.	Limestone	Dilworth, Powhatan	Gonzales
Dieckmann, C.	Galveston	Dimitt, Mrs.	
Dieckmann, Cyrus	Grimes	Mariah	Guadalupe
Diercks, J. C.	Galveston	Dimitt, Philip	Guadalupe
Dieterick, Francis	Goliad	Dimon, M. O.	Grimes
Dieterick, Francis	Travis	Dimon, M. O.	Montgomery
Dieterick, Teol	Bexar	Dinkelaker, J.	Galveston
Dietz, Ph. H.	Comal	Dinsmore, J.	Henderson
Dikeman, C.	Montgomery	Dinsmore, John	Galveston
Dikes, Dennis	Houston	Dinsmore, John	Grimes
Dikes, George P.	Henderson	Dinsmore, Silas	Matagorda
Dikes, George T.	Nacogdoches	Dircks, J. H.	Red River
Dikes, Levi	Henderson	Dircks, Leonard	Galveston
Dikes, Levi B.	Nacogdoches	Dirden, Hilliard	Tyler
Dikes, Miles G.	Gonzales	Dismuke, A. W.	Liberty
Dikes, Thomas	Dallas	Dix, John	Washington
Dillard, Allen	San Augustine	Dixon, F. B.	San Augustine
Dillard, Cintha	Panola	Dixon, F. H.	San Augustine
Dillard, Daniel B.	DeWitt	Dixon, J.	Collin
Dillard, E.	Cass	Dixon, J. S.	San Augustine
Dillard, George W.	Panola	Dixon, John M.	Washington
Dillard, Howard	Panola	Dixon, M.	Fannin
Dillard, J. B.	Bowie	Dixon, R. C.	Henderson
Dillard, John	Bowie	Dixon, Solomon	Dallas
Dillard, John L.	Panola	Doak, J. A.	Washington
Dillard, Joseph	San Augustine	Doak, Owen	Cass
Dillard, Joseph C.	San Augustine	Dobbs, C.	Cass
Dillard, Lewis H.	Panola	Dobbs, Lauriana	Newton
Dillard, Susan	DeWitt	Dobie, R. N.	Harris
Dillard, Thomas	Burleson	Dobings, Clare A.	Milam
Dillard, W. H.	San Augustine	Dobson, William	Harrison
Dillard, W. N.	Red River	Dockery, Mathew	Walker
Dillard, William	Houston	Dockhill, Jarvis	Brazoria
Dillard, William		Dodd, A. C.	Milam
M.	San Augustine	Dodd, A. D.	Harrison
Dillard, Z.	Houston	Dodd, Aaron	Harris
Dillingham, J.	Collin	Dodd, E. H.	Fannin
Dillingham, J. A.	Lamar	Dodd, J. J.	Anderson
Dillingham, J. C.	Red River	Dodd, James S.	Travis
Dillingham, James	Lamar	Dodd, John	Washington
Dillingham, James		Dodd, John B.	Tyler

45

NAME	COUNTY	NAME	COUNTY
Dodd, Thomas	Liberty	Dooly, M. A.	Comal
Dodd, William	Grimes	Doom, R. C.	Travis
Dodge, Joseph	Victoria	Dornstin, Joseph	Hunt
Dodge, W. L.	Harrison	Dorothy, Patrick	Lavaca
Dodson, Charles	Harrison	Dorr, F. F.	Galveston
Dodson, James	Rusk	Dorsett, Asa	Nacogdoches
Dodson, Laben	Rusk	Dorsett, Charles	Liberty
Doe, J. A.	Galveston	Dorsett, Theo. M.	Liberty
Doen, B. J.	Henderson	Dorsett, Theodore	Henderson
Doerfinger, George	Austin	Dorsett, Theodore	Liberty
Doeser, J. C.	Henderson	Dorsett, William	Galveston
Doherty, John	Fayette	Dorsey, J. W.	Victoria
Doil, Justin	Lavaca	Dorsimer, Andrew	Jackson
Doke, Nelson		Dosree, Charles	Montgomery
Dolge, E.	Walker	Doss, B. H.	Lamar
Dolin, William	Victoria	Doss, J. W.	Fannin
Dollahite, A.	Cass	Doss, John E.	Houston
Dollahite, J. P.	Cass	Doss, Parker	Lamar
Dollahite, James	Smith	Doss, Richard	Shelby
Dollahite, John M.	Smith	Doss, Thomas C.	Lamar
Dollahite, Wiley	Harrison	Dosset, J. T.	Rusk
Dolph, Simeon	Walker	Dosset, John	Rusk
Dolph, William	Walker	Dossey, William	Lamar
Dominguy, Coste	Bexar	Doswell, J. T.	Bexar
Donaho, Charles	Austin	Doswell, J. T.	Galveston
Donaho, Daniel	Liberty	Doswell, R. B.	Galveston
Donaho, Isaac	Austin	Dotson, C. L.	Leon
Donaho, Isaac E.	Cherokee	Doty, J. W.	Bowie
Donaho, Lewis	Newton	Dougharty, G. M.	Cherokee
Donaho, Mattamore	Austin	Dougharty, George	Newton
Donaho, Mortimore	Grimes	Dougharty, James	
Donaho, Moses	Liberty	M.	Cherokee
Donaho, William	Cass	Dougharty, William	Cherokee
Donaho, William	Cherokee	Douglas, Ann A.	Polk
Donaho, William	Sabine	Douglas, Freemen	Goliad
Donaho, Willis	Walker	Douglas, John	Robertson
Donaho, Wyson	Walker	Douglas, Richard	Goliad
Donald, John B.	Panola	Douglass, Andrew	Jackson
Donaldson, Stephen	Nacogdoches	Douglass, August	Jackson
Donaldson, W.	Matagorda	Douglass, F. W.	Brazoria
Donbough, Jacob	Fannin	Douglass, Hezekiah	Dallas
Donelson, S. E.	Collin	Douglass, K. H.	Henderson
Doningburger, D.		Douglass, Thadeus	Jackson
E.	Liberty	Douthet, B. W.	Anderson
Donnell, C. B.	Titus	Douthet, J. M.	Anderson
Donnell, S. F.	Lamar	Douthet, James	Anderson
Donnellan, Tim F.	Harris	Douthett, Ambrose	Bowie
Doolittle, Berry	DeWitt	Douthett, J. C.	Bowie
Dooly, G. W.	Fannin	Douthett, James	Henderson
Dooly, L. J.	Rusk	Dove, A.	Titus

NAME	COUNTY	NAME	COUNTY
Dove, J. C.	Titus	Driscol, Daniel B.	Goliad
Dove, J. T.	Titus	Droddy, Sarah	Burleson
D'Owanne, Bourgois	Galveston	Droddy, William	Henderson
Dowdle, David, Sr.	Lamar	Droddy, William A.	Newton
Dowdle, Davie F.	Lamar	Dryden, Thomas H.	Brazoria
Dowdle, John	Lamar	Dubose, Amasa H.	Harrison
Dowdy, H. B.	Limestone	Dubose, E. D.	Gonzales
Dowell, G. A.	Jackson	Dubose, Elias	Burleson
Dowlam, Pat	DeWitt	Dubose, Jesse K.	Harrison
Downeig, G. W.	Hopkins	Dubose, John D.	Gonzales
Downey, John B.	Bowie	Dubose, Mrs. Leah	Harrison
Downing, George	Fannin	Dubose, W. L.	Gonzales
Downing, J. B.	Cass	Dubose, Willis V.	Harrison
Downing, John	Hunt	Dubrouner, Tobias	Austin
Downing, Timy	Bowie	Duckworth, A.	Sabine
Downing, William	Hunt	Duckworth, Samuel	Leon
Downs, Absalom	Limestone	Dudges, William	Navarro
Downs, L. E.	Houston	Duer, C. F.	Harris
Doyal, Jackson	Nacogdoches	Duff, James	Austin
Doyal, Nimrod	Nacogdoches	Duff, James	DeWitt
Doyal, Thomas	Montgomery	Duff, James C.	Austin
Doyal, Winchester	Nacogdoches	Duffan, F. T.	Milam
Doyle, Festus	Refugio	Duffield, W.	San Augustine
Doyle, James	Smith	Dufner, James	Lavaca
Doyne, Thomas	San Augustine	Dufner, Joseph	Lavaca
Dozier, F. A.	Polk	Dufong, Joseph	Brazoria
Dragoo, J. B.	Upshur	Dugan, D. V.	Grayson
Drake, George	Tyler	Dugan, Daniel	Grayson
Drake, Hiram	Nacogdoches	Dugan, G. C.	Grayson
Drake, James	Jefferson	Dugan, H. P.	Grayson
Drake, Orin	Fayette	Dugan, Richard	Refugio
Draper, Daniel	Fannin	Dugan, William	Walker
Draper, James M.	Nacogdoches	Dugat, C. E.	Liberty
Draper, John S.	Nacogdoches	Dugat, J. L.	Liberty
Draper, Michael	Nacogdoches	Dugat, L. P.	Liberty
Dreiss, Gustar	Comal	Dugat, Peter	Liberty
Dreissinger,		Duke, Hamilton	Titus
Conrad	Travis	Duke, J. H.	Red River
Drennen, D.	Fannin	Duke, Thomas M.	Calhoun
Drennen, David	Bowie	Duke, W. G.	Red River
Drennen, Thomas	Bowie	Duke, Woodson E.	Bowie
Drennen, William		Dulancy, Dulaney	Fannin
J.	Calhoun	Dulancy, John	Fannin
Dresser, Thomas	Sabine	Dulancy, W. H.	Fannin
Drew, Edward	Galveston	Dumas, James P.	Grayson
Drew, Gilbert	Liberty	Dun, John C.	Harrison
Drew, Josiah	Montgomery	Dunagin, Isaac	Angelina
Drew, Monroe	Polk	Dunagin, Seth	Angelina
Dreyer, Henry	Colorado	Dunaway, G. O.	Rusk
Driggers, William	Lamar	Dunbar & Price	Galveston

47

NAME	COUNTY	NAME	COUNTY
Duncan, Apsilla	Shelby	Dunn, H. C.	Shelby
Duncan, Ben F.	Gonzales	Dunn, Jacob	Hunt
Duncan, G. B.	Robertson	Dunn, James, Jr.	Robertson
Duncan, G. H.	Anderson	Dunn, James, Sr.	Robertson
Duncan, G. W.	Hunt	Dunn, John	Hunt
Duncan, George H.	Robertson	Dunn, John	Refugio
Duncan, George J.	Washington	Dunn, Matthew	Brazos
Duncan, H.	Shelby	Dunn, Sarah	Collin
Duncan, J.	Henderson	Dunn, Tola	Collin
Duncan, J. M.	Henderson	Dunn, W. H.	Shelby
Duncan, J. T.	Shelby	Dunn, William Y.	Dallas
Duncan, James	Cass	Dunston, John	Fort Bend
Duncan, Jane	Henderson	Dupree, F. G.	Grimes
Duncan, John	Matagorda	Dupree, J. C.	Leon
Duncan, Lewis	Brazoria	Dupree, Jesse	Grimes
Duncan, Mahala	Robertson	Dupree, Joel	Grimes
Duncan, Matthew	Shelby	Dupree, John	Grimes
Duncan, Meredith	Liberty	Dupree, Lewis	Grimes
Duncan, Peter J.	Harris	Dupree, Lewis G.	Washington
Duncan, Smith	Robertson	Dupuy, A. G.	Rusk
Duncan, T. L.	Henderson	Dupuy, John B.	Washington
Duncan, Thomas	Robertson	Duran, E.	Grimes
Duncan, W. B.	Liberty	Durand, F. A.	Comal
Duncan, William	Red River	Durfee, Charles	Red River
Duncan, William B.	Shelby	Durham, B. H.	Cass
Duncan, William B.	Smith	Durham, Eli	Grimes
Dungan, Francis	Harris	Durham, George J.	Travis
Dunham, D. A.	Grimes	Durham, James C.	Cass
Dunham, Daniel T.	Grimes	Durham, L. A.	Jasper
Dunham, J. H.	Grimes	Durham, M. S.	Washington
Dunica, John	Walker	Durham, Thomas	Grimes
Dunken, James	Henderson	Durham, William	Grimes
Dunken, Robert L.	Austin	Durham, William D.	Goliad
Dunlap, Archibald	Cass	Durmet, Samuel J.	Brazoria
Dunlap, George W.	Harrison	Durocher, C. L.	Goliad
Dunlap, John	Burleson	Durr, John	Galveston
Dunlap, John C.	Polk	Durrett, S. M.	Limestone
Dunlap, Richard	Houston	Durst, C. P. B.	Leon
Dunlap, Robert	Cass	Durst, H. M.	Leon
Dunlap, William	Grimes	Durst, H. M.	Leon
Dunlap, William	Montgomery	Durst, Isaac	Cherokee
Dunman, Henry	Galveston	Durst, James H.	Cherokee
Dunman, Henry	Harris	Durst, John	Leon
Dunman, John	Galveston	Durst, John S.	Leon
Dunman, Joseph	Harris	Durst, John W.	Galveston
Dunman, Joseph	Galveston	Durst, Louis O.	Leon
Dunman, M.	Galveston	Durst, M. B.	Leon
Dunman, Robert	Galveston	Dusen, Wiley	DeWitt
Dunman, Robert	Harris	Dutches, A.	Henderson
Dunn, Charles	Cass	Duty, Henry	Titus

NAME	COUNTY	NAME	COUNTY
Duty, Joseph	Travis	Easters, A. K.	Cherokee
Duty, Phil	Red River	Easters, M. L.	Cherokee
Duty, Philip	Cass	Easters, S. R.	Cherokee
Duty, Richard	Anderson	Easthman, Henry	Fayette
Duty, Solomon	Burleson	Eastwood, A.	Henderson
Duval, Thomas	Travis	Eastwood, Leonard	Henderson
Duvall, A. F.	Galveston	Eastwood, Luther	Henderson
Dwight, George E.	Anderson	Eastwood, W.	Henderson
Dwitmer, Jacob	Bexar	Eatherton, George	Fayette
Dwyer, Edward	Bexar	Eaton, B.	Anderson
Dwyer, Martin	Bexar	Eaton, Calvin	Rusk
Dyce, G. J.	Nacogdoches	Eaton, Daniel	Limestone
Dye, Raymey	Grayson	Eaton, G. W.	Sabine
Dyer, B. F.	Walker	Eaton, J. C.	Galveston
Dyer, Dickson	Cass	Eaton, Joel	Rusk
Dyer, G. W.	Red River	Eaton, Richard,	
Dyer, Isadore	Galveston	Jr.	Limestone
Dyer, Leon	Galveston	Eaton, Richard,	
Dykes, Mark W.	Washington	Sr.	Limestone
Dykes, William C.	Jefferson	Eaton, T. H.	Henderson
Dysart, E. B.	Shelby	Eaton, Thomas H.	Refugio
		Eaves, Burwell	San Augustine
		Eaves, John	San Augustine
Eacalua, Man.	Bexar	Eazley, C. W.	Sabine
Eagan, G.	Wharton	Eazley, James	Sabine
Eaker, William	Panola	Eazley, John	Sabine
Eakey, Robert	Grayson	Eberley, A. B.	Travis
Eakin, E. M.	Henderson	Eberley, William	Liberty
Eakin, James	Nacogdoches	Eblen, John	Bastrop
Earhart, J. B.	Grayson	Eccles, James C.	Fayette
Earle, David	Nacogdoches	Echols, James T.	Shelby
Earle, Eli J.	Cherokee	Echols, John	Burleson
Earle, Elvira	Leon	Eckel, William	Brazoria
Earle, Nancy	Sabine	Ecklum, Peter	Bexar
Earle, Orville	Colorado	Eddings, Benjamin	Anderson
Earle, Thomas	Leon	Eddings, S.	San Augustine
Earle, Thomas, Sr.	Harris	Eddings, William	Anderson
Earle, William	Sabine	Edds, Joseph S.	Grimes
Earle, William E.	Gonzales	Eddy, Z. William	Jasper
Earley, F. S.	Washington	Eden, Alfred R.	Houston
Earley, John	Milam	Eden, John	Houston
Earley, Thomas	Washington	Eden, John B.	Houston
Earnst, T. F.	Fayette	Edenburgh, C. C.	Walker
Earp, J.	Upshur	Edens, D. H.	Anderson
Earp, R.	Upshur	Edens, Gulie	Anderson
Eashers, James	Henderson	Edens, J. R.	Anderson
Easly, Elbert	Lamar	Edens, S.	Henderson
East, Edward W.	Washington	Edgar, Alexander	Galveston
East, William	Cass	Edgar, M. B.	Galveston
Eastep, Daniel	Sabine	Edgar, Nicholas	San Augustine

NAME	COUNTY	NAME	COUNTY
Edgar, William	San Augustine	Eichelberger,	
Edmiston, D. C.	Travis	William	Milam
Edmundson, Henry	Cass	Eidson, James	Nacogdoches
Edmundson, J. M.	Houston	Eikel, Andreas	Comal
Edmundson, John	Burleson	Eimke, Henry	Comal
Edmundson, T. B.	Lamar	Eisel, George	Brazoria
Edmundson, W.	Walker	Eixon, Edward	Goliad
Edmundson, William	Cass	Elage, Joel	Lamar
Edmundson, William	Red River	Elam, G. W.	Montgomery
Edny, Newton J.	Washington	Elam, William B.	Dallas
Edny, Samuel	Washington	Elary, Elisha	Denton
Edoms, Balis	Anderson	Eldridge, A.	Burleson
Edrington, James		Eldridge, H. B.	Washington
F.	Washington	Eldridge, H. N.	Washington
Edwards, Arthur	Robertson	Eldridge, H. R.	Bexar
Edwards, B. E.	Bexar	Eldridge, John	Gonzales
Edwards, Benjamin	Limestone	Eldridge, Matilda	Shelby
Edwards, C. O.	Grimes	Eldridge, Peter	Sabine
Edwards, Charles	Montgomery	Eldridge, Samuel	Shelby
Edwards, Charles	San Patricio	Elen, Frederick	Harris
Edwards, E.	Henderson	Elgin, Elija	Hopkins
Edwards, Edwin A.	Harrison	Elgin, John	Washington
Edwards, Gustavus	Wharton	Elgin, Mrs. Mary	
Edwards, H.	Upshur	A.	Washington
Edwards, Hyden	Nacogdoches	Eliot, George	Goliad
Edwards, James	Montgomery	Eliot, S.	Dallas
Edwards, John	Brazoria	Elkins, A.	Limestone
Edwards, John	Travis	Elkins, Bennet	San Augustine
Edwards, John	Shelby	Elkins, Erasmus	San Augustine
Edwards, L. L.	Upshur	Elkins, J. J.	Montgomery
Edwards, M. H.	Upshur	Elkins, J. M.	Montgomery
Edwards, N.	Montgomery	Elkins, James, Sr.	Montgomery
Edwards, N.	Upshur	Elkins, Miles	Montgomery
Edwards, P.	Cass	Elkins, Preston	Hopkins
Edwards, S.	Upshur	Elkins, William	Montgomery
Edwards, T.	Austin	Ellett, A. K.	Bowie
Edwards, T. R.	Galveston	Ellett, John	Cherokee
Edwards, W.	Wharton	Ellett, John W.	Bowie
Edwards, William		Ellett, Joseph W.	Bowie
C.	Jackson	Ellett, William	Bowie
Edwards, William		Elley, G. A.	Bexar
C.	San Augustine	Ellington, Martha	
Efinger, Francis		B.	Grimes
F.	Austin	Ellington, Thomas	Grimes
Egbert, Charles	Sabine	Ellington, Thomas	Grimes
Eggleston, Horace	Gonzales	Elliott, B.	Titus
Eggleston, Julia	Bastrop	Elliott, B. E.	Bowie
Ehlinger, Charles	Colorado	Elliott, Elias	Austin
Ehlinger, Mary	Colorado	Elliott, George	Goliad
Ehrhardt, Anton	Bexar	Elliott, George	Matagorda

NAME	COUNTY	NAME	COUNTY
Elliott, Humphrey	Harrison	Emberson, Elijah	Lamar
Elliott, J.	Cass	Emerson, Joseph	Galveston
Elliott, James H.	Cass	Emory, William	Harris
Elliott, John	Henderson	Engelback, Philip	Travis
Elliott, John N.	Gonzales	Engledow, C. S.	Nacogdoches
Elliott, Peter J.	Goliad	Engledow,	
Elliott, S. L.	Bowie	Elizabeth	Nacogdoches
Elliott, William	Bexar	Engledow, Elom	Nacogdoches
Elliott, William	Panola	Engledow, J. W.	Nacogdoches
Elliott, William		Engledow, Oscar	Henderson
A.	Bowie	Engledow, Osker	Nacogdoches
Elliott, William		Engleking, F.	Austin
A.	Harris	English, A. H.	Houston
Elliott, William		English, Abram	Houston
K.	Shelby	English, George	Houston
Elliott, William		English, Isaac	Grayson
M.	Bowie	English, J. C.	Red River
Elliott, William		English, James	Houston
S.	Bowie	English, James	Shelby
Ellis, Ann Maria	Rusk	English, John	Houston
Ellis, B. B.	Houston	English, John	Polk
Ellis, B. F.	Liberty	English, John	Shelby
Ellis, Benjamin	Houston	English, Jonah	Shelby
Ellis, C. M. C. H.	Houston	English, Joseph	Shelby
Ellis, Chris	Harrison	English, Joshua	Shelby
Ellis, G. L.	Upshur	English, Levi	Grimes
Ellis, G. W.	Polk	English, Myra	Shelby
Ellis, Ira	San Augustine	English, William	
Ellis, Mary J.	Brazos	J.	Panola
Ellis, John	Burleson	Enloe, Benjamin	Tyler
Ellis, John L.	Brazoria	Enloe, D. C.	Tyler
Ellis, N. D.	Bowie	Ennis, Alexander	Grayson
Ellis, Peter	Milam	Ennis, Cornelius	Harris
Ellis, Q. L.	Liberty	Enniston, James E.	Travis
Ellis, Richard	Bowie	Enochs, Jason	Lamar
Ellis, Stephen H.	Bowie	Enochs, Miles	DeWitt
Ellis, Thomas	Dallas	Epperson, Caro	Bowie
Ellis, William	Upshur	Epperson, Faustain	Grimes
Ellison, Ewing	Titus	Epperson, Mark	Bowie
Ellison, James	San Augustine	Epperson, T. S.	Polk
Ellison, John	San Augustine	Epps, C.	Henderson
Ellison, Martin	Brazos	Epps, Charles	San Augustine
Ellison, W.	Anderson	Epps, Elbert	Montgomery
Elmendorff,		Epps, Henry	Montgomery
Charles	Comal	Epps, Isham	Montgomery
Elmore, Charles	Hopkins	Epps, Robert C.	Limestone
Elmore, J. M.	Hopkins	Erath, G. B.	Milam
Elmore, William	Hopkins	Erath, George B.	Burleson
Elvy, George R.	Cherokee	Erickson, Gustavus	Harris
Emanuel, E.	Henderson	Ernst, Fred	Austin

NAME	COUNTY	NAME	COUNTY
Erskine, Ab.	Guadalupe	Evans, E. A. J.	Jasper
Erskine, D. M.	Galveston	Evans, E. D.	Fannin
Erskine, Michael	Guadalupe	Evans, Edward	Bastrop
Ervendberg, G. C.	Comal	Evans, Emma	Fayette
Ervendberg, Peter	Comal	Evans, F. W.	Polk
Ervins, James	Austin	Evans, Gregg	Harrison
Ervins, John	Houston	Evans, H. C.	Sabine
Erwin, A. J.	Fannin	Evans, Henry	Houston
Erwin, Mrs. C. M.	Harrison	Evans, J.	Henderson
Erwin, L. J.	Henderson	Evans, J. K.	Cass
Erwin, T. J.	Harrison	Evans, James	Sabine
Erwin, T. R.	Matagorda	Evans, Jesse	Houston
Erwin, Samuel	Fannin	Evans, Jesse	Lamar
Escarena, Y.	Bexar	Evans, John	Sabine
Escaton, L.	Henderson	Evans, Joseph	Grimes
Escavaro, F.	Victoria	Evans, Josiah	Jackson
Esker, Casper	Brazoria	Evans, June	Galveston
Eskridge, R. J.	Nacogdoches	Evans, Key	Harrison
Esley, Benjamin	Nacogdoches	Evans, Mackijah	Henderson
Eson, W.	Titus	Evans, Mackijah	Lamar
Espada, Fr.	Bexar	Evans, Mary	Harris
Espy, Thomas	Polk	Evans, Matt. R.	Bexar
Esquerdo, Justo	Bexar	Evans, Moses	Grimes
Esta, Nathan	DeWitt	Evans, S. T.	Lamar
Esta, Nathan	Goliad	Evans, T. D.	Jasper
Estel, Milton	Walker	Evans, William	Lamar
Estes, Anderson	Brazoria	Evans, William	Navarro
Estes, B.	Shelby	Evans, William G.	Goliad
Estes, D. M.	Washington	Evans, William G.	Harris
Estes, Edmund T.	Washington	Evans, William M.	Fayette
Estes, James D.	Washington	Evens, A.	Angelina
Estes, James M.	Washington	Evens, Absalom	Hopkins
Estes, John	Washington	Evens, Edward	Titus
Estes, John B.	Brazoria	Evens, Eliza	Hopkins
Estes, John H.	Calhoun	Evens, Henry	Titus
Estes, Robert	Harrison	Evens, J. M.	Montgomery
Estes, W. H.	Cass	Evens, J. P.	Henderson
Estill, James	Bowie	Evens, James	Hopkins
Ethridge, Howard	Fannin	Evens, Jesse	Walker
Ethridge, John	Smith	Evens, John	Angelina
Ethridge, Thomas	Upshur	Evens, Lucy	Austin
Eubanks, A. B.	Nacogdoches	Evens, Robert B.	Rusk
Eubanks, E. N.	Nacogdoches	Evens, Turney	Walker
Eubanks, James	Lamar	Evens, W. F.	Walker
Eubanks, John T.	Grimes	Evens, William	Rusk
Eubanks, R. A.	Nacogdoches	Evens, William M.	San Augustine
Eubanks, W.	Lamar	Everett, Altezira	Jasper
Eutaw, M.	Hunt	Everett, J. B.	Bowie
Evans, Annstia	Henderson	Everett, James	Rusk
Evans, D. M.	Harris	Everett, John C.	Cass

NAME	COUNTY	NAME	COUNTY
Everett, Samuel	Fayette	Falvel, Luke	Galveston
Everett, Sylvanus	Rusk	Fanas, Antonio	Bexar
Everett, William	Liberty	Fanas, Pablo	Bexar
Everhart, James	Grayson	Fannin, J. W.	Goliad
Evertd, G. A.	Fannin	Fannin, W.	Hopkins
Evetts, Samuel G.	Austin	Fanthorp, Henry	Grimes
Evetts, T. H.	Austin	Farish, Oscar	Galveston
Evins, Chereola	Leon	Farish, Oscar	Goliad
Evins, James C.	Leon	Farley, Catherine	Liberty
Evins, O.	Leon	Farley, H. V.	Liberty
Evins, W. M.	Leon	Farmer, Alexander	Galveston
Evins, William P.	Leon	Farmer, Allen	Grayson
Ewer, Lemuel	Lamar	Farmer, James	Washington
Ewing, Alexander	Harris	Farmer, Mary Ann	Grayson
Ewing, C. L.	Titus	Farmer, R.	Anderson
Ewing, Edley	San Augustine	Farmer, Samuel W.	Smith
Ewing, J. M.	Titus	Farnash, John	Burleson
Ewing, J. R. S.	Titus	Farnsworth, Sol	Cass
Ewing, J. S.	Titus	Farquhar, Alfred	Washington
Ewing, James L.	Angelina	Farquhar, James L.	Washington
Ewing, James L.	Angelina	Farral, Jesse	Washington
Ewing, John	Washington	Farrell, Evan	Austin
Ewing, R. M.	Leon	Farrell, Francis	Fayette
Ewing, Samuel	Leon	Farrell, Griffin	Austin
Ewing, T. J.	Harris	Farrell, Hiram	Fayette
Ewing, W. E.	Titus	Farris, Aaron	Cherokee
Ewing, W. H.	Washington	Farris, Daniel	Cherokee
Ewing, William	Titus	Farris, E.	Walker
Ewing, William G.	Calhoun	Farris, Ellen	Cass
Eyery, Cyrus W.	Refugio	Farris, H.	Walker
		Farris, Werity	Cass
		Farris, William	Walker
Fadden, Patrick	San Patricio	Farris, William A.	Fayette
Faeson, N. W.	Fayette	Farror, Alfred	Houston
Fagan, George	Goliad	Farror, F. L.	Shelby
Fagan, John	Victoria	Farror, John	Shelby
Fagan, Nicholas	Refugio	Farror, Simon B.	Shelby
Fahl, George	Fannin	Farrow, John	Travis
Fahn, John	Comal	Farrow, John M.	Galveston
Fahrenkamp, B.	Colorado	Fasoner, Hulet	Rusk
Fahrenkamp, G.	Colorado	Fatheree,	
Fain, Mercer	Shelby	Jefferson	Gonzales
Faircloth, H. C.	Sabine	Fatheree, William	Hopkins
Faith, A. B.	Fayette	Faulk, Henry M.	Harris
Faley, Nathaniel	Angelina	Faulk, Jacob	Rusk
Falkerson, James		Faulk, Jesse	Harris
P.	Calhoun	Faulkenburg, J. T.	Limestone
Falks, E. B.	Lavaca	Faulkenburg, Nancy	Limestone
Fall, John M.	Nacogdoches	Fauquhar, Joseph	Fayette
Falson, D.	Henderson	Fauquhar, Wright	Fayette

NAME	COUNTY	NAME	COUNTY
Fay, Valentin	Comal	Fields, M. W.	Montgomery
Faynes, Thomas	Calhoun	Fields, Sarah	Liberty
Fegaria, Juan	Bexar	Fields, William	Liberty
Fellows, A. G.	Rusk	Fields, William	Rusk
Fellows, George	Galveston	Fields, William A.	Harrison
Fellows, L. S.	Galveston	Fifer, Jacob	Goliad
Fellows, Marion	Rusk	Fifer, Jacob	Jackson
Fellows, R. G.	Rusk	Fight, J.	Liberty
Felton, G. W.	Rusk	Files, David S.	Grimes
Fennier, Yg.	Bexar	Finch, John H.	Gonzales
Fenmietz, B.	Polk	Finch, R. B.	Houston
Fenn, Eli	Grimes	Fine, Levi	Jackson
Fenn, J. R.	Fort Bend	Fink, J.	Fayette
Fenton, Harrison	Rusk	Fink & Derr	Fayette
Fentress, James	Bastrop	Finley, Hetty	Hopkins
Ferguson, Alston	Harrison	Finley, Isaac	Hunt
Ferguson, David	Harrison	Finley, J. B.	Titus
Ferguson, Edward	Galveston	Finley, John	Panola
Ferguson, Isaac	Harrison	Finley, Milton	Hunt
Ferguson, James	Walker	Finley, J. D.	Harrison
Ferguson, Mrs.		Finley, W. L.	Titus
Jane	Harrison	Finley, William	Hunt
Ferguson, Joseph	Bowie	Finley, William N.	Angelina
Ferguson, Robert	Brazos	Finney, A. D.	Walker
Ferguson, Rollin	Sabine	Finney, Richard A.	Rusk
Ferguson, Thomas	Bowie	Finney, Thomas	Walker
Ferguson, William	Harris	Fischer, Albert	Bexar
Feris, George A.	Fort Bend	Fischer, G.	Comal
Fernandez, Antonio	Guadalupe	Fischer, Peter	Bexar
Fernandez, Cecilio	Henderson	Fish, Joseph	Newton
Fernandez, Juan	Bexar	Fishback, J. H.	Cass
Ferrell, Edward H.	Cass	Fishback, J. H.	Titus
Ferrell, Perrer	Colorado	Fisher, David	Bastrop
Ferrell, Silas	Hopkins	Fisher, George	Travis
Ferrell, Thomas B.	Washington	Fisher, Henry F.	Harris
Ferry, James	Lamar	Fisher, Israel R.	Colorado
Fewel, P. B.	Nacogdoches	Fisher, J.	Collin
Fewell, James	Washington	Fisher, Jeremiah	Liberty
Fielder, Henry	Travis	Fisher, Jesse	Red River
Fielder, James	Lamar	Fisher, John	Washington
Fields, Cooper W.	Panola	Fisher, King	Hunt
Fields, D.	Upshur	Fisher, M. T.	Austin
Fields, D. B. H.	Grimes	Fisher, Moses	Hopkins
Fields, D. L.	Upshur	Fisher, S. W.	Matagorda
Fields, Isiah	Liberty	Fisher, Samson D.	Panola
Fields, J. N.	Harrison	Fisher, T.	Collin
Fields, J. W.	Red River	Fisher, Thomas D.	Colorado
Fields, James	Harrison	Fisher, W.	Collin
Fields, Joseph	Harrison	Fisher, W. H.	Bastrop
Fields, L. N.	Jasper	Fisher, William C.	Washington

NAME	COUNTY	NAME	COUNTY
Fisk, J. P.	Bexar	H.	Burleson
Fisnon, John	Henderson	Flarity, Michael	Navarro
Fitch, C. H.	Grayson	Flato, William	Austin
Fitch, William	Grayson	Flavens, James	Hunt
Fitchet, Mary	Austin	Flavens, T. S.	Hunt
Fitz, Nancy	Harrison	Fleck, Isaac	Grayson
Fitz, O. H.	Harrison	Fleck, William	Fort Bend
Fitzallen, O.	San Augustine	Fleenisee, Thomas	Lavaca
Fitzgerald, A.	Colorado	Flemin, J. D.	Red River
Fitzgerald, Chris.	Henderson	Fleming, Caleb	Grimes
Fitzgerald,		Fleming, E. K.	Red River
Christopher	Fayette	Fleming, J. W.	Bowie
Fitzgerald, E.	Henderson	Fleming, Pat	Colorado
Fitzgerald, Ganet,		Fleming, R. C.	Cass
Jr.	Fannin	Fleming, W. H.	Red River
Fitzgerald, Ganet,		Flemmons, William	
Sr.	Fannin	P.	Cherokee
Fitzgerald, J.	San Augustine	Fletcher, James	Navarro
Fitzgerald, J. D.	Fannin	Fletcher, Robert	Polk
Fitzgerald,		Flint, Gideon	Harrison
Jackson	Henderson	Flint, Luther	Bastrop
Fitzgerald, Jesse	Cass	Flint, Thomas	Harrison
Fitzgerald, John	Harris	Floid, James	Austin
Fitzgerald, John		Florence, J. R.	Galveston
S.	Polk	Florence, John	Brazoria
Fitzgerald,		Flores, Edwardo	Guadalupe
Obediah	Fayette	Flores, Esme	Bexar
Fitzgerald, S. W.	Fannin	Flores, Francisco	Bexar
Fitzgerald, Samuel	Fayette	Flores, Gregorio	Goliad
Fitzgerald, T. R.	Liberty	Flores, Jesus	Nacogdoches
Fitzgerald, Wm.	Anderson	Flores, Jose	Bexar
Fitzgerald, Wm.	Colorado	Flores, Juan	Jackson
Fitzgerald, Wm. R.	Fannin	Flores, Manuel	Bexar
Fitzgerald, Wm. W.	Polk	Flores, Manuel	Guadalupe
Fitzhugh, G.	Collin	Flores, Miguel	Nacogdoches
Fitzhugh, J.	Collin	Flores, Napoleon	Bexar
Fitzhugh, W.	Collin	Flores, Pedro	Bexar
Fitzpatrick, M. A.	Victoria	Flores, Policarpie	Nacogdoches
Fitzpatrick, Rene	Harrison	Flores, Salvador	Bexar
Fitzsimmons,		Flores, Vital	Nacogdoches
Edward	Houston	Florida, Pasacola	Calhoun
Fitzsimmons, N.	Galveston	Flot, William	Henderson
Fitzsimmons,		Flotan, L. M.	Henderson
Patrick	Refugio	Flournoy, S. A.	Henderson
Fiveash, E. H.	Cherokee	Flournoy, S. L.	Nacogdoches
Flack, C. P.	Brazoria	Floyd, Elisha	Grimes
Flack, R. D.	Brazoria	Floyd, Elisha	Nacogdoches
Flagge, Andreas	Comal	Floyd, Francis	Nacogdoches
Flanigan, John	Anderson	Floyd, George	Grimes
Flannekin, Robert		Floyd, J. B.	Bowie

NAME	COUNTY	NAME	COUNTY
Floyd, R. F.	Nacogdoches	Ford, Henry	Walker
Floyd, T.	Grimes	Ford, J. B.	Grimes
Flutcher, Joshua	Austin	Ford, J. H.	Nacogdoches
Flynt, John S.	Robertson	Ford, James	Red River
Fmhoff, Henry	Comal	Ford, James, Sr.	Montgomery
Foerster, Eduard	Comal	Ford, James B.	Montgomery
Fogg, James W.	Harris	Ford, John	Anderson
Fogleman, W.	Anderson	Ford, John	Walker
Foley, Green L.	Lavaca	Ford, John A.	Galveston
Foley, H. Stewart	Lavaca	Ford, John H.	Newton
Foley, John N.	Brazos	Ford, John P.	Brazos
Foley, Mason	Lavaca	Ford, John S.	Henderson
Folks, A. M.	Montgomery	Ford, L.	Henderson
Folks, Abigal	Burleson	Ford, Levi	Nacogdoches
Folks, Daniel	Burleson	Ford, Maria V.	Newton
Folks, John	Milam	Ford, Obedience	Grimes
Foller, J. E.	Grimes	Ford, P. W.	Nacogdoches
Follett, Mrs.	Brazoria	Ford, Raleigh G.	Grimes
Follett, Alex	Brazoria	Ford, W. J. B.	Houston
Follett, Alonzo	Brazoria	Ford, W. W.	Montgomery
Follett, Robert	Limestone	Ford, William	Walker
Folse, John	Nacogdoches	Ford, William G.	Washington
Folsom, E. B.	Grimes	Foreas, Eusebie	Bexar
Folsom, E. L.	Grimes	Foreman, Edward	Houston
Folsom, Nathaniel	Grimes	Foreman, Green L.	Cherokee
Folt, James	Hunt	Foreman, J. B.	Cherokee
Foncall, Henry	Austin	Foreman, John H.	Houston
Foote, G. A.	Collin	Foreman, W. W.	Red River
Forber, D.	Bastrop	Foreman, William	
Forber, J.	Bastrop	K.	Galveston
Forbis, George	Fayette	Forena, Gertrudus	Bexar
Forbis, J. M.	Rusk	Foreo, B. W.	Lavaca
Forbis, James	Harris	Forester, James	DeWitt
Forbis, James	Rusk	Forgeois, Nicolas	Bexar
Forbis, John	Nacogdoches	Forguson, C.	Upshur
Forbis, R. M.	Calhoun	Forguson, E. A.	Henderson
Forbis, Richard	Shelby	Fork, Ingal	Bexar
Forbs, Jackson	Shelby	Forke, A.	Comal
Forbs, Thomas C.	Red River	Forker, F. E.	Colorado
Forbus, A. R.	Henderson	Forquhar, William	Brazos
Forbus, C.	Henderson	Forsythe, David	Cass
Forck, Joshua	Panola	Forsythe, James	Panola
Ford, Alfred	Brazos	Forsythe, P. C.	Red River
Ford, Allison	Brazoria	Forsythe, William	San Augustine
Ford, Cramer	Walker	Fort, Fred	Sabine
Ford, E. L.	Wharton	Fort, J. W.	Bowie
Ford, Elizabeth	Grimes	Fort, James L.	Bowie
Ford, G. W.	Collin	Fort, W. D.	Travis
Ford, H. P.	Henderson	Forteny, John	Galveston
Ford, Hazel P.	Smith	Fortner, M. F.	Dallas

NAME	COUNTY	NAME	COUNTY
Fortran, Charles	Austin	Fowler, W. C.	Leon
Fortune, George W.	Cass	Fowler, W. H.	Montgomery
Fortune, J.	Henderson	Fowler, William	Leon
Fossett, John	Bastrop	Fowler, William H.	Grimes
Foster, Benjamin	Newton	Fox, Charles	Galveston
Foster, Charles	Walker	Fox, Christopher	Galveston
Foster, David	Leon	Fox, Daniel	Refugio
Foster, F. W.	Washington	Fox, Edwin	Montgomery
Foster, George P.	Fort Bend	Fox, Garret	Refugio
Foster, Isaac	Sabine	Fox, J. A.	Walker
Foster, J.	Cass	Fox, Jacob	Victoria
Foster, James	Colorado	Fox, James	Refugio
Foster, James	Walker	Fox, John	Limestone
Foster, James F.	Gonzales	Fox, John	Refugio
Foster, James W.	Washington	Fox, Michael	San Patricio
Foster, Jane	Tyler	Fox, Michall	Refugio
Foster, John	Bastrop	Fox, Sabina	Refugio
Foster, John	Brazoria	Foy, W. D.	Sabine
Foster, John	Wharton	Foyfogle, J.	Cass
Foster, John C.	Newton	Frade, Francis	Fayette
Foster, John R.	Lavaca	Fraley, A. J.	Nacogdoches
Foster, John S.	Shelby	Frampton, William	Austin
Foster, Lee	Lamar	France, Alfred	Hopkins
Foster, M.	Brazos	Francis, James P.	Harris
Foster, M. R.	Collin	Francis, John	Brazoria
Foster, Norris	Walker	Francis, Miller	Austin
Foster, R.	Houston	Francis, R. A.	Galveston
Foster, R.	Travis	Francis, R. B.	Lamar
Foster, R. B. S.	Washington	Francis, S.	San Augustine
Foster, Rachel	Wharton	Frank, Lowie	Austin
Foster, Randolph	Fort Bend	Franklin, Allen	Jefferson
Foster, T. J.	Cass	Franklin, G. F.	Limestone
Foster, Virginia		Franklin, Henry	Brazoria
W.	Galveston	Franklin, James B.	Harrison
Foster, William L.	Gonzales	Franklin, Josiah	
Foulbough, L.	Victoria	R.	Washington
Foulhouze, James	Galveston	Franklin, Reason	Cherokee
Fountaine, H. W.	Goliad	Franklin, W. R.	Titus
Foutrel, Danis	Bexar	Franks, Elijah	Limestone
Fowler, Fannin	Fannin	Frasure, B. E.	Nacogdoches
Fowler, Fannin	Fannin	Frazier, Deniel	Cass
Fowler, J. B.	Cass	Frazier, Ebenezer	Harrison
Fowler, J. W.	Grimes	Frazier, Eli	Cass
Fowler, J. W.	Montgomery	Frazier, Esquire	Cass
Fowler, John M.	Refugio	Frazier, F. W.	Fort Bend
Fowler, Josiah	Grayson	Frazier, G. F.	Tyler
Fowler, L.	Henderson	Frazier, G. W.	Harris
Fowler, M. M.	Sabine	Frazier, Harmon	Tyler
Fowler, Samuel	Montgomery	Frazier, Hartwell	Shelby
Fowler, Samuel L.	Fayette	Frazier, J. W.	Cherokee

NAME	COUNTY	NAME	COUNTY
Frazier, James	Cass	Frosh, Laurence	Galveston
Frazier, John, Jr.	Newton	Frost, B. P.	Leon
Frazier, John, Sr.	Newton	Frost, H.	Anderson
Frazier, M. D.	Cass	Frost, Joseph	Panola
Frazier, Richard	Cherokee	Fruh, Charles Wm.	Galveston
Frazier, Robert E.	Cass	Frust, S. M.	Fort Bend
Frazier, Simon	Gonzales	Fry, Benjamin	Walker
Frazier, Stephen	Milam	Fry, Delila	San Augustine
Frazier, W. C.	Jasper	Fry, George	Bexar
Frazier, William B.	Sabine	Fry, R. L.	Houston
Frazier, William C.	Panola	Fry, R. T.	Walker
Freeman, Burrell	Lamar	Fry, S.	Walker
Freeman, David B.	Newton	Fuentes, Gertrudus	Bexar
Freeman, E.	Lamar	Fulbright, David	Red River
Freeman, Harry H.	Smith	Fulcher, Elizabeth	Burleson
Freeman, Ira M.	Harrison	Fulcher, Franklin	Burleson
Freeman, Ira M.	Houston	Fulcher, Solomon	Burleson
Freeman, J. B.	Lamar	Fulcher, Tluna	Angelina
Freeman, James	Cass	Fulcher, Z. M.	Burleson
Freeman, Jeremiah	Lamar	Fulchur, Churchill	Fort Bend
Freeman, John	Cass	Fulchur, John	Milam
Freeman, T. J.	San Augustine	Fulgham, E. T.	Tyler
Freese, F. H.	Bowie	Fulgham, George F.	Gonzales
Freese, Gerd.	Bowie	Fulgham, Henry	Tyler
French, Daniel	Travis	Fulgham, Jesse	Tyler
French, G. T.	Austin	Fulgham, Purces	Nacogdoches
French, James	Cass	Fulgham, R. C.	Tyler
French, Lefford	Lamar	Fulgham, Rayford	Nacogdoches
French, Richard J.	Washington	Fulgham, Thomas	Victoria
French, W. C.	San Augustine	Fullenwider, P. H.	Grimes
French, Z. M. T.	Bastrop	Fullenwider, R. H.	Montgomery
Fretillina, Auguste	Bexar	Fuller, Allen J.	Nacogdoches
Friar, Daniel B.	DeWitt	Fuller, Benjamin	Nacogdoches
Fridge, John, Jr.	Montgomery	Fuller, C. J.	Fannin
Fridge, John, Sr.	Montgomery	Fuller, Desdemona	Washington
Friend, L. S.	San Augustine	Fuller, Ilsey	Henderson
Friene, William	Montgomery	Ruller, Ira	Fort Bend
Fries, John	Bexar	Fuller, Joel C.	Fannin
Friesenham	Comal	Fuller, John	Washington
Frillman, Conrad	Victoria	Fuller, Matthew	Rusk
Frisbie, Abram	Houston	Fuller, Nathan	Harris
Frisbie, Charles	Galveston	Fuller, R. W.	Washington
Frisby, F.	Matagorda	Fuller, Samuel	Washington
Fritcher, Charles	Harris	Fuller, T. H.	Nacogdoches
Fritz, Louis	Victoria	Fullerton, Henry	Robertson
Frizzell, W. W.	Cherokee	Fullerton, John	Robertson
Frizzell, W. W.	Henderson	Fullerton, Margaret	Brazos
		Fulls, Gerald	Colorado
		Fulls, Herman	Colorado

NAME	COUNTY	NAME	COUNTY
Fulls, William	Colorado	Gahagan, John C.	Titus
Fulton, James	Goliad	Gaily, James	Fannin
Fulton, L.	Goliad	Gaines, John B.	Sabine
Fulton, L. B.	Anderson	Gaines, William B.	
Fulton, S. K.	Calhoun	P.	Brazoria
Fulton, Samuel M.	Lamar	Gaither, F. G.	Austin
Fulton, William	Navarro	Galaspa, Thomas	Hopkins
Fulton, William M.	Lamar	Gality, Robert	Goliad
Fung, Phillipp	Comal	Gallaher, E.	Wharton
Fuqua, A. M.	Grimes	Gallan, M.	Victoria
Fuqua, Ephraim	Grimes	Gallaton, A.	Milam
Fuqua, H. H.	Grimes	Gallet & Brown	Lamar
Fuqua, Lucas	Gonzales	Galley, Anton	Bexar
Fuqua, Stephen	Washington	Gallion, J. C.	Houston
Furguson, Alston	Rusk	Galliot, H.	Bexar
Furguson, Isaac	Rusk	Galloway, C. A.	Grayson
Furguson, J. D.	Rusk	Galloway, George	
Furguson, James	Cherokee	G.	Anderson
Furguson, Joseph	Limestone	Galloway, J. B.	Grayson
Furguson, Joseph	Rusk	Galloway, John F.	Robertson
Furguson, N. K.	Rusk	Galloway, Peter	Angelina
Furguson, P. M.	Titus	Galveston,	
Furguson, R. A.	Fayette	Fernando	Guadalupe
Furguson, William	Rusk	Galyan, Franswar	Jefferson
Furguson, William,		Galyan, Joseph	Jefferson
Sr.	Tyler	Gamage, T. T.	Harrison
Furguson, William		Gambel, William,	
A.	Tyler	Jr.	Fannin
Fury, M.	Montgomery	Gambel, William,	
Fusl, Joseph	Bexar	Sr.	Fannin
Futch, A.	Austin	Gamble, Ann	San Patricio
Futch, Fertinant	Austin	Gamble, Arthur	Refugio
Futch, R. A.	Grayson	Gamble, E. H.	Cass
Fyffe, James H.	Harrison	Gamble, George	Bastrop
Fyffe, Nancy	Harrison	Gamble, Joseph	Red River
		Gamble, W. L. F.	Bastrop
		Gamble, William	San Patricio
Gable, J. M.	Rusk	Gamble, Wm.	Victoria
Gaffield, William	Harris	Gambo, J.	Henderson
Gafney, Owen	Victoria	Gammel, William	Harris
Gage, B.	Upshur	Gammon, Smith M.	Smith
Gage, Calvin	Fannin	Gann, John D.	Angelina
Gage, Calvin	Henderson	Gann, Solomon	Angelina
Gage, David	Gonzales	Gann, William W.	Angelina
Gage, David	Rusk	Gano, F. R.	Walker
Gage, E. N.	Red River	Gant, John J.	Rusk
Gage, Joseph	Bastrop	Gant, Matthew	Rusk
Gage, Moses	Bastrop	Garant, D. B.	Walker
Gage, Shirley	Bastrop	Garcia, Cas.	Bexar
Gahagan, James	Titus	Garcia, Dolores	Bexar

NAME	COUNTY	NAME	COUNTY
Garcia, Greg	Bexar	Garret, John	Hopkins
Garcia, Guadalupe	Bexar	Garret, Michael	Hopkins
Garcia, Juan	Henderson	Garret, William	Hopkins
Garcia, M.	Galveston	Garrett, A.	Bastrop
Garcia, M de	Victoria	Garrett, Charles	Harris
Garcia, Marcus	Henderson	Garrett, Charles	Smith
Garcia, Meguil	Bexar	Garrett, H. N.	Anderson
Garcia, Pilar	Bexar	Garrett, Hosea	Washington
Gardiner, Charles		Garrett, Howell	Sabine
H.	Nacogdoches	Garrett, J. B. F.	Houston
Gardiner, J. B.	Galveston	Garrett, J. S.	Sabine
Gardiner, John	Galveston	Garrett, Julius N.	Shelby
Gardiner, L.	Sabine	Garrett, Milton	San Augustine
Gardiner, Thomas		Garrett, O. H. P.	Washington
G.	Smith	Garrett, T. M.	Anderson
Gardino, Charles	Jefferson	Garrett, Thomas D.	Nacogdoches
Gardner, G. G.	Sabine	Garrett, W. H.	Bastrop
Gardner, G. W.	Colorado	Garrett, William	San Augustine
Gardner, J. W.	Anderson	Garrett, William	
Gardner, James A.	Lamar	S.	Smith
Gardner, O. H. P.	Rusk	Garrison, Jacob	Goliad
Gardner, Roxana	Lamar	Garrison, James	Lamar
Gardner, Sebastian	Leon	Garrison, Mitchel	Panola
Gardner, T. H.	Leon	Garrison, P. S.	Bowie
Gardner, Thomas	Lamar	Garton, Joseph	Victoria
Gardner, W. M.	Rusk	Garvin, Neiman	Guadalupe
Garland, James	Grayson	Garvin, S. M.	Grimes
Garlnad, James	Lamar	Gary, H. S.	Titus
Garlick, Catharine	Galveston	Gary, John	Robertson
Garner, Arthur D.	Polk	Gary, Seamon	DeWitt
Garner, Bradley	Jefferson	Garza, Andreas	Bexar
Garner, David	Jefferson	Garza, C.	Bexar
Garner, George S.	Harris	Garza, Fraylan	Bexar
Garner, Henry P.	Nacogdoches	Garza, Jose de la	Bexar
Garner, Isaac	Jefferson	Garza, Jose	
Garner, J. F.	Henderson	Antonio	Bexar
Garner, J. R.	Shelby	Garza, Josefa	Bexar
Garner, Jacob	Polk	Garza, Manuel	Bexar
Garner, Jacob H.	Jefferson	Garza, Ped.	Goliad
Garner, James	Polk	Garza, R. C.	Bexar
Garner, John	San Augustine	Gaskin, J. W.	Grayson
Garner, Solomon	Cass	Gass, J. A.	Henderson
Garner, Wesley	Jefferson	Gass, J. M.	Henderson
Garner, William	Shelby	Gaston, Hudson	Fort Bend
Garner, William H.	Polk	Gates, Amos	Grimes
Garnett, G. W.	Victoria	Gates, Amos	Washington
Garnett, John R.	Fannin	Gates, Benjamin P.	Jefferson
Garnett, William		Gates, Samuel H.	Washington
R.	Fannin	Gates, William L.	Polk
Garret, Jane	Hunt	Gates, William P.	Washington

NAME	COUNTY	NAME	COUNTY
Gatewood, William	Anderson	George, David	Wharton
Gatlen, Thomas H.	Bastrop	George, Easly	Navarro
Gatliff, Timothy	Anderson	George, Ezekiel	Fort Bend
Gautier, Peter	Brazoria	George, Freeman	Gonzales
Gautier, Peter W.	Brazoria	George, Hesekiah	Rusk
Gautier, William	Brazoria	George, Holman	Goliad
Gay, Appleton	Montgomery	George, J. W.	Houston
Gay, Edward	Cass	George, J. W.	Limestone
Gay, G. D.	Montgomery	George, J. W.	Wharton
Gay, G. W.	Austin	George, James	Goliad
Gay, Thomas A.	Montgomery	George, James	Navarro
Gayle, A. T.	Jackson	George, Joseph	Goliad
Gayle, B.	Liberty	George, Joseph	Wharton
Gayle, R. W.	Liberty	George, Joseph J.	Brazoria
Gaylord, G. D.	Colorado	George, Nicholas	Wharton
Gayton, Estevan	Bexar	George, Philip	Navarro
Gayton, Philipe	Bexar	George, Presley	Bowie
Gazley, T. J.	Bastrop	George, Stephen	Rusk
Gebins, Epps	Lamar	George, Wiley	Victoria
Gedry, Joshua	Jefferson	George, William	Goliad
Gedry, Ursan	Jefferson	George, William E.	Cherokee
Gee, A.	Grimes	George, William J.	Angelina
Gee, Alfred	Washington	George, Winston	Wharton
Gee, C.	Burleson	Gephart, Peter	Lavaca
Gee, Elizabeth	Burleson	Germany, J.	Cass
Gee, M. S.	Burleson	Gerrighty, John	Goliad
Gee, N. A.	Burleson	Gerwin, Henry	Comal
Gee, Richard N.	Washington	Gestzer, Frank	Liberty
Gee, S. R.	Burleson	Ghilbrett, E.	Henderson
Geer, Mrs.		Gholson, A. G.	Limestone
Permeila	Red River	Gholson, Britania	Harrison
Geescke, Charles	Colorado	Gholson, Jacob	Rusk
Geescke, Edward	Brazoria	Ghormley, J. S.	Henderson
Geline, John	Grimes	Ghossett, J. L.	Henderson
Gellatty, Robert	Sabine	Ghossett, James	Henderson
Gelt, James	Liberty	Gibbs, Alonso F.	Tyler
Genard(?), William	Brazoria	Gibbs, E. W.	Panola
Genn, Marshall	Anderson	Gibbs, J. L.	Panola
Gentry, F. B.	Washington	Gibbs, Jesse	Austin
Gentry, George	Limestone	Gibbs, Jonathan P.	Panola
Gentry, George W.	Washington	Gibbs, P. F.	Panola
Gentry, James	Washington	Gibbs, Thomas	Grimes
Gentry, R. K.	Cherokee	Gibbs, Thomas	Walker
Geor, Peter	Victoria	Gibbs, William	Tyler
George, Aaron	Tyler	Gibens, William	
George, Alfred	Grimes	Fitz	Panola
George, B. M.	Harris	Gibony, John	Grimes
George, Cary	Angelina	Gibson, A.	Cherokee
George, D. A.	Travis	Gibson, A. P.	Walker
George, David	Goliad	Gibson, Archibald	Goliad

NAME	COUNTY	NAME	COUNTY
Gibson, Archibald	Gonzales	Giles, S. B.	Washington
Gibson, Elizabeth	Cherokee	Giles, Smith	Henderson
Gibson, Isom	Leon	Giles, William	Cass
Gibson, Ivy	Bowie	Gill, James M.	Harrison
Gibson, J. N.	Henderson	Gill, John P.	Brazoria
Gibson, J. T.	Hunt	Gill, Joshua	Panola
Gibson, Jesse	Cherokee	Gill, Presley	Liberty
Gibson, Jesse	Denton	Gill, William	Goliad
Gibson, John N.	Denton	Gill, William C.	Goliad
Gibson, M.	Anderson	Gill, William H.	Red River
Gibson, R. A.	Fannin	Gillard, Adolph	Liberty
Gibson, R. T.	Sabine	Gillard, Anna	Liberty
Gibson, T.	Hunt	Gillard, C.	Liberty
Gibson, William	Denton	Gillard, E. E.	Liberty
Gibson, William H.	Anderson	Gillard, J. M.	Liberty
Gibson, William H.	Denton	Gillard, John B.	Liberty
Giddings, Calvry	Hopkins	Gillard,	
Giddings, Edward	Hopkins	Petronvilla	Liberty
Giddings, J. D.	Washington	Gillard, R.	Liberty
Gideon, Joseph F.	Cherokee	Gillespie, Bexar	Bexar
Gideon, L. H.	Cherokee	Gillespie, Grimes	Grimes
Gideon, L. H.	Henderson	Gillespie, J. H.	Bastrop
Gideon, R. F.	Cass	Gillespie, J. H.	Houston
Gideon, R. F.	Red River	Gillespie, J. L.	San Augustine
Gideon, W. W.	Red River	Gillespie, James	Walker
Gidry, Lefty	Liberty	Gillett, Revd.	
Gil, Yguacia	Bexar	Charles	Harris
Gilbert, D. W.	San Augustine	Gillett, Henry F.	Harris
Gilbert, David	Galveston	Gillett, Roswell	Grimes
Gilbert, J. M.	Grimes	Gillett, S. S.	Grimes
Gilbert, John F.	Sabine	Gilley, Charles	Nacogdoches
Gilbert, Jonas	Grimes	Gilley, H. B.	Washington
Gilbert, Joseph L.	DeWitt	Gilley, John B.	Smith
Gilbert, Joseph T.	Grimes	Gilliam, F. B.	Lamar
Gilbert, L. A.	Henderson	Gilliam, James C.	Red River
Gilbert,		Gilliam, James S.	Red River
Lorzneaski	Washington	Gilliam, L. W.	Henderson
Gilbert, Mabel	Fannin	Gilliam, L. W. L.	San Augustine
Gilbert, R. N.	San Augustine	Gilliam, William	
Gilbert, R. S.	Red River	L.	Montgomery
Gilbert, T. Y.	Grimes	Gilliland, Allen	
Gilbert, Thomas	Fannin	T.	Hopkins
Gilbreath, John A.	Robertson	Gilliland, D.	Grimes
Gilbreath, Mary	Henderson	Gilliland, D.	Montgomery
Gilcrist, A.	Newton	Gilliland, Diannah	Travis
Gilcrist, W. C.	Newton	Gilliland, Henry	Washington
Gildersleeve, T.	Galveston	Gilliland, J.	Travis
Gildon, Charles	Cherokee	Gilliland, James	Angelina
Giles, J. J.	Cass	Gilliland, John T.	Angelina
Giles, Robert	Henderson	Gilliland,	

NAME	COUNTY	NAME	COUNTY
Nathaniel	Washington	Glass, Martha	Burleson
Gilliland, S.	Henderson	Glass, Shelby	Shelby
Gilliland, Samuel	Angelina	Glass, Wiley B.	Red River
Gilliland, William	Montgomery	Glass, William S.	Victoria
Gillum, Dudley	Cass	Glaze, Que	Navarro
Gilmer, Betsy G.	Fannin	Glenn, Alexander	Austin
Gilmer, James G.	Fannin	Glenn, Alexander	Washington
Gilmore, Caroline		Glenn, E. M.	Jackson
P.	Grimes	Glenn, G. R.	Walker
Gilmore, Charles	Anderson	Glenn, J. B.	Lamar
Gilmore, D. C.	Bexar	Glenn, J. D.	Lamar
Gilmore, D. J.	Leon	Glenn, M. S.	Austin
Gilmore, Thomas	Grimes	Glenn, Mrs. P.	Jackson
Gilmore, William	Goliad	Glenn, Silas S.	Lamar
Gilmore, William	Grimes	Glenn, W. Y.	Cherokee
Gilpin, B.	Henderson	Glenn, William	Lamar
Gilpin, R.	Henderson	Glidewell, A.	Cherokee
Gipson, J. T.	Henderson	Glosing, Henry	Guadalupe
Gipson, John T.	Henderson	Glover, E. C.	Jefferson
Gipson, Leroy	Henderson	Glover, G. H.	Bowie
Gipson, William	Henderson	Glover, G. W.	Dallas
Girard, Emile	Harris	Glover, J.	Shelby
Girdes, G.	Cass	Glover, John W.	Grayson
Gist, Joseph	Titus	Glover, Joseph	Red River
Given, C. C.	Galveston	Glover, M.	Cass
Given, G. W.	Burleson	Glover, Martin	Bowie
Given, J. J.	Travis	Glover, William	Bowie
Given, William	Houston	Glover, William B.	Galveston
Glanis, Prudence	Goliad	Gocher, H. P.	Nacogdoches
Glascock, E. J.	Rusk	Godbolt, J. C.	Cass
Glascock, Fred	Cass	Godfrey, Robert	Henderson
Glascock, George		Godman, James J.	Dallas
D.	Travis	Godsey, B. J.	Fannin
Glascock, George		Godsir, E.	Henderson
J.	Travis	Godwin, Rufus	Titus
Glascock, George		Goff, Henry N.	Montgomery
W.	Travis	Goff, Monroe	Jackson
Glascock, James A.	Travis	Goheen, Stacey M.	Grimes
Glascock, S. B.	Fort Bend	Gohsen, M. R.	Harris
Glascock, T. C.	Travis	Goldbeck, Theo	Comal
Glascock, Thomas		Golden, James	Shelby
W.	Travis	Golden, Philip J.	Travis
Glascock, Thomas		Golden, Richard	Panola
W.	Travis	Gomer, Augustus	Sabine
Glascock, W. D.	Bastrop	Gomez, Francisco	Bexar
Glascock, Z. T.	Bastrop	Gomez, Jairana	Goliad
Glass, D. S.	Cherokee	Gomez, Jesus	Henderson
Glass, H. D.	Red River	Gomez, Luis	Bexar
Glass, J. B.	Bowie	Gomez, M. D.	Henderson
Glass, John C.	Bowie	Gomez, Martina	Bexar

NAME	COUNTY	NAME	COUNTY
Gomez, N. B.	Henderson	Goodwin, Cathy	Angelina
Gomez, N. M.	Henderson	Goodwin, G. W.	Galveston
Gomex, W. B.	Henderson	Goodwin, James R.	Cherokee
Gomoines, F.	Bexar	Goodwin, John J.	Dallas
Goney, John	Travis	Goodwin, Joseph	Angelina
Gonzales, Agapo	Bexar	Goodwin, Micajah	Dallas
Gonzales, Andrew	Henderson	Goodwin, Robert	Angelina
Gonzales, Antonio	Bexar	Goodwin, Robert	Shelby
Gonzales, C.	Bexar	Goodwin, Robert,	
Gonzales, Carlos	Bexar	Jr.	Shelby
Gonzales, F.	Henderson	Goodwin, Shirley	Angelina
Gonzales, Leonardo	Goliad	Goodwin, William	Angelina
Gonzales, Mastine	Nacogdoches	Goodwin, William	Shelby
Gonzales, Pedro	Goliad	Gookin, Thomas M.	
Gonzales, T.	Henderson	S.	Grayson
Gooch, B.	Titus	Goolsby, C. M.	Houston
Gooch, James	Travis	Goolsby, H. M.	Cherokee
Good, Edward	Jasper	Goolsby, J. A.	Houston
Good, Hanibal	Jasper	Goosley, William	
Good, James B.	Jasper	G.	Brazoria
Good, Joseph W.	Jasper	Gorbet, C. S.	Grimes
Good, Matthew	Jasper	Gordes, G.	Bowie
Good, Minor J.	Jasper	Gordon, George	Red River
Good, Thomas B.	Tyler	Gordon, J. R.	Grimes
Goodbread, P.	Walker	Gordon, James	Harrison
Goodbread, P. K.	Walker	Gordon, John	Lamar
Goodbread, Philip	Grimes	Gordon, Joseph	Titus
Goode, G. J.	Jasper	Gordy, Catherine	Bowie
Goode, Harriet C.	Harrison	Gordy, Liston	Bowie
Goode, Noble M.	Harrison	Gore, H. V. N.	Matagorda
Goode, Richard N.	Harrison	Gore, T. W.	Hunt
Goode, Samuel	Jasper	Gorman, Churchill	Harrison
Goodin, Elijah	Rusk	Gorman, J. P.	Burleson
Goodin, Warren	Jefferson	Gorman, James	Harrison
Goodin, William	Brazoria	Gorman, Joab	Houston
Goodloe, R. K.	Sabine	Gorman, Ross	Houston
Goodman, J. B.	Jasper	Gormley, James S.	Anderson
Goodman, J. J.	Walker	Gosa, William	Anderson
Goodman, James	Bexar	Goshen, Alison	Lamar
Goodman, John S.	Fort Bend	Goshen, William	Grayson
Goodman, Lewis	Walker	Goslin, John	Harris
Goodman, M. D.	Fort Bend	Goslin, Levi	Harris
Goodman, Sarah	Walker	Goss, C. S.	Wharton
Goodman, Stephen	Fort Bend	Goss, John	Gonzales
Goodman, T. J.	Liberty	Goss, N. H.	Austin
Goodman, W. B.	Grimes	Goss, Thomas	Cherokee
Goodman, W. B.	Montgomery	Gossett, A. E.	Houston
Goodrich, B. B.	Grimes	Gossett, Elijah	Houston
Goodrich, E. W.	Grimes	Gossett, J. L.	Grimes
Goodrich, James M.	Grimes	Gossett, John V.	

NAME	COUNTY	NAME	COUNTY
D.	Houston	Granada, Mariano	Robertson
Gotcher, H. B.	Lamar	Granada, Pereira	Robertson
Gotcher, James	Bastrop	Graner, J. H.	Henderson
Gould, William C.	Galveston	Grant, G. W.	Houston
Gound, Joseph	Cherokee	Grant, Joel	Washington
Goune, F.	Victoria	Grant, Stephen	Red River
Gourland, Edward	Galveston	Grant, T. A.	Harris
Gowen, Henry	Houston	Grant, William W.	Goliad
Gowen, Jeremiah	Houston	Granville,	
Goyins, William	Nacogdoches	Benjamin	Austin
Grace, B. M.	Upshur	Grasmeyer, F. W.	Bastrop
Grace, Benjamin	Cass	Graves, Charles H.	Harris
Grace, J. E.		Graves, Edward	Goliad
(decd)	Austin	Graves, Elizabeth	Henderson
Grace, John	Rusk	Graves, G. W.	Shelby
Grace, Morgan	Shelby	Graves, J. B.	Wharton
Grace, Thomas	Rusk	Graves, J. K.	Polk
Grady, Daniel	Fayette	Graves, John	Harrison
Graff, J.	Henderson	Graves, Joseph	Panola
Gragg, Samuel	Cass	Graves, Philip	Panola
Graham, ----	Victoria	Graves, Ralph	Grimes
Graham, A.	Fayette	Graves, Robert R.	Shelby
Graham, Alex.	Lamar	Graves, S. J.	Harrison
Graham, Andrew	Shelby	Graves, Thomas F.	Harris
Graham, B.	Red River	Graviel, S.	Refugio
Graham, Henry	Goliad	Gray, A. F.	San Augustine
Graham, J.	Cass	Gray, Ben W.	Titus
Graham, J. N.	Travis	Gray, Daniel	Bastrop
Graham, J. R.	Goliad	Gray, Elizabeth T.	Harrison
Graham, James	Collin	Gray, Hanson L.	Hopkins
Graham, James	Hopkins	Gray, Harvey	Rusk
Graham, James	Lamar	Gray, J. L.	Bastrop
Graham, James	Red River	Gray, J. W.	Titus
Graham, James H.	Rusk	Gray, James	Tyler
Graham, James M.	Shelby	Gray, James	Washington
Graham, John	Robertson	Gray, James W.	Bexar
Graham, John D.	Titus	Gray, Jesse	Grimes
Graham, John H.	Angelina	Gray, John	Washington
Graham, John L.	Angelina	Gray, Joshua	Bastrop
Graham, R. C.	Cass	Gray, P.	Walker
Graham, R. H.	Red River	Gray, Peter W.	Harris
Graham, Robert	Brazoria	Gray, S. S.	Bastrop
Graham, Robert	Cass	Gray, Tarlton	Lamar
Graham, Spencer	Denton	Gray, Thomas	Bastrop
Graham, T. W.	Cass	Gray, Uriah	Harrison
Graham, Thomas	Red River	Gray, W. F.	Grimes
Graham, William	Fannin	Gray, W. W.	San Augustine
Graham, Wm.	Hopkins	Gray, Westley	Bastrop
Grammar, Joseph	Anderson	Gray, William	Tyler
Granada, Fran.	Bexar	Gray, William	Walker

NAME	COUNTY	NAME	COUNTY
Gray, William J.	Grimes	Green, Michael	Goliad
Grayham, Arch. C.	Nacogdoches	Green, Nathan	Houston
Grayham, John H.	Nacogdoches	Green, Quincy	Nacogdoches
Grayham, John F.	Nacogdoches	Green, R. G.	Houston
Grayham, William		Green, Rolin	Titus
C.	Nacogdoches	Green, Thomas	Washington
Grayson, Benjamin	Austin	Green, Thomas J.	Brazoria
Grayson, Charles	Nacogdoches	Green, Tom	Tyler
Grayson, Jackson	Nacogdoches	Green, Will B.	Henderson
Grayson, T. W.	Fayette	Green, William	Navarro
Grayson, William		Green, William	Sabine
S.	Colorado	Green, William B.	DeWitt
Grayton, W. D.	Harrison	Greenhaw, B. F.	Bowie
Greathouse, Archie	Dallas	Greenman, S. P.	Red River
Greathouse,		Greenwald, Francis	Bexar
Archilas	Dallas	Greenwell, William	Bowie
Green, Aaron	Tyler	Greenwood, B. C.	Lavaca
Green, Allen	Grimes	Greenwood,	
Green, B. S.	Washington	Franklin J.	Grimes
Green, Benjamin	Bexar	Greenwood,	
Green, Genjamin	Cass	Garrison	Gonzales
Green, Benjamin	Tyler	Greenwood, H. A.	Lavaca
Green, Berry	Rusk	Greenwood, J.	Grimes
Green, Cassa	Smith	Greenwood, John	Lavaca
Green, David G.	Polk	Greer, A.	Henderson
Green, E. F.	Galveston	Greer, Alexander	Nacogdoches
Green, Ellis	Tyler	Greer, D. D.	Grimes
Green, Ezekiel	Tyler	Greer, David	Shelby
Green, F. F.	Harrison	Greer, E. C.	Fannin
Green, F. L.	San Augustine	Greer, Felix	Wharton
Green, F. M.	Anderson	Greer, G.	Henderson
Green, Fritz	Polk	Greer, Gilbert	Washington
Green, G. B.	Anderson	Greer, H. H.	Henderson
Green, George	Burleson	Greer, J. A.	Grimes
Green, Henry	Fannin	Greer, J. A.	San Augustine
Green, J. L.		Greer, J. H.	Henderson
Womack	Grimes	Greer, Joseph	DeWitt
Green, J. W.	Cass	Greer, Joseph	Harrison
Green, J. W.	Red River	Greer, L. V.	San Augustine
Green, James	Houston	Greer, M. D.	Harrison
Green, James	Matagorda	Greer, N. B.	Grimes
Green, James	Navarro	Greer, Nathaniel	
Green, James, Jr.	Tyler	H.	Washington
Green, James, Sr.	Tyler	Greer, Solomon	Grimes
Green, James O.	Burleson	Greer, W.	Henderson
Green, John A.	Fayette	Greer, William S.	Nacogdoches
Green, Jones	Dallas	Gregary, Charles	
Green, Joseph	Tyler	E.	Harris
Green, Lonting	Tyler	Gregary, Jacob	Burleson
Green, M. H.	San Augustine	Gregary, Jesse	Burleson

NAME	COUNTY	NAME	COUNTY
Gregary, Richard, Jr.	Tyler	Griffith, Henry	Liberty
		Griffith, Henry	Wharton
Gregary, Richard, Sr.	Tyler	Griffith, J.	Washington
		Griffith, J. C.	San Augustine
Gregary, W.	Fayette	Griffith, James S.	Shelby
Gregg, A. J.	Washington	Griffith, John	Goliad
Gregg, Cf. F.	Brazoria	Griffith, Joshua	Montgomery
Gregg, Darias	Grimes	Griffith, Noah	Montgomery
Gregg, Darius	Harris	Griggs, D. C.	Red River
Gregg, Ellis, Sr.	Burleson	Grigsby, C.	Anderson
Gregg, G. G.	Harrison	Grigsby, E. W.	Jasper
Gregg, Harrison	Colorado	Grigsby, Elijah	Rusk
Gregg, Jacob	Houston	Grigsby, G. H. B.	Nacogdoches
Gregg, Jacob	Red River	Grigsby, John	Anderson
Gregg, Jeremiah	Travis	Grigsby, John P.	Rusk
Gregg, John	Burleson	Grigsby, Mark	Rusk
Gregg, John	Hopkins	Grigsby, Sally M.	Jasper
Gregg, John	Houston	Grigsby, Solomon	Rusk
Gregg, John	Red River	Grigsby, W.	Jasper
Gregg, Josiah	Hopkins	Grigsby, William	Anderson
Gregg, Milon	Titus	Grimes, Albert	Montgomery
Gregg, Samuel	Titus	Grimes, Fred	Austin
Gregg, William	Red River	Grimes, G. W.	Nacogdoches
Greggson, Jacob	Victoria	Grimes, George	Austin
Gresham, Edward L.	Washington	Grimes, H.	Cass
Gresham, William	Washington	Grimes, Jesse	Grimes
Grey, Daniel H.	Panola	Grimes, R.	Matagorda
Grey, Eli	Cass	Grimes, R. H.	Bastrop
Grey, James	Goliad	Grimes, Rufus	Grimes
Grey, Joseph	Henderson	Grimes, Thomas R.	DeWitt
Grey, T. M.	Fort Bend	Grimes, Washington	Austin
Grier, Walter	Smith	Grimes, William	Austin
Griffin, Allen	Washington	Grinage, A. M.	Guadalupe
Griffin, Elizabeth	Angelina	Grinder, William	Fannin
Griffin, J. F.	Lamar	Griner, John	Cherokee
Griffin, J. H.	Liberty	Grisham, G. W.	Harrison
Griffin, Jackson	Limestone	Grisham, John W.	Sabine
Griffin, Jesse	Wharton	Grisham, Joseph	Lamar
Griffin, John	Fayette	Grisman, A.	Travis
Griffin, John, Sr.	Washington	Grissom, L. B.	Brazoria
Griffin, L.	Limestone	Grissom, W. H.	Lamar
Griffin, Moses	Robertson	Griswold, Elijah	Panola
Griffin, Solomon	Goliad	Groce, F.	Victoria
Griffin, Sylvanus	Cherokee	Groce, George W.	Rusk
Griffin, Thomas J.	Cass	Groce, J. E.	Grimes
Griffin, William	Angelina	Groce, John	Rusk
Griffin, William	Rusk	Groce, L. W.	Austin
Griffin, William, Jr.	Robertson	Groce, Leonard	Grimes
		Groce, Thomas	Rusk
Griffith, Ewin	Titus	Groen, Seddon	Titus

67

NAME	COUNTY	NAME	COUNTY
Groesbeck, James D.	Harris	Gunther, Charles	Bexar
Grooms, A.	Travis	Gupton, N.	Cass
Grooms, Elizabeth	Walker	Curberry, Albert	Goliad
Grooms, Horacio	Travis	Gurley, John	Dallas
Grooms, Jane	Travis	Gurling, J.	Henderson
Grooms, R. E.	Bowie	Gusicke, Charles A.	Brazoria
Grooms, W.	Walker	Gusten, Samuel	Cass
Gross, Jacob	Milam	Guteones, Antonio	Bexar
Grove, Henry	Comal	Guthrie, George W.	Burleson
Grove, William	Brazoria	Guthrie, John F.	Burleson
Grover, B. H.	Fayette	Guthrie, Nancy	Newton
Grover, DeWitt	Victoria	Guthrie, William	Goliad
Grover, James	Victoria	Guthrie, William A.	Jackson
Grover, Nathan	Victoria	Guthrie, William C.	Burleson
Grow, G. F.	Bowie	Guy, John	Liberty
Grown, Goerge	Houston	Guy, Rafael	Bexar
Grubbs, Thomas	Polk	Guylls, Horace	Bexar
Grumbles, John J.	Travis	Guyman, William	Goliad
GuaJarda, Ignatio	Goliad	Guyton, J. B.	Limestone
Guderion, C. F. M.	Fannin	Guzabo, Luis	Bexar
Gudson, G. H.	Leon	Guzmann, S.	Bexar
Guerrero, Alex	Bexar	Gwaltney, John	Fannin
Guerrero, Juan	Bexar	Gwolworth, Adam	Henderson
Guerrero, Marcus	Bexar		
Guest, James	Cass		
Guest, Joseph	Titus		
Guest, Martin, Jr.	Red River		
Guest, Martin, Sr.	Red River	Haardt, H.	Comal
Guest, William	Red River	Gabbrooks, H. G.	Titus
Guffey, John	Lamar	Habermacker, Casper	Harris
Guilder, John L.	Colorado	Habermacker, Conrad	Harris
Guinn, Amos	Liberty	Habermacker, S.	Harris
Guinn, B. M.	Liberty	Habermacker, Thomas	Harris
Guinn, John	Cherokee	Haby, Jacob	Bexar
Guinn, Malcolm	Cherokee	Haby, Joseph	Bexar
Guinn, Richard	Liberty	Hackett, J. W.	Walker
Guinn, Sarah	Liberty	Hackworth, W. W.	Washington
Guinn, Thomas M.	Anderson	Hadaway, Samuel	Goliad
Guinn, Thornton	Anderson	Hadden, Anna	Colorado
Guinn, W. L.	Liberty	Hadden, Elizabeth	Colorado
Guinn, William	Anderson	Hadden, Henry	Colorado
Guisa, Charles	Bexar	Hadden, J. E.	Wharton
Guiterre, B.	Bexar	Hadden, William	Wharton
Gullins, Alex.	Harris	Haden, Robert	Panola
Gumble, George W.	Washington	Haden, Day & Co.	Austin
Gundeman, F.	Galveston	Hadgeons, William	Lavaca
Gunn, F. B.	Bowie		
Gunn, Henry	Harris		
Gunter, M.	Nacogdoches		

NAME	COUNTY	NAME	COUNTY
Hadley, A.	Grimes	Haley, Thomas T.	Harris
Hadley, B. Q.	Goliad	Halfpenny, James	Bastrop
Hadley, B. Q.	Grimes	Halins, T. B.	Grimes
Hadley, Dennis P.	Grimes	Haljan, Antonio	Jackson
Hadley, F. B. J.	Harris	Hall, Allen	Austin
Hadley, G. H.	Grimes	Hall, Ambrose	Galveston
Hadley, Henry F.	Grimes	Hall, Bartlett M.	Nacogdoches
Hadley, Joice V.	Grimes	Hall, Britton	Newton
Hadley, Joshua	Grimes	Hall, C. K.	Harris
Hadley, Simon	Grimes	Hall, Charles C.	Houston
Hadley, T. K.	Grimes	Hall, Charles M.	Harrison
Haga, Joel W.	Lamar	Hall, Edward	Galveston
Haga, John R.	Lamar	Hall, Edward H.	Brazoria
Hagan, Adam	Fort Bend	Hall, George	Lamar
Hagan, Austin	Fort Bend	Hall, H. H.	San Augustine
Hagan, J. W.	Grimes	Hall, Harrison	Walker
Hagan, John	Houston	Hall, Isaac W.	San Augustine
Hageman, Simon	Fort Bend	Hall, J. J.	Houston
Hagerlund, John P.	Fort Bend	Hall, J. M.	Lamar
Hages, Mrs.	Matagorda	Hall, J. M. W.	Polk
Haggerty, J.	Cass	Hall, Jackson J.	Burleson
Haggerty, S. M.	Harrison	Hall, James	Washington
Hagin, T. C.	Upshur	Hall, James, 3rd	Austin
Hagood, Thomas G.	Fannin	Hall, James M.	Houston
Hagood, W. A.	Nacogdoches	Hall, Jane	Shelby
Hail, Gatewood	Harris	Hall, John	Colorado
Hailley, Mary	San Patricio	Hall, John	Shelby
Hailley, Michael	San Patricio	Hall, John	Washington
Hailley, W. F.	Matagorda	Hall, John B.	Harrison
Haines, William J.	Harrison	Hall, John L.	Houston
Hairbolt, James	Grayson	Hall, John P.	Montgomery
Hairston, Richard	Washington	Hall, John S.	Brazoria
Halbaden, J. B.	Bexar	Hall, Joyce	Houston
Halbert, Jowel	Sabine	Hall, Juliette	Brazoria
Halbert, Stephen	Sabine	Hall, Layton	Brazoria
Hale, J. C.	Red River	Hall, M. J.	Harrison
Hale, J. W.	Red River	Hall, Mary	Montgomery
Hale, Jonas J.	San Augustine	Hall, Mary A.	Brazoria
Hale, Mason	Washington	Hall, N. H.	Bastrop
Hale, W. C.	San Augustine	Hall, Priscilla	Grimes
Haley, Allen	Shelby	Hall, R.	Henderson
Haley, James W.	Harris	Hall, Richard G.	Cherokee
Haley, John, Jr.	Shelby	Hall, Robert	Gonzales
Haley, John R.	Leon	Hall, S.	Henderson
Haley, Mark	Leon	Hall, S. P.	Harrison
Haley, Mary A.	Shelby	Hall, Samuel	Bexar
Haley, R. B.	Leon	Hall, Solomon	Goliad
Haley, Richard	Shelby	Hall, T. D.	Harris
Haley, Richard,		Hall, T. J.	Walker
Jr.	Shelby	Hall, Thomas J.	Brazoria

NAME	COUNTY	NAME	COUNTY
Hall, W. B.	Burleson	Hard, Mrs. S.	Galveston
Hall, Warren	Brazoria	Hardaway, A.	Red River
Hall, William	Galveston	Hardaway, Nancy	Grayson
Hall, William	Harrison	Hardaway, T. E.	Grayson
Hall, William	Shelby	Harden, A.	Sabine
Hall, William A.	Gonzales	Harden, A. R.	Leon
Hall, William A.	Houston	Harden, Asher	Titus
Hall, William G.	Grimes	Harden, B. P.	Polk
Hallam, Margaret	Houston	Harden, H.	Upshur
Haller, Jacob	Washington	Harden, J. D.	Shelby
Hallet, Margaret	Lavaca	Harden, J. P.	Henderson
Hallford, James P.	Denton	Harden, Jane	Panola
Hallmark, A. M.	Houston	Harden, Leon	Shelby
Hallmark, G. W.	Houston	Harden, Martha	Polk
Hallmark, John B.	Houston	Harden, Nancy	Newton
Hallmark, Richard	Houston	Harden, Nopoleon	
Hanie, S. G.	Travis	B.	Newton
Hankins, Eli	Gonzales	Harden, S. H.	Panola
Hankla, R. A.	Sabine	Harden, Sam	Brazoria
Hannks, George	Anderson	Harden, William B.	Polk
Hanks, B.	Angelina	Harder, George	Colorado
Hanks, Eli	Anderson	Harder, H.	Colorado
Hanks, George W.	Anderson	Hardest, John	Brazos
Hanks, H. M.	San Augustine	Hardgrove, F. C.	Cherokee
Hanks, Hansford	Anderson	Hardiman, B.	Henderson
Hanks, J. S.	Anderson	Hardiman, Const.	Nacogdoches
Hanks, James	Shelby	Hardiman, D.	Brazoria
Hanks, Mortimer	Anderson	Hardiman,	
Hanks, Peter	Hunt	Elizabeth	Gonzales
Hanks, S. G.	San Augustine	Hardiman, J. J.	Bastrop
Hanks, W. W.	Angelina	Hardiman, John M.	Washington
Hanks, Wyatt	Tyler	Hardiman, Owen B.	Bastrop
Hanna, Amariah	Dallas	Hardiman, T. M.	Bastrop
Hanna, Archibald	Henderson	Hardiman, W. M.	Henderson
Hanna, David	Gonzales	Hardiman, W. T.	Bastrop
Hanover, A.	Victoria	Hardin, A. B.	Liberty
Hanover, Hiram	Robertson	Hardin, B. W.	Liberty
Hansbrough, J.	Brazoria	Hardin, Franklin	Liberty
Hansbrough, W. S.	Brazoria	Hardin, J. B.	Limestone
Hansel, G. W.	Fort Bend	Hardin, M. A.	Liberty
Hanson, Henry F.	Brazoria	Hardin, Robert E.	Limestone
Hanson, James	Brazoria	Hardin, Thomas P.	Cass
Hanson, Mary A.	Brazoria	Harding, D. G.	San Augustine
Hanson, N.	Henderson	Harding, J. R.	Robertson
Hapirmil, George	Travis	Harding, T. B.	Milam
Harbour, Elijah	Grimes	Hardison, Thomas	Lamar
Harbour, George W.	Washington	Hardwick, G. B.	Houston
Harbour, James	Grimes	Hardwick, George N.	
Harbour, James M.	Washington	N.	Cherokee
Harbour, Mary	Washington	Hardy, G. J. P.	Jasper

NAME	COUNTY	NAME	COUNTY
Hardy, G. M. P.	Newton	Harper, Jacob	Newton
Hardy, Mrs.		Harper, James	Bowie
Harriet	Harris	Harper, William	Hopkins
Hardy, J. P.	Jasper	Harper, Willis	Harrison
Hardy, James	Washington	Harrell, A. J.	Travis
Hardy, Jesse	Polk	Harrell, A. W.	Galveston
Hardy, M. H.	Victoria	Harrell, Benjamin	
Hardy, Massa	Tyler	C. P.	Nacogdoches
Hardy, Richard	Tyler	Harrell, Henry	Navarro
Hardy, Theo.	Robertson	Harrell, J. M.	Travis
Hargas, F.	Titus	Harrell, John	Anderson
Hargas, Lary	Shelby	Harrell, John	Cherokee
Hargraves, E. G.	Hopkins	Harrell, John	Travis
Hargraves, J. P.	Hopkins	Harrell, John B.	Polk
Hargraves, James	Hopkins	Harrell, Josiah T.	Harris
Hargraves, James		Harrelson, A. J.	Travis
R.	Hopkins	Harrelson, J. C.	Harrison
Hargraves, Robert	Hopkins	Harrelson, Silas	Harrison
Hargraves, William	Hopkins	Harrington, E. M.	Shelby
Hargrove, Solliman	Anderson	Harrie, L. B.	Bastrop
Hargrove, W. D.	Washington	Harris, A. J.	Goliad
Harison, S. M.	Henderson	Harris, Allen	Red River
Harkins, James	Harrison	Harris, Ausborn	Sabine
Harkness, Benjamin	Shelby	Harris, B. F.	Harris
Harland, Joasph	Robertson	Harris, Buckner	DeWitt
Harlin, Isaiah	Montgomery	Harris, C. A.	Shelby
Harlis, Hiram	Lavaca	Harris, C. M.	Harris
Harman, D.	Harris	Harris, Carter	Travis
Harman, David	Jefferson	Harris, D.	Victoria
Harman, Francis	Harrison	Harris, D. W. C.	Harris
Harman, J. T.	Lamar	Harris, Daniel	Dallas
Harman, Jacob	Lamar	Harris, David	Harris
Harman, John	Austin	Harris, David	Henderson
Harman, John	Jefferson	Harris, E. C.	Jefferson
Harman, John	Lamar	Harris, E. R.	Sabine
Harman, Lewis	Lamar	Harris, Eldridge	
Harman, Michael	Lamar	C.	Henderson
Harman, M. P.	Fayette	Harris, F. W.	Brazos
Harman, Thomas	Goliad	Harris, G. B.	Burleson
Harmes, F. W.	Brazos	Harris, George	Montgomery
Harmes, Julius	Leon	Harris, H.	Anderson
Harp, George	Fort Bend	Harris, H. B.	Red River
Harper, A.	Montgomery	Harris, Harrison	Grayson
Harper, Andrew	Grimes	Harris, J. A.	Anderson
Harper, B. J.	Cherokee	Harris, J. A.	Colorado
Harper, C. A.	Bexar	Harris, J. A.	Harris
Harper, Daniel E.	Grimes	Harris, James	Goliad
Harper, E. S.	Travis	Harris, Jane	Harris
Harper, E. W.	Newton	Harris, Jas.	
Harper, Elizabeth	Bowie	Madison	Washington

NAME	COUNTY	NAME	COUNTY
Harris, Jesse	Goliad	Harrison, J. W.	Lamar
Harris, John	Cherokee	Harrison, Jacob	Shelby
Harris, John	Dallas	Harrison, James	Shelby
Harris, John	Sabine	Harrison, James G.	Fannin
Harris, John B.	Grimes	Harrison, John	Navarro
Harris, John C.	Hopkins	Harrison, John H.	Harrison
Harris, John W.	Shelby	Harrison, John S.	Grimes
Harris, Lewis	Lamar	Harrison, John S.	Navarro
Harris, Lewis B.	Harris	Harrison, Joseph	Fannin
Harris, Lisal	Gonzales	Harrison, L.	Hunt
Harris, Mary	Nacogdoches	Harrison, Mary	Bastrop
Harris, McNiny	Cass	Harrison, Peter	Newton
Harris, N. T.	Navarro	Harrison, Sam	Harrison
Harris, R. C.	Bowie	Harrison, Samuel	Cass
Harris, R. C.	Cass	Harrison, Terry	Bastrop
Harris, R. D.	Washington	Harrison, Thomas	
Harris, Reuben	Burleson	H.	Fannin
Harris, Samuel	Brazoria	Harrison, Vincent	Polk
Harris, Samuel M.	Harris	Harrison, W. C.	Lamar
Harris, Sarah	Sabine	Harrison, W. P.	Harrison
Harris, Seaborn	Sabine	Harrison, William	Grimes
Harris, T. A.	Harrison	Harrison, William	
Harris, Thomas	Washington	G.	Anderson
Harris, Thomas H.	Harris	Harrison, William	
Harris, V. N.	Jefferson	R.	Lamar
Harris, W. D.	Harrison	Harrison, Zada	Lamar
Harris, W. D.	Sabine	Harrold, Josiah	Lamar
Harris, W. G.	Grimes	Harruff, Henry	Cherokee
Harris, Wiley	Bastrop	Hart, A. J.	Henderson
Harris, William	Dallas	Hart, Bridget	San Patricio
Harris, William	Grimes	Hart, C.	Collin
Harris, William	Hunt	Hart, Claiborne	Newton
Harris, William A.	Guadalupe	Hart, Edward	Grayson
Harris, William H.	Fannin	Hart, Free L.	Fannin
Harris, William R.	Anderson	Hart, G. W.	Red River
Harris & Pease	Brazoria	Hart, Harden	Grayson
Harrison, B. S.	Austin	Hart, Hardin	Fannin
Harrison, Curtis	Fayette	Hart, J. C.	Red River
Harrison, Eleanor	Shelby	Hart, J. K.	Titus
Harrison, Elsey	Brazoria	Hart, John	Grayson
Harrison, F. E.	Fannin	Hart, John	Hopkins
Harrison, G. H.	Washington	Hart, John	Hunt
Harrison, G. P.	Harrison	Hart, John	San Patricio
Harrison, G. W.	Victoria	Hart, Jonathan	Fannin
Harrison, Isabel	Shelby	Hart, Josiah	Hunt
Harrison, J. C.	Montgomery	Hart, Luke	San Patricio
Harrison, J. C.	Washington	Hart, M. D.	Fannin
Harrison, J. M.	Walker	Hart, Meredith	Hopkins
Harrison, J. P.	Bowie	Hart, Meredith,	
Harrison, J. P.	Walker	Jr.	Fannin

NAME	COUNTY	NAME	COUNTY
Hart, Miles	Fannin	Harwood, A. M.	Dallas
Hart, O. P.	Polk	Hasha, Marsla	Jefferson
Hart, Patrick	San Patricio	Haskins, Francis	Goliad
Hart, S.	Henderson	Haskins, James	Goliad
Hart, Silas	Fannin	Haskins, R.	Brazoria
Hart, Thomas	Hunt	Hass, G. L.	Bexar
Hart, Thomas W.	Jasper	Hassel, D. D.	Anderson
Hart, Timothy	Refugio	Hassel, J. W.	Goliad
Hart, Timothy	San Patricio	Hassel, John	Anderson
Hart, W. F. T.	Fannin	Hassel, Phebe	Anderson
Hart, W. H.	Upshur	Hastings, G. W.	Rusk
Hart, William	Grayson	Hastings, Lymon	Henderson
Harter, Daniel	Cass	Haston, J. C.	Jefferson
Harter, Henry	Dallas	Haswell, Charles	
Hartgroves, H. W.	Titus	F.	Fayette
Hartin, J. B.	Harrison	Haswell, J. S.	Houston
Hartless, --	Rusk	Hatch, E. H.	Fayette
Hartoss, William	Henderson	Hatch, F. L.	Walker
Hartson, E.	Travis	Hatch, George W.	Goliad
Hartung, Christian	Comal	Hatch, Orsen	Rusk
Harty, John	Cass	Hatch, Sylvanus	Goliad
Harven, A.	Travis	Hatcher, Isham	Panola
Harven, P. W.	Shelby	Hatcher, Solomon	Grayson
Harven, W. W.	Dallas	Hatfield, B. M.	Washington
Harvey, B. W.	San Augustine	Hathaway, W.	Victoria
Harvey, Calvin	San Augustine	Hathaway, W. L.	Wharton
Harvey, Edward R.	Burleson	Hatley, T. B.	Harrison
Harvey, Edward R.,		Hattix, T. H.	Fayette
Jr.	Burleson	Hatton, Rudolph R.	Lavaca
Harvey, F.	Matagorda	Hatton, William E.	Jefferson
Harvey, H. C.	Fayette	Hau, F.	Harrison
Harvey, J. M. A.	Sabine	Haught, Samuel	Dallas
Harvey, J. W.	Burleson	Haughton, Kenady	Sabine
Harvey, Jane	Burleson	Haun, Jawris	Dallas
Harvey, John	Bastrop	Haupmann, W. R.	Comal
Harvey, John	Burleson	Haven, Eben	Gonzales
Harvey, John H.	Burleson	Haven, Silas	Hopkins
Harvey, John J.	Harrison	Haven, Smith S.	Grimes
Harvey, R. E.	Burleson	Haven, Thomas, Jr.	Hopkins
Harvey, Robert	Sabine	Haven, Thomas,	
Harvey, Samuel H.	Burleson	Senr.	Hopkins
Harvey, William J.	Harrison	Haveneor, Charles	Brazoria
Harvey, William R.	Grayson	Hawkins, A. B.	Fannin
Harvick, Adam	Smith	Hawkins, Henry	Rusk
Harvick, King	Smith	Hawkins, J. D.	Matagorda
Harvick, Martin	Fannin	Hawkins, J. D.	Rusk
Harwell, Mrs.		Hawkins, J. T.	Brazoria
Delilah	Harrison	Hawkins, J. W.	Grimes
Harwell, Thomas	Limestone	Hawkins, Jacob	Navarro
Harwood, A.	Dallas	Hawkins, R.	Harris

NAME	COUNTY	NAME	COUNTY
Hawkins, S. M.	Fannin	Haywood, W. W.	Henderson
Hawkins, Thomas M.	Smith	Haze, John	Lamar
Hawkins, Tim	Harris	Hazeltine, H.	Limestone
Hawkins, William		Hazlett, Samuel	Travis
W.	Burleson	Head, James	Cherokee
Hawley, Fierce	Travis	Head, James A.	Brazos
Hawley, James C.	Harrison	Head, Jennet	Brazos
Hawpe, G. C.	Dallas	Head, William	Cass
Haws, Thomas	Titus	Headstream, Z.	Fannin
Hay, Thomas	Henderson	Heal, Simon	Cass
Hay, William J.	DeWitt	Heard, E. F.	Walker
Hayden, Gerard	Fayette	Heard, G. W.	Limestone
Haygood, D. S.	Cass	Heard, J. A.	Limestone
Haygood, H. H.	Jasper	Heard, James G.	Washington
Haynes, Charles	Goliad	Heard, T. J.	Grimes
Haynes, Charles	Gonzales	Heard, Thomas J.	Washington
Haynes, G. M.	Rusk	Heard, W. J. E.	Wharton
Haynes, J. P.	Henderson	Hearn, Benjamin	Harrison
Haynes, James C.	Rusk	Hearn, John	Bastrop
Haynes, James T.	Nacogdoches	Hearn, Joseph	Fannin
Haynes, John	Jasper	Hearn, William R.	Cherokee
Haynes, L. A.	Grimes	Heart, James R.	Houston
Haynes, M. H.	Nacogdoches	Heartgraves, --	Houston
Haynes, Mathew	Jasper	Heath, Beverly	Rusk
Haynes, Thomas	Calhoun	Heath, James	Red River
Haynes, Thomas H.	Goliad	Heath, P. S.	Walker
Haynes, Thomas M.	Jackson	Heath, R. D.	Cass
Haynes, William	Rusk	Heath, S. P.	Henderson
Haynie, James A.	Fayette	Heath, Thomas	Rusk
Haynie, John	Fayette	Heath, William	Goliad
Haynie, S. A. J.	Bastrop	Heath, William	Grimes
Hays, D.	Henderson	Heath, William	Walker
Hays, Henry	Cass	Heatherby, H. B.	Lamar
Hays, J. C.	Bexar	Hector, Asty	Guadalupe
Hays, Jacob	Grimes	Hector, James R.	Travis
Hays, Jacob	Jefferson	Hedgepeth, H. D.	Austin
Hays, John	Jackson	Hefflefinger,	
Hays, Leonard	Jefferson	James	Lamar
Hays, P. H.	Leon	Hefford, J. T.	Matagorda
Hays, P. N.	Victoria	Heflin, David	Nacogdoches
Hays, Thomas	Goliad	Heflin, Joseph	Montgomery
Hays, Thomas	Houston	Hefner, Alfred	Titus
Hays, Thomas	Jackson	Hefner, W.	Upshur
Hays, Thomas J.	Smith	Hegman, Joseph	Bowie
Hays, William C.	Houston	Heiman, Casper	Colorado
Hays, William J.	Bowie	Heidemeir, Fred	Comal
Hays, William R.	Houston	Heins, Jacob	Comal
Haytor, A. W.	Fort Bend	Heins, Otto	Comal
Haytor, William	Nacogdoches	Heitcamp, Henry	Comal
Haytor, William D.	Nacogdoches	Heith, Louis	Bexar

NAME	COUNTY	NAME	COUNTY
Heitman, D. A.	Austin	Henderson, James	
Heitman, L.	Austin	P.	Nacogdoches
Helfenstein, F.	Galveston	Henderson, John	Cherokee
Helibrant, C. L.	Jefferson	Henderson, John	Fannin
Helibrant,		Henderson, John T.	Shelby
Christian	Jefferson	Henderson, L. D.	Red River
Helm, Jacob	Dallas	Henderson, L. R.	Harrison
Helm, Thomas J.	Dallas	Henderson, Robert	Shelby
Helms, Abram	Grimes	Henderson, Samuel	Nacogdoches
Helms, T.	Collin	Henderson, T. J.	Lavaca
Helton, Henry	Rusk	Henderson, Tyre G.	Panola
Helton, Joseph H.	Rusk	Henderson, William	
Helum, G. W.	Lamar	B.	Nacogdoches
Helviss, Lewis	Houston	Hendick, H.	Henderson
Hemander, H. M.	Victoria	Hendley, J. J.	Galveston
Hemby, J. W.	Lamar	Hendley, William	Galveston
Hemby, James	Lamar	Hendrick, Edwin	Cherokee
Hemby, John	Anderson	Hendrick, H. G.	Fannin
Hemby, Jonathan	Lamar	Hendrick, J.	Cass
Hemby, Joseph	Panola	Hendrick, Joel F.	Fannin
Hemingway, R. C.	Red River	Hendrick, John	Gonzales
Hemnerle, Francis	Comal	Hendrick, O.	Harrison
Hemphill, --	Grimes	Hendrix, Elija	Tyler
Hemphill, A.	Montgomery	Hendrix, John	Grayson
Hemphill, C. M.	Gastrop	Hendrix, Reuben	Grayson
Hemphill, John	Galveston	Hendrix, T. D.	Leon
Hemphill, John	Washington	Hendry, John H.	Anderson
Hemphill, M. L.	Bastrop	Henkel, A.	Comal
Hemphill, Samuel	Red River	Henley, Daniel	Hunt
Hemphill, W. S.	Bastrop	Henley, Hiram	Harrison
Hemphill, Z. J.	Bastrop	Henne, F. L.	Comal
Henaker, Francis	Colorado	Hennings, John	Harris
Hench, John	Lavaca	Hennings, Josiah	Rusk
Hench, M. H.	Lavaca	Hennings, Lewis	Shelby
Henckle, Samuel	Brazoria	Henninton, Thomas	
Henderson, A.	San Augustine	E.	Jasper
Henderson,		Hennis, J. J.	Houston
Brinkley	Panola	Henrietta, Patrick	Galveston
Henderson, David	Nacogdoches	Henriques, Juana	Henderson
Henderson, F.	Brazos	Henry, A. F.	Grimes
Henderson, F. J.	Lavaca	Henry, E.	Montgomery
Henderson, H. G.	Guadalupe	Henry, Elizabeth	Brazos
Henderson, H. G.	Titus	Henry, Hugh	Brazos
Henderson, Henry	Hopkins	Henry, J. W.	Rusk
Henderson, Hugh	Anderson	Henry, James	Austin
Henderson, J. J.	Galveston	Henry, John	San Augustine
Henderson, J. P.	San Augustine	Henry, John R.	Robertson
Henderson, J. W.	Harris	Henry, Robert	Brazos
Henderson, James	Bastrop	Henry, W.	Henderson
Henderson, James	Red River	Henry, William	Brazos

NAME	COUNTY	NAME	COUNTY
Henry, William	Harris	Herndon, John B.	Fort Bend
Henry, William	Robertson	Herndon, Robert S.	Brazoria
Hensey, Hugh	Harrison	Heron, John	Bastrop
Henshaw, Jesse	Henderson	Herrald, Dennis	Washington
Hensley, A. J.	Washington	Herrald, John H.	Washington
Hensley, Charles	Washington	Herrald, W.	Fayette
Hensley, James	Henderson	Herrall, William	San Augustine
Hensley, James N.	Washington	Herrera, Ajs.	Bexar
Hensley, Johnson	Washington	Herrera, Blas	Bexar
Hensley, William		Herrera, Manuel	Bexar
R.	Calhoun	Herrera, Rafael	Bexar
Henson, A. J.	Grimes	Herrera, Teodor	Bexar
Henson, Absalom	Grimes	Herrera, Victor	Bexar
Henson, David	Robertson	Herrick, Daniel	Galveston
Henson, Henry	Rusk	Herrin, Ferdinand	Lamar
Henson, J., Jr.	Upshur	Herrin, W. H.	Collin
Henson, J. B.	Upshur	Herrin, William	Anderson
Henson, Joseph	Montgomery	Herrin, William	Newton
Henson, Montgomery	Montgomery	Herring, B. F.	Bowie
Henson, R. L.	Upshur	Herring, J.	Upshur
Henson, Terrell	Panola	Herring, Jacob	San Augustine
Henson, W. N.	Rusk	Herring, John S.	Bowie
Hensworth, Thomas	Brazoria	Herring, Prior	Titus
Hepple, Robert	Montgomery	Herring, William	
Herald, Richard	Fannin	L.	Shelby
Herald, Robert	Fannin	Herrington,	
Herams, Sam C.	Polk	Arabell	Washington
Herbert, C. C.	Colorado	Herrington, Ewell	Shelby
Herbert, P. T.	Fort Bend	Herrington, G.	Cass
Herbert, W. J.	Colorado	Herrington, John	Washington
Herbruger, Emil	Austin	Herrington, S.	Angelina
Herbst, Henry	Comal	Herrington,	
Herd, Stepher	Jasper	William	Angelina
Hereford, Charles	San Augustine	Herron, Abner, Jr.	Panola
Hereford, Charles		Herron, Abner,	
P.	San Augustine	Senr.	Panola
Hereford, W. H.	San Augustine	Herron, Lemuel	Panola
Herenden, E.	Collin	Herron, William M.	Panola
Herenden, J.	Collin	Herter, George W.	Washington
Herlock, Vincent	Walker	Hertz, H.	Henderson
Herman, Aiken	Harris	Hervey, Samuel S.	Red River
Herman, John	Harris	Hervie, Clayton	Navarro
Hernandez, Eulogio	Goliad	Heskew, Moses	Gonzales
Hernandez, Geraldi	Bexar	Heskew, William	Gonzales
Hernandez, Jesus	Bexar	Hess, Cyrus	Sabine
Hernandez, Jose	Victoria	Hessly, John	Galveston
Hernandez, Juan	Bexar	Hester, D. G.	Rusk
Hernandez, Ricardo	Bexar	Hester, John A.	Rusk
Hernandez, Santa	Bexar	Hester, William	Rusk
Hernandez, Vincent	Goliad	Hester, Willis	Cass

NAME	COUNTY	NAME	COUNTY
Hester & Ferguson	Comal	Higgins, Henry	Washington
Heujan, Bruno	Bexar	Higgins, J. C.	Bastrop
Heujan, Francisca	Bexar	Higgins, James	San Augustine
Heujan, Pablo	Bexar	Higgins, M. P.	Bowie
Heujan, Sefina	Bexar	Higgins, Moses	Wharton
Heusted, Hanson	Dallas	Higgins, William	
Heuston, Walter	Shelby	A.	Washington
Hewett, J. L.	Bexar	Higgs, George	Brazos
Hewett, J. L.	Cass	Higgs, Jonathan	Galveston
Hewett, Martha	Shelby	High, James	Bowie
Hewett, William	Washington	High, James	Cass
Hewett, William M.	Shelby	High, Peter	Henderson
Hewett, William		Highnote, Anderson	Navarro
M., Jr.	Shelby	Highnote, Philip	Navarro
Hewth, William	Cass	Highsmith, L.	Bastrop
Hext, Joseph B.	Newton	Highsmith, Samuel	Travis
Heynds, Clement	Gonzales	Highton, Levi	Lamar
Hiatt, W. L.	Panola	Hightower, C.	Red River
Hibbert, John B.	Dallas	Hightower, J. B.	Red River
Hibbert, William	Grayson	Hightower, Mrs.	
Hick, R. D.	Washington	Jane A.	Harrison
Hickey, Isaac	Titus	Hightower, John	Titus
Hickey, W. W.	Titus	Hightower, Robert	
Hicklen, William	Dallas	S.	Harrison
Hickman, Asa	Sabine	Hightower, T. P.	Red River
Hickman, James	Newton	Hihler, Conrad	Burleson
Hickman, Jesse	Houston	Hiland, Joseph	Burleson
Hickman,		Hiland, Sarah E.	Burleson
Theophilus	Newton	Hilburn, J.	Navarro
Hickman, William,		Hilburn, Mathias	Lamar
Jr.	Houston	Hilburn, R.	Bexar
Hickman, William,		Hilderbrand, F.	Cass
Sr.	Houston	Hill, A. J.	Fannin
Hickman, Wyatt	Newton	Hill, A. W.	Bastrop
Hicks, A. W.	Lavaca	Hill, Aaron	Grayson
Hicks, Alfred	Robertson	Hill, Abner	Lamar
Hicks, Edwin, Jr.	Lamar	Hill, Albert	Fayette
Hicks, Edwin, Sr.	Lamar	Hill, Alex A.	Nacogdoches
Hicks, Elbert	Grimes	Hill, Allen	Limestone
Hicks, Francis	Rusk	Hill, Bernard	Titus
Hicks, Stephen	Lavaca	Hill, D. R.	Milam
Hicks, William C.	Polk	Hill, David	Harrison
Hidgon, Ezekiel	Henderson	Hill, David S.	Grimes
Higdon, E.	Anderson	Hill, Elizabeth L.	Polk
Higginbotham, C.	Liberty	Hill, F. E.	Houston
Higginbotham, L.	Anderson	Hill, Fielden	Panola
Higginbotham, R.		Hill, Francis	Angelina
T.	Bexar	Hill, G. W.	Robertson
Higgins, E.	Brazoria	Hill, George W.	Cherokee
Higgins, Elijah	Colorado	Hill, H. J. A.	Robertson

NAME	COUNTY	NAME	COUNTY
Hill, H. T.	Bastrop	Hillbert, William	Liberty
Hill, Hanah	Sabine	Hillburn, Rebecca	Fayette
Hill, Harrison H.	Panola	Hiller, Francis	Fayette
Hill, J. B.	Fayette	Hilliard, C. T.	Shelby
Hill, J. B.	Lamar	Hilliard, William	Matagorda
Hill, J. L.	Austin	Hillman, Charles	Colorado
Hill, J. L.	Robertson	Hillman, Herman	Colorado
Hill, James C.	Smith	Hillyard, James	Austin
Hill, James M.	Fayette	Hindman, W. K.	Victoria
Hill, James O.	Grayson	Hinds, Genins	Brazoria
Hill, Jesse	Cherokee	Hinds, Thomas S.	Brazoria
Hill, Joel	Walker	Hines, David	Sabine
Hill, John	Nacogdoches	Hines, Davis	Sabine
Hill, John W.	Shelby	Hines, Elbert	Sabine
Hill, Jordan	Brazoria	Hines, J. A.	Sabine
Hill, L. A.	Fayette	Hines, James R.	Washington
Hill, Lemuel B.	Grayson	Hines, R. E.	Bowie
Hill, Libby	Fayette	Hines, William	Sabine
Hill, M. M.	Bastrop	Hinkley, Walter	Lavaca
Hill, Margaret	Bowie	Hinley, C. B.	Houston
Hill, Martha	Fayette	Hinshaw, J.	Hunt
Hill, Mary	Austin	Hinton, David	Shelby
Hill, Massouri	Harrison	Hinton, S. S.	Houston
Hill, Nicholas S.	Galveston	Hinton, Z.	Shelby
Hill, O. B.	Matagorda	Hipp, Janis	Guadalupe
Hill, O. H. T.	Walker	Hisaw, Fred	Fannin
Hill, Peter	Henderson	Hitch, N. B.	Anderson
Hill, R. H.	Jackson	Hitchcock, L. M.,	
Hill, Robert	Red River	Jr.	Galveston
Hill, Samuel	Walker	Hitchcock, M. M.	Burleson
Hill, T. B. J.	Bastrop	Hitchens, Merrit	Goliad
Hill, T. D.	Red River	Hitson, Alexander	Rusk
Hill, Theophelus	Panola	Hitson, William H.	Rusk
Hill, Thomas	Fannin	Hix, Isaac	Limestone
Hill, Thomas J.	Grayson	Hnesee, Thomas	Lavaca
Hill, Thomas M.	Panola	Hobbs, Abel	Anderson
Hill, W.	Upshur	Hobbs, Edward	Grimes
Hill, W. C.	Robertson	Hobbs, James	Hunt
Hill, W. C. J.	Grimes	Hobbs, John	Bastrop
Hill, W. C. J.	Washington	Hobbs, Robert	Grimes
Hill, W. F.	Milam	Hobbs, Thomas	Fannin
Hill, W. W.	Burleson	Hobbs, W. W.	Hunt
Hill, Warren J.	Fayette	Hobbs, William	Anderson
Hill, William	Cass	Hobbs, William	Grimes
Hill, William	Smith	Hobdy, Hoses	San Augustine
Hill, William C.	Goliad	Hobert, C.	Travis
Hill, William G.	Brazoria	Hobson, John	Milam
Hill, William G.	Goliad	Hocker, Henry	Red River
Hill, William J.	Burleson	Hodge, F. M.	Liberty
Hillbert, John	Liberty	Hodge, Henry	Liberty

NAME	COUNTY	NAME	COUNTY
Hodge, Hopkins	Hopkins	Holbert, Thomas	Bowie
Hodge, James	Liberty	Holbrooks, R.	Lamar
Hodge, T. M.	Liberty	Holbrooks, Uri	Houston
Hodge, William J.	Goliad	Holcomb, George	Cherokee
Hodges, A. E., Jr.	Fort Bend	Holcomb, H.	Navarro
Hodges, A. E., Sr.	Fort Bend	Holcomb, Joseph	Cherokee
Hodges, A. M.	Lamar	Holcomb, L.	Cass
Hodges, Abram H.	Fort Bend	Holcomb, M.	Navarro
Hodges, Archie	Fort Bend	Holcomb, Marshall	Polk
Hodges, Benjamin	Houston	Holcomb, W. B.	Cass
Hodges, David	Gonzales	Holden, James	Nacogdoches
Hodges, Elizabeth	Gonzales	Holderman, David	Bastrop
Hodges, Fleming	Cass	Holderman, Jesse	Bastrop
Hodges, Isaac	Houston	Holdes, Joseph	Travis
Hodges, J. C. M.	Collin	Holding, I. W.	Lamar
Hodges, J. M.	Wharton	Holdridge, Hanson	DeWitt
Hodges, James	Gonzales	Holeman, Catherine	Fayette
Hodges, John	Brazoria	Holeman, H. C.	Fayette
Hodges, John F.	Harris	Holeman, J. B.	Fayette
Hodges, John S.	Gonzales	Holeman, John T.	Fayette
Hodges, Joshua	Dallas	Holland, Charles	
Hodges, N. O.	Rusk	S.	Jasper
Hodges, Robert	Brazoria	Holland, Devro D.	Panola
Hodges, Robert	Fort Bend	Holland, E. D.	Wharton
Hodges, S. M.	Lamar	Holland, James K.	Panola
Hodges, Thomas	Gonzales	Holland, Levi H.	Jasper
Hodges, William F.	Fayette	Holland, Nacy	Panola
Hoffman, Charles	Galveston	Holland, Spearman	Panola
Hoffman, F. P.	Harris	Holland, Spearman	Panola
Hoffman, Gustav	Comal	Holland, W. A.	Shelby
Hoffman, John	Bexar	Holley, H.	Lamar
Hoffman, Joseph	Comal	Holliman, Howell	
Hoffman, Mary	Goliad	H.	Liberty
Hoffman, Owen	Sabine	Holliman, James	Liberty
Hoffman, Susanah	Harris	Holliman, N. B.	Liberty
Hoffuggs, Anthony	Bexar	Hollin, John F.	Austin
Hogale, Joseph	Bexar	Hollinsworth,	
Hogan, G. M.	Nacogdoches	James H.	Burleson
Hogan, James B.	Harris	Hollinsworth,	
Hogan, John W.	Burleson	Joicy	Rusk
Hogan, M. D.	Nacogdoches	Hollinsworth,	
Hogan, Robert R.	Titus	Stephen	Rusk
Hogan, Thomas	Bexar	Hollis, David	Walker
Hogan, Thomas M.	Harris	Hollis, William	San Augustine
Hogan, William	Harris	Holman, C. K.	Lamar
Hogan, William	Nacogdoches	Holman, J. H.	Grimes
Hogard, Richard	Navarro	Holman, James	Lamar
Hoggue, McKnight	Rusk	Holman, Jeremiah	Shelby
Hoggue, Robert M.	Rusk	Holman, John	Austin
Holbert, John	Colorado	Holman, Luther	Hopkins

NAME	COUNTY	NAME	COUNTY
Holman, T. H.	Guadalupe	Honor, Isaac	Henderson
Holman, W. W.	San Augustine	Hood, Alexander	Lamar
Holman, William	Austin	Hood, Carolina	Fort Bend
Holmes, Charles	Newton	Hood, Jeremiah	Burleson
Holmes, Charles	San Augustine	Hood, Thomas	Washington
Holmes, E. J.	Cass	Hooker, James	Hunt
Holmes, Francis G.	Bexar	Hooker, Jesse M.	Harris
Holmes, J. C.	Gonzales	Hooker, Robert	Polk
Holmes, James	Anderson	Hooks, William M.	Tyler
Holmes, Jane A.	Shelby	Hooper, J. J.	Shelby
Holmes, Joseph	Lamar	Hooper, J. M.	Shelby
Holmes, L.	Nacogdoches	Hooper, Richard	Shelby
Holmes, Milton	Anderson	Hooper, Washington	Shelby
Holmes, Thomas	Newton	Hoover, Daniel C.	Guadalupe
Holmes, Thomas C.	Newton	Hope, Mrs.	
Holmes, W. H. J.	Newton	Elizabeth	Harrison
Holmes, William	Anderson	Hope, H. S.	Harrison
Holmes, William S.	Burleson	Hope, Oscar	Harrison
Holmstrom, Charles	Galveston	Hope, Richard	Washington
Holoway, Daniel	San Augustine	Hope, Thomas	Wharton
Holoway, James	Bowie	Hope, William	Colorado
Holoway, Lewis	San Augustine	Hoper, James	Henderson
Holoway, Mary A.	Fayette	Hopkins, A. N.	Lamar
Holoway, Simpson	San Augustine	Hopkins, David	Hopkins
Holoway, William	Bowie	Hopkins, Dicy	Travis
Holsclaw, Eli	Houston	Hopkins, E.	Hopkins
Holshousen, C.	Polk	Hopkins, James	Anderson
Holshouser, M.	Upshur	Hopkins, James E.	Hopkins
Holsom, Hiram	Burleson	Hopkins, Levi	Anderson
Holstein, King	Brazoria	Hopkins, R.	Cass
Holster, Felix	Lavaca	Hopkins, R. M.	Red River
Holster, Mary	Lavaca	Hopkins, Solliman	Anderson
Holt, A. G.	Panola	Hopkins, William	Anderson
Holt, F. S.	Titus	Hoppe, M.	Milam
Holt, J. J.	Jackson	Hoppe, Seburn	Hopkins
Holt, James M.	Panola	Hopson, C. K.	Harris
Holt, John	Cherokee	Hopson, Elvira Y.	Colorado
Holt, Littleton	Fannin	Hopson, Hardy	Tyler
Holt, R. G.	Panola	Hopson, Zacariah	Tyler
Holt, S. F.	Shelby	Horan, John	Travis
Holt, William	Anderson	Horath, R. D.	Cass
Holt, William	Shelby	Hord, James	Harris
Holtes, V.	Henderson	Hord, Jesse	Wharton
Holton, W. J.	Bastrop	Hord, William H.	Dallas
Holzapfel, John	Comal	Horne, G.	Collin
Homan, V. C.	Victoria	Horne, J.	Collin
Homes, John	Anderson	Horne, Jacob	Houston
Homsley, Duke	Houston	Horne, Jacob	San Augustine
Honetcut, Roland	Goliad	Horne, John	Shelby
Honk, H.	Collin	Horne, Peter	Comal

NAME	COUNTY	NAME	COUNTY
Horne, R. H.	San Augustine	Hotchkiss, W.	Fayette
Horne, Valentin	Comal	Hough, Samuel	Jasper
Horne, Valentine	Fayette	Hough, Thomas	Panola
Horne, W.	Collin	Houghton, B. R.	Fannin
Horne, William B.	San Augustine	Houghton, William	
Hornsby, Josephus	Travis	S.	Titus
Hornsby, Reuben	Travis	Houk, Daniel	Hopkins
Hornsby, Reuben,		Houk, John	Hopkins
Jr.	Travis	Houk, John, Jr.	Hopkins
Hornsby, T. M.	Burleson	Houndshell, Joseph	Lamar
Hornsby, William	Travis	House, J. B.	Lamar
Horrie, Isaac	Red River	House, James	Harris
Horseley, Thomas	Walker	House, James	Brazos
Horst, Lewis	Travis	House, John	Brazos
Horton, A. C.	Matagorda	House, John T.	Washington
Horton, Alex	San Augustine	House, L. W.	Bowie
Horton, C. B. M.	Houston	House, Munford	Harris
Horton, Calvin	Tyler	House, Ransom	Harris
Horton, Enoch	Dallas	House, Simon	Panola
Horton, J. R.	Lamar	House, Thomas W.	Harris
Horton, James	Dallas	Houson, Windfield	Henderson
Horton, John	Dallas	Houston, C. M.	Nacogdoches
Horton, John	Sabine	Houston, David	Walker
Horton, Robert	Dallas	Houston, F. E.	Montgomery
Horton, S. W.	San Augustine	Houston, H.	Montgomery
Horton, Stephen	Sabine	Houston, J.	Henderson
Horton, W. B.	Austin	Houston, James	Bastrop
Horton, W. W.	San Augustine	Houston, James H.	Burleson
Horton, William P.	Dallas	Houston, John	DeWitt
Hoskins, Elizabeth	Gonzales	Houston, John	Jefferson
Hoskins, Hugh	Walker	Houston, Margaret	Navarro
Hoskins, Isaac C.	Brazoria	Houston, Peter	Bastrop
Hoskins, J. H.	Lavaca	Houston, Robert	DeWitt
Hoskins, John	Brazoria	Houston, T.	Montgomery
Hoskins, Julian	Shelby	Houth, Fletcher	Rusk
Hoskins, Nancy	Brazoria	Houth, Harvey	Rusk
Hoskins, P. H.	Shelby	Houth, Nelson	Rusk
Hoskins, Thomas	Gonzales	Houth, Tandy	Rusk
Hoskinson, T. B.	Walker	Houth, Thomas	Rusk
Hosse, James	Brazos	Houth, William	Rusk
Hossfeld, C.	Henderson	Houx, James M.	Dallas
Hossfeldt,		Houx, Michael	Dallas
Christian	Nacogdoches	Hover, Calvin H.	Grayson
Hossley, Thomas	Henderson	Hoving, John	Lamar
Hotchkiss, A.	Galveston	Hoving, Thomas	Lamar
Hotchkiss,		Howard, Arrington	Lamar
Archibald	Nacogdoches	Howard, C.	Collin
Hotchkiss, Charles	Nacogdoches	Howard, D.	Collin
Hotchkiss, R.	Henderson	Howard, E. H.	Nacogdoches
Hotchkiss, Renaldo	Nacogdoches	Howard, Edmon	Angelina

NAME	COUNTY	NAME	COUNTY
Howard, Elizabeth	Brazoria	Hoyt, Benjamin	Liberty
Howard, Elizabeth		Hoyt, Mrs. M. D.	
G.	Galveston	F.	Galveston
Howard, Gary	Lavaca	Hoyt, Nathaniel	Galveston
Howard, Hartwell	Shelby	Hoyt, Timothy	Liberty
Howard, Henry	Goliad	Hubbell, H.	Galveston
Howard, Isaac	Nacogdoches	Hubble, John	Henderson
Howard, Isaac	San Augustine	Hubble, John	Shelby
Howard, J. M.	Lamar	Hubby, C. M.	Milam
Howard, J. P.	Walker	Hubby, F. C.	Milam
Howard, J. Q. A.	Newton	Hubert, Benjamin	Galveston
Howard, James K.	Lamar	Hubert, F. W.	Washington
Howard, Jesse	Nacogdoches	Hubert, Matthew	Polk
Howard, John	DeWitt	Hubert, Sarah N.	Nacogdoches
Howard, John	San Augustine	Hubner, J. A.	Fayette
Howard, Lacy	Navarro	Huckaby, John P.	Fort Bend
Howard, Mordica	Polk	Huckins, James	Galveston
Howard, Phillip	Lavaca	Huckins, John	Austin
Howard, Ransom	Houston	Huddleston, John	Jefferson
Howard, Robert	Nacogdoches	Huddleston, P.	Shelby
Howard, S.	Collin	Huddleston,	
Howard, Thomas	Gonzales	William N.	Anderson
Howard, Thomas B.	Brazoria	Hudgens, J. W.	Rusk
Howard, Volney C.	Bexar	Hudgens, Joel	Wharton
Howard, William	Navarro	Hudnall, Baldwin	Houston
Howard, William R.	Limestone	Hudnall, Elizabeth	
Howard, William T.	Nacogdoches	S.	Houston
Howe, John	Galveston	Hudnall, H. E.	Smith
Howe, William R.	Navarro	Hudnall, Leroy	Houston
Howell, Alfred	Grimes	Hudnall, Robert	Smith
Howell, Asa	Grimes	Hudson, A. B.	Hopkins
Howell, D.	Collin	Hudson, D. P.	Hopkins
Howell, F. E.	Fayette	Hudson, David	Burleson
Howell, Ned	Rusk	Hudson, H. G.	Brazos
Howell, Robert F.	Harris	Hudson, J. D.	Rusk
Howerton, D. E. V.	Brazoria	Hudson, J. J.	Cass
Howland, E. P.	Fayette	Hudson, J. P.	Fayette
Howland, James	Refugio	Hudson, Jackson	Sabine
Howlet, James	Burleson	Hudson, James	Shelby
Howth, Mary Ann	Washington	Hudson, John	Bowie
Howth, Walstun	Washington	Hudson, Leonard	Brazos
Howth, William E.	Washington	Hudson, Obediah	Rusk
Hoxie, Asa	Washington	Hudson, P. B.	Shelby
Hoy, Catherine	San Patricio	Hudson, R. E. W.	Brazos
Hoy, Joseph	Rusk	Hudson, Thomas	Anderson
Hoy, Thomas W.	Montgomery	Hudson, Thomas	Lamar
Hoy, William J.	Refugio	Hudson, Eilliam	Rusk
Hoy, William S.	Fannin	Hudson, William D.	Polk
Hoya, Joseph	Nacogdoches	Hudson, Eilliam M.	Galveston
Hoyle, Nancy	Galveston	Huested, Titus B.	Fannin

NAME	COUNTY	NAME	COUNTY
Huey, G. H.	Anderson	Hughes, Ruse	Cass
Huey, William K.	Brazoria	Hughes, Samuel	Bowie
Huey, Willis G.	Brazoria	Hughes, Susan	Brazoria
Huff, D. G.	Harrison	Hughes, T. S.	Burleson
Hugg, Elen	Austin	Hughes, Tessie	Hopkins
Huff, George	Fort Bend	Hughes, Thomas M.	Cass
Huff, Henry	Fayette	Hughes, Thomas M.	Washington
Huff, John	Wharton	Hughes, Uriah	Burleson
Huff, M. T.	Austin	Hughes, W. B.	Guadalupe
Huff, William T.	Austin	Hughes, W. V.	Cass
Huffer, Jacob	Nacogdoches	Hughes, William	Brazoria
Huffman, A.	Jasper	Hughes, William	Navarro
Huffman, B.	Austin	Hughes, William B.	Bowie
Huffman, Charles B.	Anderson	Hughes, WIlliam B.	Cass
		Huitt, A. J.	Dallas
Huffman, Elisa R.	Sabine	Huitt, J.	Dallas
Huffman, Nathan	Lamar	Huitt, Rolen	Dallas
Huffmeyer, Henry	Bexar	Hulett, James	Tyler
Huffstutter, J.	Cass	Hulett, Obadiah	Tyler
Hufington, James G.	Austin	Huling, Elizabeth	Jasper
		Huling, Marcus	Bastrop
Huggins, J. H.	San Augustine	Huling, Thomas	Lamar
Huggins, W. H.	Liberty	Huling, Thomas B.	Jasper
Hughart, Edward	Red River	Huling, William	Montgomery
Hughes, Benjamin	Brazoria	Hull, Jonathan	Harris
Hughes, D.	Henderson	Hull, William	Liberty
Hughes, Daniel H.	Nacogdoches	Hulme, A. L.	Bowie
Hughes, Evaline	Cass	Hulse, Silas	Nacogdoches
Hughes, George	Cherokee	Humberson, W. F.	Anderson
Hughes, Grigsby	Burleson	Humbuckle,	
Hughes, J.	Brazoria	Elizabeth	Shelby
Hughes, James	Navarro	Hume, John	Walker
Hughes, James	Shelby	Hume, Margaret	Walker
Hughes, James A.	Burleson	Humphrey, DeCalb	Panola
Hughes, Joel	Cass	Humphrey, George	Brazos
Hughes, John J.	Shelby	Humphrey, J. F.	Nacogdoches
Hughes, L. A. J.	Rusk	Humphrey, James	Houston
Hughes, Matilda	Cass	Humphrey, Joseph	Panola
Hughes, Mikaga	Titus	Humphrey, Joseph	Red River
Hughes, Moses, Jr.	Burleson	Humphrey, Owen	Navarro
Hughes, Moses, Sr.	Burleson	Humphrey, Sarah	Panola
Hughes, P. M.	Fort Bend	Humphries, Berry	Washington
Hughes, Rebecca	Burleson	Humphries, Jesse	Polk
Hughes, Rhody	Burleson	Humphries, Jesse	
Hughes, Robert	Newton	C.	Henderson
Hughes, Robert, Jr.		Humphries, William	Red River
	Cass	Hundley, James	Fayette
Hughes, Robert, Sr.		Hundley, William	Burleson
	Cass	Huneyman, --	Milam
Hughes, Robert L.	Cass	Hunnicutt, G. B.	Lavaca

NAME	COUNTY	NAME	COUNTY
Hunnicutt, William	Burleson	Hunter, Thaddeus	Guadalupe
Hunt, A. C.	Fayette	Hunter, Thomas	Fort Bend
Hunt, A. D.	Bastrop	Hunter, W. H.	Fort Bend
Hunt, Benjamin F.	Nacogdoches	Hunter, W. L.	Matagorda
Hunt, Charles S.	Newton	Hunter, William	Brazoria
Hunt, D. P.	Bastrop	Hunter, William	Fannin
Hunt, E. P.	Galveston	Hunter, William	Goliad
Hunt, Mrs.		Huntington, J. F.	Galveston
Elizabeth	Washington	Huntsman, W. C.	Houston
Hunt, F. K.	Austin	Huntsman, William	
Hunt, Francis	Brazoria	R.	Galveston
Hunt, George G.	Cass	Hurd, James G.	Galveston
Hunt, Henry	San Augustine	Hurdman, James	Galveston
Hunt, J. W.	Gonzales	Hurlburt, Mrs.	Galveston
Hunt, John	San Augustine	Hurley, John	Harris
Hunt, John	Washington	Hurley, W. H.	Cass
Hunt, Lydia	Bastrop	Hurst, Joseph	Wharton
Hunt, Nathaniel	San Augustine	Hurst, Stephen	Goliad
Hunt, Robert	Milam	Hurt, W. K.	Nacogdoches
Hunt, Samuel	Henderson	Huson, W.	Henderson
Hunt, T. W.	Fayette	Hussey, T.	Jasper
Hunt, Thomas	Henderson	Huston, E. S.	San Augustine
Hunt, Thomas	San Augustine	Huston, Elizabeth	San Augustine
Hunt, Thomas D.	Grayson	Huston, Rufus	Shelby
Hunt, Thomas N.	Washington	Huston, Samuel A.	Shelby
Hunt, Toby C.	Bastrop	Huston, W.	San Augustine
Hunt, W. A.	Lamar	Hutchins, H. B.	Upshur
Hunt, W. E.	Leon	Hutchins, Merritt	Colorado
Hunt, W. R.	Colorado	Hutchins, William	
Hunt, Wilkins	Victoria	J.	Harris
Hunt, William	Bastrop	Hutchinson, B. B.	Washington
Hunt, William	Washington	Hutchinson, James	Grimes
Hunt, William G.	Colorado	Hutchinson, John	
Hunt, William H.	Fannin	C.	Harris
Hunt & Black	Fannin	Hutchinson, T. M.	
Hunter, A. J.	Henderson	W.	Harris
Hunter, B. B. B.	Harrison	Hutchinson,	
Hunter, Charles	Leon	William	Titus
Hunter, G. E.	Walker	Hutchinson,	
Hunter, G. M.	Brazos	William D.	Harris
Hunter, J. S.	Walker	Hutton, James H.	Smith
Hunter, James	Calhoun	Hutton, V. J.	Dallas
Hunter, Jehu	Navarro	Hyde, A. C.	Victoria
Hunter, John	Cherokee	Hyde, A. G.	San Augustine
Hunter, John F.	Henderson	Hyde, Archibald C.	Goliad
Hunter, John F.	Fannin	Hyde, Charles M.	Goliad
Hunter, Johnson	Fort Bend	Hyde, George S.	Nacogdoches
Hunter, L. L.	Fort Bend	Hyde, John C.	Fort Bend
Hunter, R. N.	Guadalupe	Hyde, John H.	Nacogdoches
Hunter, Samuel	Gonzales	Hydon, G.	Henderson

NAME	COUNTY	NAME	COUNTY
Hyer, Nancy	Sabine	Isaac, James M.	Jasper
Hyett, Solomon	Fannin	Isaac, William	Cherokee
Hynes, Charles	Travis	Isbell, George	Hopkins
Hynes, John	Nacogdoches	Isbell, George D.	Harrison
Hynes, John	Refugio	Isbell, John H.	Harris
Hytener, W. N.	Leon	Isbell, William	Washington
		Isham, Ira	Fannin
		Isham, James	Fannin
Idle, George	Austin	Ivantt, J.	Collin
Ijams, B. G.	Colorado	Ives, C. S.	Matagorda
Ijams, George W.	Harris	Ives, David	Lavaca
Ijams, Isaac D.	Harris	Ives, Henry C.	Liberty
Ijams, John	Harris	Ivey, Isiah	Panola
Ijams, L. C.	Colorado	Ivey, Jeremiah	Panola
Iles, P. B.	Matagorda	Ivey, Margaret	Hunt
Ilvey, Albert	Shelby	Ivey, Mary	Panola
Inglis, James	Jefferson	Ivey, Micajah	Panola
Inglish, Bailey	Fannin	Ivey, Wyatt	Grimes
Ingraham, Robert C.	Harris		
Ingram, I.	Matagorda	Jack, S. H.	Grimes
Ingram, James	Victoria	Jack, Mrs. William H.	Brazoria
Ingram, M.	Cass		
Ingram, Seth	Matagorda	Jackson, Abner	Brazoria
Ingram, Wiley	Harrison	Jackson, Alden A. M.	Travis
Inman, Hiram	Shelby		
Inman, John H.	Shelby	Jackson, B. H.	Walker
Irby, J. H.	Henderson	Jackson, C. L.	Cass
Irby, John H.	Cherokee	Jackson, Calvin	Lamar
Irens, Edward	Panola	Jackson, Charles	Cass
Irion, R. A.	Nacogdoches	Jackson, Curtis M.	Sabine
Irish, Milton	San Augustine	Jackson, E.	Hopkins
Irons, Elisha	Bastrop	Jackson, E. Davis	Washington
Irons, William	Bastrop	Jackson, E. S.	Brazoria
Irvin, J. T. P.	Nacogdoches	Jackson, E. T.	Fannin
Irvine, B. F.	Montgomery	Jackson, E. T.	Limestone
Irvine, J. A.	Guadalupe	Jackson, Edward	Liberty
Irvine, James	Henderson	Jackson, F. M.	Brazoria
Irvine, Jane	Henderson	Jackson, Gabriel	Burleson
Irvine, Josephus S.	Neston	Jackson, Gilbert	Washington
		Jackson, Hasford	Dallas
Irvine, Samuel	Grimes	Jackson, Henry	Grimes
Irvine, Samuel	San Augustine	Jackson, Hezekiah	Grimes
Irwin, James	Shelby	Jackson, Hugh	Liberty
Irwin, L. J.	Brazos	Jackson, J.	Collin
Irwin, Mesia	Panola	Jackson, J.	Grimes
Irwin, Mowry	Panola	Jackson, James	Cass
Isaac, Alfred	Jasper	Jackson, James	Liberty
Isaac, Elijah	Jasper	Jackson, James J.	Austin
Isaac, F. M.	Cherokee	Jackson, James M.	Washington

NAME	COUNTY	NAME	COUNTY
Jackson, John	Liberty	James, Margaret	Grimes
Jackson, John	Red River	James, T.	Gonzales
Jackson, John	Sabine	James, T. D.	Guadalupe
Jackson, Joseph	Dallas	James Thomas	Montgomery
Jackson, Joseph	Washington	James, William	Dallas
Jackson, Joseph M.	Washington	James, William H.	Limestone
Jackson, Mrs.		Jamie, Filipe	Bexar
Julia	Washington	Jamison, Allen	Sabine
Jackson, Michael	Lavaca	Jamison, C. H.	Wharton
Jackson, Mrs.		Jamison, D. K.	Red River
Nancy	Washington	Jamison, J. N.	Sabine
Jackson, S.	Collin	Jamison, James	Brazoria
Jackson, Samuel	Cass	Jamison, Thomas	Hunt
Jackson, Semantha	Washington	Jamison, Thomas	Matagorda
Jackson, Solomon	Navarro	Jamison, W. S.	Lamar
Jackson, Stephen	Jefferson	Janes, John E.	Bowie
Jackson, T. A.	Washington	Janes, M. H.	Bowie
Jackson, T. J.	Sabine	Janes, S. H.	Bowie
Jackson, T. J.	Washington	January, B.	Navarro
Jackson, William	Austin	January, George G.	Panola
Jackson, William	Washington	January, S. P.	Harrison
Jackson, William		January, Samuel A.	Panola
B.	Austin	Jaques, William B.	Bexar
Jackson, William		Jarboe, H.	Harris
E.	Washington	Jarmon, John	Fort Bend
Jackson, Zac.	Nacogdoches	Jarmon, R. B.	Fayette
Jacobs, Henry	Nacogdoches	Jarmon, Richard	Goliad
Jacobs, J. G.	Cherokee	Harods, Nathan	Henderson
Jacobs, J. J.	Harris	Jarrell, Charles	
Jacobs, James	Nacogdoches	E.	Colorado
Jacobs, John	Cass	Jarrell, Claborn	Washington
Jacobs, John	Navarro	Jarrett, David	Bowie
Jacobs, Madison G.	DeWitt	Jarvis, George O.	Brazoria
Jacobs, W.	Henderson	Jarvis, Rezin	Washington
Jacobs, William	Harris	Jasper, Martha	Houston
Jacobs, William	Rusk	Jasper, S. L. B.	Houston
Jaen, Thomas	Houston	Jay, G. S.	Red River
James, A. F.	Galveston	Jeanbrow(?), L.	Liberty
James, A. T.	Galveston	Jefferies, Elija	Navarro
James, Antonio	Bexar	Jefferies, J. B.	Montgomery
James, Asberry	Victoria	Jefferies, S. O.	Harrison
James, B. F.	Harrison	Jeffers, A. M.	Lamar
James, G. W.	Montgomery	Jeffers, James A.	Lamar
James, J.	Houston	Jeffers, John C.	Navarro
James, James	Limestone	Jeffers, Samuel	Lamar
James, Jesse R.	Polk	Jeffers, Sarah	Navarro
James, John	Bexar	Jeffrey, Caleb H.	Goliad
James, John	Brazoria	Jeffrey, Elijah	Nacogdoches
James, John	Guadalupe	Jeffrey, Mary	Cherokee
James, John	Victoria	Jeffries, William	

NAME	COUNTY	NAME	COUNTY
W.	Bexar	John, M. L.	Panola
Jenkins, Dallas	Dallas	John, N. N.	Galveston
Jenkins, Edward	Bastrop	John, Stephen	Grimes
Jenkins, G. B.	Cherokee	Johns, Sarah	Liberty
Jenkins, J. C.	Washington	Johns, William	Liberty
Jenkins, James R.	Washington	Johnson, A.	Collin
Jenkins, John	Bastrop	Johnson, A. A.	San Augustine
Jenkins, Ralph	Travis	Johnson, A. J.	Grayson
Jenkins, S. M.	Montgomery	Johnson, A. M.	San Augustine
Jenkins, Thomas	Washington	Johnson, A. S.	Henderson
Jenkins, William		Johnson, Adam	Houston
M.	Washington	Johnson, B. B.	Walker
Jenks, H. B.	Henderson	Johnson, B. C. H.	Rusk
Jenks, W. C.	Gonzales	Johnson, B. F.	Travis
Jennings, C. B.	Henderson	Johnson, B. F.	Washington
Jennings, H. L.	Fannin	Johnson, B. W.	Cass
Jennings, James	Red River	Johnson, Bede	Sabine
Jennings, John	Grayson	Johnson, Chaney	Bastrop
Jennings, Joseph	Travis	Johnson, Charles	
Jennings, L. C.	Fort Bend	A.	Burleson
Jennings, T. J.	Nacogdoches	Johnson, Cyrus	Hopkins
Jennings, Stephen	Hopkins	Johnson, E. D.	Grimes
Jergan, J. H.	Bastrop	Johnson, E. J.	Bowie
Jernigan, H. B.	Panola	Johnson, Elias	Sabine
Jernigan, W. P.	San Augustine	Johnson, Eliza	Austin
Jernigan, William		Johnson, Elizabeth	Houston
A.	Panola	Johnson, Enoch	Bastrop
Jessup, Curtis	San Augustine	Johnson, Enos	Lamar
Jessup, Israel	San Augustine	Johnson, F.	Houston
Jester, Andrew	Grimes	Johnson, Fred	Bastrop
Jetson, Nathan	Tyler	Johnson, Gabriel	Brazos
Jett, Absalom	Jefferson	Johnson, H. G.	Montgomery
Jett, James	Navarro	Johnson, H. S.	Cherokee
Jewel, C.	Lavaca	Johnson, Henry	Colorado
Jewel, David	Colorado	Johnson, Hiram A.	Nacogdoches
Jewel, G. W.	Lamar	Johnson, J. A.	Rusk
Jewitt, E.	Liberty	Johnson, J. B.	San Augustine
Jewitt, M.	Liberty	Johnson, J. F.	Guadalupe
Jewitt, S. G.	San Augustine	Johnson, J. H.	Washington
Jiles, Thomas	Bowie	Johnson, J. L. H.	Cass
Jinks, John	Fayette	Johnson, J. W.	Nacogdoches
Jobe, James	Bastrop	Johnson, J. W.	Shelby
Jobine, John S.	Brazoria	Johnson, Jacob	Grimes
Joel, James A.	Rusk	Johnson, James	Cass
Joel, John D.	Rusk	Johnson, James	Fort Bend
John, Christian	Rusk	Johnson, James	Hopkins
John, David	Nacogdoches	Johnson, James	Houston
John, Henry	Jackson	Johnson, James	Shelby
John, James F.	Panola	Johnson, James A.	Navarro
John, John	Fannin	Johnson, James E.	Galveston

NAME	COUNTY	NAME	COUNTY
Johnson, James F.	Travis	Johnson, William	Sabine
Johnson, James N.	Cass	Johnson, William	Titus
Johnson, Jesse	Gonzales	Johnson, William	Travis
Johnson, Jesse	Montgomery	Johnson, William	Walker
Johnson, John	Bastrop	Johnson, William	
Johnson, John	Dallas	C.	Nacogdoches
Johnson, John	Lamar	Johnson, William	
Johnson, John	Walker	H.	Grayson
Johnson, John A.	Gonzales	Johnson, William	
Johnson, John L.	Gonzales	M.	Cherokee
Johnson, John R.	Polk	Johnson, Z. C.	Shelby
Johnson, Jonathan	Shelby	Johnston, A. S.	Fannin
Johnson, Lindley	Lamar	Johnston, A.	
Johnson, Luke	Houston	Sidney	Brazoria
Johnson, Luke	Shelby	Johnston, A. W.	Liberty
Johnson, M.	Walker	Johnston, B. C.	Red River
Johnson, M. D.	Galveston	Johnston, Benjamin	Jefferson
Johnson, M. J.	Rusk	Johnston, Claiborn	DeWitt
Johnson, M. N.	Cass	Johnston,	
Johnson, M. T.	Shelby	Elizabeth	Jefferson
Johnson, Martin	Polk	Johnston, G. S.	Titus
Johnson, Mary	Cass	Johnston, H. B.	Liberty
Johnson, Mary	Grimes	Johnston, Hampton	Cherokee
Johnson, O. D.	Galveston	Johnston, J. F.	Red River
Johnson, P.	Goliad	Johnston, J. S.	Henderson
Johnson, Peter	Montgomery	Johnston, J. W.	Colorado
Johnson, Purvis	Washington	Johnston, James	Leon
Johnson, R. D.	Galveston	Johnston, James M.	San Augustine
Johnson, R. J.	Guadalupe	Johnston, John	Grimes
Johnson, Rapier	Galveston	Johnston, John	Leon
Johnson, Robert	Brazos	Johnston, John	Titus
Johnson, S. M.	Grayson	Johnston, Malcom	Calhoun
Johnson, Sam	Sabine	Johnston, Mary	Red River
Johnson, Samuel	Cherokee	Johnston, Nathan	Fannin
Johnson, Samuel	Fannin	Johnston, P. B.	Red River
Johnson, Sol L.	Washington	Johnston, Thomas	
Johnson, Solomon	Grimes	D.	Brazoria
Johnson, Susan A.	Shelby	Johnston, William	Brazoria
Johnson, T. D.	Washington	Johnston, William	Leon
Johnson, T. J.	Nacogdoches	Johnston, William	Titus
Johnson, Thomas	Galveston	Joiner, Calib	Lavaca
Johnson, Thomas	Washington	Joiner, L.	Grimes
Johnson, W. F.	Houston	Jolley, Vardey	Smith
Johnson, W. H.	Walker	Jones, A. C.	Panola
Johnson, W. S.	Lamar	Jones, A. H. W.	Anderson
Johnson, W. S.	Red River	Jones, A. J.	Grimes
Johnson, Wilks	Washington	Jones, A. J.	Red River
Johnson, William	Cass	Jones, A. S.	Washington
Johnson, William	Fort Bend	Jones, Alfred	Lamar
Johnson, William	Grimes	Jones, Allen	Grimes

NAME	COUNTY	NAME	COUNTY
Jones, Andrew	Shelby	Jones, Jefry	Nacogdoches
Jones, Archibald	Gonzales	Jones, Jesse	Fort Bend
Jones, Augustus	Gonzales	Jones, Jesse G.	Cherokee
Jones, B. F.	Navarro	Jones, John	Fannin
Jones, B. F.	Titus	Jones, John	Galveston
Jones, Beneniah	Grimes	Jones, John	Harris
Jones, Benjamin	Grimes	Jones, John	Jackson
Jones, C. B.	Grimes	Jones, John	Wharton
Jones, C. T.	Panola	Jones, John B.	Harris
Jones, Charles	Shelby	Jones, John B.	Polk
Jones, Charles	Titus	Jones, John F.	Angelina
Jones, Clisby	Polk	Jones, John N.	Brazos
Jones, D. M.	Matagorda	Jones, John R.	Goliad
Jones, Daniel	Cass	Jones, John R.,	
Jones, Daniel	Grimes	Jr.	Fayette
Jones, E.	Bastrop	Jones, John S.	Galveston
Jones, Eli	Guadalupe	Jones, John S.	Washington
Jones, Eli	Milam	Jones, Joseph	Walker
Jones, Elisa	Cass	Jones, Joseph W.	Burleson
Jones, Enoch	Polk	Jones, L.	Cherokee
Jones, Ezekiel	Panola	Jones, L. B.	Anderson
Jones, Fielding	Victoria	Jones, L. C.	Navarro
Jones, Fleming	Cass	Jones, L. S.	Grimes
Jones, G. H.	Bexar	Jones, Levi	Galveston
Jones, G. J.	Walker	Jones, Levi	Polk
Jones, George W.	San Augustine	Jones, Louis	Shelby
Jones, H. W.	Fannin	Jones, M.	Travis
Jones, H. W.	Titus	Jones, M. M.	Cass
Jones, Hamilton	Polk	Jones, Maria	Walker
Jones, Hardy	Grimes	Jones, Martin	Titus
Jones, Hardy	Shelby	Jones, Merryman	Rusk
Jones, Henry	Fort Bend	Jones, Milres F.	Austin
Jones, Henry	Matagorda	Jones, Moses	Fannin
Jones, Hiram	Cherokee	Jones, N.	Harrison
Jones, Isaac	Polk	Jones, Nancy	Shelby
Jones, Isaac	Titus	Jones, Oliver	Austin
Jones, Isham G.	Gonzales	Jones, Oliver	Cass
Jones, J. C.	Navarro	Jones, Peter	Grimes
Jones, J. D.	Angelina	Jones, R. D.	Harrison
Jones, J. G.	Lamar	Jones, R. P.	Brazoria
Jones, J. H.	Matagorda	Jones, Randall	Fort Bend
Jones, J. J.	Henderson	Jones, Rees	Rusk
Jones, J. N.	Leon	Jones, Richard	Galveston
Jones, J. W.	San Augustine	Jones, Robert	Titus
Jones, James	Bastrop	Jonew, Mrs. Rosa	Harris
Jones, James	Harrison	Jones, Russell	Gonzales
Jones, James H.	Walker	Jones, S. L.	Galveston
Jones, James M.	Angelina	Jones, Sam	Henderson
Jones, James R.	Burleson	Jones, Samuel	Fort Bend
Jones, James W.	Fort Bend	Jones, Samuel	Milam

NAME	COUNTY	NAME	COUNTY
Jones, Sarah	Burleson	Jowel, R. R.	Sabine
Jones, Simon	Grimes	Jowers, G. W.	Anderson
Jones, Sophia	Gonzales	Jowess, W. G. W.	Henderson
Jones, Stephen W.	Fort Bend	Joy, G.	Collin
Jones, Theodóre D.	Fannin	Joyce, Festus	Lavaca
Jones, Thomas	Rusk	Judd, H. B.	San Augustine
Jones, Thomas	Smith	Juett, H. J.	Robertson
Jones, Timothuy	Goliad	Juett, J. G.	Fannin
Jones, W.	Henderson	Juett, N.	Fannin
Jones, W. E.	Guadalupe	Juinan, J. H.	Houston
Jones, Wiley	Milam	Jukins, Gerhart	Bexar
Jones, William	Anderson	Junall, Robert	Titus
Jones, William	Bastrop	Juneman, L.	Galveston
Jones, William	Bexar	Junker, Isaiah	Jefferson
Jones, William	Bowie	Jurgens, Fred	Colorado
Jones, William	Fannin	Jurgens, Ultman	Houston
Jones, William	Harris	Jurgens, William	Houston
Jones, William	Shelby	Justice, Eli	Brazoria
Jones, William	Walker	Justice, S. J.	Brazoria
Jones, WIlliam C.	Limestone	Justis, James	Fannin
Jones, William H.	Refugio	Jwonsky, C. K.	Comal
Jones, William J.	Colorado		
Jones, William P.	Fayette		
Jones, William S.	Fort Bend	Kaderle, A.	Comal
Jones, Wyly	Fort Bend	Kail, John P.	Liberty
Joplin, George B.	Austin	Kail, Peter	Harris
Jordan, A. M.	Bowie	Kaller, John	Galveston
Jordan, C.	Matagorda	Kaller, Stephen	Galveston
Jordan, Elizabeth	Anderson	Hannady, Sally	Brazoria
Jordan, Fred	Austin	Kannady, William	Brazoria
Jordan, G. W.	Fayette	Kansler, Daniel	Rusk
Jordan, J. F.	San Augustine	Karnes, John	Robertson
Jordan, John	DeWitt	Kartz, Edward	Comal
Jordan, John	Henderson	Kassler, James	Bexar
Jordan, Michael	Galveston	Kastine, Louise	Bexar
Jordan, Thomas J.	Smith	Kattenborn, H.	Milam
Jordan, William	Jackson	Kaufman, ---	Walker
Jordan, WIlliam	Jasper	Kaufman, D. S.	Sabine
Joslin, Martha C.	Newton	Kaufman, E.	Galveston
Jost, A.	Anderson	Kaufman, J. A.	Galveston
Jourdan, Curtas	Hopkins	Kavanaugh, Nelson	Washington
Jourdan, Curtis	Lamar	Kay, John	Fayette
Jourdan, Francis	Panola	Kay, Willey	Fayette
Jourdan, Gary	Lavaca	Keaghey, William	
Jourdan, James	Hopkins	S.	Jasper
Jourdan, John	Lamar	Keath, George	Jefferson
Jourdan, Redding		Keathly, Silas	Jasper
A.	Cherokee	Keating, Ellen	Refugio
Jourdan, Samuel	Shelby	Keating, John	Goliad
Jourdan, W. H.	Shelby	Keating, L. P.	Liberty

NAME	COUNTY	NAME	COUNTY
Keating, Michael	Liberty	Kellogg, Samuel B.	Robertson
Keeble, Albert F.	Polk	Kelloway, Allen	Anderson
Keefer, George	Liberty	Kellum, Allen D.	Harris
Keel, Terry	San Augustine	Kellum, N. K.	Harris
Keeling, Charles	Bastrop	Kelly, Mrs.	Harris
Keene, Edward Y.	Washington	Kelly, Alexander	Jasper
Keenon, C. G.	Walker	Kelly, Barbery	Jasper
Keenon, John	Walker	Kelly, Catherine	Harris
Keese, Thomas T.	Gonzales	Kelly, Charles	Gonzales
Keifer, Benjamin	Dallas	Kelly, Charles S.	Fort Bend
Keigwin, WIlliam	Leon	Kelly, Daniel	Jasper
Keilmann, George	Galveston	Kelly, Daniel	Leon
Kegans, Hamilton	Fort Bend	Kelly, Eliga	Lavaca
Kegans, John	Fort Bend	Kelly, Elvira	Lavaca
Kegans, W. S.	Fort Bend	Kelly, Francis	Travis
Keighlow, Allen	Anderson	Kelly, H. B.	Henderson
Keilough, S. B.	Robertson	Kelly, H. B.	San Augustine
Keith, Abijah	Titus	Kelly, Hugh	Galveston
Keith, Ely	Titus	Kelly, J. H.	Cass
Keith, Gabriel	Titus	Kelly, James	Smith
Keith, James	Titus	Kelly, James G.	Panola
Keith, John J.	Titus	Kelly, Jane	Harris
Keith, Joseph	Titus	Kelly, Jeremiah	Cass
Keith, N.	Titus	Kelly, Jesse	Cass
Keith, Stephen	Titus	Kelly, John W.	Fayette
Keith, William	Titus	Kelly, Sary	Lavaca
Keith, William S.	Titus	Kelly, Stephen	Hunt
Keizer, John	Polk	Kelly, Thomas	Upshur
Keizer, William	Jackson	Kelly, W. C.	Rusk
Kelch, Christian	Colorado	Kelly, William	Lavaca
Kell, Archibald	Rusk	Kelsey, A. W.	Colorado
Kell, James	Rusk	Kelsey, Cyrus	Angelina
Kellaugh, Isaac	Fayette	Kelsey, H. B.	Harrison
Keller, Andrus	Bexar	Kelso, Alfred	DeWitt
Keller, B. M.	Titus	Kelso, James	Galveston
Keller, Fred G.	Jackson	Kelton, B. F.	Montgomery
Keller, J. W.	Matagorda	Kelton, Mrs. Sarah	
Keller, John	Galveston	Ann	Harris
Keller, Joseph	Bexar	Kelton, Warren	Rusk
Keller, Martin	Galveston	Kemp, Jonathan	Fort Bend
Keller, Michael T.	Lamar	Kemp, Thomas	Goliad
Keller, Samuel	Dallas	Kemper, Eliza	Victoria
Keller, W.	Matagorda	Kendall, A. D.	Grayson
Kellett, J. M.	Montgomery	Kendall, H. A.	San Augustine
Kellett, T. J.	Montgomery	Kendall, Troy	Henderson
Kellett, William		Kendrick, B.	Matagorda
C.	Montgomery	Kendrick, Harvey	Matagorda
Kellman, F.	Galveston	Kendrick, Isaac D.	Harrison
Kellner, Justus	Comal	Kendrick, J. H.	San Augustine
Kellogg, George H.	Harris	Kenley, Mrs. R. A.	Harrison

NAME	COUNTY	NAME	COUNTY
Kennard, A. D., Jr.	Grimes	Kerr, James	Jackson
Kennard, A. D., Sr.	Grimes	Kerr, John B.	Newton
Kennard, Marquis L.	Grimes	Kerr, N. M.	Henderson
		Kerr, Peter	Travis
Kennard, Michael M.	Grimes	Kerr, Robert	Fannin
Kennard, Mrs. S. A. M.	Grimes	Kerr, William	Leon
		Kerr, William	Shelby
Kennard, William C.	Grimes	Kerr, William H.	Bexar
		Kerr, William P.	Bexar
Kennedy, A. S.	Fayette	Kerr, William P.	Washington
Kennedy, Alfred	Cherokee	Kerr, Yelberton	Fannin
Kennedy, Cyresa	Henderson	Kester, Sithery C.	Colorado
Kennedy, Frederick	Shelby	Ketchum, James	Dallas
Kennedy, George	Lamar	Kewley, John H.	Grimes
Kennedy, James	Milam	Keys, Eliza N.	Houston
Kennedy, Jacob	Cherokee	Keys, John P.	Washington
Kennedy, Jesse	Cherokee	Keys, M. T.	Houston
Kennedy, John	Galveston	Keys, Reuben	Walker
Kennedy, John	Harris	Keys, Thomas W.	Liberty
Kennedy, John J.	Harrison	Keys, William	Polk
Kennedy, McLain	Cherokee	Kezea, B.	Hunt
Kennedy, Robert	Washington	Kezea, William	Hunt
Kennedy, S. E.	Houston	Kichen, H. C.	Goliad
Kennedy, Sarah	Shelby	Kilgore, Charles	Robertson
Kennedy, Seth	Panola	Kilgore, J. T.	Harris
Kennedy, T. D.	Lamar	Kilgore, John	Cherokee
Kennedy, T. G.	Lamar	Kilgore, Joseph	Goliad
Kennedy, W. W.	Fannin	Kilgore, Robert	Galveston
Kenon, Thomas	Dallas	Killcrease, Charles	Jefferson
Kent, Borman	Lavaca	Killion, Goodwin	Nacogdoches
Kent, David	Lavaca	Killion, N.	Navarro
Kent, Joseph	DeWitt	Killion, P. F.	Nacogdoches
Keough, Edward	Galveston	Killion, William	Rusk
Kepler, F.	Montgomery	Killough, Isaac	Cherokee
Kepler, William	Grimes	Killough, Nathaniel	Cherokee
Kepton, Nathan	DeWitt	Killough, Nathaniel	Henderson
Kepper, Jacob	Bexar	Killough, W. C.	Leon
Kerby, George	Walker	Kilpatrick, E.	Victoria
Kerby, J. W.	Collin	Kimbell, A. G.	Henderson
Kerby, Josiah	Walker	Kimbell, Henry	Cass
Kern, A. S.	Matagorda	Kimbell, J. M.	Bowie
Kern, W.	Henderson	Kimbell, S. C.	Henderson
Kerr, A. B. F.	Washington	Kimberling, Benjamin	Harrison
Kerr, A. T.	Washington	Kimble, E. T.	Austin
Kerr, David A.	Newton	Kimble, V. A.	Austin
Kerr, George A.	Fayette	Kimble, W.	Henderson
Kerr, George A.	Goliad		

NAME	COUNTY	NAME	COUNTY
Kimbro, Daniel	Bastrop	King, John G.	Gonzales
Kimbro, T.	Hunt	King, John H.	Grimes
Kimbro, William	San Augustine	King, John J.	Grimes
Kimbrocke,		King, John R.	Guadalupe
Benjamin	Cass	King, John W.	Denton
Kimbrocke, W.	Cass	King, John W.	Nacogdoches
Kimley, Michael	Galveston	King, Joseph	Nacogdoches
Kincade, G. W.	Walker	King, M. H.	Henderson
Kincade, J. M.	Collin	King, Madison T.	Nacogdoches
Kincade, P. B.	Cass	King, Miles	Brazos
Kincade, Polly	Navarro	King, Nathaniel	Titus
Kincade, S. M.	Red River	King, Norris	Titus
Kincannon, Jesse		King, O. H.	Cass
C.	Smith	King, Peter	Cherokee
Kincannon, Wm. P.	Grimes	King, R. B.	Leon
Kincheloe,		King, Rebecca	Burleson
Augustus	Wharton	King, S. M.	Titus
Kincheloe, Daniel	Wharton	King, Samuel	Henderson
Kincheloe, G.	Cherokee	King, Thomas	Goliad
Kincheloe,		King, Thomas	Lamar
Lawrence	Wharton	King, Thomas	Walker
Kincheloe, Lewis		King, Thomas B.	Galveston
King, A. W.	Red River	King, V. S.	Titus
King, C. F.	Bexar	King, William, Jr.	Leon
King, C. F.	Nacogdoches	King, William, Sr.	Leon
King, D.	Nacogdoches	King, William A.	Burleson
King, D. T.	Titus	King, William G.	Guadalupe
King, David	Henderson	King, William H.	Harris
King, Elizabeth	Cass	King, William T.	Leon
King, Enoch	Austin	King, Wm. H.	Nacogdoches
King, Frank	Galveston	Kingeade, David G.	Polk
King, G. B.	Grimes	Kinison, D. W.	Navarro
King, Gray B.	Henderson	Kinison, S. G.	Henderson
King, H. B.	Guadalupe	Kinney, John	Leon
King, H. C. A.	Burleson	Kinney, John W.	Austin
King, Hardy	Lavaca	Kinney, M. W. Mc.	Brazoria
King, Hilsman	Leon	Kinsey, E. R.	Grayson
King, Isaiah	Red River	Kinsey, H. M.	San Augustine
King, J. W.	Henderson	Kinsey, Samuel	Grayson
King, James	Fannin	Kipp, Abram	Harris
King, James	Shelby	Kirbee, J. M.	Montgomery
King, James H.	Red River	Kirby, W.	Austin
King, James W.	Harris	Kirchopper, J. D.	Houston
King, John	Gonzales	Kirchopper, John	
King, John	Polk	H.	Henderson
King, John	Rusk	Kiren, James	Henderson
King, John	Shelby	Kirgan, A.	Fannin
King, John	Victoria	Kirk, Ann R.	Milam
King, John A.	Washington	Kirk, J. N.	Bastrop
King, John E.	Burleson	Kirk, Lewis	Fannin

NAME	COUNTY	NAME	COUNTY
Kirk, Margaret	Fannin	Knight, Lewis	Nacogdoches
Kirkbrod, Pollard	Navarro	Knight, S. R.	Shelby
Kirkham, S.	Montgomery	Knight, W. J.	Polk
Kirkland, Joseph	Cass	Knight, William	Cass
Kirkland, Stephen	Galveston	Knolle, E.	Austin
Kirkman, John M.	Brazoria	Knott, Joseph	Grimes
Kirkpatrick, Hiram	Shelby	Knox, George W.	Nacogdoches
Kirkpatrick, Ira	Rusk	Knox, James	Anderson
Kirkpatrick, J. D.	Goliad	Knox, Jesse	Lavaca
Kirkpatrick, John	Smith	Knox, R. K.	Harrison
Kirkpatrick,		Koch, F. A.	Comal
Thomas	Smith	Koker, George	San Augustine
Kirksey, W.	Houston	Kokernott, D. L.	Liberty
Kirkwood, Goerge	Tyler	Kolb, William G.	Limestone
Kirkwood, Thomas		Koller, John	Austin
L.	Limestone	Kone, S. R.	Montgomery
Kirtley, A.	Grimes	Kone, Stephen	Brazos
Kiser, J. H.	Henderson	Konida, Joseph	Anderson
Kiser, John	Dallas	Koontz, Henry	Comal
Kisler, Charles	Colorado	Koop, John	Harris
Kissam, A.	Grimes	Koop, William	DeWitt
Kitchel, Aaron	Leon	Korn, Levi	Grayson
Kitchens, D.	Collin	Kornegay, D. S.	Fayette
Kitchens, F.	Cass	Koster, Theodore	Comal
Kitchens, Henry	Calhoun	Kounce, Gotlieb	Bexar
Kitchens, Jane	Grimes	Kroner, Francis	Galveston
Kitchens, John	Fannin	Krose, Melchoir	Colorado
Kitchens, John S.	Cass	Krum, Jacob	Victoria
Kitchens, Wilson	Cass	Kughen, Andrew	Cass
Kittrell, John	Bowie	Kuhn, Adam	Colorado
Kizer, B. P.	Fort Bend	Kuhn, J. C.	Galveston
Kizer, Daniel J.	Washington	Kuhn, L.	Anderson
Kizer, John	Fort Bend	Kuhner, Charles A.	Bexar
Klaener, D. H.	Galveston	Kuykendall, Abner	Fayette
Kleberg, Ernst	Austin	Kuykendall,	
Kleberg, Lowie	Austin	Absolem	Fayette
Kleberg, Robert	Austin	Kuykendall,	
Kleen, Stephen	Comal	Benjamin	Nacogdoches
Klein, Joseph	Comal	Kuykendall,	
Kline, C. F.	Henderson	Brazela	Austin
Klotz, Jacob	Victoria	Kuykendall, Gibson	Austin
Knapp, John	Burleson	Kuykendall, Gran	Fannin
Knapp, John G.	Washington	Kuykendall, J. A.	Fannin
Kneeland, Isaac	Henderson	Kuykendall, J. H.	Austin
Knetoch, John	Comal	Kuykendall, J. W.	Fannin
Knibbe, Dedrick	Comal	Kuykendall, Joseph	Fort Bend
Knight, Anna	Lamar	Kuykendall, John	Austin
Knight, D. F.	Fayette	Kuykendall, John	Cass
Knight, James	Liberty	Kuykendall, John	Harris
Knight, John R.	Shelby	Kuykendall, M.	Rusk

NAME	COUNTY	NAME	COUNTY
Kuykendall, M. C.	Fannin	Lagrone, Jacob,	
Kuykendall,		Sr.	Harrison
Matthew	Limestone	Lagrone, M.	Upshur
Kuykendall, O.	Cass	Lagrone, William	
Kuykendall, Robert	Harris	A.	Panola
Kuykendall, Simon	Nacogdoches	Lague, Neely	Panola
Kuykendall,		Lain, Green	Jasper
Thornton	Austin	Lain, Joseph	Jasper
Kuykendall,		Laird, J. R.	Tyler
William	Refugio	Laird, Robert	Jasper
Kuykendall,		Lake, Thomas	Dallas
William L.	Nacogdoches	Lake, William	Liberty
Kyle, James	Panola	Lakey, J. T.	San Augustine
Kyle, Robert	Panola	Lakey, William	San Augustine
Kyle, Robert E.	Nacogdoches	Lakin, George W.	Cass
Kyle, William J.	Brazoria	Lakin J. W.	Cass
Kyle, WIlliam J.	Grimes	Lakin, Samuel	Cass
		Lakin, W. D.	Cass
		Lall, Joel	Washington
Labadie, N. D.	Galveston	Lamar, L.	Cass
Labinska, V. L.	Bastrop	Lamar, Samuel	Cass
Lackey, George	Fannin	Lamb, James	Travis
Lackey, John J.	Wharton	Lamb, John C.	Colorado
Lackin, Benjamin	Houston	Lamb, M.	Henderson
Lackin, Thomas M.	Houston	Lamb, Medy	Leon
Lacy, Daniel	Henderson	Lamb, R. S.	Leon
Lacy, George B.	Houston	Lamb, Richard	Grimes
Lacy, H.	Houston	Lamb, Thomas	Walker
Lacy, J. R.	Bowie	Lambert, John	Nacogdoches
Lacy, Jacob M.	Harrison	Lambert, Joseph	Navarro
Lacy, Joseph H.	Houston	Lambert, Thomas T.	Gonzales
Lacy, M.	Cherokee	Lambert, Walter	Refugio
Lacy, Martin	Grimes	Lambrans, H.	Goliad
Lacy, R. J.	Red River	Lambright, G.	Walker
Lacy, S.	Houston	Lamkins, Aston	Milam
Lacy, S. B.	Houston	Lamkins, James	Grayson
Lacy, W. D.	Matagorda	Lamkins, P. Y.	Anderson
Lacy, William B.	Houston	Lamkins, William	Milam
Lacy, William H.	Panola	Lamon, James C.	Comal
Lacy, William Y.	Cherokee	Lancaster, Joseph	
Lado, Napoleon	Harris	D.	Grimes
Ladd, C. D.	Titus	Lancaster, Matthew	Red River
Ladd, R. R.	Titus	Lancaster,	
Ladd, William	Navarro	Sterling	Red River
Lafferty, W. D.	Fayette	Lancaster, Thomas	Grimes
Lagrone, A. J.	Panola	Lance, Henry	Bastrop
Lagrone, Adam	Panola	Land, J. R.	Victoria
Lagrone, G. W.	Upshur	Land, John	Cass
Lagrone, Jacob,		Land, Joseph	Gonzales
Jr.	Harrison	Land, P. B.	Cass

NAME	COUNTY	NAME	COUNTY
Land, Thomas J.	Brazoria	Langley, Thomas	Dallas
Landers, F. G.	Harrison	Langston, Hiram	Smith
Landers, Henry	Smith	Langston, J. T.	Lamar
Landers, L.	Henderson	Langston, Jacob	Leon
Landers, Levi	Harrison	Langthorpe,	
Landfaire, Robert		William	Galveston
L.	Polk	Langum, Benjamin	Walker
Landingham, Irvin	Lamar	Langum, Charles	Walker
Landrum, B. L.	Montgomery	Langum, William	Walker
Landrum, J. T.	Leon	Lanier, A. H.	Henderson
Landrum, Jane	Leon	Lanier, A. H., Sr.	Shelby
Landrum, John	Grimes	Lanier, B. F.	Cass
Landrum, John	Rusk	Lanier, Lamiel	Liberty
Landrum, Larkin	Leon	Lanier, W. W.	Henderson
Landrum, W. H.	Sabine	Lanier, William H.	Shelby
Landrum, W. P.	Shelby	Lankford, Mrs. E.	Cass
Landrum, William	Montgomery	Lankford, Eleasor	Cass
Landy, Nathaniel	Henderson	Lankford, G. F.	Grayson
Lane, Ann S.	Rusk	Lankford, P. Lee	Grayson
Lane, David	Cass	Lankford, W. T.	Grayson
Lane, David	Fannin	Lann, J. W.	Matagorda
Lane, J. A.	Shelby	Lansdell, John	Bowie
Lane, J. C.	Henderson	Lansing, James	Victoria
Lane, James	Robertson	Lapolean, Luis	Brazoria
Lane, James F.	Rusk	La Prelle, John	Bowie
Lane, John C.	Rusk	Larabee, ----	Henderson
Lane, John M.	Shelby	Lard, A. J.	Shelby
Lane, Margaret	Fayette	Lard, Jesse	Tyler
Lane, Martin	Robertson	Lardner, Nicholas	Bexar
Lane, Robert	Rusk	Larimore, J.	Collin
Lane, W.	Hunt	Larimore, John	Sabine
Lane, William	Houston	Larison, Joel	Walker
Lang, Daniel	Liberty	Larkins, A.	Fannin
Lang, George W.	Liberty	Larkins, James	Grayson
Lang, L.	Walker	Larner, William	Dallas
Lang, Sara	Shelby	Lars, Florentius	Guadalupe
Langacre, W. J.	Shelby	Larue, Isam	Fannin
Lange, W. G.	Angelina	Lasavine, Antonio	Nacogdoches
Langford, G. M.	Red River	Lasavine, Maria	
Langford, H.	Hunt	Josefa	Nacogdoches
Langham, J. M.	Leon	Laster, James	Harrison
Langham, Joel	Leon	Laster, Jane	Harrison
Langham, M. H.	Henderson	Latamore, J. M.	Red River
Langham, M. H.	Leon	Latamore, James	Red River
Langham, Monroe	Henderson	Latamore, A. H.	Red River
Langham, Monsow	Henderson	Latham, Enoch	Grimes
Langham P. C.	Henderson	Latham, King	Henderson
Langham, P. C.	Leon	Latham, King H.	Shelby
Langham, W. D.	Leon	Latham, James	Shelby
Langhorn, Melvin	Brazos	Latham, L. J.	Harris

NAME	COUNTY	NAME	COUNTY
Latham, Lewis	Sabine	Lawson, J. W. B.	Jackson
Latham, Lewis	Shelby	Lawson, James	Grimes
Latham, Martin,		Lawson, John	Bexar
Jr.	Sabine	Lawson, N. P.	Fannin
Latham, Martin,		Lawson, Peter	Galveston
Sr.	Sabine	Lawson, Ruffin	Limestone
Latham, William	Nacogdoches	Lawton, G. F.	Red River
Latham, William	Shelby	Lay, A. W.	Guadalupe
Latimer, A. H.	Cass	Lay, William C.	Harrison
Latimer, H. R.	Cass	Layo, Antonio	Goliad
Latimer, H. R.	Lamar	Layton, H. A.	Milam
Latimer, R. W.	Nacogdoches	Layton, J. C.	Milam
Lattimore, John	Colorado	Layton, L. W.	Milam
Laude, A.	Galveston	Layton, W.	Matagorda
Lauderdale, S. J.	Limestone	Lea, D. D.	Jasper
Laughlin, David	Lavaca	Lea, Major	Jasper
Laughlin, John J.	Lavaca	Lea, V. P.	Liberty
Laut, M. V.	Panola	Leach, A.	Collin
Lavgie, Abe	Sabine	Leach, John	Houston
Lavigne, Jose	Henderson	Leach, P.	Upshur
Lawhon, David	Jafferson	Leach, W.	Collin
Lawhon, John C.	Newton	League, Thomas M.	Harris
Lawler, L. W.	Houston	Leake, A. M.	Dallas
Lawrence, Adam	Burleson	Leake Samuel	Dallas
Lawrence, Charles	Galveston	Leal, Antonio	Bexar
Lawrence,		Leal, Antonio	Victoria
Claiborne	Washington	Leal, Jesus	Bexar
Lawrence, D.	Burleson	Leal, Jose	Bexar
Lawrence, G. W.	Grimes	Leal, Juan	Bexar
Lawrence, G. W.	Walker	Leath, J. G.	Henderson
Lawrence, H. C.	Nacogdoches	Leath, Jeremiah	Houston
Lawrence, James	Harris	Leath, R. J.	Rusk
Lawrence, Joseph	Fayette	Leathers, Joel D.	Houston
Lawrence, Joseph	Liberty	Leathers, Samuel	Leon
Lawrence, M. G.	Grimes	Leauerman, Luis	Austin
Lawrence, Perry	Burleson	Leavitt, J. W.	Matagorda
Lawrence, Richard	Smith	Leavitt, R.	Matagorda
Lawrence, Samuel	Burleson	Leavy, Robert	Henderson
Lawrence, T.	Robertson	Le Clere, J. S.	Galveston
Lawrence, W. H.	Anderson	Ledbetter, Absalom	Hopkins
Lawrence, W. Moore	Burleson	Ledbetter,	
Lawson, A. R.	Wharton	Hamilton	Fayette
Lawson, Amanda M.	Rusk	Ledbetter, Joseph	Fannin
Lawson, Harvey	Fannin	Le Duc, J.	Galveston
Lawson, Henry M.	Rusk	Lee, A., Jr.	Brazos
Lawson, Irvine	Rusk	Lee, A. A.	Victoria
Lawson, Irwin	Jackson	Lee, Abner	Washington
Lawson, J. D.	Red River	Lee, Abram	Harris
Lawson, J. H.	Wharton	Lee, Alfred	Hunt
Lawson, J. T.	Nacogdoches	Lee, Alfred	Liberty

NAME	COUNTY	NAME	COUNTY
Lee, Alfred J.	Rusk	Leiter, Samuel	Austin
Lee, Charles	Fannin	Leja, Jose	Bexar
Lee, D. W.	Lamar	Lelurkule, Antonia	Austin
Lee, David	Upshur	Leman, J. H.	Walker
Lee, H. B.	Shelby	Lemmenstite, F.	Colorado
Lee, Isaac	Nacogdoches	Lemmon, Robert A.	Dallas
Lee, Isom	Upshur	Lenard, George L.	Dallas
Lee, J. B.	Dallas	Lenard, Leo S. C.	Dallas
Lee, Jacob	Hunt	Lenningham, Z.	Fayette
Lee, James	Montgomery	Leon, Francisco	Goliad
Lee, James B.	Bexar	Leonard, Alfred M.	Cherokee
Lee, Jeremiah	Grimes	Leonard, Charles	Brazoria
Lee, John	Fannin	Leonard, John A.	Dallas
Lee, John	Fort Bend	Leonard, Joshua	Dallas
Lee, John C.	Austin	Leonard, Rachel	Cherokee
Lee, John H.	Harrison	Lepert, J. H.	Galveston
Lee, Joseph	Travis	Leslie, A. J.	Bexar
Lee, Larkin G.	Nacogdoches	Lester, A. D.	Harrison
Lee, M. C.	Grimes	Lester, Fountain	Harrison
Lee, Martin	Henderson	Lester, James S.	Fayette
Lee, Mary	Rusk	Lester & Barnes	Grimes
Lee, Owen	Shelby	Letcher, John	Lavaca
Lee, Peter	Hunt	Letney, Lewis	Jasper
Lee, R. W.	Fannin	Lettis, Cornelius	Goliad
Lee, Robert	Hopkins	Leuter, Jonathan	Rusk
Lee, Stewart	Nacogdoches	Levender, William	Dallas
Lee, T. D.	Red River	Levenhager, Henry	Harris
Lee, T. S.	Gonzales	Levering, John	Goliad
Lee, W. G.	Hopkins	Levery, A. M.	Matagorda
Lee, William	Nacogdoches	Levis, H. J.	Galveston
Lee, William D.	Harris	Levitre, Mishael	Galveston
Leeg, C.	Henderson	Levitt, Israel	Cass
Leelier, Dominik	Bexar	Levy, James	Washington
Leeper, G. J.	Collin	Levy, Lewis A.	Harris
Leeper, Samuel	Liberty	Levy, Parker	Washington
Leftwick, T.	Matagorda	Lewaine, Phillip	Goliad
Leger, T.	Grimes	Lewellen, A.	Shelby
Legg, G.	Bowie	Lewellen, James	Anderson
Le Grande, J. B.	San Augustine	Lewellen, Thomas	Lamar
Legrasse, John B.	Harris	Lewis, A. L. D.	Liberty
Legrone, Emanuel	Sabine	Lewis, Dr. A. M.	Anderson
Lehea, Timothy	Harris	Lewis, Asa M.	Washington
Lehman, F.	Galveston	Lewis, C. F.	Panola
Lehr, J. T.	Walker	Lewis, C. T.	Matagorda
Leicester, E.	Liberty	Lewis, Charles	Bowie
Leicester, George		Lewis, Charles	Fort Bend
F.	Grimes	Lewis, Daniel	Jefferson
Leigh, James	Walker	Lewis, David	Nacogdoches
Leigh, John	Walker	Lewis, F. J. A.	Washington
Leikner, William	Comal	Lewis, Francis	Bastrop

NAME	COUNTY	NAME	COUNTY
Lewis, Franklin	Fayette	Liddy, William	Panola
Lewis, George	Harris	Liendecker, John	Colorado
Lewis, Harrison	Grimes	Light, Peter E.	Lamar
Lewis, Harry M.	Bexar	Light, Robert	Lamar
Lewis, J.	Angelina	Light, W. R.	Lamar
Lewis, J. R.	Matagorda	Lightfoot, W. T.	Fort Bend
Lewis, Jacob	Nacogdoches	Lilburn, James S.	Goliad
Lewis, James	Hopkins	Liles, William	Nacogdoches
Lewis, James	Tyler	Lilley, H. B.	Titus
Lewis, James B.	Matagorda	Lilley, Joseph D.	Titus
Lewis, Jared	Bowie	Lilley, R. P.	Grimes
Lewis, Joel	Jefferson	Lilley, W. C.	Titus
Lewis, John	Galveston	Lillie, J. E.	Harris
Lewis, John	Harris	Lillie, J. W.	Wharton
Lewis, John E.	Fayette	Lillie, P. R.	Rusk
Lewis, John H.	San Augustine	Lin, Jacoba	Bexar
Lewis, John M.	Montgomery	Linam, J. W.	Victoria
Lewis, John T.	Newton	Lincoln, J. G.	Fannin
Lewis, Joshua	Jefferson	Lincoln, William	
Lewis, L. L.	Collin	A.	Harrison
Lewis, Lacy T.	Lamar	Linderman, Henry	Guadalupe
Lewis, Lucretia E.	Harris	Lindheimer,	
Lewis, M. B.	Jasper	Ferdinand	Comal
Lewis, Mary	Fayette	Lindley, Eli	Hopkins
Lewis, Nathaniel	Bexar	Lindley, Samuel	Hopkins
Lewis, Newton	Shelby	Lindley, Samuel	Montgomery
Lewis, R. B.	Houston	Lindmuller, W. H.	Comal
Lewis, Robert	Harris	Lindsey, B.	Henderson
Lewis, S. K.	Austin	Lindsey, Ben F.	Fannin
Lewis, S. T.	Collin	Lindsey, Catherine	Panola
Lewis, Sarah	Jasper	Lindsey, George W.	Burleson
Lewis, Sarah	Panola	Lindsey, Isaac	San Augustine
Lewis, Thomas H.	Jefferson	Lindsey, Isaac M.	Henderson
Lewis, W.	Anderson	Lindsey, J. L.	Shelby
Lewis, W. C.	Collin	Lindsey, James	Washington
Lewis, William	Anderson	Lindsey, James M.	Fannin
Lewis, William	Fayette	Lindsey, James S.	Cherokee
Lewis, William	Jefferson	Lindsey, Micaga	Shelby
Lewis, William C.	Washington	Lindsey, R. M.	Bowie
Lewis, William G.	Nacogdoches	Lindsey, T. E.	Nacogdoches
Lewis, William J.	Brazos	Lindsey, Thomas	Fannin
Lewis, William J.	Galveston	Lindsey, Thomas	Shelby
Lewis, William		Lindsey, Thomas J.	Cherokee
McF., Jr.	Newton	Lindsey, Tyler	Burleson
Lewis, William T.	Polk	Lindsey, William	Fayette
Lewis, William W.	Brazos	Lindsey, William	
Licett, John	Colorado	H.	Fannin
Liday, Andrew	Fannin	Linley, William	Walker
Liday, Isaac	Fannin	Linn, Charles	Cass
Liddy, Francis	Panola	Linn, J. J.	Victoria

NAME	COUNTY	NAME	COUNTY
Linn, James S.	Nacogdoches	Lively, Philip	Rusk
Linn, Edward	Victoria	Lively, Susan	Rusk
Linscomb, Joseph	Jefferson	Livingston,	
Linsey, Alfred	Rusk	Charles	Harrison
Linsey, C. B.	Rusk	Livingston, T.	Brazoria
Linsey, Claborn B.	Anderson	Lock, James	Rusk
Linsey, Michael	Liberty	Lock, L. H.	Rusk
Linscum, G. R.	Jackson	Lock, Leander	Lamar
Linthecum, Bird	Panola	Lock, R. H.	Fannin
Linton, John	Harrison	Lock, Samuel	Galveston
Lipscomb, A. S.	Washington	Lockamy, H.	Leon
Lipscomb, Joel	Harrison	Lockett, Richard	Colorado
Lipscomb, L. R.	Harrison	Lockhart, C. J. C.	Washington
Lipscomb, Mary P.	Washington	Lockhart, C. M.	Washington
Lipscomb, W. B.	Austin	Lockhart, Charles	Goliad
Lister, E. J.	Washington	Lockhart, John W.	Washington
Lister, J. H.	Shelby	Lockhart, K. B.	Gonzales
Lister, Josiah	Washington	Lockhart, L. C.	Washington
Lister, Milton	Washington	Lockhart, Robert	Grimes
Lister, Thomas H.	Shelby	Lockhart, Robert	Harris
Lister, William H.	Washington	Lockhart, William	
Lister, Z. F.	Shelby	A.	Washington
Lith, Harvey M.	Brazoria	Lockhart, William	
Lith, John W.	Brazoria	B.	Gonzales
Litteken, Henry	Brazoria	Lockley, George	Liberty
Littig, Joshua	Lavaca	Locklin, William	
Little, E. D.	Washington	L.	Milam
Little, Erastis	Brazoria	Lockman, Antonio	Bexar
Little, Henry	Red River	Lockridge, H. H.	Henderson
Little, Hiram	Walker	Lockridge, Mrs.	
Little, J. D.	Nacogdoches	Rebecca	Washington
Little, Jane	Fort Bend	Lockridge, William	Anderson
Little, John	Anderson	Lockwood, A. A.	Bexar
Little, John	Fort Bend	Lockwood, C.	Travis
Little, John	Leon	Lockwood, W. R.	Liberty
Little, Matthew	Rusk	Loffler, Christian	Comal
Little, Samuel	Anderson	Loftis, B. H.	Rusk
Little, Seth	Grimes	Lofton, William B.	Grimes
Little, Thomas	Anderson	Logan, A. M.	Austin
Little, William	Leon	Logan, Abel	Houston
Littlefield, J. G.	San Augustine	Logan, Charles	Lamar
Littlefield,		Logan, Elizabeth	Austin
Joseph	Lamar	Logan, J. H.	Liberty
Littlefield,		Logan, John	Victoria
Hudson	Liberty	Logan, P. E.	Lamar
Littleton, Samuel		Logan, William	Lamar
M.	Grayson	Logan & Stern	Victoria
Litton, John	Bastrop	Logdin, Alben	Austin
Litton, Mary B.	Bastrop	Loggins, Martin	San Augustine
Litton, Thomas	Grayson	Loggins, Sam	San Augustine

NAME	COUNTY	NAME	COUNTY
Loggins, W. H.	San Augustine	Look, E. S.	Red River
Logre, Edmund	Galveston	Looney, David	Bowie
Logsden, John	Rusk	Looney, George	Austin
Logwood, T. Y.	Bowie	Looney, H. E.	Jackson
Lohrnubler, G.	Galveston	Looney, J. A.	Bowie
Loid, Elizabeth	Austin	Loop, John	Bowie
Loid, Benjamin	Rusk	Loose, David	Cherokee
Loller, Henry	Rusk	Loose, Hardin	Cherokee
Loller, Isaac	Rusk	Loose, Jesse	Cherokee
Loller, James	Smith	Loose, John	Cherokee
Loller, John	Smith	Loose, Joseph	Cherokee
Loman, H.	Travis	Loose, William	Cherokee
Lombard, James	Brazoria	Lopes, Calisto	Bexar
Lonas, G. W.	Guadalupe	Lopes, Corrila	Leon
Lonas, James C.	Brazoria	Lopes, Cos	Bexar
Lonas, William L.	Brazoria	Lopes, Feliciana	Angelina
London, David E.	Washington	Lopes, J. C.	Houston
Long, A. H.	Grimes	Lopes, Mary	Houston
Long, A. J. W.	Houston	Lorance, Hiram	Smith
Long, Benjamin	Harrison	Lorance, M. Donato	Smith
Long, C.	Harrison	Loring, John	Fannin
Long, C. S. (decd)	Lamar	Loring, Joseph	Bexar
Long, George W.	Rusk	Losoyo, Felis	Besar
Long, Henry C.	Dallas	Losoyo, Juan	Bexar
Long, J.	Henderson	Lott, Absolom	Polk
Long, Jackson	Polk	Lott, Arthur	Limestone
Long, Jacob	Burleson	Lott, Arthur	Smith
Long, Jacob	Lamar	Lott, Mrs. C. S.	Jackson
Long, James	Titus	Lott, Calvin	Polk
Long, James H.	Fort Bend	Lott, Celia	Limestone
Long, James M.	Travis	Lott, E. E.	Smith
Long, John	Houston	Lott, Jesse	Limestone
Long, John	Nacogdoches	Lott, John	Harrison
Long, Mary J.	Montgomery	Lott, John, Jr.	Limestone
Long, Mary M.	Nacogdoches	Lott, John, Sr.	Limestone
Long, Rheuben	Hunt	Lott, Joshua	Polk
Long, W. T.	Henderson	Lott, Miller	Limestone
Long, William	Cherokee	Lott, R. M.	Jackson
Long, William	Liberty	Lott, Robert A.	Washington
Long, William	Smith	Lott, Thomas	Jackson
Long, William D.	Nacogdoches	Lothlin, A. Y.	Burleson
Long, William E.	Houston	Loudon, Thomas	Hopkins
Long, Wyly	Cherokee	Lout, Bailey	Shelby
Longbottom, B. B.	Grimes	Love, A. A.	Henderson
Longbottom, John	Grimes	Love, A. C.	Houston
Longcope, Charles		Love, A. D.	Henderson
S.	Fayette	Love, Allen	Washington
Longcope, Virginia	Fayette	Love, David	Travis
Longly, Campbell	Austin	Love, David M.	Brazos
Looby, M.	Red River	Love, G. H.	Brazos

NAME	COUNTY	NAME	COUNTY
Love, James	Galveston	Lowery, Thomas	San Augustine
Love, James	Washington	Lowrenz, J. G.	Polk
Love, James M.	Robertson	Lowy, Aaron	Shelby
Love, John	Rusk	Lowy, Alfred	Rusk
Love, John G.	San Augustine	Lowy, G. R.	Rusk
Love, Joseph	Brazos	Lowy, S. H.	Rusk
Love, M. P.	Goliad	Loyd, Berry G.	Henderson
Love, M. P. H.	Victoria	Loyd, E. R.	Rusk
Love, Mrs. N.	Matagorda	Loyd, G. W.	Grayson
Love, R. H.	Henderson	Loyd, L.	Cass
Love, Robert D.	San Patricio	Loyd, Richard	Grimes
Love, Wade	Rusk	Loyd, Richard J.	Grayson
Love, William	Washington	Loyd, S.	Upshur
Love, Young E.	Grimes	Loyd, S. M.	Leon
Loveing, George S.	Liberty	Loyd, Thomas	Fort Bend
Loveing, James	Lamar	Loyd, Thomas C.	Nacogdoches
Loveing, Lidy	Sabine	Loyd, W.	Upshur
Loveing, M. W.	Sabine	Loyless, R. J.	Leon
Loveing, Martha	Liberty	Lubbock, F. R.	Harris
Loveing, O.	Collin	Lubbock, Thomas	Harris
Lovis, Sarah	Goliad	Lucas, Charles	Washington
Lovejoy, C. A.	Henderson	Lucas, D. C.	San Augustine
Lovejoy, John L.	Lamar	Lucas, G. H.	Collin
Lovejoy, Samuel	Nacogdoches	Lucas, George E.	San Augustine
Lovel, Benoni	Panola	Lucas, John	San Augustine
Lovel, David	San Augustine	Lucas, John H.	San Augustine
Lovel, Felix G.	San Augustine	Lucas, P. H.	Collin
Lovel, G. W.	Henderson	Lucas, Wilson	Washington
Lovelace, Ralph	Goliad	Luce, William	Houston
Lovelady, J.	Collin	Luck, Joseph	Lamar
Lovelady, James	Cass	Luckett, A. C.	Travis
Loverin, W. H.	Matagorda	Luckett, A. W.	Travis
Lowe, Alfred D.	DeWitt	Luckett, N. D.	Nacogdoches
Lowe, B. C.	Jasper	Luckett, N. M.	Travis
Lowe, Barney	Jasper	Luckie, M. W.	Houston
Lowe, Benjamin F.	DeWitt	Luckie, S. H.	Bexar
Lowe, D. M.	Jasper	Ludlow, ---	Henderson
Lowe, Eli	Sabine	Ludwig, J. W.	Comal
Lowe, Elijah	Polk	Luesch, John H.	Houston
Lowe, G. L.	Anderson	Luke, William	Colorado
Lowe, Isaac	Sabine	Lumly, Thomas	Dallas
Lowe, J. H.	Sabine	Lumnesdon, E. J.	Anderson
Lowe, Jesse	Sabine	Lumpkin, William	San Augustine
Lowe, Joel	Polk	Lund, C. C.	Liberty
Lowe, John	Guadalupe	Luner, Silvester	Nacogdoches
Lowe, John	Harrison	Lunie, Stephen	Brazoria
Lowe, John C.	Sabine	Lunsford, John	Navarro
Lowe, John M.	Cherokee	Luntzel, M.	Comal
Lowe, P. M.	Jasper	Lupton, J. W.	Bowie
Lowery, Thomas	Henderson	Lupton, Joseph	Red River

NAME	COUNTY	NAME	COUNTY
Lusey, D. H.	Rusk	Lyon, Seymore C.	Fayette
Lusk, Mrs. A. W.	Washington	Lyon, William	Fayette
Lusk, G. V.	Leon	Lyon, William N.	Harris
Lusk, R. O.	Leon	Lytle, William	Bexar
Lusk, Samuel	Washington	Lytle, William L.	Goliad
Luster, James	Titus		
Lutenbacker, L.	Bexar		
Luther, Samuel	Nacogdoches	McAda, J. S.	Polk
Lutrell, Shelton	Denton	McAda, J. N.	San Augustine
Lutze, Mrs.	Galveston	McAdams, George	Bowie
Lutze, Peter	Burleson	McAdams, Henry	Cass
Lux, Albertus	Comal	McAdams, Jeptha J.	Smith
Lyel, Thomas	Sabine	McAdams, John	Walker
Lyell, Mrs. S.	Washington	McAdams, Samuel	Bowie
Lyday, Jacob	Lamar	McAdams, Samuel	Shelby
Lyford, John	Goliad	McAdams, W. R.	Harrison
Lynch, Andrew	Wharton	McAdams, W. R.	Henderson
Lynch, B. F.	Harris	McAdams, William	Bowie
Lynch, E. B.	Brazoria	McAdams, William	Cass
Lynch, E. O.	Galveston	McAdams, William,	
Lynch, Francis	Harris	Jr.	Smith
Lynch, Jacob	Red River	McAdams, William,	
Lynch, James	Goliad	Sr.	Smith
Lynch, James	Hunt	McAdams, William	
Lynch, John J.	Harris	C.	Harrison
Lynch, John R.	Jasper	McAdoo, J. D.	Cass
Lynch, Joseph Penn	Washington	McAdoo, William C.	Bowie
Lynch, N.	Liberty	McAfee, Ezekiel	Henderson
Lynch, Patrick	Grimes	McAhron, William	Fayette
Lynch, Patrick	Lamar	McAlister, William	Rusk
Lynch, R. J.	Liberty	McAlpin, M. S.	Jefferson
Lynch, S.	Upshur	McAmus, James	Lamar
Lynch, Thomas	Red River	McAnally, J. E.	Nacogdoches
Lynch, W. C. C.	Brazoria	McAnety, John	Angelina
Lynch, William	Harris	McAnier, Alver	Red River
Lynd, John	Robertson	McAnier, J. B.	Red River
Lynhart, Antonio	Bexar	McAnnully, C.	Harris
Lynn, Arthur	Galveston	McAnnully, P.	Walker
Lynn, B. F.	Red River	McAnulty, James	Nacogdoches
Lynn, Isaac	Hunt	McAnulty, Richard	Nacogdoches
Lynn, Jesse D.	Liberty	McAnulty, Sarah	Nacogdoches
Lyon, A.	Liberty	McArn, A.	Henderson
Lyon, Alfred	Newton	McArthur, John	Grimes
Lyon, Ben F.	Washington	McArthur, N.	Travis
Lyon, D. C.	Fayette	McAshan, E.	Fayette
Lyon, G. W.	Fayette	McBarclay, Jenny	Tyler
Lyon, James M.	Panola	McBarclay, John	Tyler
Lyon, Joseph G.	Brazos	McBeath, A. P.	Sabine
Lyon, Martha	Fayette	McBee, A. T.	Henderson
Lyon, Samuel C.	Brazoria	McBee, Jordan	Henderson

NAME	COUNTY	NAME	COUNTY
McBee, Vardre	Jackson	McClain, William	Navarro
McBee, W. H.	Henderson	McClanahan, J.	Victoria
McBride, Alex	Grimes	McClane, Robert	Lavaca
McBride, James	Grayson	McClary, S. S.	Fannin
McCain, William	Nacogdoches	McClellan, W. B.	Washington
McCaleb, A.	Washington	McClellan, William	
McCaleb, G. W.	Montgomery	D.	Fayette
McCaleb, John	Washington	McClelland, A.	Galveston
McCaleb, Z.	Montgomery	McClelland, A. J.	Bexar
McCall, D.	Titus	McClelland, John	
McCallister, John		S.	Bexar
R.	Robertson	McClelland,	
McCallister,		William	Shelby
Michael	Robertson	McClendon, Hiram	Fort Bend
McCallister,		McClendon, Jackson	Titus
Thomas	Robertson	McClendon, Jason	Titus
McCally, John	San Augustine	McClendon, William	Tyler
McCamley, J. W.	Matagorda	McClenney, Mary	Grimes
McCamy, Marcellus	Rusk	McClosky, J. J.	Bowie
McCanlays, D. P.	Robertson	McClure, A. E.	Anderson
McCanlays, David	Robertson	McClure, Levi	Fayette
McCann, Samuel	Fannin	McClure, Susan	Fayette
McCardell, Thomas	Polk	McClure, William	
McCarley, John P.	Grimes	F.	Nacogdoches
McCarty, Mrs. A.		McCoen, Hugh	Nacogdoches
F.	Harrison	McCollum, Mrs.	Grimes
McCarty, D. F.	Harrison	McCollum, T. J.	Grimes
McCarty, Edward	Liberty	McComb, Samuel	Polk
McCarty, J. M.	Anderson	McComb, Thomas W.	Harris
McCarty, James	Brazos	McComes, James	Navarro
McCarty, James R.	Harrison	McComes, Phebe	Navarro
McCarty, Jarred	Grayson	McCommas, Aaron	Dallas
McCarty, John H.	Henderson	McCommas, James	Dallas
McCarty, Joseph	Lamar	McCommas, John C.	Dallas
McCarty, Samuel	Rusk	McCommas, Stephen	
McCarty, Thompson	Rusk	B.	Dallas
McCarty, William	Titus	McConnell, D. B.	Goliad
McCasky, G. B.	Travis	McConnell, John	Grayson
McCaslin, William	San Augustine	McConnell, John	Harris
McCaul, Matthew	Hopkins	McConnell, William	Harris
McCaul, Robert	Hopkins	McCorkle, A.	Austin
McCauly, John	Navarro	McCormick, --	Goliad
McCay, A.	Harrison	McCormick, J. M.	Brazoria
McCay, Green	Robertson	McCormick,	
McCay, John	Shelby	Margaret	Harris
McCay, John R.	Henderson	McCormick, Mishael	Harris
McCerly, Pleaseedo	Grimes	McCowan, A.	Grimes
McChriston, J. S.	Bowie	McCowan, Alexander	Montgomery
McChriston,		McCowan, J.	Henderson
William	Titus	McCowan, James	Harrison

NAME	COUNTY	NAME	COUNTY
McCowan, Nancy	Montgomery	McCullough, Robert	Dallas
McCoy, B. D.	DeWitt	McCune, H. J.	Rusk
McCoy, Catherine	Gonzales	McCune, James	Rusk
McCoy, Daniel	DeWitt	McCune, William	Nacogdoches
McCoy, G. S.	Cass	McCurley, Caleb	Harris
McCoy, Green	DeWitt	McCurley, G. W.	Red River
McCoy, John	DeWitt	McCurley, John	Cass
McCoy, John C.	Dallas	McCurry, Jackson	Rusk
McCoy, Juanita	DeWitt	McCutcheon,	
McCoy, Kimber	DeWitt	William H.	Anderson
McCoy, O. C.	Fayette	McDade, Ales.	Washington
McCoy, Prospect	DeWitt	McDade, James W.	Washington
McCoy, William	Grimes	McDade, John A.	Washington
McCrabb, John	DeWitt	McDaniel, C. T.	Sabine
McCracken, Anson	Dallas	McDaniel, George	Robertson
McCracken, John B.	Cherokee	McDaniel, H.	Houston
McCracken, Samuel	Bowie	McDaniel, J.	Henderson
McCracken, Samuel	Cass	McDaniel, J. H.	San Augustine
McCraven, William	Harris	McDaniel, John T.	Nacogdoches
McCreary, J. K.	Matagorda	McDaniel, Judith	Travis
McCreary, James	Red River	McDaniel, Levi	Sabine
McCreary, John	Red River	McDaniel, R. C.	San Augustine
McCreary, Samuel	Titus	McDaniel, William	Gonzales
McCreary, William	Dallas	McDaniel, William	Nacogdoches
McCrite, M.	Upshur	McDaniel, William	
McCrory, William		L.	Nacogdoches
G.	Travis	McDermot, J. B.	Fannin
McCuiston, Elisha	Lamar	McDermot, John	Goliad
McCuiston, J. C.	Robertson	McDivit, John	Travis
McCuiston, James	Robertson	McDonald, A.	Houston
McCuiston, John	Lamar	McDonald, A. J.	Colorado
McCuiston, N.	Robertson	McDonald, A. J.	Rusk
McCuiston, Otho	Lamar	McDonald, A. W.	Titus
McCuiston, Robert	Robertson	McDonald,	
McCuller, John	Titus	Alexander	Harrison
McCuller, Robert	Titus	McDonald, Andrew	Hunt
McCuller, Samuel	Titus	McDonald, D.	San Augustine
McCuller, William	Titus	McDonald, D. R.	Lamar
McCullock, David	Walker	McDonald, Donald	Harris
McCullock, G. R.	Grimes	McDonald, Elisha	Brazos
McCullock, J. H.	Grimes	McDonald, Francis	Liberty
McCullock, W. H.	Grimes	McDonald, Green	Limestone
McCullough, Ben	Guadalupe	McDonald, H. G.	Lamar
McCullough, Dlila	Milam	McDonald, J. M.	Henderson
McCullough, H. E.	Guadalupe	McDonald, J. W.	Matagorda
McCullough, John	Bexar	McDonald, James	Henderson
McCullough, John		McDonald, James C.	Gonzales
L.	Harris	McDonald, John	Liberty
McCullough,		McDonald, John	Nacogdoches
Margaret	Galveston	McDonald, John C.	Travis

105

NAME	COUNTY	NAME	COUNTY
McDonald, John S.	Nacogdoches	M.	Harris
McDonald, M.	Montgomery	McFarland, A. W.	Lamar
McDonald, Orson	Houston	McFarland, Albert	Fannin
McDonald, Rebecca	Brazos	McFarland, J. B.	Fayette
McDonald, T.	Collin	McFarland, J. D.	Montgomery
McDonald, Thomas	Grimes	McFarland, J. F.	Montgomery
McDonald, Thomas	Polk	McFarland, Jackson	Fannin
McDonald, W. B. D.	Grimes	McFarland, Jacob	Bowie
McDonald, William	Anderson	McFarland, James	Fannin
McDonald, William	Grimes	McFarland, Manuel	Leon
McDonald, William	Nacogdoches	McFarland, R. C.	Lamar
McDonald, William	Polk	McFarland, S. H.	Bowie
McDonald, William	Walker	McFarland, Samuel	Fannin
McDonald, William		McFarland, Samuel	
G.	Walker	T.	Newton
McDonnell, B.	Galveston	McFarland, Thomas	
McDougall, John	Galveston	S.	Newton
McDougel, George	Harris	McFarland, W. Y.	Washington
McDowell, John	Washington	McFarland, William	Leon
McDowell, Robert	Fannin	McFarland, William	
McDowell, William	Washington	M.	Newton
McDudley, C. W.	Titus	McGaffey, John	Jefferson
McElrath, James	Hunt	McGaffey, N.	Jasper
McElroy, B. H.	Rusk	McGaffey, Otis	Jefferson
McElroy, Harrison	Rusk	McGaffey, W.	Jefferson
McElroy, Henry P.	Fort Bend	McGahey, A.	Brazos
McElroy, William	Rusk	McGahey, J. W.	Brazos
McElwee, William	Montgomery	McGahey, James S.	Grimes
McEntire, A.	Henderson	McGarrah, J.	Collin
McEnturff, A. B.	Henderson	McGarrick, G.	Collin
McEnturff, D. R.	Henderson	McGary, D. H.	Montgomery
McEnturff, George	Henderson	McGary, Isaac	Walker
McEnturff, William	Henderson	McGary, J. A.	Walker
McFaddin, David	Jefferson	McCauhey, L. G.	Jasper
McFaddin, Eliza	Washington	McGee, A. S.	Polk
McFaddin, J.	Henderson	McGee, Daniel	Washington
McFaddin, N. A.	Washington	McGee, Duncan	Houston
McFaddin, William	Jefferson	McGee, Holden	Jasper
McFaddin, William	Polk	McGee, James P.	Harris
McFadin, D. H.	Bastrop	McGee, Jesse	Polk
McFadin, Jane	Panola	McGee, Joseph	Newton
McFadin, Josephine	Bastrop	McGee, Kich	Goliad
McFadin, Samuel	Panola	McGee, N.	Cass
McFadin, William	Panola	McGee, Norman	Titus
McFarlan, D. M.	Harris	McGee, Ralph	Polk
McFarlan, J. C.	Victoria	McGee, Richard	Rusk
McFarlan, James	Harris	McGee, William	Polk
McFarlan, W. B.	Refugio	McGehee, E. T.	Bastrop
McFarlan, William	Lamar	McGehee, Richard	
McFarlan, William		A.	Fayette

NAME	COUNTY	NAME	COUNTY
McGehee, Thomas G.	Bastrop	McHines, D. C.	Shelby
McGehee, W. B.	Bastrop	McHogan, James	Cherokee
McGervin, John	Angelina	McIntire, Margaret	Grimes
McGill, A. B.	Travis	McIntire, Robert	Grimes
McGill, W. H.	Bastrop	McIntire, William	Grimes
McGinty, John C.	Henderson	McIntosh, Daniel	Angelina
McGloine, James	San Patricio	McIntosh, Jesse	Angelina
McGlothlin, Samuel	Grayson	McIntree, James	Harris
McGonigill, G. J.	Henderson	McInturff, Andrew	Lamar
McGonigill, J. C.	Bowie	McIntyre, Hugh	Washington
McGovern, Edward	Washington	McIntyre, Rachel	
McGowan, A.	Harris	R.	Grayson
McGowan, B.	Walker	McIntyre, Thomas	
McGowan, Elizabeth		H.	Goliad
A.	Grimes	McIver, David	Grimes
McGowan, G. W.	Sabine	McIver, James	Leon
McGowan, James	Red River	McIver, Joseph	Grimes
McGowan, Samuel	Fannin	McIver, T. T.	Montgomery
McGowan, William		McJimsey, George	
C.	Grimes	D.	Panola
McGraw, John H.	Harrison	McKabe, William	Navarro
McGraw, Sterling	Newton	McKain, John	Liberty
McGreal, Patrick	Brazoria	McKay, Alexander	Rusk
McGreal, Peter	Brazoria	McKay, Daniel	Milam
McGreal, Thomas	Brazoria	McKay, J. L.	Henderson
McGregor, Bartlett	Washington	McKay, John L.	Fayette
McGrew, Alex	Sabine	McKay, Samuel M.	Gonzales
McGrew, Elizabeth	Robertson	McKee, A. A.	Fannin
McGrew, J. H.	Sabine	McKee, Andrew A.	Tyler
McGrew, Jefferson	Guadalupe	McKee, F. V.	San Augustine
McGrew, John	Victoria	McKee, J. R.	Fannin
McGrew, John F.	Robertson	McKee, John	Fannin
McGrew, Sarena	Robertson	McKee, John	Galveston
McGrew, Thomas	Robertson	McKee, S. W.	Fannin
McGrew, Thomas	Victoria	McKee, Samuel E.	Fannin
McGrew, William	Victoria	McKee, Samuel L.	Shelby
McGriffin, H.	Montgomery	McKee, Thomas	Navarro
McGriffin, J. F.	Montgomery	McKeen, E.	Burleson
McGriffin, Samuel	Grimes	McKeen, Hugh	Burleson
McGruder, Mrs. M.	Harris	McKeen, James	Navarro
McGuire, G. W.	Rusk	McKeen, John B.	Burleson
McGuire, H. B.	Sabine	McKeen, John C.	Gonzales
McGuire, H. T.	Bowie	McKeen, William W.	Burleson
McGuire, John	Grimes	McKelvy, Hezekiah	Shelby
McGuire, Lawrence	Sabine	McKelvy, James	Rusk
McGuire, S.	Henderson	McKelvy, Jesse	Shelby
McHaffey, Isaac H.	Sabine	McKennon, Murdock	Burleson
McHall, Levin	Nacogdoches	McKenzie, Alex	Nacogdoches
McHam, W. B.	Cass	McKenzie, J. W. P.	Red River
McHenry, L. A.	Austin	McKenzie, J. W. P.	Wharton

NAME	COUNTY	NAME	COUNTY
McKenzie, James	Harris	McKnight, David	Nacogdoches
McKenzie, S. B.	Red River	McKnight, Francis	Nacogdoches
McKeown, Dick	Goliad	McKnight, J. H.	San Augustine
McKey, John	Leon	McKnight, James	Nacogdoches
McKim, Charles	Polk	McKnight, James A.	Nacogdoches
McKim, James	Polk	McKnight, John	Washington
McKimpson, Joseph	Red River	McKnight, P.	Robertson
McKinley, James	Galveston	McKnight, William	Robertson
McKinley, John N.	Smith	McKnight, William	
McKinley, P. S.	Fannin	D.	Nacogdoches
McKinley, William		McKoy, David	Shelby
B.	Gonzales	McKy, Naemi	Sabine
McKinley, William		McLane, Edward J.	Bexar
L.	Smith	McLane, Hannah	Houston
McKinney,		McLane, James	Houston
Archibald	Bowie	McLane, William Z.	Houston
McKinney, Ashley	Grayson	McLaughlin, James	Harrison
McKinney, C.	Collin	McLaughlin, James	Washington
McKinney, Cary	Galveston	McLaughlin, John	Harrison
McKinney, Collin	Bowie	McLaughlin, Levi	Harrison
McKinney, Daniel	Cass	McLaughlin,	
McKinney, G. Y.	Collin	William	Harris
McKinney, H.	San Augustine	McLaughlin,	
McKinney, H. C.	Grayson	William T.	Grimes
McKinney, J.	Collin	McLaurin, Agness	Travis
McKinney, J. B.	Cass	McLean, Hanson	Liberty
McKinney, J. N.	Cass	McLean, Harrison	Harris
McKinney, J. W. N.	Cass	McLean, James B.	Limestone
McKinney, James	Cass	McLean, N.	Harrison
McKinney, Marcus	Grayson	McLelland, John J.	Cherokee
McKinney, Mary	Grayson	McLennan, John	Milam
McKinney, Rolin	Milam	McLennan, Neill	Milam
McKinney, T. F.	Burleson	McLemore, A.	Shelby
McKinney, T. F.	Galveston	McLemore, Richard	Lamar
McKinney, W. C.	Collin	McLeod, H.	Henderson
McKinney, William	Harrison	McLeod, J. A.	Sabine
McKinney, William	Milam	McLeod, John D.	Travis
McKinney, William		McLeroy, J. W.	Sabine
C.	Bowie	McLure, John F.	Nacogdoches
McKinney, Y. X.	Bowie	McMahan, A. W.	Henderson
McKinsey, John	Houston	McMahan, D. F.	Bastrop
McKinsey, Lacy	Houston	McMahan, Daniel	Grimes
McKinsey, Richard	Limestone	McMahan, Friend,	
McKinsey, Rowland	Limestone	Jr.	Newton
McKinsey, William	San Augustine	McMahan, George W.	Fort Bend
McKisick, John W.	Fayette	McMahan, Isaac	Newton
McKisick, M. J. D.	Grimes	McMahan, James	Newton
McKisick, W. Y. H.	Grimes	McMahan, Martin,	
McKnight, A. E. T.	Washington	Jr.	Fort Bend
McKnight, C. D.	Nacogdoches	McMahan, S. W.	Harrison

NAME	COUNTY	NAME	COUNTY
McMahan, Sam D.	Sabine	McNeal, Sarah E.	Travis
McMahan, T. H.	Fort Bend	McNeal, T. S.	Matagorda
McMahan, W. W.	Fort Bend	McNeal, W.	Collin
McMahan, William,		McNeese, Delancy	Washington
Jr.	Newton	McNeese, Ivy	Montgomery
McMahan, William,		McNeese, John	Washington
Sr.	Newton	McNeese, P. W.	Washington
McManus, Jacob	Lamar	McNeese, William	Titus
McManus, R. O. W.	Liberty	McNeill, A.	Grimes
McMaster, ---	Goliad	Mcneill, Angus	Colorado
McMaster, William	Brazoria	Mcneill, Archibald	Colorado
McMeans, Eleazer	Nacogdoches	McNeill, Daniel B.	Brazoria
McMelon, A.	Austin	McNeill, Hector	Bastrop
McMenneny, Isaac		McNeill, James W.	Cherokee
A.	Fannin	McNeill, John G.	Brazoria
McMenneny, John	Fannin	McNeill, John	
McMenneny, William	Fannin	Shelby	Brazoria
McMichael, J. H.	Bexar	McNeill, Leander	
McMicken, Andrew	Fayette	H.	Brazoria
McMillion, A.	Collin	McNeill, Neill	San Augustine
McMillion, William	Nacogdoches	McNeill, P. B.	Brazoria
McMillon, Andrew	Brazos	McNeill, W. P.	Cass
McMillon, Edward	Robertson	McNulty, Joseph	Robertson
McMillon, George	Brazos	McNutt, H.	Nacogdoches
McMillon, Hiram	Lamar	McNutt, J.	Grimes
McMillon, Isham	Fayette	McNutt, Robert	Austin
McMillon, J.	Victoria	McPeters, Jonathan	Smith
McMillon, James	Brazos	McPeters, Thomas	Fayette
McMillon, Jeremiah	Rusk	McPeake, William	Fannin
McMillon, John	Colorado	McPhail, A. E.	Fannin
McMillon, John	Panola	McPhail, R. N.	Fannin
McMillon, Lrew	Walker	McPhail, Robert	Fannin
McMillon, M. A.	Walker	McQueen, H. F.	Panola
McMillon, Newton	Colorado	McQueen, John F.	Jasper
McMillon, S. B.	Titus	McQueen, Jonathan	Shelby
McMillon, Thomas	Walker	McRae, Alexander	Montgomery
McMillon, William	Harris	McRae, Archibald	Refugio
McMillon, William	Panola	McRae, James	Montgomery
McMillon, William,		McRae, John H.	Sabine
Jr.	Panola	McReynolds, J. M.	Collin
McMinn, John	Lamar	McReynolds, John	Fayette
McMullen, John	Bexar	McRhea, William	Grimes
McMurry, James L.	Robertson	McRory, Wilson	Shelby
McMurry, Joseph A.	Burleson	McShan, William B.	San Augustine
McMurry, Thomas	Austin	McTenarl, S.	Goliad
McNabb, Jackson	Travis	McVain, Daniel	Shelby
McNabb, John	Fort Bend	McVey, William	Rusk
McNair, James	Colorado	McWhirter, J. R.	Cass
McNeal, G.	Collin	McWhorter, A. A.	Grimes
McNeal, Jesse	Red River	McWhorter, A. F.	Grimes

NAME	COUNTY	NAME	COUNTY
McWhorter, C. L.	Grimes	Maine, Elisha	Anderson
McWhorter, J. B.	Bowie	Maine, Makin	Anderson
McWhorter, James		Maine, William	Anderson
H.	Grimes	Maismer, B.	Colorado
McWhorter, John R.	Grimes	Makinsey, Cully	Anderson
Maass, Peter	Bexar	Malden, J.	Cass
Maass, Samuel	Galveston	Maley, George D.	Liberty
Maass, Samuel	Henderson	Maley, William	Liberty
Maberry, David	Rusk	Mall, Caleb	Fayette
Maberry, J. H.	Rusk	Mall, Jonathan	Fayette
Maberry, John W.	Burleson	Mallerd, E.	Henderson
Mabry, E.	Bastrop	Mallerd, J. B.	Anderson
Mabry, J. K.	Harris	Mallich, Edward	Gonzales
Mabry, S. W.	Bastrop	Mallich, Paul	Colorado
Mackey, Elias	Limestone	Mallon, N. R.	Bexar
Mackey, James	Austin	Mallory, James H.	Nacogdoches
Mackey, John	Matagorda	Mallory, Joel H.	Nacogdoches
Macle, Francois	Bexar	Mallory, John H.	Harrison
Macrea, William	Washington	Malone, D. C.	Grimes
Maculkister, M. D.	Anderson	Malone, Isaac	Limestone
Madden, D. B.	Washington	Malone, John	Lavaca
Madden, Lucinda	Houston	Malone, S. B.	Liberty
Madden, R. W.	Fannin	Malone, Thomas	Anderson
Madden, Robert	Anderson	Maloy, Andrew	Harrison
Maddox, Jesse	Burleson	Maloy, John	Harrison
Maddox, Nicholas	Grayson	Malpoose, William	Fayette
Maddox, T.	Walker	Maltly, Thomas D.	Bexar
Maddox, W.	Lamar	Malugen, Joseph	Fannin
Madeley, G. B.	Harris	Man, Hugh	DeWitt
Madgen, Francis I.	Burleson	Man, J. W.	Harrison
Magee, Daniel	Grimes	Manadin, W. H.	Brazoria
Magee, Ervin	Limestone	Manard, Peter J.	Polk
Magee, Felix W.	Grimes	Mancha, Jose	Goliad
Magee, Martha C.	Grimes	Mancha, Jose S.	Henderson
Magee, Nehemiah	Grimes	Mancha, Tomias	Goliad
Magee, Philip	Grimes	Mancon, Andrew	Anderson
Mageen, Bryan	Galveston	Mandiola, Yg.	Bexar
Mageen, James	Galveston	Manford, James	Rusk
Magg, Adam	Bexar	Mangham, M. B.	Grimes
Magia, Nestro	Guadalupe	Manier, William	Anderson
Magill, John H.	Galveston	Manion, A. B.	Lamar
Magness, J. B.	Shelby	Manis, S.	Limestone
Magness, T. H.	Lamar	Manis, Shadrack	Limestone
Magrill, J. R.	Upshur	Manker, Allen	Cass
Magrill, S. D.	Upshur	Manlove, B.	Bastrop
Mahafey, Amos	Jasper	Manly, A. P.	Fayette
Mahan, Andrew	Brazos	Manly, Asbury	Fannin
Mahan, P., Jr.	Harris	Manly, Daniel	Bowie
Mahone, William M.	Cass	Mann, James E.	Grimes
Mahoney, Peter	San Patricio	Mann, M. V.	Panola

110

NAME	COUNTY	NAME	COUNTY
Mann, Thomas B.	Washington	Marsh, Shubel	Washington
Mann, W.	Washington	Marsh, William R.	Montgomery
Mann, W. T.	Tyler	Marshall, Benjamin	
Mannin, A. C.	Dallas	G.	Fort Bend
Mannin, J.	Collin	Marshall, Bexar	Bexar
Manning, B.	Milam	Marshall, Elijah	Austin
Manning, G. S.	Cass	Marshall, Elijah	Goliad
Manning, J. W.	Austin	Marshall, Elvira	Grimes
Manning, Levi	Grimes	Marshall, Isom	DeWitt
Manning, Levi	Limestone	Marshall, J. C.	Shelby
Manning, Mark	Walker	Marshall, J. D.	Milam
Manning, May	Grimes	Marshall, J. L.	Fayette
Manning, R. J.	Harris	Marshall, James	Leon
Manning, Stephen	Gonzales	Marshall, John	Anderson
Manor, Charles	Brazoria	Marshall, John	Shelby
Manshaca, Antonio	Robertson	Marshall, John R.	Galveston
Mansher, Sebastian	Cherokee	Marshall, Joseph	Grimes
Manson, L. C.	Brazoria	Marshall, Samuel	Austin
Manton, Edward	Fayette	Marshall, Thomas	
Manuel, David	Tyler	W.	Galveston
Manur, John A.	San Augustine	Marshall, William	Newton
Manwaring, William	Nacogdoches	Marston, Daniel,	
Many, J. B.	Rusk	Jr.	Galveston
Marble, Lewis	Burleson	Marston, T. R.	Grimes
Marble, Stephen R.	Jefferson	Martain, James	Henderson
March, D. T.	Cass	Martain, T.	Henderson
March, William H.	Harris	Martell, Henry	Fayette
Marcha, Agapo	Goliad	Martin, A.	Montgomery
Marchal, Joel G.	Titus	Martin, A. W.	Smith
Marchal, Stephetre	Titus	Martin, Aaron	Cherokee
Marcus, Pearl	Austin	Martin, Albert	Goliad
Mardoff, Henry	Bastrop	Martin, Alex	Guadalupe
Marey, Polly	Sabine	Martin, Alexander	Gonzales
Mariner, C.	Grimes	Martin, Andrew	Cass
Markey, James K.	Grimes	Martin, Camilon	Galveston
Marks, Joseph	Panola	Martin, Caroline	Grimes
Marley, W.	Grimes	Martin, Charles	Harris
Marlor, H. W.	Red River	Martin, Daniel	Panola
Marlor, R. W.	Harrison	Martin, E.	Burleson
Marlow, Edward	Fayette	Martin, E. D.	Sabine
Marr, Kinzy	Hunt	Martin, E. L.	San Augustine
Marr, Lewis	Hunt	Martin, E. W.	Harrison
Mars, J. R.	Fannin	Martin, G.	Collin
Mars, James	Newton	Martin, G. L.	Polk
Mars, James H.	Grayson	Martin, G. W.	Harrison
Marsh, C. C.	Goliad	Martin, G. W.	Henderson
Marsh, H. C.	Dallas	Martin, George	Harris
Marsh, M.	Collin	Martin, Harriet	Sabine
Marsh, R.	Montgomery	Martin, Henry	Harrison
Marsh, Shubel	Grimes	Martin, Isaiah	Brazos

NAME	COUNTY	NAME	COUNTY
Martin, J.	Angelina	Martin, William G.	Harris
Martin, J.	Matagorda	Martin, William N.	
Martin, J. F.	Brazos	P.	Limestone
Martin, J. G.	Titus	Martin, Zadok	Hopkins
Martin, J. S.	Anderson	Martinas,	
Martin, J. S.	Leon	Guadalupe	Henderson
Martin, James	Limestone	Martinas,	
Martin, James	San Augustine	Perfector	Guadalupe
Martin, James B.	Polk	Martinez, Aus.	Bexar
Martin, James H.	Sabine	Martinez,	
Martin, James R.	Liberty	Francisco	Nacogdoches
Martin, Janice	Anderson	Martinez, Gabriel	Bexar
Martin, Job R.	Anderson	Martinez,	
Martin, John	Grayson	Guadalupe	Henderson
Martin, John	Limestone	Martinez, Jose	Bexar
Martin, John	Nacogdoches	Martinez, Jose	Nacogdoches
Martin, John F.	Grimes	Martinez, Manuel	Goliad
Martin, Joseph	Cass	Martinez, Ramon	Bexar
Martin, Joseph	Goliad	Mashpack, R. P.	Washington
Martin, Joseph S.	Gonzales	Mason, A. H.	Walker
Martin, Josiah	Angelina	Mason, Charles	Travis
Martin, Keziah	Lamar	Mason, Elija	Tyler
Martin, Lewis	Colorado	Mason, G.	Grimes
Martin, Lucy	Liberty	Mason, G. W.	Montgomery
Martin, M. C.	Cass	Mason, H. D.	Red River
Martin, Matthew M.	Lamar	Mason, J. A.	Bexar
Martin, Neal	Nacogdoches	Mason, James	Sabine
Martin, P. C.	Panola	Mason, Job	Sabine
Martin, Peter	Fort Bend	Mason, John	Sabine
Martin, Peter	Galveston	Mason, Joseph A.	Harris
Martin, Peter S.	Rusk	Mason, Joseph V.	Brazoria
Martin, R. B.	Montgomery	Mason, Lewis	San Augustine
Martin, R. P.	Liberty	Mason, Reddin	Harrison
Martin, R. W.	San Augustine	Mason, Richard	Sabine
Martin, Richard	Gonzales	Mason, Samuel	Austin
Martin, Robert	Liberty	Mason, William	Harrison
Martin, Robert	Rusk	Mason, William	Henderson
Martin, S. W.	Limestone	Mason, William	Hopkins
Martin, Thomas	Sabine	Mason, William	Sabine
Martin, Toliver	Grimes	Massa, A. D.	Harrison
Martin, Vincent	Lamar	Massa, D. M.	Harrison
Martin, W.	Collin	Massa, George W.	Harrison
Martin, W. B.	Bastrop	Massey, J. N.	Fort Bend
Martin, W. C.	Anderson	Massey, V.	Liberty
Martin, William	Cass	Massey, William S.	Walker
Martin, William	Colorado	Massengill, George	Angelina
Martin, William	Grayson	Massengill, H.	Houston
Martin, William	Nacogdoches	Massengill, Henry	Angelina
Martin, William	Smith	Massengill, Isaac	Angelina
Martin, William B.	Navarro	Massengill, John	Angelina

NAME	COUNTY	NAME	COUNTY
Massengill, Nathan	Angelina	Matson, Jacob	Galveston
Massie, J. C.	Grimes	Matson, James	Washington
Massie, J. W.	Rusk	Matson, William	Washington
Massie, Mary	Rusk	Matterson, Thomas	Nacogdoches
Massie, W. W.	Washington	Matterson, William	
Mast, Jacob	Nacogdoches	P.	Nacogdoches
Masters, Henry	Houston	Mattheson, W.	Lamar
Masters, Jacob,		Matthews, A.	Robertson
Jr.	Houston	Matthews, Barton	
Masters, Jacob,		H.	Hopkins
Sr.	Houston	Matthews, F. C.	Hopkins
Masters, Wm.	Henderson	Matthews, F. S.	Red River
Masterson, Thomas		Matthews, George	Nacogdoches
G.	Brazoria	Matthews, Henry	Austin
Mastyn, H. F.	Goliad	Matthews, Isaac	Smith
Matheny, Samuel	Lamar	Matthews,	
Mather, Edmund	Harris	Jefferson	Limestone
Mather, Joseph	Red River	Matthews, John	Hopkins
Mathews, Abner	Travis	Matthews, John	Walker
Mathews, Catherine	Panola	Matthews, L. H.	Henderson
Mathews, D. M.	Galveston	Matthews, M. W.	Hopkins
Mathews, David W.	Harrison	Matthews, R. H.	Robertson
Mathews, E. W.	Limestone	Matthews, R. T.	Walker
Mathews, J. B.	Collin	Matthews, Robert	Robertson
Mathews, J. R.	Montgomery	Matthews, Robert	
Mathews, James	Panola	E.	Hopkins
Mathews, James	Travis	Matthews, W.	Harris
Mathews, John	Colorado	Matthews, W. G.	San Augustine
Mathews, John	Nacogdoches	Matthews, William	
Mathews, John G.	Travis	C.	Hopkins
Mathews, John H.	Bexar	Matthews, William	
Mathews, Martin	Nacogdoches	H.	Henderson
Mathews, Nathan	Shelby	Matthews, William	
Mathews, R.	Harrison	H.	Hopkins
Mathews, Robert	Limestone	Matthews, Z. W.	Austin
Mathews, Robert L.	Titus	Mattox, Wade H.	Newton
Mathews, Simon	Harrison	Maulding, E. C.	Shelby
Mathews, Simon	Houston	Maulding, J. W.	Victoria
Mathews, Simon H.	Harrison	Maulding, P.	Bowie
Mathews, William	Cherokee	Maulding, Richard	Harrison
Mathews, William	Panola	Maux, D. O.	Henderson
Mathews, William		Mauzy, W. H.	Lamar
H.	Harrison	Maverick, S. A.	Matagorda
Mathews, Wm. A.	Gonzales	Maxamilian, A.	Henderson
Mathis, August	Houston	Maxey, Elisha	Brazoria
Mathis, D. K.	Red River	Maxey, Sarah	Brazoria
Mathis, Daniel	Red River	Maxey, William	Polk
Mathis, Lidy	Leon	Maxfield, William	Nacogdoches
Mathus, Samuel	Dallas	Maxim, David	Shelby
Matson, Jacob	Brazoria	Maximillio,	

NAME	COUNTY	NAME	COUNTY
Antonio	Grimes	Meador, B. W.	Sabine
Maxon, Lyons	Panola	Meador, Catherine	
Maxwell, J. W.	Collin	M.	Sabine
Maxwell, James	Cass	Meador, Nancy	Liberty
Maxwell, James	Hopkins	Meador, Richard	Sabine
Maxwell, R.	Fayette	Meadors, Joel	Navarro
Maxwell, Thomas	Austin	Meadows, Daniel	Washington
Maxwell, Thomas	Fayette	Meadows, Elijah	Smith
Maxwell, Thomas	Rusk	Meadows, Jacob	Shelby
Maxwell, William	Austin	Meadows, James	Fort Bend
May, A. J.	Fannin	Meadows, Richard	
May, G. P.	Jasper	E.	Smith
May, Grosvener H.	Gonzales	Meagles, Moses	Rusk
May, James	DeWitt	Mealor, Mary A.	Colorado
May, John	DeWitt	Means, William	DeWitt
May, John J.	DeWitt	Measles, James	Rusk
May, Joshua	Fannin	Mebane, Abner	Lamar
May, Morris	Gonzales	Mebane, J. A.	Lamar
Maybee, George	Goliad	Mebane, J. H.	Lamar
Mayes, Andrew	Bastrop	Mebane, James	Lamar
Mayes, John D.	Polk	Mebane, R. W.	Lamar
Mayes, Squire	Lamar	Meberry, S. S.	Henderson
Mayes, Thomas H.	Bastrop	Meckel, F. Ph.	Comal
Mayes, Watson P.	Fort Bend	Medford, Isom	Angelina
Mayfield, Joseph		Medford, Isom	Cherokee
S.	Fayette	Medford, J.	Henderson
Mayfield, Michael	Harris	Medford, John A.	Rusk
Mayfield, S. C.	Grimes	Medford, Jonathan	Cherokee
Mayfield, Sanders	Bowie	Medford, Levi	Cherokee
Mayfield, Sophia		Medi, M. P.	Anderson
Ann	Fayette	Medlin, G. B.	Upshur
Mayfield, T.	Navarro	Medlin, P.	Victoria
Mayfield, William	Brazos	Medlock, Thomas	Houston
Mayfield, William	Navarro	Meek, James M.	Washington
Maynard, C. O.	Matagorda	Meek, John M.	Fort Bend
Maynard, Harvey	Matagorda	Meek, W. D.	Washington
Maynard, W. J.	Matagorda	Meen, D. D.	Henderson
Mays, Abner	Liberty	Megginson, J. C.	Montgomery
Mays, Garner	Liberty	Megina, Rocinto	Nacogdoches
Mays, George	Liberty	Meirs, E. R.	Polk
Mays, John	Shelby	Meirs, Nel	Navarro
Mays, John J.	Liberty	Meisner, Andress	Comal
Mays, Joshua	Liberty	Mellor, Robert	Galveston
Mays, Matthew	Shelby	Melown, Eleazer	San Augustine
Mays, Robert	Shelby	Melown, James	San Augustine
Mays, T. S.	Travis	Melown, Thomas	San Augustine
Mays, William	Shelby	Melton, Jeremiah	Navarro
Mayson, Joseph	Harrison	Melton, Jonathan	Robertson
Maze, Thomas	Sabine	Melton, S.	Walker
Mead, George W.	Panola	Menard, M. B.	Galveston

NAME	COUNTY	NAME	COUNTY
Menard, Midard	Galveston	A.	Washington
Menard, Mrs. P.	Galveston	Merrell, David	Dallas
Mendis, Antonio	Nacogdoches	Merrell, Eli	Cass
Mendosa, Jose	Nacogdoches	Merrell, Eli, Jr.	Dallas
Mendosa, Lewis	Goliad	Merrell, Eli, Sr.	Dallas
Menefee, George S.	Jackson	Merrell, Nelson	Milam
Menefee, J. S.	Goliad	Merrell, W. B.	Fannin
Menefee, Jarat	Limestone	Merrick, George	Lamar
Menefee, John	Wharton	Merrick, James	Hunt
Menefee, John S.	Jackson	Merrimon, ---	Henderson
Menefee, Susan	Leon	Merrimon, F. H.	Galveston
Menefee, Thomas	Jackson	Merrit, Ann	Washington
Menefee, Thomas	Wharton	Merrit, Daniel	Liberty
Menefee, Thomas S.	Limestone	Merrit, J. E.	Nacogdoches
Menefee, William	Limestone	Merrit, R.	Liberty
Menefee, William	Wharton	Merrit, Robert	Washington
Mengs, T. J.	Upshur	Merrit, T. G.	Galveston
Meniel, Lewis	Travis	Merritt, G. B.	Harrison
Mercer, Celia K.	Burleson	Merritt, Josiah	Walker
Mercer, E. G.	Wharton	Merriwether, F. L.	Harrison
Mercer, Eli	Wharton	Merriwether, W. H.	Bexar
Mercer, Jesse	Milam	Merriwether,	
Mercer, Levi	Wharton	William B.	Fayette
Mercer, Silvester	Polk	Merton, J.	Cass
Merchant, B.	Titus	Merts, E. C.	Austin
Merchant, E. A.	Hopkins	Mertz, C. C.	Comal
Merchant, J. S. W.	Nacogdoches	Mertz, John	Comal
Merchant, John D.	Henderson	Messer, Charles	Wharton
Merchant, John D.	Nacogdoches	Metcalf, John	Fort Bend
Merchant, Sarah P.	Nacogdoches	Metcalf, Silas	Rusk
Merchison, John	Anderson	Methvin, O. N.	Upshur
Merchison, John	Fayette	Metz, George	Travis
Merchison, L.	Houston	Metz, H. W.	Travis
Merchison, Martin	Houston	Meux, Thomas O.	Galveston
Meredith, Daniel	Cherokee	Mewcuir, Aug.	Bexar
Meredith, David	Houston	Meyer, Daniel H.	Goliad
Meredith, George		Meyer, Joseph	Bexar
W.	Houston	Meyerbrough, L.	Colorado
Meredith, H. J.	Guadalupe	Meyo, E.	Victoria
Meredith, James L.	Rusk	Mhoon, William M.	San Augustine
Meredith, Joseph	Guadalupe	Micham, Hezekiah	Anderson
Meredith, P.	Henderson	Michell, J.	
Meredith, William	Grayson	Vinciento	Henderson
Mergel, Peter	Comal	Michell, Vicente	Nacogdoches
Merida, Samuel	Grayson	Michels, Berry	Titus
Merrell, A. F.	Fannin	Michels, Henry	Harris
Merrell, Benjamin	Cass	Michlick, C.	Harris
Merrell, Benjamin	Dallas	Mickleborough, E.	Grimes
Merrell, Brandon	Goliad	Mickleborough, H.	Grimes
Merrell, Charles		Mickler, Jacob	Anderson

NAME	COUNTY	NAME	COUNTY
Middlebrook,		Miller, David	DeWitt
Anderson	Nacogdoches	Miller, David	Goliad
Middlebrook, Ibzan	Nacogdoches	Miller, Drury	Burleson
Middleton, Benona	Leon	Miller, E. M.	Lamar
Middleton, John W.	Washington	Miller, Elizabeth	Colorado
Middleton, R. D.	Cherokee	Miller, Elizabeth	Rusk
Middleton, S.	Henderson	Miller, F. H.	Harrison
Middleton, S. P.	Jasper	Miller, F. L.	Leon
Middleton, Samuel	Brazos	Miller, George	Lavaca
Middleton, Thomas	Leon	Miller, George	San Augustine
Middleton, W. B.	Leon	Miller, George W.	Washington
Middleton,		Miller, Greene	Titus
Washington	Brazos	Miller, Henry	Dallas
Middleton, William	Tyler	Miller, Isaac	Shelby
Middleton, William		Miller, J. C.	Rusk
H.	Cherokee	Miller, J. P.	Sabine
Middleton, William		Miller, J. W.	Harris
R.	Grayson	Miller, Jacob A.	DeWitt
Midkiff, P. D.	Harrison	Miller, James	Grayson
Midlin, Walter	Galveston	Miller, James B.	Fort Bend
Milam, E. S.	Collin	Miller, James F.	Fayette
Milburn, D. H.	Brazoria	Miller, James M.	Cherokee
Milby, Henry H.	Harris	Miller, James T.	Dallas
Milby, Robert	Goliad	Miller, Jesse	Guadalupe
Milby, Robert	Jackson	Miller, John	Panola
Milender, Jane	Anderson	Miller, John D.	Anderson
Miles, Edward	Bexar	Miller, John F.	Colorado
Miles, Francis	Bexar	Miller, John F.	Goliad
Miles, G. W.	Liberty	Miller, John F.	Travis
Miles, John	Houston	Miller, John H.	Travis
Miles, Sarah	Fayette	Miller, John R.	Fayette
Miley, Daniel	Grimes	Miller, John R.	Fort Bend
Milford, John	Anderson	Miller, John W.	Lamar
Milholland, B. W.	Hopkins	Miller, Joseph	Brazoria
Milhorn, Francis	Jasper	Miller, Joseph	San Augustine
Millard, Alfred	Galveston	Miller, Joseph	Victoria
Millard, D. J.		Miller, Leroy	San Augustine
Otho	Jefferson	Miller, Lorance	Austin
Millard, Massa	Nacogdoches	Miller, Lucretia	Limestone
Millard, Nancy	Jefferson	Miller, M.	Limestone
Millard, R. F.	Nacogdoches	Miller, Madison M.	Dallas
Millemon, J. S.	Montgomery	Miller, Mark M.	Harrison
Miller, Adam	Hopkins	Miller, Martin	Titus
Miller, Alsey S.	Gonzales	Miller, Michael	DeWitt
Miller, Andrew	Rusk	Miller, N. G.	Lamar
Miller, Arnold	Fort Bend	Miller, N. H.	Montgomery
Miller, B.	Harris	Miller, Philip	Fayette
Miller, C.	Colorado	Miller, Philip	Liberty
Miller, C. W.	Bastrop	Miller, Richard	Lamar
Miller, Daniel	Colorado	Miller, Riley C.	Washington

NAME	COUNTY	NAME	COUNTY
Miller, Robert	Grimes	Milliken, George	
Miller, Robert	Limestone	H.	Houston
Miller, Robert	San Augustine	Milliken, H. C.	Houston
Miller, S. A.	Cass	Milliken, John	Houston
Miller, S. A.	Houston	Mills, D. G.	Brazoria
Miller, S. L.	Guadalupe	Mills, Edward L.	Jackson
Miller, S. R.	Guadalupe	Mills, F. E.	Austin
Miller, Samuel	Bastrop	Mills, Henry	Liberty
Miller, Samuel	Fayette	Mills, J. S.	Liberty
Miller, Samuel	Grimes	Mills, James	Goliad
Miller, Sarah L.	Fayette	Mills, James L.	Jackson
Miller, Simon	Burleson	Mills, John R.	Galveston
Miller, Solomon	San Augustine	Mills, Mary C.	Liberty
Miller, Stephen	Austin	Mills, N. T.	Shelby
Miller, Theo.	Goliad	Mills, R.	Brazoria
Miller, Thomas R.	Gonzales	Mills, Rebecca	Jackson
Miller, Travis	Colorado	Mills, Robert	Grimes
Miller, W. G.	Red River	Mills, Robert G.	Galveston
Miller, W. P.	Victoria	Mills, Robert H.	Newton
Miller, W. T.	Anderson	Mills, S. M.	Shelby
Miller, William	Fayette	Mills, S. P.	Liberty
Miller, William	Montgomery	Mills, S. P.	Liberty
Miller, William	Panola	Mills, W. J.	Liberty
Miller, William	Washington	Mills, William	Henderson
Miller, William P.	Goliad	Mills, William	Walker
Miller, Z. B.	Lamar	Mills, William J.	Galveston
Millett, S.	Grimes	Mills, William P.	Goliad
Millican, Andrew,		Millsap, Thomas	Grayson
adm.	Brazos	Millsap, William	Cass
Millican, C. C.	Galveston	Millstead, John	Titus
Millican, Charity,		Mims, Gid	Red River
adm.	Brazos	Mims, Henry	Cass
Millican, Creed T.	Burleson	Mims, Henry	Lavaca
Millican, D. L.	Brazos	Mims, S. L.	Brazoria
Millican, Diadem,		Mims, Stephen W.	Harrison
adm.		Mims, William D.	Cass
Millican, E. M.	Brazos	Mims, William H.	Houston
Millican, James	Brazos	Minchew, J. G.	Nacogdoches
Millican, James D.	Brazos	Minchew, Jonas	Nacogdoches
Millican, John	Brazos	Minchew, Sarah	Liberty
Millican, John N.	Brazos	Minor, Henry	Bowie
Millican, Robert		Minor, J.	Travis
G.	Goliad	Minor, J. J.	Travis
Millican, Wesley	Brazos	Minor, James	Travis
Millican, William	Goliad	Minor, Jarvis	Travis
Millican, William		Minter, G. W.	Dallas
L.	Jackson	Minton, Alfred	Austin
Milligan, J. H.	Titus	Mirando, Macedonio	Cass
Milligan, T. S.	Upshur	Mires, L. S.	Anderson
Milligan, W. G.	Upshur	Miskell, George A.	DeWitt

NAME	COUNTY	NAME	COUNTY
Miskell, Martha C.	DeWitt	Mitchell, William	
Miskell, William	DeWitt	L.	Gonzales
Mitchell, A. G.	Sabine	Mitchell, William	
Mitchell, Alfred	Panola	R.	Montgomery
Mitchell, Asa	Washington	Mitchinson, J. R.	Washington
Mitchell, Bluford	Angelina	Mixon, J. B.	Victoria
Mitchell, D. R.	Robertson	Mixon, Jeremiah	Jefferson
Mitchell, David	Navarro	Mixon, Noel	Harris
Mitchell, E.	Shelby	Mixon, Simon S.	Milam
Mitchell, E. C.	Walker	Mobiety, Myers	Navarro
Mitchell, Eli	Gonzales	Mock, L. W.	Walker
Mitchell, G. W.	Harrison	Mockford, William	Travis
Mitchell, George		Mode, William	Hunt
B., Jr.	Cass	Modin, J.	Anderson
Mitchell, H. B.	Matagorda	Modley, J.	Cass
Mitchell, Harvey	Brazos	Moffitt, Anna C.	Galveston
Mitchell, Henry	Houston	Moffitt, J. H.	Nacogdoches
Mitchell, Isaac	Lavaca	Moffitt, J. P.	Wharton
Mitchell, J. H.	Bexar	Moffitt, J. W.	Nacogdoches
Mitchell, J. N.	Jackson	Moffitt, Paul G.	Grimes
Mitchell, J. N.	Victoria	Moffitt, Thomas	Grimes
Mitchell, J. W.	Collin	Moirs, Joseph	Titus
Mitchell, James	Shelby	Mojanas, Eusebe	Bexar
Mitchell, James	Walker	Mojanas, Francois	Bexar
Mitchell, James H.	Montgomery	Mojanas, Manuel	Bexar
Mitchell, James H.	Robertson	Molavis, Carlos	Goliad
Mitchell, Jesse A.	San Augustine	Molyneaus, John	Brazoria
Mitchell, John	Panola	Moncrief, John A.	Houston
Mitchell, John	Titus	Monday, Benjamin	Lamar
Mitchell, John H.	Rusk	Mondiola,	
Mitchell, John R.	Dallas	Ferdinand	Goliad
Mitchell, John S.	Cass	Money, John H.	Washington
Mitchell, Jonathan	Goliad	Mongala, Clemente	Bexar
Mitchell, Joseph	Fannin	Monk, J. H.	Lamar
Mitchell, M. A.	Robertson	Monk, J. W.	Lamar
Mitchell, M. M.	Cass	Monk, Jerym	Red River
Mitchell, M. M.	Harrison	Monkhouse, John	Red River
Mitchell, Martha	Robertson	Monod, C.	Calhoun
Mitchell, N. J.	Harrison	Monroe, Aaron	Fayette
Mitchell, Peter	Harrison	Monroe, Daniel	Milam
Mitchell, R.	Cass	Monroe, Jane	Shelby
Mitchell, R. P.	Red River	Monroe, William	Milam
Mitchell, Reuben	Red River	Montague, Daniel	Fannin
Mitchell, Robert	Travis	Montague, John F.	Harris
Mitchell, S. T.	Harrison	Monteithe, Jesse	Henderson
Mitchell, Stephen	Panola	Monteithe, Jesse	Nacogdoches
Mitchell, Thomas		Monteithe, Samuel	Angelina
S.	Henderson	Montel, Charles	Bexar
Mitchell, W. S.	Cass	Montes, C.	Bexar
Mitchell, W. S.	Rusk	Montes, Jose	Nacogdoches

NAME	COUNTY	NAME	COUNTY
Montgomery, Andrew	Grimes	Moor, Richard	Titus
Montgomery, Benson	Henderson	Moor, Standford	Titus
Montgomery, C.	Henderson	Moor, William	Fayette
Montgomery, Edly	Grimes	Moore, A.	Burleson
Montgomery, F.	Henderson	Moore, A.	Henderson
Montgomery, Farriss	Nacogdoches	Moore, A.	Nacogdoches
		Moore, A.	Washington
Montgomery, J. M.	Harris	Moore, A. H.	Anderson
Montgomery, J. S.	Colorado	Moore, A. M.	Henderson
Montgomery, James	Hopkins	Moore, A. W.	Washington
Montgomery, John	Fort Bend	Moore, B. W.	Red River
Montgomery, John	Henderson	Moore, C.	Fannin
Montgomery, John	Hopkins	Moore, Cyrus A.	Titus
Montgomery, John	Red River	Moore, D.	Cass
Montgomery, R. W.	Travis	Moore, D. C.	Cherokee
Montgomery, S. R.	Harrison	Moore, D. C.	Harrison
Montgomery, Samuel	Wharton	Moore, E. D.	Red River
Montgomery, Stephen	Rusk	Moore, Eli	Cass
		Moore, Elisha	Shelby
Montgomery, T. M.	Red River	Moore, Elizabeth	Bowie
Montgomery, W. T.	Red River	Moore, Elizabeth	Navarro
Montgomery, William	Rusk	Moore, G. W.	Shelby
		Moore, George W.	DeWitt
Montgomery, William	Sabine	Moore, Guilford	Washington
		Moore, H.	Cass
Montigue, George	Travis	Moore, H. A.	Bowie
Montrose, M. A.	Grimes	Moore, H. B.	Cass
Montz, Z.	Victoria	Moore, Isaac	Shelby
Moody, A.	Upshur	Moore, J. B.	Navarro
Moody, J. A.	Victoria	Moore, J. B. M.	Newton
Moody, J. H.	Cherokee	Moore, J. C.	Bowie
Moody, John D.	Brazos	Moore, J. C.	Milam
Moody, John M.	Grimes	Moore, J. D.	Harrison
Moody, William C.	Grimes	Moore, J. H.	Cass
Moon, G. L.	Shelby	Moore, J. P.	Henderson
Moon, James	Polk	Moore, J. W.	Grimes
Moon, Jesse	Dallas	Moore, James	Cass
Moon, Jonas	Cass	Moore, James	Harris
Moon, Malcolm	Shelby	Moore, James W.	Harris
Mooney, Edward	Hopkins	Moore, James W.	Limestone
Mooney, John	Nacogdoches	Moore, John	Grimes
Mooneyhan, James	Dallas	Moore, John	Matagorda
Mooneyhan, William	Dallas	Moore, John	Panola
Moor, A. P.	Travis	Moore, John	San Augustine
Moor, Burrel	Titus	Moore, Joseph	Houston
Moor, David	Titus	Moore, Joseph H.	Limestone
Moor, Edwin L.	Fayette	Moore, Josephus	Houston
Moor, Haywood	Fayette	Moore, Lemuel L.	Burleson
Moor, John H.	Fayette	Moore, Lovie P.	Washington
Moor, Lamar	Travis	Moore, Martha	Panola

NAME	COUNTY	NAME	COUNTY
Moore, Martin	Travis	Mora, Jose	Nacogdoches
Moore, Mrs. Mary		Mora, Juan	Nacogdoches
E.	Harrison	Mora, Maria Jose	Nacogdoches
Moore, Morris	Milam	Mora, Mariana	Nacogdoches
Moore, N. J.	Nacogdoches	Morales, Jose R.	Henderson
Moore, Nathaniel	Travis	Morales, M.	Goliad
Moore, Pheba	Robertson	Moran, Mary	Lamar
Moore, R.	Henderson	Moran, W. H.	Lamar
Moore, R. B.	Victoria	Morar, Sary	Titus
Moore, R. N.	Cass	Moray, William	Wharton
Moore, R. R.	Panola	More, J. B.	Walker
Moore, Ransel	Milam	More, James	Jasper
Moore, Richard	Limestone	More, Jovie	Goliad
Moore, Robert	Fort Bend	More, Simeon	Jasper
Moore, Robert	Washington	More, Thomas C.	Anderson
Moore, Robert C.	DeWitt	Moreno, Г.	Victoria
Moore, S.	Burleson	Morey, F. P.	Harris
Moore, S. F.	Cass	Morey & Harvey	Harris
Moore, S. F.	Red River	Morgan, A.	Hopkins
Moore, Samuel	Bowie	Morgan, A. J.	Anderson
Moore, Samuel	Limestone	Morgan, Anthony	Galveston
Moore, Samuel	Walker	Morgan, Barba	Limestone
Moore, T. J.	Nacogdoches	Morgan, Charles	Goliad
Moore, Thomas	Grimes	Morgan, Charles	Hopkins
Moore, Thomas	Leon	Morgan, Charles	Jefferson
Moore, Thomas A.	Travis	Morgan, Daniel	Anderson
Moore, Uriah	Smith	Morgan, Daniel	Hopkins
Moore, W.	Henderson	Morgan, David	Cass
Moore, W.	Hunt	Morgan, Edward	Hopkins
Moore, W.	Liberty	Morgan, G.	Upshur
Moore, W. J.	Nacogdoches	Morgan, G. W.	Limestone
Moore, W. R.	Polk	Morgan, Gabriel	Fannin
Moore, Whit	Red River	Morgan, George	Harris
Moore, William	Cass	Morgan, H. S.	Bastrop
Moore, William	Red River	Morgan, Hugh	Liberty
Moore, William B.	Harrison	Morgan, Isaac	Red River
Moore, William B.	Nacogdoches	Morgan, J. L.	Bowie
Moore, William H.	Cass	Morgan, J. V.	Anderson
Moore, William M.	Nacogdoches	Morgan, J. W.	Lamar
Moore & Blessing	Travis	Morgan, James	Cherokee
Moores, Anderson		Morgan, James	Harris
R.	Bowie	Morgan, John	Anderson
Moores, Charles	Bowie	Morgan, John	Galveston
Moores, E. H.	Bowie	Morgan, John	Washington
Mooring, G. W.	Grimes	Morgan, John T.	Hopkins
Mooring, L. G.	Grimes	Morgan, Joseph	Limestone
Moorman, C. W.	Panola	Morgan, Joshua	Fannin
Moorman, Charles	Panola	Morgan, Levi	Grimes
Mora, Anastacion	Nacogdoches	Morgan, Margaret	Hopkins
Mora, E.	Henderson	Morgan, Nathaniel	Cass

NAME	COUNTY	NAME	COUNTY
Morgan, R. B.	Harris	Morris, William C.	Shelby
Morgan, R. G.	Colorado	Morris, William H.	Dallas
Morgan, R. P.	Washington	Morris, William T.	Montgomery
Morgan, S. H.	Red River	Morris & Reilly	San Augustine
Morgan, Silas	Walker	Morrison, A.	Collin
Morgan, Thomas N.	Red River	Morrison, Andrew	Red River
Morgan, W. M.	Upshur	Morrison, C. L.	Henderson
Morgan, William J.	Limestone	Morrison, Daniel	Fannin
Morgan, Zachias	Hopkins	Morrison, Daniel	
Morman, James T.	Rusk	M.	Fannin
Morrell, A.	Cass	Morrison, Edward	Travis
Morrell, Amos	Red River	Morrison, Edward	
Morrell, John	Navarro	P.	Newton
Morrell, Reese V.	Navarro	Morrison, Francis	Lamar
Morrell, William		Morrison, G.	Montgomery
M.	Navarro	Morrison, Gwyn	Grimes
Morrell, Z. W.	Robertson	Morrison, J. P.	Fannin
Morris, Alfred	Sabine	Morrison, J. W.	Montgomery
Morris, Alfred W.	Newton	Morrison, James M.	Nacogdoches
Morris, B. F.	Montgomery	Morrison, John	Harris
Morris, Burrel	Polk	Morrison, John	Nacogdoches
Morris, David	Shelby	Morrison, John C.	Cherokee
Morris, Elijah	Shelby	Morrison, John C.	Shelby
Morris, Elisha	Shelby	Morrison, Joseph	Fannin
Morris, G. W.	San Augustine	Morrison, Joseph	
Morris, George	Bowie	H.	Fannin
Morris, George	Cass	Morrison, M.	Matagorda
Morris, H.	Cass	Morrison, William	
Morris, Isaac	Rusk	H.	Fannin
Morris, James	Shelby	Morrow, ---	Henderson
Morris, James	Walker	Morrow, Alfred	Fayette
Morris, James H.	Cass	Morrow, B. C. L.	Red River
Morris, James W.	Shelby	Morrow, Jacob	Anderson
Morris, John	Panola	Morrow, James	Fayette
Morris, John	Victoria	Morrow, James G.	Brazoria
Morris, John P.	Harris	Morse, John W.	Matagorda
Morris, Joseph	Lamar	Mortimer, Thomas	
Morris, Lee	Bowie	N.	Harris
Morris, Mary	Bowie	Morton, J. P.	Colorado
Morris, Mary	Galveston	Morton, Jessey	Anderson
Morris, R.	Harris	Morton, John	Anderson
Morris, R. D.	Bowie	Morton, John	Titus
Morris, Robert C.	Henderson	Morton, John W.	Jefferson
Morris, Seth	Bowie	Morton, Levi	Anderson
Morris, Seth	Cass	Morton, Rufus	Titus
Morris, Spencer	Leon	Morton, Rusion	Titus
Morris, Thomas	Colorado	Morton, Sinda	Titus
Morris, Thomas	Panola	Mosely, A.	Upshur
Morris, Washington	Panola	Mosely, Dandridge	Harrison
Morris, William	Victoria	Mosely, Daniel	Harrison

121

NAME	COUNTY	NAME	COUNTY
Mosely, E.	Cherokee	Mudgett, M.	Grayson
Mosely, J. H.	Shelby	Muldrow, J. H.	Grimes
Mosely, M.	Upshur	Muldrow, William	Grimes
Mosely, Marvel H.	Shelby	Mullen, Peter	Washington
Mosely, Wade C.	Harrison	Mullen, W. B.	Hunt
Moses, J. C.	San Augustine	Muller, Joseph	Galveston
Moses, William M.	Angelina	Mullikin, F. G.	Dallas
Mosgen, Christian	Comal	Mullins, B. F.	Titus
Moss, A. F.	Robertson	Mullins, Mary A.	Cass
Moss, Fred	Dallas	Mullins, Henry	Houston
Moss, G. W.	Grimes	Mullins, Isaac	Fayette
Moss, James	Montgomery	Mullins, M. S.	Cass
Moss, James L.	Robertson	Mullins, Mary A.	Cass
Moss, John	Grayson	Mullins, William	Fayette
Moss, John	Jasper	Mulvy, James	Austin
Moss, M.	Houston	Mumett, M. L.	Henderson
Moss, Mathew	Travis	Mumford, David	Burleson
Moss, Matthew	Fayette	Munchacha, Santos	Bexar
Moss, Samuel	Grasyson	Mundel, Henry	Fayette
Moss, Samuel R.	Robertson	Mundine, John C.	Washington
Moss, William L.	Robertson	Munger, D. Albert	Austin
Mosser, Joanna	Galveston	Munger, N. H.	Austin
Mosser, John B.	Galveston	Munger, Nelson	Austin
Mosser, Peter	Galveston	Munger, S. S.	Austin
Motherill, G. J.	Henderson	Munke, Fred	Comal
Mott, Eliza	Galveston	Munoz, Jose	Bexar
Mott, Frank	Tyler	Munoz, Julian	Bexar
Mott, John	Grimes	Munoz, Lucas	Bexar
Mott, Joseph	Tyler	Munson, Henry J.	Burleson
Mountford, Jesse	Milam	Munson, Ira	Travis
Mounts, J. H.	Collin	Munson, W. W.	Houston
Mounts, J. V.	Dallas	Munson, William B.	Brazoria
Mounts, Thomas A.	Dallas	Murcheson, A.	Bastrop
Mouser, Dana	Nacogdoches	Murcheson, E. F.	Henderson
Mouser, Henry, Sr.	Fannin	Murphree, D.	Victoria
Mower, M.	San Augustine	Murphree, John B.	Washington
Mowery, N.	Red River	Murphy, A.	Cass
Moyer, David	Newton	Murphy, Dalbert	Hopkins
Moyer, Peter D.	Newton	Murphy, Edmond	Lavaca
Mozano, Philipe	Refugio	Murphy, Harvey	Grimes
Muckleroy, D.	Henderson	Murphy, Henderson	Denton
Muckleroy, David	Nacogdoches	Murphy, J. D.	Walker
Muckleroy, Mike	Colorado	Murphy, James	Fayette
Mudd, B. X.	Jasper	Murphy, James	Goliad
Mudd, Eleanor	Goliad	Murphy, James	Houston
Mudd, Elenor	Fort Bend	Murphy, James	Sabine
Mudd, Francis	Lavaca	Murphy, John	Liberty
Mudd, George	Fort Bend	Murphy, Joseph	DeWitt
Mudd, Joseph P.	Fort Bend	Murphy, Michael	Lavaca
Mudd, T. N.	Fort Bend	Murphy, Priscilla	Sabine

NAME	COUNTY	NAME	COUNTY
Murphy, Thomas	Anderson	Nabers, Robert	Fayette
Murphy, Thomas G.	Grayson	Nagele, Michael	Bexar
Murphy, W. G.	Cherokee	Nail, Abraham	Houston
Murphy, William	Fayette	Nail, Anna	Fannin
Murrah, William C.	Leon	Nail, John	Fannin
Murray, A. L.	Milam	Nail, Joseph	Fayette
Murray, Benjamin	Anderson	Nail, Lewis	Fayette
Murray, James F.	Cherokee	Nail, Nicholas	Anderson
Murray, John B.	Henderson	Nail, William	Fannin
Murray, Soloman	Red River	Nail, William A.	Colorado
Murray, Thomas	Fayette	Naja, Gua	Bexar
Murray, W.	Cass	Nale, Abner	Panola
Murray, W. L.	Fort Bend	Nale, Elizabeth	Panola
Murray, Walter	Nacogdoches	Nale, George	Panola
Murray, William	Cherokee	Nale, William	Panola
Murray, William	Fayette	Nall, John	Titus
Mursa, John	Brazoria	Nall, John H.	Cass
Musenkelter	Washington	Nall, M. G.	Red River
Musgrave, J. J.	Red River	Nall, Robert	Titus
Musgrave, Quinby	Lamar	Nance, Benjamin	Nacogdoches
Musick, William S.	Cherokee	Nance, John	Bexar
Musler, Charles	Goliad	Nance, R. J.	Jackson
Mustin, Elijah D.	DeWitt	Nann, William	Rusk
Myar, Casper	Colorado	Nanny, Charles	Limestone
Myers, A.	Cass	Naramore, Tyre	Harrison
Myers, A.	Henderson	Nash, Cooper B.	Nacogdoches
Myers, Abrum	Cherokee	Nash, Eleazar	Navarro
Myers, Benjamin	Jefferson	Nash, F. M.	Bastrop
Myers, Benjamin	Walker	Nash, James	Guadalupe
Myers, Charles		Nash, James T.	Galveston
Myers, Gibson	Cass	Nash, John D.	San Augustine
Myers, Gideon	Cass	Nash, Lorenzo D.	Harris
Myers, H. C.	Harrison	Nash, Martha	Bastrop
Myers, Henry	Lamar	Nash, W. J.	Bastrop
Myers, J. J.	Smith	Nash, William	San Augustine
Myers, J. W.	Wharton	Nations, Joseph	Nacogdoches
Myers, Jesse	Grayson	Naul, John	Walker
Myers, John	Cass	Navaritto, J.	Goliad
Myers, John	Cass	Navarro, Antonio	Bexar
Myers, John	Fayette	Navarro, J.	
Myers, John	Newton	Antonio	Guadalupe
Myers, Mary	Jefferson	Navarro, Lucians	Guadalupe
Myers, N. T.	Lamar	Navarro, Lydia	Robertson
Myers, Rease	Jefferson	Navasota, Calig.	Bexar
Myers, T. D.	Fayette	Nave, Jesse	Cass
Myres, David	Dallas	Naylor, A. W.	San Augustine
Myrick, Abram	Harrison	Nea, Henry	Comal
Myrick, D. B.	Shelby	Neabling, F.	Burleson
Myrick, James	Harrison	Neal, Benjamin F.	Refugio
		Neal, L. W.	Cass

NAME	COUNTY	NAME	COUNTY
Neal, Lewis	Montgomery	Nethery, Wesly	Lamar
Nealin, Middleton	Jefferson	Nettles, Joseph R.	Nacogdoches
Nealy, H.	Victoria	Nettles, M. T.	Polk
Neblett, R. C.	Grimes	Nettles, Shadrack	Fayette
Neecham, Enoch	Angelina	Nevels, F.	Leon
Needham, Gordon	San Augustine	Nevill, Alex	Titus
Needham, John	Brazos	Nevill, H. W.	Anderson
Needham, John	Titus	Nevill, Hardin	Brazos
Needham, Louis	Cass	Nevill, James	Houston
Needham, Samuel	Angelina	Nevill, R. C.	Houston
Neely, John E.	San Augustine	Nevill, T. M.	Titus
Neely, Wilson	San Augustine	Nevill, Tolliver	Titus
Negendank, Lewis	Comal	New, Mary	Polk
Negley, J. S.	Bastrop	New, William	Jackson
Neil, Cruheny	Gonzales	Newancroft, A.	Colorado
Neil, Dennis	Harris	Newborn, Thomas J.	Lamar
Neil, George J.	Travis	Newby, George	Cass
Neil, John	Guadalupe	Newby, J. F.	Cass
Neill, A.	Guadalupe	Newby, Jonathan	Navarro
Neill, H.	Upshur	Newcomb, James	Bexar
Neill, J. C.	Grimes	Newcomb, Thomas	Bexar
Neill, John	Washington	Newcomb, William	Red River
Neiman, H.	Galveston	Newel, J. C.	Henderson
Neiman, T. H.	Fayette	Newel, J. J.	Lamar
Nelis, Thomas	Harris	Newel, Samuel	Henderson
Nellams, A.	Leon	Newel, W. R.	Henderson
Nellams, J. H.	Rusk	Newell, J. C.	Hunt
Nellams, William		Newell, J. D.	Wharton
W.	Leon	Newell, S.	Hunt
Nelson, A. A.	Nacogdoches	Newell, T.	
Nelson, Elias	Cherokee	Virginia	Wharton
Nelson, G. C.	Leon	Newland, James	Galveston
Nelson, Horatio	Nacogdoches	Newland, James	Goliad
Nelson, James	Limestone	Newland, John	Harris
Nelson, James M.	Nacogdoches	Newland, W. H.	Lamar
Nelson, Nelson	Dallas	Newman, B. S.	Henderson
Nelson, R. A.	Houston	Newman, John C.	Fort Bend
Nelson, S.	Walker	Newman, Jonathan	Washington
Nelson, Samuel	Limestone	Newman, Rachel	Wharton
Nelson, Thomas	Goliad	Newman, Thomas	Wharton
Nelson, William	Colorado	Newman, W. R.	Wharton
Nelson, William S.	Panola	Newman, W. W.	Jackson
Nemiller, J. A. B.	Austin	Newman & Levi	Sabine
Nesbit, Henry C.	Shelby	Newsom, Nathaniel	Leon
Nesbit, Samuel	Bowie	Newton, Anderson	Dallas
Nesta, Bernardino	Bexar	Newton, John	Washington
Netherland, Joseph	Polk	Newton, M. A.	San Augustine
Netherly, Ab.	Hopkins	Newton, Mary L.	Galveston
Netherly, T. S.	Gonzales	Newton, Samuel R.	Polk
Netherly, William	Shelby	Nibbs, A. R.	Fort Bend

NAME	COUNTY	NAME	COUNTY
Nicholas, C.	Anderson	Noble, J. M.	Nacogdoches
Nicholas, W.	Matagorda	Noble, J. S.	Sabine
Nichols, E. B.	Harris	Noble, Levi	Nacogdoches
Nichols, Elizabeth	Leon	Noble, S. E.	Sabine
Nichols, Henry	Sabine	Noble, S. F.	Harris
Nichols, James	Austin	Noblitt, John	Nacogdoches
Nichols, James W.	Guadalupe	Noe, Keziah	Navarro
Nichols, John	Austin	Noel, James	San Augustine
Nichols, John	San Augustine	Nogees, Elizabeth	Jasper
Nichols, John W.	Guadalupe	Noguest, John	Jefferson
Nichols, Q. J.	Bastrop	Noland, Beckwith	Harris
Nichols, S.	Henderson	Noland, Edward	Tyler
Nichols, S. G.	Guadalupe	Noland, John	Harrison
Nichols, Stephen	Nacogdoches	Noll, John M.	Harris
Nichols, T. G.	Nacogdoches	Nolte, Henry	Galveston
Nichols, William	Nacogdoches	Norbasco, Jose	Bexar
Nichols, William		Norbeck, N.	Henderson
C.	Austin	Norboe, John	Dallas
Nicholson, D. M.	Lamar	Norboe, Peter	Dallas
Nicholson, Daniel	Bastrop	Nordain, James N.	Henderson
Nicholson, G. M.	Fayette	Nordham, William	Harris
Nicholson, J. D.	Lamar	Nordmann, C.	Galveston
Nicholson, James	Bastrop	Norfore, J. A.	Sabine
Nicholson, James	Lamar	Norman, J.	Henderson
Nicholson, John	San Augustine	Norman, William H.	Montgomery
Nicholson, John R.	Fannin	Norris, Allen	Rusk
Nicholson, L. W.	Fannin	Norris, H. C.	Brazoria
Nicholson, N.	Navarro	Norris, Mrs. H. C.	Brazoria
Nicholson, T. J.	Victoria	Norris, J. B.	Titus
Nicholson, Thomas	Goliad	Norris, J. M.	Washington
Nicks, G. W.	Henderson	Norris, James	Titus
Nicks, G. W.	Polk	Norris, John	Nacogdoches
Nidever, Henry	Lamar	Norris, John B.	Brazoria
Night, Frederic	Walker	Norris, William	Washington
Night, John E.	Houston	North, Isom R.	DeWitt
Niles, Mrs.	Harris	Northampton, A.	Grimes
Nix, Ben	Grayson	Northcut, J. W. C.	Washington
Nix, Elisha	Anderson	Northcut, James W.	Shelby
Nix, John	Anderson	Northcut, N. W.	Shelby
Nix, Jonathan	Grayson	Northington, A.,	
Nix, Samuel	Anderson	Jr.	Wharton
Nix, Sarah	Bowie	Northington, A.,	
Nison, Mahala	Grimes	Sr.	Wharton
Nixon, Richard	Grimes	Northington, H. W.	Titus
Nobels, Henry	Victoria	Northington,	
Nobels, Thomas	Victoria	Minter	Wharton
Nobels, William	Victoria	Norton, D. O.	Hopkins
Noble, A.	Tyler	Norton, Mrs. H. E.	Harris
Noble, C.	Harris	Norton, H. W.	Henderson
Noble, G. B.	Harris	Norton, H. W.	Hopkins

NAME	COUNTY	NAME	COUNTY
Norton, Henry	Refugio	O'Connar, James	Goliad
Norton, Lydia A.	Hopkins	O'Connar, John	Galveston
Norton, P. A.	Red River	O'Connar, Richard	Galveston
Norton, William P.	Galveston	O'Connar, T. B.	Grimes
Norvell, Lipscomb	Sabine	O'Connar, Thomas	Refugio
Norwood, Nathaniel	Washington	Oconnell, Susan	Travis
Nowell, B. G.	Lamar	Oconnell, William	Travis
Nowland, Jesse R.	Rusk	O'Daniel, James	Fayette
Nowland, John	Travis	O'Daniel, Josiah	Fayette
Nowland, Lewis	Rusk	O'Daniel, Lucinda	Fayette
Nowland, Richard	Rusk	Odell, A.	Nacogdoches
Nuckles, F. J.	Brazoria	Odell, James	Navarro
Nuckles, Martin L.	Brazoria	Odell, James	San Augustine
Nugent, John	Red River	Odell, Joel	Hunt
Nuishopper, A.	Liberty	Odell, John	Hunt
Nunn, John B.	Washington	Odell, Nehemiah	Hunt
Nunn, Simpson H.	Washington	Odell, Peter	Bexar
Nunn, Thomas	Washington	Odell, Simon	Hunt
Nunnely, A.	Grimes	Oden, A. L.	Guadalupe
Nunnely, A. A.	Grimes	Oden, Bishop	Travis
Nunnely, A. D.	Fannin	Oden, Lucinda	Panola
Nunnely, Caroline	Grimes	Odine, J. M.	Galveston
Nutt, J. C.	Upshur	Odle, John	Cherokee
Nutt, Nicholas W.	Jackson	O'Docharty,	
Nutt, Walter	Cherokee	Margaret	San Patricio
		O'Docharty,	
		William	San Patricio
Oakey, S. W.	Galveston	Odom, Bennett W.	Smith
Oaks, Charles	Limestone	Odom, Britton	Goliad
Oatis, James W.,		Odom, James	Cherokee
Sr.	Harris	Odom, Kinchen	Panola
Oatis, William	Cass	Odom, Margaret	DeWitt
Obanion, J. W.	Walker	Odom, R. R.	Washington
O'Bar, Alfred	Fayette	Odom, Randol	Cherokee
O'Bar, Mary	Fayette	Odom, Richard	Newton
Obenhus, Arnold	Colorado	Odom, Simeon	Navarro
Obenhus, H. C.	Colorado	Odom, Walker	Newton
O'Boyle, Patrick	Refugio	Odom, William	Newton
O'Brien, Irwin	Fannin	O'Driscoll, Daniel	Refugio
O'Brien, John	Refugio	Oest, M. R.	Colorado
O'Brien, Morgan	Refugio	Officeur, Antonio	Galveston
O'Brien, Solomon	Galveston	Offield, James	Washington
O'Brien, W.	Wharton	Offutt, H. J.	Galveston
Obrine, Owey	Travis	Ogburn, John C.	DeWitt
O'Bryan, A.	Fannin	Ogden, C. A.	Tyler
Ochiltree, Hugh	San Augustine	Ogden, F. W.	Jefferson
Ochiltree, W. B.	Nacogdoches	Ogg, Adolph	Bexar
O'Connar, C.	Galveston	Ogg, H. R.	Angelina
O'Connar, E. J.	Liberty	Ogg, Thomas	Grimes
O'Connar, Eugene	Travis	Ogle, David	Fannin

NAME	COUNTY	NAME	COUNTY
Ogle, Jeremiah	Harrison	Oneal, G. W.	Grayson
Ogletree, B. S.	Montgomery	Oneal, G. W.	Titus
O'Goode, Martin	Refugio	Oneal, James	Goliad
Ohair, Jonathan	Rusk	Oneal, James R.	Grayson
Ohair, Michael	Rusk	Onstat, David	Navarro
Ohair, Washington	Rusk	Onstat, John	Lamar
Ohair, William	Rusk	Onstat, Joshua	Navarro
Ohara, John	Cass	Onstat, William	Lamar
Oker, Anson	Colorado	Orander, Henry	Houston
Old, S. W.	Harrison	Orchard, Jesse	Cherokee
Oldes, Lucinda	Jasper	O'Reilly, Michael	Refugio
Oldham, B. F.	Hunt	Organ, Archibald	Washington
Oldham, James		Orlis, Antonio	Bexar
Thomas	Burleson	O'Rourke, James	Galveston
Oldham, John	Burleson	Orr, Green	Lamar
Oldham, Moses	Burleson	Ortega, Firman	Bexar
Oldham, S. W.	Burleson	Ortega, Fran	Bexar
Oldham, W.	Brazoria	Ortiz, Jesus	Bexar
Oldham, William	Burleson	Ortiz, Juan	Bexar
O'Leary, Patrick	Refugio	Orton, S. B.	Lamar
Oliba, Polina	Bexar	Orton, S. M.	Nacogdoches
Oliphant, A. D.	Sabine	Osborn, Bush	Cass
Oliphant, B. A.	Walker	Osborn, E.	Henderson
Oliphant, M.	Henderson	Osborn, Edward	Harris
Oliphant, S. J.	Sabine	Osborn, Eyerial	Wharton
Oliphant, Wilfred	Sabine	Osborn, J. M.	Wharton
Oliphant, William	Walker	Osborn, Milton	Guadalupe
Olivarre, Georgina	Bexar	Osgood, C.	Matagorda
Olivarre, Placido	Bexar	O'Steen, Abram	Titus
Oliver, A. G.	Henderson	Ostermann, Joseph	Galveston
Oliver, A. G.	Sabine	Oswalt, William R.	Nacogdoches
Oliver, Andrew	Henderson	Ott, William	Liberty
Oliver, Boston	Fannin	Ottranger, Volney	Harris
Oliver, E. O.	Grimes	Ottwell, William	
Oliver, G.	Cass	H.	Bexar
Oliver, J. W.	Sabine	Oualline, F.	Galveston
Oliver, James	Fayette	Outlaw, L. B.	Milam
Oliver, John	Shelby	Outlaw, N. S.	Henderson
Oliver, John C.	Houston	Overland, G. G.	Harris
Oliver, John E.	Limestone	Overland, John F.	Harris
Oliver, John P.	Grimes	Overman, John	Harris
Oliver, Mo	Shelby	Overstreet,	
Oliver, Nancy	Sabine	Stephen	Harrison
Oliver, R. F.	Montgomery	Overton, ---	
Oliver, W. F.	Matagorda	Overton, Aaron	Dallas
Olney, Joseph	Burleson	Overton, C. C.	Dallas
Olney, Mary A.	Burleson	Overton, Cass	Cass
Olphin, R. A.	Walker	Overton, David	Travis
Olphin, R. R.	Walker	Overton, J. D.	Brazos
Oneal, Francis	Harrison	Overton, John	Anderson

NAME	COUNTY	NAME	COUNTY
Overton, John F.	Henderson	Pace, R. E.	Montgomery
Overton, William		Pace, Twitty	Fannin
P.	Dallas	Pace, William B.	Rusk
Overell, T.	Upshur	Pack, Jeremiah	Nacogdoches
Overell, William	Fannin	Paddock, Jonathan	Red River
Owens, Anthony F.	Grimes	Paddock, William	Red River
Owens, Augustin	Limestone	Padello, Antonio	Bexar
Owens, B. W.	Harris	Padello, Rafael	Bexar
Owens, Bird G.	Bastrop	Page, Benjamin	Harris
Owens, C. C.	Limestone	Page, Bury	Fannin
Owens, Clark L.	Jackson	Page, Elias G.	Harrison
Owens, David F.	Bastrop	Page, H.	Upshur
Owens, Francis	Harris	Page, J. H.	Matagorda
Owens, Harrison		Page, Mrs. Jenetty	Harrison
Owens, Henry	Red River	Page, John	Gonzales
Owens, J. J.	Robertson	Page, John	Harrison
Owens, James D.	Goliad	Page, Richard	Walker
Owens, John B.	Panola	Page, Solomon	Fort Bend
Owens, Jonathan	Titus	Pagitt, John	Cherokee
Owens, Mrs. Mary	Limestone	Pagitt, Pleasant	Cherokee
Owens, Nelson	Montgomery	Pahll, Henry	Grimes
Owens, Nelson F.	Bastrop	Paigre, John M.	Anderson
Owens, O. M.	Polk	Paine, John W.	Nacogdoches
Owens, Pinkney	Walker	Painter, William	
Owens, Richard	Victoria	C.	Fannin
Owens, Robert B.	Bastrop	Palethorp, William	Hunt
Owens, S. B.	Walker	Palker, John	Titus
Owens, Smallwood	Robertson	Pallais, D. H.	Galveston
Owens, Tyler	Harris	Palm, S. W.	Brazoria
Owens, William	Cass	Palmer, G. W.	Victoria
Owens, William	Titus	Palmer, H. D.	Nacogdoches
Owens, William E.	Bastrop	Palmer, H. S.	Cass
Owings, Thomas D.	Washington	Palmer, Isham	Walker
Oxford, Claborne		Palmer, J. C.	Grimes
Oxsheer, W. W.	Milam	Palmer, J. F.	San Augustine
		Palmer, T. E.	Walker
		Palmer, Thomas	Walker
Pace, A. E.	Fannin	Palmer, W. H.	Liberty
Pace, Dempsey	Colorado	Palmer, William	Walker
Pace, George L.	Polk	Palvador, John	
Pace, Hardy	Jasper	Batist	Nacogdoches
Pace, J. F.	Sabine	Palvador, Joseph	Nacogdoches
Pace, James	Travis	Pamer, A. C.	Jasper
Pace, Joel	Cherokee	Pamer, Martin	Jasper
Pace, John	Goliad	Pancoast, Josiah	Dallas
Pace, John S.	Fannin	Pane, William	Dallas
Pace, K. H.	Lamar	Pangburn, Ganet	Grayson
Pace, M. D.	Fannin	Pankey, F. A.	Montgomery
Pace, M. J.	Montgomery	Pankey, H. E.	Henderson
Pace, Paris	Panola	Pankey, J. W.	Grimes

128

NAME	COUNTY	NAME	COUNTY
Panky, Mary A.	Washington	Parker, Joseph	Anderson
Pannel, H. G.	Harris	Parker, Joseph	Sabine
Pannell, V.	Henderson	Parker, Joseph	San Augustine
Pantalion, R.	Nacogdoches	Parker, L. J.	Harris
Panther, George W.	Cherokee	Parker, Lucy	Grimes
Parchman, H. C.	Harrison	Parker, Matthew	Sabine
Parchman, J. D.	Harrison	Parker, Moses	Sabine
Parchman, James W.	Harrison	Parker, N. B.	Galveston
Parchman, Jesse	Harrison	Parker, Nancy B.	Shelby
Parchman, P. B.	Harrison	Parker, Paton	Anderson
Parchman, W. J.	Harrison	Parker, Richard	Navarro
Parchman, Wesley		Parker, Samuel	Fannin
J.	Harrison	Parker, T. S.	Anderson
Parchum, Ruth	Henderson	Parker, Thomas	Shelby
Parham, Edmund,		Parker, W.	Henderson
Jr.	Tyler	Parker, W. W.	Henderson
Parham, James	Bowie	Parker, Warren	Harrison
Parham, Lewis L.	Panola	Parker, Wiley	Walker
Paris, E. P.	Grayson	Parker, William	Anderson
Parish, A. W.	Shelby	Parker, William E.	Houston
Park, A. C.	Cherokee	Parker, William L.	Galveston
Park, Cyrus	Cherokee	Parker, Willis	Anderson
Park, Ellen	Galveston	Parkerson, H. J.	Fort Bend
Park, Moses	Washington	Parkerson, M. M.	Travis
Park, William J.	Cherokee	Parkinson, G.	Victoria
Parker, A.	Harrison	Parks, Andrew	Montgomery
Parker, A. G.	Fannin	Parks, G. S.	Cass
Parker, A. G.	Tyler	Parks, G. S.	Red River
Parker, Asa	Polk	Parks, J.	Collin
Parker, B.	Anderson	Parks, J. D.	Matagorda
Parker, Benjamin	Navarro	Parks, J. W.	Montgomery
Parker, D.	Anderson	Parks, John W.	Polk
Parker, D.	Henderson	Parks, William	Harrison
Parker, Daniel,		Parks, William S.	Red River
Jr.	Anderson	Parks, Willis E.	Hunt
Parker, David	San Augustine	Parmalee, Atalia	
Parker, Dickinson	Anderson	A.	Nacogdoches
Parker, Dickinson	Henderson	Parmalee, Richard	Nacogdoches
Parker, George D.	Fort Bend	Parmeley, E. M.	Nacogdoches
Parker, George D.	Washington	Parmeley, Samuel	Nacogdoches
Parker, Henry	Galveston	Parmeley, Samuel,	
Parker, Isaac	Anderson	Jr.	Nacogdoches
Parker, Isaac	Houston	Parmenter, H. A.	Shelby
Parker, Isaac D.	Houston	Parmer, J. S.	Upshur
Parker, Isaac G.	Shelby	Parmer, Matilda	Henderson
Parker, J. A.	Henderson	Parmer, Robert	Shelby
Parker, Jesse	Walker	Parmer, Thomas	Henderson
Parker, John	Anderson	Parmer, William	Shelby
Parker, John	Anderson	Parr, Samuel	Galveston
Parker, John R.	Houston	Parrish, George W.	Panola

NAME	COUNTY	NAME	COUNTY
Parrish, J. C.	Fannin	Patterson, Anthony	Grimes
Parrish, Samuel C.	Panola	Patterson, Isaac	
Parrish, William		H.	Red River
G.	Panola	Patterson, J. M.	Dallas
Parrott, C. W.	Fort Bend	Patterson, Jacob	Grimes
Parrott, H.	Montgomery	Patterson, James	Jefferson
Parry, Samuel M.	Panola	Patterson, James	
Parsons, Abel	Robertson	T.	Grimes
Parsons, B. S.	Galveston	Patterson, John	Grimes
Parsons, David	Hunt	Patterson, P. W.	Sabine
Parsons, Eliza	Navarro	Patterson, R. S.	Upshur
Parsons, Hugh	Hopkins	Patterson, W. B.	Bexar
Parsons, J. A. S.	Rusk	Patterson, W. T.	Leon
Parsons, J. B.	Henderson	Patterson, William	DeWitt
Parsons, J. W.	Collin	Patterson, Wm.	Montgomery
Parsons, John	Hunt	Patterson, Wm. P.	Goliad
Parsons, Kenneth	Tyler	Patton, A. B.	Henderson
Partridge, Worthy	Jefferson	Patton, A. B.	San Augustine
Pascal, G. R.	Henderson	Patton, Andrew	Navarro
Pascal, Sam	Harris	Patton, Andrew B.	Lamar
Paschal, G. W.	Bexar	Patton, C. R.	Brazoria
Paschal, J. A.	Bexar	Patton, Charles F.	Brazoria
Paschal, James	Lamar	Patton, G. W.	Houston
Paschal, Samuel	Henderson	Patton, J. L. R.	Robertson
Passnele, R.	Henderson	Patton, James	Harrison
Pasture, William		Patton, James C.	Navarro
E.	San Augustine	Patton, John	Fort Bend
Patching, T.	Harris	Patton, John	Henderson
Pate, A.	Hunt	Patton, John	Navarro
Pate, Daniel M.	Nacogdoches	Patton, John M.	Fannin
Pate, G. B.	Houston	Patton, Moses L.	Nacogdoches
Pate, John	Nacogdoches	Patton, N. B.	Bowie
Pate, William	Anderson	Patton, Pickens	Bastrop
Patillo, G. A.	Jefferson	Patton, R. S.	Houston
Patillo, G. C.	Upshur	Patton, Robert	Lamar
Patillo, G. C.,		Patton, Robert S.	Nacogdoches
Jr.	Upshur	Patton, S. B.	Upshur
Patillo, George A.	Grimes	Patton, St. C.	Henderson
Patillo, James H.	Jefferson	Patton, Samuel	Harrison
Patillo, Simeon	Jefferson	Patton, Samuel	Houston
Patillo, T. A.	Harrison	Patton, T.	Leon
Patloe, Joseph	Sabine	Patton, W. H.	Henderson
Patman, William	Goliad	Patton, Wm.	Navarro
Patrick, George M.	Grimes	Paul, Andrew	Houston
Patrick, H.	Upshur	Paul, Barton	Shelby
Patrick, J. T.	Polk	Paul, James	Grimes
Patrick, James B.	Gonazles	Paul, John	Houston
Patrick, William	Grimes	Paul, S. B.	Shelby
Patrick, William		Paul, Z. M.	Lamar
W.	Leon	Paulett, Edgar	Smith

NAME	COUNTY	NAME	COUNTY
Paxton, J. N.	Cass	Pearson, James	Grayson
Paxton, W. G.	Bowie	Pearson, Lorenzo	
Payer, Thomas	Anderson	D.	Nacogdoches
Payne, A. J.	Harrison	Pearson, P. H.	Henderson
Payne, A. J.	Henderson	Pearson, P. R.	Upshur
Payne, Alvah	Washington	Pearson, William	Dallas
Payne, Ben W.	Sabine	Pease, Elisha M.	Brazoria
Payne, C. B.	Harrison	Peck, Joseph	Bexar
Payne, Charlton	San Augustine	Pedro, Martin	Henderson
Payne, D. C.	San Augustine	Peebles, R. R.	Austin
Payne, George W.	San Augustine	Peebles, Robert	DeWitt
Payne, J. G.	Cherokee	Peebles, Robert	Grimes
Payne, Jean C.	Sabine	Peek, A. C.	Hopkins
Payne, Jesse M.	Harrison	Peek, Barton	Goliad
Payne, John	Fayette	Peek, Barton	Jackson
Payne, John	Sabine	Peek, Ben B.	Gonzales
Payne, John F.	Goliad	Peek, Nathaniel	Fort Bend
Payne, John K.	Fort Bend	Peel, Thomas R.	Montgomery
Payne, John M.	Sabine	Peer, James B.	Austin
Payne, John M.	Washington	Peery, Crocket	Fayette
Payne, P. A.	Fannin	Peevyhouse,	
Payne, Thomas T.	San Augustine	Preston	Austin
Payne, William	Anderson	Pegues, George H.	Dallas
Payne, William H.	San Augustine	Pelham, Joseph M.	Panola
Payne, William H.	Washington	Pelkington, T. K.	Fort Bend
Payton, A. R.	Victoria	Pemberton, Gideon	Dallas
Peace, Skiny	Harris	Pemleton, J. J.	Tyler
Peacock, Allen	Cass	Pena, C.	Henderson
Peacock, C. C.	Titus	Pena, Calistro	Bexar
Peacock, George S.	Calhoun	Pence, Singular	Fannin
Peacock, James	Colorado	Pendexter, George	
Peacock, John	Titus	W.	Brazoria
Peacock, Ralph W.	Bexar	Pendleton, W. N.	Goliad
Peacock, William	Titus	Pengenot, J.	Bexar
Pearce, B. B.	Jackson	Penn, David P.	Harris
Pearce, Dona H.	Refugio	Penn, G. F.	Rusk
Pearce, Mrs. E. J.	Grimes	Penn, S. C.	Rusk
Pearce, George R.	Refugio	Pennick, William	Houston
Pearce, James	Jackson	Pennick, Wm. J.	Houston
Pearce, Jesse	Jackson	Pennington, Elias	Fannin
Pearce, Philip R.	Fayette	Pennington, Elijah	Washington
Pearce, Thomas	Harris	Pennington, J.	Rusk
Pearce, W. D.	Jasper	Pennington, John	Henderson
Pearce, W. J. C.	Grimes	Pennington,	
Pearce, William	Harrison	Richard	Houston
Pearman, George R.	Refugio	Pennington, Riggs	Washington
Pearson, Charles		Penny, Thomas	Galveston
H.	Refugio	Penper, John B.	Anderson
Pearson, Dudley F.	Dallas	Pentercost, A. W.	Fort Bend
Pearson, E. A.	Victoria	Pentercost, S.	Fort Bend

NAME	COUNTY	NAME	COUNTY
Peoples, Thomas	Shelby	Perry, J. C.	Bexar
Pepper, W.	Upshur	Perry, J. D.	Harrison
Perdido, Tomas	Bexar	Perry, James	Fort Bend
Perez, Hernando	Bexar	Perry, James	Galveston
Perez, Jose	Bexar	Perry, James F.	Brazoria
Perez, Teodo	Bexar	Perry, L. W.	Red River
Perie, James	Bexar	Perry, Lawrence	Grimes
Peris, Valentine	Goliad	Perry, Middleton	Dallas
Perkins, Alvey	Walker	Perry, N. B.	Harrison
Perkins, B. W.	Bastrop	Perry, Patric	Fort Bend
Perkins, Daniel	Cass	Perry, S. R.	Harrison
Perkins, Daniel,		Perry, S. W.	Robertson
Jr.	Cass	Perry, Stuart	Refugio
Perkins, Daniel,		Perry, Thomas	Fayette
Sr.	Cass	Perry, W. B.	Colorado
Perkins, E. S.	Harris	Perry, W. D.	Harrison
Perkins, J. C.	Grimes	Perry, William	Anderson
Perkins, J. R.	Bastrop	Perry, William	Cass
Perkins, James	Grayson	Perry, William	Lamar
Perkins, James	Houston	Perry, Wm. M.	Bastrop
Perkins, James	San Augustine	Perryhouse, J.	Goliad
Perkins, James H.	Galveston	Perryman, A. J.	Lamar
Perkins, Jesse	Houston	Perryman, Austin	Lamar
Perkins, Jourdan	Houston	Perryman, E. L.	Austin
Perkins, L. S.	Galveston	Perryman, James G.	Cherokee
Perkins, Matt	Cass	Perryman, Wm. J.	Austin
Perkins, P.	Navarro	Perryton, W.	Goliad
Perkins, Samuel	Cass	Persons, Benjamin	Shelby
Perkins, Samuel W.	Brazoria	Persons, Hiram	Colorado
Perkins, W. E.	Bastrop	Pervis, J. L.	Shelby
Perkins, William	Harris	Pervis, Joseph	Shelby
Perkinson, B. H.	Red River	Peski, Martin	Brazoria
Peronis, Elijah	Goliad	Peters, James	Bowie
Perrin, A. B.	Collin	Peters, Joseph	Comal
Perrin, James M.	Lamar	Peters, L. H.	Colorado
Perrin, W.	Collin	Peters, Lemuel	Bowie
Perrin, W.	Lamar	Peters, O. H.	Fort Bend
Perrin, William C.	Gonzales	Peters, R.	Cass
Perry, A. G.	Grimes	Peters, R. F.	Bowie
Perry, A. W.	Dallas	Peters, Stephen	Cass
Perry, Alfred	Harrison	Peterson, John	Grimes
Perry, C. R.	Bastrop	Peterson, John	Leon
Perry, Daniel	Fort Bend	Peterson, Mary	Grimes
Perry, Mrs. E. E.	Washington	Petree, Peter	Walker
Perry, E. W.	Colorado	Pettet, Ben, Jr.	Fannin
Perry, Edward	Refugio	Pettet, John G.	Houston
Perry, Elisha	Harris	Pettet, Robert T.	Fannin
Perry, Ett.	Grimes	Pettet, Walker	Shelby
Perry, H. E.	Grimes	Pettigrew, J. C.	Red River
Perry, H. P.	Harrison	Pettigrew, Jason	

NAME	COUNTY	ANME	COUNTY
H.	Fannin	Phillips, L. M.	Wharton
Pettis, Edward C.	Austin	Phillips, N. B.	Panola
Pettis, John	Austin	Phillips, Nelson	Goliad
Pettis, Martha	Austin	Phillips, Sam S.	Jackson
Pettis, Mary	Austin	Phillips, Sidney	Fort Bend
Petty, George W.	Washington	Phillips, T.	Collin
Petty, J. T.	Washington	Phillips, Thomas	Harris
Petty, Newton	Wharton	Phillips, W. C.	Sabine
Petty, P. H.	Wharton	Phillips, W. J.	Matagorda
Petty, Thomas	Bastrop	Phillips, William	Upshur
Pevehouse, D.	Montgomery	Phillips, William	
Pevehouse, M.	Montgomery	M.	Gonzales
Pevehouse, T.	Grimes	Phillips, Z.	Brazos
Peveler, David	Fannin	Phillips, Z. B.	Rusk
Pevetone, Ougen	Harris	Phillips, Zeno	Brazoria
Pevits, J. D.	Jefferson	Philly, Bortus	Lamar
Pevits, John N.	Jefferson	Philpott, H.	Limestone
Pew, Samuel	Lamar	Philpott, J. P.	Limestone
Pew, Thomas	San Patricio	Philsby, Abraham	Nacogdoches
Peyburn, R. W.	Grayson	Phipps, E. G.	Galveston
Pfeiffer, J. G.	Comal	Phipps, John	Galveston
Pfeiffer, John	Galveston	Pholoford, James	Henderson
Phairison, P. B.	Henderson	Phuffer, Samuel	Henderson
Phan, Augustus	Brazoria	Piburn, John	Panola
Pharr, Samuel	Fort Bend	Pickens, Allen B.	Shelby
Phelan, M.	Fannin	Pickens, John	Cass
Phelps, J. S.	Dallas	Pickens, John H.	Fort Bend
Phelps, James A.		Pickens, Leonard	Colorado
E.	Brazoria	Pickens, M. D.	Henderson
Phelps, M. H.	Austin	Picket, William	Red River
Phenoy, ----	Henderson	Pieper, Anton	Comal
Phifer, Bradley	Limestone	Pierce, H. E.	Limestone
Phifer, Forest	Limestone	Pierce, John	Wharton
Phillippi, C.	Bexar	Pierce, Joseph	Rusk
Phillips, A. H.	Victoria	Pierce, Lewis	Montgomery
Phillips, Abner	Bastrop	Pierce, R. A.	Houston
Phillips, Alfred	Lamar	Pierce, Silas C.	Goliad
Phillips, Benjamin	Fayette	Pierce, William	Harris
Phillips, C.	Bastrop	Pierce, William	Shelby
Phillips, David	Lamar	Pierce, William C.	Rusk
Phillips, Elias	Lamar	Pierson, Isaac	Travis
Phillips, F. B.	Galveston	Pierson, J. G. W.	Grimes
Phillips, F. J.	Matagorda	Pike, Samuel	Rusk
Phillips, Henry S.	Bastrop	Piland, E.	Lamar
Phillips, J.	Collin	Piland, J.	Lamar
Phillips, Jacob	San Augustine	Piland, M.	Navarro
Phillips, James R.	Fort Bend	Piland, Mills	Lamar
Phillips, John	Anderson	Pilant, J. W.	Harris
Phillips, John	Bexar	Pile, John	Cherokee
Phillips, John T.	Grimes	Pile, Joseph	Rusk

NAME	COUNTY	NAME	COUNTY
Pilgrim, Benjamin	Guadalupe	Ploughman, Thomas	
Pilgrim, Thomas J.	Guadalupe	R.	Harris
Pilkenton, C.	Montgomery	Plovis, Juan	Goliad
Pillana, P. J.	Fannin	Pluker, William	Nacogdoches
Pillar, Richard	Washington	Plummer, L. T. M.	Limestone
Pillot, Claude N.	Harris	Plunket, E. J.	Sabine
Pillot, Eugene	Harris	Poag, J. A.	Bastrop
Pillows, H.	Goliad	Poag, William	Panola
Pilsbury, Timothy	Brazoria	Poe, J.	Henderson
Pincham, P.	Montgomery	Poe, Jed	Anderson
Pincham, William	Guadalupe	Poe, John	Nacogdoches
Pinchard, F.	Galveston	Poer, David	Dallas
Pinchback, James	Grimes	Poer, James	Bowie
Pinchback, John	Colorado	Poer, John C.	Bowie
Pinchback, L.	Grimes	Poer, Martin A.	Bowie
Pinckney, Thomas		Poer, Nancy	Bowie
S.	Grimes	Poer, Solomon	Bowie
Pinkard, M. P.	Brazoria	Poer, Wm. B.	Bowie
Pinson, J. J.	Anderson	Pogue, John H.	DeWitt
Pinson, J. J.	Houston	Poinsett &	
Piper, Peter	Colorado	Brassette	DeWitt
Pipkin, S.	Travis	Poland, George	Titus
Pipkin, S. W.	Travis	Poland, John	Victoria
Pipkin, W. R.	Washington	Polk, Alfred	San Augustine
Pirtle, Albert	Rusk	Polk, Andrew	San Augustine
Pirtle, B.	Titus	Polk, Charles	San Augustine
Pirtle, William	Titus	Polk, Headley	Bastrop
Pirtle, Wm.	Titus	Polk, J.	Henderson
Pistole, A.	Cass	Polk, J. M.	Henderson
Pitman, L. J.	Red River	Polk, John	Nacogdoches
Pitman, Willis	Cass	Polk, John	San Augustine
Pitts, Alex	Galveston	Polk, Lucius	San Augustine
Pitts, E. T.	Grimes	Polk, Thomas	DeWitt
Pitts, Edward H.	Grimes	Polk, Thomas A.	Limestone
Pitts, John D.	Grimes	Pollan, Anson	Polk
Pitts, John G.	Washington	Pollard, James	Galveston
Pitts, Levi	Washington	Pollard, Wiley	Brazoria
Pitts, Obediah	Grimes	Polley, John	Sabine
Pix, Christopher		Polley, Joseph H.	Brazoria
H.	Galveston	Polley, Robert	Sabine
Plank, Christian	Harrison	Polley, Thomas	Sabine
Plankhouse, F.	Harris	Pollock, Henry	Goliad
Plasters, Thomas		Polly, James	Hopkins
P.	Grimes	Pomeroy, Samuel D.	Henderson
Platt, James	San Augustine	Pomplin, William	Jasper
Pleasants, John	Galveston	Pomroy, W.	Henderson
Pleasants, L. C.	Limestone	Poncelet, J. C.	Bexar
Pleasants, Q. W.	Fort Bend	Pond, Carlisle	Leon
Pledger, Mary Ann	Matagorda	Ponton, Andrew	Lavaca
Plemans, James	Cherokee	Ponton, Joel	Lavaca

NAME	COUNTY	NAME	COUNTY
Pool, A. N.	San Augustine	Potter, L. J.	Harrison
Pool, Beverly	Washington	Potter, M. M.	Galveston
Pool, J. C.	Walker	Potter, M. W.	Goliad
Pool, John C.	Milam	Potter, M. W.	Matagorda
Pool, O. L.	Bowie	Potter, R. L.	Cass
Pool, Robert	Harrison	Potter, R. M.	Travis
Pool, Sedley	Harrison	Potts, John H.	Leon
Poor, Ira S.	Red River	Pouncy, A. W.	Travis
Poor, James	Red River	Pounds, S. J.	Shelby
Pope, Clarence	Harrison	Powel, E. R.	Jasper
Pope, J. J.	Leon	Powel, Elisha	Jasper
Pope, James	Panola	Powel, W. R.	Henderson
Pope, James	Red River	Powel, William R.	Walker
Pope, Jesse	Panola	Powel, Wyley	Panola
Pope, L.	Titus	Powell, C. B.	San Augustine
Pope, L. M. F.	Nacogdoches	Powell, Dorcas	Fort Bend
Pope, Thomas	Titus	Powell, Enoch	Fort Bend
Pope, William A.	Panola	Powell, Homer M.	Tyler
Porter, Amanda	Grimes	Powell, Isaac	Sabine
Porter, B. T.	Titus	Powell, J.	Goliad
Porter, David	Cass	Powell, J. H.	Robertson
Porter, Dempsey	Jackson	Powell, J. S.	Harrison
Porter, Henry	Cass	Powell, James	Fort Bend
Porter, Humphrey	Goliad	Powell, James B.	Brazos
Porter, Isom B.	Burleson	Powell, John	Robertson
Porter, J. B.	Walker	Powell, M.	Cass
Porter, J. L.	Cass	Powell, Nathan	Navarro
Porter, James	Cass	Powell, Peter	Guadalupe
Porter, John	Shelby	Powell, S. G.	Matagorda
Porter, John T.	Burleson	Powell, T. D.	Harrison
Porter, John W.	Burleson	Powell, Thomas	Goliad
Porter, Joseph W.	Hopkins	Powell, Wiley	Robertson
Porter, Samuel	Shelby	Powell, Wm. R.	Nacogdoches
Porter, T. D.	Newton	Power, Annette	Liberty
Porter, W. W.	Fannin	Power, Benjamin	DeWitt
Porter, William L.	Walker	Power, E.	Matagorda
Porterfield, M. H.	Henderson	Power, F. B.	Matagorda
Portice, D. Y.	Austin	Power, H. C.	Cherokee
Portice, Rebecca	Austin	Power, Isaac	Houston
Portwood, L. T. J.	Nacogdoches	Power, James	Refugio
Posey, Bennet	Cherokee	Power, John	Burleson
Posey, Jinsy	Anderson	Power, John	Liberty
Posey, L. P.	Red River	Power, John H.	Houston
Posey, Terry	Red River	Power, Josiah	DeWitt
Posey, William	Anderson	Power, Josiah	Panola
Poston, James H.	Fayette	Power, Mary	DeWitt
Poteet, S.	Lamar	Power, Michael	DeWitt
Poteet, T. R. H.	Lamar	Power, Samuel	Refugio
Potter, Daniel	Limestone	Powers, Elijah,	
Potter, H. N.	Galveston	Jr.	Limestone

NAME	COUNTY	NAME	COUNTY
Powers, Elijah, Sr.	Limestone	Price, John T.	Lamar
Powers, Francis	Limestone	Price, Joseph T.	Gonzales
Powers, L. B.	Limestone	Price, P. C.	Leon
Powers, Wm. C.	Limestone	Price, P. M.	Lamar
Poy, Peter B.	Jasper	Price, Perry	Fayette
Pralla, L.	Brazoria	Price, R. C.	Titus
Prather, A.	Walker	Price, Reece	Leon
Prather, Freeman	San Augustine	Price, S. M.	Lamar
Prather, James	Fort Bend	Price, Samuel C.	Lamar
Prator, Dorothy	Galveston	Price, Thomas	Milam
Prator, Philip	Milam	Price, Thomas	Washington
Pratt, John	DeWitt	Price, W. M.	Henderson
Pratt, T.	Galveston	Price, William	Fayette
Pratt, Thomas	Fort Bend	Price, William	Shelby
Pratt, William	Harrison	Price, William C.	Navarro
Prendergast, L. B.	Robertson	Price, William W.	Harrison
Prescher, George	Liberty	Price, Williamson	Washington
Prescott, William	Jasper	Price, Wm. D.	Galveston
Prescott, Wm.	Refugio	Price, Willis	Angelina
Pressley, Joseph	Harris	Price, Willis A.	Limestone
Pressley, Wm.	Nacogdoches	Prichard, Sion	Houston
Presnal, Luke	Rusk	Prichett, G.	Robertson
Prewitt, A. S.	Navarro	Pride, John	Cass
Prewitt, C. W.	Nacogdoches	Pridgeon, H. M. B.	Harrison
Prewitt, G. W.	Houston	Pridgeon, R. S.	Harrison
Prewitt, H. R.	Milam	Pridgeon, Wiley W.	Harrison
Prewitt, Ira	Anderson	Pridham, P. M.	Victoria
Prewitt, J.	Anderson	Priest, William	Hopkins
Prewitt, James A.	Burleson	Priestly, James	DeWitt
Prewitt, Jesse	Houston	Prigmore, Joseph	Dallas
Prewitt, John M.	Brazoria	Prim, W.	Fayette
Prewitt, Joseph	Hunt	Primrose, Elizabeth	Galveston
Prewitt, Martin T.	Anderson	Primrose, M.	Galveston
Price, Charles L.	Rusk	Primrose, William	Galveston
Price, D.	Henderson	Prince, G. W.	Nacogdoches
Price, Elijah	San Augustine	Prince, Philip W.	Harris
Price, Elisha	Angelina	Prior, Benjamin	Navarro
Price, Ellen	Cass	Prior, Richard	Shelby
Price, F.	Henderson	Pritchard, Thomas	Galveston
Price, F. W.	Titus	Procilla, Jose	Nacogdoches
Price, George W.	Guadalupe	Procilla, Louis	Nacogdoches
Price, Isom	Hopkins	Proctor, H. S.	Titus
Price, J. H.	Montgomery	Proctor, Isaac	Sabine
Price, James	Fayette	Proctor, N.	Bowie
Price, James	Shelby	Proctor, Thomas	Hopkins
Price, James M.	Brazos	Proctor, W. S.	Bowie
Price, John	Galveston	Proskey, D.	Sabine
Price, John	Henderson	Prosous, H.	Goliad
Price, John T.	Goliad	Provine, Wm. M.	Red River

NAME	COUNTY	NAME	COUNTY
Pruett, B.	Liberty	Purson, Wm. H.	Washington
Pruett, C.	Liberty	Purvis, Hiden	Houston
Pruett, Fields	Rusk	Purvis, William	Harris
Pruett, Jesse	Henderson	Putman, M.	Upshur
Pruett, Martha	Liberty	Putman, Mrs. Mary	Washington
Pruett, Mattison		Putman, Michael	Gonzales
G.	Rusk	Putman, Wm.	Gonzales
Pruett, William	Red River	Pyle, M. Edward	Henderson
Pruett, Winifred	Rusk	Pyle, John	Henderson
Pruett, Wm. M.	Tyler	Pyle, John	Montgomery
Pruit, J. S. H.	Cass	Pyle, S. E.	Montgomery
Pruit, William	Leon		
Pruitt, Anselm	Cass		
Pruitt, Caroline	Cass	Quace, John	Leon
Pruitt, George W.	Cass	Quasheimer,	
Pruitt, Levi	Henderson	Patrick	Rusk
Pruitt, William	Dallas	Quick, Edmond	Galveston
Pryor, John S.	Washington	Quillin, Charles	
Puckett, Jackson	Limestone	C.	Grayson
Puckett, L. D.	Travis	Quinin, George	Wharton
Puckett, M. W.	Rusk	Quinn, G. B.	San Augustine
Puckett,		Quinn, James	Bexar
Montgomery	Henderson	Quinn, James	Harris
Puckett, Robert	Goliad	Quinn, James O.	Grimes
Puckett, Thomas	Travis	Quinton, Nathaniel	Rusk
Pugh, F. W.	Harrison	Quirido, Guil	Goliad
Pugh, John	Red River	Quonones, Antonio	Bexar
Pullam, George W.	Tyler		
Pullam, M. S.	Collin		
Pullam, S.	Collin	Rabb, Andrew	Fayette
Pullam, W. H.	Collin	Rabb, John, Jr.	Fayette
Pullen, B. S.	Washington	Rabb, John, Sr.	Fayette
Puller, John	Henderson	Rabb, Thomas J.	Fayette
Pulliam, Benjamin		Rabb, William	Fayette
H.	Nacogdoches	Rabio, Santia	Nacogdoches
Pulliam, John L.	Dallas	Raborn, Levi	Polk
Pulliam, Thomas D.	Cass	Raburn, Hodge	Shelby
Pulsifer, J. T.	Jefferson	Raburn, Matthew	Cass
Punchard,		Raburn, Susan	Shelby
Louisiana	Austin	Racener, Henry	Harris
Punchard, S. W.	Austin	Rachel, C.	Liberty
Punchard, William	Austin	Raden, Aaron C.	Henderson
Punderson, Austin	Washington	Radan, Otto Van	Austin
Purcell, Charles	Brazoria	Rader, Davis	Cass
Purcell, Edward	Brazoria	Radican, John A.	Washington
Purcell, S.	Galveston	Rado, N. V.	Austin
Pursley, Wm.	Walker	Rae, Daniel	Polk
Purson, C. C.	Washington	Rae, Edward	Polk
Purson, G. W.	Washington	Raford, Robert	Burleson
Purson, P. H.	Washington	Ragan, Adam R.	Fayette

NAME	COUNTY	NAME	COUNTY
Ragan, C.	Cass	Ramsdale, G. L.	Houston
Ragan, G.	Cass	Ramsdale, John F.	Houston
Ragan, Gilbert	Red River	Ramsey, Andrew H.	Harrison
Ragan, Hamilton	Cass	Ramsey, Isaac	Dallas
Ragan, J. B.	Cass	Ramsey, James	Gonzales
Ragland, B. V.	Cass	Ramsey, John	Denton
Raglin, Edward	Victoria	Ramsey, John	Washington
Raglin, H. W.	Grimes	Ramsey, Lawrence	Wharton
Raglin, J. B.	Victoria	Ramsey, M.	Colorado
Raglin, J. T.	Titus	Ramsey, M. D.	Colorado
Raglin, William	Victoria	Ramsey, Richard	Harrison
Ragsdale, C. C.	Fayette	Ramsour, Michael	Denton
Ragsdale, Edward		Randall, Hannah	Austin
B.	Sabine	Randall, J. H.	San Augustine
Ragsdale, G. B.	Polk	Randall, Jonas	Fayette
Ragsdale, James C.	Fayette	Randall, Leonard	San Augustine
Ragsdale, M. H.	Lamar	Randall, O. W.	Nacogdoches
Ragsdale, Peter C.	Guadalupe	Randle, Barnett	Gonzales
Ragsdale, Thomas	Lamar	Randle, Wilson	Guadalupe
Ragsdale, W. R.	Cass	Randolph, C. H.	Houston
Ragsdale, Wm. J.	Sabine	Randolph, H.	Henderson
Raguet, Condy	Nacogdoches	Randolph, Harvey	Walker
Raguet, H. W.	Nacogdoches	Randolph, J. W.	Gonzales
Raguet, Henry	Nacogdoches	Randolph, John	Rusk
Raguet, Mary	Nacogdoches	Randolph, John	Walker
Railey, Charles	Austin	Random, John	Fort Bend
Rainbolt, Wm.	Lamar	Raney, Joseph	Anderson
Rainer, S. M.	San Augustine	Raney, David	Red River
Rains, Charles B.	Nacogdoches	Raney, Joseph	Anderson
Rains, Emery	Shelby	Raney, S. D.	Red River
Rains, George C.	Galveston	Rankin, D. H.	Fayette
Rains, George R.	Shelby	Rankin, F. B.	Montgomery
Rains, J. D.	San Augustine	Rankin, F.H.	Polk
Rains, J. H.	Bowie	Rankin, Hannah	Fayette
Rains, Joel D.	Henderson	Rankin, J. M.	San Augustine
Rains, John	Navarro	Rankin, James M.	Polk
Rains, R. P.	Red River	Rankin, M.	Brazoria
Rajas, Francisco	Bexar	Rankin, Peggy	Polk
Ralls, Benjamin	Tyler	Rankin, Wm., Jr.	Harris
Ralls, M.	Red River	Rankin, William M.	Montgomery
Ralph, Nancy	Walker	Ransom, A.	Galveston
Ralph, S. W.	Jasper	Ransom, Farman	Bastrop
Ralph, Samuel	Washington	Ransom, John	Bastrop
Ralston, Joseph	Washington	Ranson, Thomas J.	Washington
Rambo, Anderson G.	Handerson	Rasback, Fatten	Austin
Rambough, J. A.	Brazoria	Rashall, John	Bexar
Rames, Hose	Victoria	Rassel, William	Polk
Ramon, Antonio	Goliad	Ratcliffe, Ann	Tyler
Ramos, Tomas	Bexar	**Ratcliffe, E. T.**	**Tyler**
Ramos, V.	Goliad	Ratcliffe, Eli.	Tyler

NAME	COUNTY	NAME	COUNTY
Ratcliffe, John	Anderson	Reagan, John H.	Henderson
Ratcliffe, John K.	Newton	Reagan, William	Rusk
Ratcliffe, R. K.	Tyler	Reager, William	Travis
Ratcliffe, William	Tyler	Reagle, Philip	Grimes
Ratcliffe, Wm. V.	Henderson	Reams, S. Y.	Austin
Rather, Mrs.		Reatherford, J. H.	Titus
Harriet	Harris	Reatherford,	
Rather, William S.	Fort Band	Thomas	Titus
Raths, H.	Henderson	Reaves, ----	Red River
Rathven, A. S.	Harris	Reaves, D. M.	Rusk
Ratlaseau, A.	Galveston	Reaves, D. W.	Rusk
Ratliff, Richard	San Augustine	Reaves, George	Sabine
Ratliff, W. D.	San Augustine	Reaves, John	Hopkins
Ratliff, William	Smith	Reaves, John H.	Red River
Rattan, Daniel	Hopkins	Record, James	Lamar
Rattan, Hyram	Hopkins	Record, Newton	Lamar
Rattan, John	Fannin	Rector, Claiborne	Brazoria
Rattan, Littleton	Hopkins	Rector, E. J.	Travis
Rattan, T.	Collin	Rector, G. W.	Nacogdoches
Rattan, Thomas T.	Hopkins	Rector, John	Nacogdoches
Raven, Ernst	Burleson	Rector, John	Walker
Ravena, M.	Galveston	Rector, Lewis	Brazos
Ravil, B. F.	Washington	Rector, M.	Brazos
Rawls, John T.	San Augustine	Rector, Morgan	Brazoria
Rawls, R. R.	San Augustine	Rector, N. S.	Travis
Ray, Edward	Grimes	Rector, Pendleton	Guadalupe
Ray, Guivens	Burleson	Rector, William R.	Walker
Ray, John W.	Henderson	Red, Allen W.	Angelina
Ray, R.	Navarro	Red, Ansel	Angelina
Ray, R. R.	Henderson	Red, Meachek	Angelina
Ray, W. B.	Walker	Red, Micah	Angelina
Rayl, William W.	Travis	Red, Thomas	Wharton
Raymond, James H.	Travis	Reddin, Joseph	Lamar
Raymond, N. C.	Burleson	Reddin, Richard	Lamar
Rayner, William S.	Fort Bend	Redding, G. W.	Angelina
Rayner, Wm. S.	Galveston	Redding, John	Hopkins
Rea, A.	Grimes	Redding, N. L.	Bastrop
Rea, John	Bexar	Redding, Nancy	Angelina
Read, A. A.	Shelby	Redding, R. B.	Henderson
Read, J. D.	San Augustine	Redding, W. R.	Bastrop
Read, J. H.	Henderson	Reden, J. F.	Dallas
Read, Joseph	Titus	Redgate, S. J.	Colorado
Read, Joseph M.	Lamar	Reding, C. W.	Henderson
Read, Miles	Red River	Reding, G. W.	Montgomery
Read, Thompson	Lamar	Reding, Iredell	Montgomery
Read, W. D.	Henderson	Reding, J. B.	Montgomery
Read, William	Liberty	Reed, Almon	Calhoun
Reader, J. H.	Hunt	Reed, Charles	Bowie
Reader, Mickajah	Hunt	Reed, Elijah	Limestone
Ready, C. C.	Liberty	Reed, Elijah R.	Burleson

NAME	COUNTY	NAME	COUNTY
Reed, Elizabeth	Burleson	Reid, James	Henderson
Reed, G. B.	Grimes	Reid, James	Nacogdoches
Reed, Harman	Lamar	Reid, James W.	Bastrop
Reed, Henry	Robertson	Reid, John	Henderson
Reed, Isaac	Panola	Reid, John	Nacogdoches
Reed, Isaac	Rusk	Reid, Joseph	Cass
Reed, J.	Matagorda	Reid, Miles	Cass
Reed, J.	Upshur	Reid, Rhoda	Bastrop
Reed, J. B.	Victoria	Reid, S. H.	Bastrop
Reed, Jacob	Burleson	Reid, Thomas	Bastrop
Reed, John	Austin	Reid, Thomas	Washington
Reed, John	Rusk	Reilly, B.	San Augustine
Reed, John	Victoria	Reilly, James	Harris
Reed, John N.	Galveston	Reinarz, F. W.	Comal
Reed, John N.	Harris	Reinertz, R. C.	Fort Bend
Reed, L.	Upshur	Reinhards, M. F.	Nacogdoches
Reed, Matthew	Lamar	Reinhards, M. J.	Nacogdoches
Reed, Michael	Milam	Reinhardt, Hunt	Leon
Reed, Natnahiel	Goliad	Reinhardt, J. P.	Leon
Reed, Nathaniel	Washington	Reininger, Henry	Comal
Reed, William	Bexar	Rellos, James	Bexar
Reed, William	Milam	Rellos, Mateo	Bexar
Reed, William	Titus	Remer, Dr. William	Comal
Reed, William	Victoria	Remierez, ----	Henderson
Reed, William D.	Rusk	Remler, Gabriel	Comal
Reed, Wilson	Brazos	Ren, John Gerlock	Comal
Reel, Barbary	Rusk	Renfro, David	Sabine
Reel, James	Rusk	Renfro, Ed	Walker
Reel, Pat	Colorado	Renfro, J. S.	Sabine
Reese, Charles R.	Brazoria	Renfro, James	Grimes
Reese, Cyrus B.	Polk	Renfro, John F.	Angelina
Reese, G. M.	Polk	Renfro, Lucey	Sabine
Reese, George	Polk	Renfro, P. F.	Sabine
Reese, J.	Grimes	Renfrow, John	Nacogdoches
Reese, John J.	Polk	Renkar, John J.	Galveston
Reese, Joseph	Brazoria	Rennert, Julius	Comal
Reese, Sarah T.	Brazoria	Renney, William	Harris
Reese, William E.	Brazroia	Renolds, Isam	Jackson
Reese, William S.	Polk	Rensan, J. F.	Houston
Reeves, Alexander		Renshaw, Arthur	Henderson
B.	Harris	Respess, Ormond	Harrison
Reeves, George	Henderson	Retens, M. W.	Henderson
Reeves, John	Bowie	Rettig, Adam	Comal
Reeves, John B.	Panola	Reubens, John	Henderson
Reeves, John H.	Cass	Reuter, Lewis	Nacogdoches
Reeves, Talbot	Burleson	Revas, Jose	Bexar
Reeves, William	Galveston	Revere, W. K.	Lamar
Reeves, William B.	Harris	Reves, Loji	Refugio
Regaldo, Jose	Bexar	Reves, Thomas	Henderson
Reid, George	Cass	Reynolds, Fabius	Harris

NAME	COUNTY	NAME	COUNTY
Reynolds, J. M.	Harris	Rice, C. A.	Houston
Reynolds, J. R.	Fayette	Rice, D.	Robertson
Reynolds, James	Anderson	Rice, Edward	Liberty
Reynolds, James	Brazroia	Rice, Elizabeth	Bowie
Reynolds,		Rice, George C.	Bowie
Jefferson	Grimes	Rice, James	Houston
Reynolds, John B.	Cherokee	Rice, James O.	Travis
Reynolds, John J.	Shelby	Rice, John G.	Washington
Reynolds, Margaret	Shelby	Rice, John M.	Burleson
Reynolds, Matilda	Henderson	Rice, Joseph	Burleson
Reynolds, R.	Houston	Rice, Joseph	Houston
Reynolds, R. W.	Lamar	Rice, Joseph	Upshur
Reynolds, S. S.	Shelby	Rice, Joseph W.	Galveston
Reynolds, Sarah	Harrison	Rice, L.	Houston
Reynolds, William		Rice, L. M.	Bowie
G.	Shelby	Rice, Levi M.	Bowie
Rhea, John	Bexar	Rice, Marshal	Washington
Rhea, John	Cass	Rice, Porter	Washington
Rhea, John R.	Harris	Rice, Saborne	Burleson
Rhea, John V.	Galveston	Rice, Solomon	Harris
Rhief, Jacob	Bexar	Rice, Spencer	Burleson
Rhodes, Adolphus	Colorado	Rice, W.	Burleson
Rhodes, Barney	Angelina	Rice, William	Polk
Rhodes, C. K.	Galveston	Rice, William M.	Harris
Rhodes, E. A.	Galveston	Rice, William S.	Robertson
Rhodes, E. A.	Grimes	Rice, Y. B.	Lamar
Rhodes, Elizabeth	Rusk	Rice & Mason	Bowie
Rhodes, Franklin	Liberty	Rich, James	Harrison
Rhodes, Jacob	Shelby	Rich, James A.	Harris
Rhodes, James	Montgomery	Rich, Peter	Liberty
Rhodes, John	Milam	Richards, Asa	Rusk
Rhodes, Josiah	Hunt	Richards, J.	Grimes
Rhodes, M. W.	Liberty	Richards, J. M.	Tyler
Rhodes, R.	Upshur	Richards, James S.	Shelby
Rhodes, Thomas	Angelina	Richards, John	Fannin
Rhodes, Thomas	Liberty	Richards, John D.	Shelby
Rhodes, William	Liberty	Richards, John S.	Shelby
Rhodes, William R.	Shelby	Richards, Levi	Fannin
Rhodins, Otto	Guadalupe	Richards, Lewis	Fannin
Rhodins, Thomas	Guadalupe	Richards, M.	Red River
Rhome, Mobley	Cherokee	Richards, Mary	Shelby
Rhorman, James	Montgomery	Richards, S. H.	Shelby
Rhuman, Edward	Colorado	Richards, Samuel	
Rials, John J.	Henderson	J.	Harris
Rias, Maria	Bexar	Richards, Stephen	Nacogdoches
Ribble, Adam	Red River	Richards, William	Shelby
Ribble, James	Red River	Richardson, A.	Milam
Ribble, John	Red River	Richardson, A. J.	Jasper
Rice, A. D.	Henderson	Richardson,	
Rice, A. P.	Burleson	Benjamin	Jasper

NAME	COUNTY	NAME	COUNTY
Richardson, D. H.	Walker	Riddell, J. L.	Montgomery
Richardson, D. L.	Grimes	Riddle, John	Bexar
Richardson, D. L.	Sabine	Riddle, L. M.	Titus
Richardson, E. F.	Angelina	Riddle, Sarah	Shelby
Richardson, George	Dallas	Riddle, William	Shelby
Richardson, George	Lamar	Riddle, Wilson J.	Bexar
Richardson, H. G.	San Augustine	Ridens, Bartlett	
Richardson, J.	Goliad	G.	Washington
Richardson, J. W.	Upshur	Ridens, John	Washington
Richardson, James	Jasper	Ridge, Isaac	Lamar
Richardson, John	Navarro	Ridgeway, A. W.	Harris
Richardson, John,		Ridgeway, Garat M.	Limestone
Jr.	Jasper	Ridgeway, J. H.	Montgomery
Richardson, John,		Ridgeway, John	Burleson
Sr.	Jasper	Ridgeway, John P.	Jefferson
Richardson,		Rieck, John	Comal
Jonathan	Navarro	Riedel, Anton	Comal
Richardson, Joshua	Navarro	Riedel, Nix	Comal
Richardson, L.	Red River	Rien, Jacob	Austin
Richardson, Lewis	Navarro	Rieves, William	Walker
Richardson, M. F.	Robertson	Riggs, Samuel	Burleson
Richardson, Paul	Dallas	Riggs, William	Navarro
Richardson, R. A.	Jasper	Right, Abner	Bastrop
Richardson, R. M.	Bowie	Right, Lewis	Bastrop
Richardson, Robert	Jasper	Rigil, William	Walker
Richardson,		Rigin, B. M.	Robertson
Stephen	Harris	Rigsby, Benjamin	Montgomery
Richardson, Thomas	Angelina	Rigsby, J. P.	Tyler
Richardson, Thomas	Navarro	Rigsby, Pheneus	Goliad
Richardson, Thomas		Rihn, Losing	Bexar
J.	Shelby	Riker, N. M.	Red River
Richardson, W. H.	Jasper	Riley, Isaac	Hunt
Richardson, Wm. S.	Harrison	Riley, James	Leon
Richardson, Zilpha	Smith	Riley, James W.	Lamar
Richie, Benjamin	Harris	Riley, John	Hunt
Richie, C.	Collin	Riley, John	Polk
Richie, Elijah	Panola	Riley, Joseph	Hunt
Richie, J.	Cass	Riley, Joseph W.	Fannin
Richie, J. S.	Upshur	Riley, Priscilla	Hunt
Richie, Thomas J.	Cass	Riley, Thomas	Hunt
Richison, Mrs. A.	Cass	Riley, William	Hunt
Richison, A. J.	Cass	Rind, G. H.	Titus
Richison, John	Anderson	Rine, Nathaniel	Houston
Richison, W. J.	Anderson	Ringer, John	Victoria
Richy, Susanah	Grimes	Ringo, Jonas	Titus
Ricketts, John S.	Harris	Ringo, Peter	Red River
Rickey, H.	Red River	Ringold, James	Grimes
Rickleth, Anyone	Bexar	Ringold, Thomas	Grimes
Rickmus, H.	Galveston	Riosdan, J.	Harris
Ricks, George W.	Travis	Ripley, A.	Cass

NAME	COUNTY	NAME	COUNTY
Ripley, Ambrose	Titus	Roberson, L.	Anderson
Ripley, William	Victoria	Roberson, Z.	Leon
Rippy, P.	Hunt	Roberts, Abram	Harris
Risley, George	San Patricio	Roberts, Allen	Henderson
Rister, F. C.	Liberty	Roberts, C. B.	Cherokee
Ritchey, Alexander	Lamar	Roberts, Charles	Walker
Ritchey, W. F.	Henderson	Roberts, Cynthia	Brazoria
Ritchey, William	Lamar	Roberts, Daniel	Sabine
Ritchie, Henry	Red River	Roberts, David	Anderson
Ritchie, James	Red River	Roberts, E. G.	Henderson
Ritchie, Sam A.	Red River	Roberts, Elisha	Houston
Ritchie, Vyrus	Red River	Roberts, Elizabeth	Washington
Ritchie, W. F.	Henderson	Roberts, F. G.	San Augustine
Ritter, John	Denton	Roberts, G. W.	San Augustine
Ritter, John L.	Newton	Roberts, George B.	Panola
Ritter, William	Denton	Roberts, George H.	Harris
Rivers, Antonio	Grimes	Roberts, Harriet	Nacogdoches
Rivers, John	Cass	Roberts, Isaac	San Augustine
Rivore, William K.	Bexar	Roberts, Isaac H.	Houston
Roach, A. J.	Liberty	Roberts, J.	Collin
Roach, B. E.	Austin	Roberts, J. E.	Shelby
Roader, A. V.	Austin	Roberts, J. S.	Harris
Roader, Ludie	Austin	Roberts, J. T.	Collin
Roader, William V.	Austin	Roberts, Jeremiah	Gonzales
Roahamder, Andrew	Austin	Roberts, John	Colorado
Roam, John	Rusk	Roberts, John	Fannin
Roan, John P.	Grimes	Roberts, John	Lamar
Roan, Mobley	Houston	Roberts, John B.	Shelby
Roan, Willia J.	Grimes	Roberts, John F.	Nacogdoches
Roan, William	Grimes	Roberts, John G.	Sabine
Roanguer, M.	Victoria	Roberts, John S.	Nacogdoches
Roark, John	Navarro	Roberts, Joseph	Hopkins
Roark, Margaret	Cherokee	Roberts, Joseph	Jefferson
Roark, Reed W.	Walker	Roberts, Joseph	Rusk
Roark, William	Cherokee	Roberts, Josiah	Jasper
Robb, Benjamin	Polk	Roberts, Luke	Cass
Robbins, George	Dallas	Roberts, Luke	Washington
Robbins, John	Red River	Roberts, Mark	Anderson
Robbins, Josh	Walker	Roberts, Mark R.	Fannin
Robbins, Penelope	Walker	Roberts, Moses F.	Shelby
Robbins, S.	Matagorda	Roberts, Noel G.	San Augustine
Robbinson, J. T.	Grimes	Roberts, O. M.	San Augustine
Robbinson, J. W.	Grimes	Roberts, Rachel	Walker
Robe, Andrew	Panola	Roberts, Ray	Grimes
Roben, J. J.	Henderson	Roberts, Redim	Burleson
Robenson, E.	Liberty	Roberts, Reuben	Fannin
Robenson, Elem	Liberty	Roberts, Robert J.	Washington
Robenson, James	Liberty	Roberts, Samuel A.	Fannin
Roberson, Harmon	Nacogdoches	Roberts, Stephen	
Roberson, J. L.	Leon	R.	Washington

NAME	COUNTY	NAME	COUNTY
Roberts, T. C.	Hopkins	Robins, John K.	Austin
Roberts, T. H.	Walker	Robins, Joseph	Houston
Roberts, Thomas	Grimes	Robinson, E. J.	Galveston
Roberts, Thomas K.	Grimes	Robinson, E. P.	Grimes
Roberts, W. E.	Shelby	Robinson, Daniel	Milam
Roberts, W. W.	Limestone	Robinson, Daniel	Montgomery
Roberts, William	Anderson	Robinson, Gabriel	Jefferson
Roberts, William	Burleson	Robinson, Hy F.	Nacogdoches
Roberts, William	Walker	Robinson, James	Bexar
Roberts, William H.	Brazoria	Robinson, James	Fayette
		Robinson, James W.	Lavaca
Roberts, William M.	Montgomery	Robinson, Jesse	Lavaca
		Robinson, Jesse J.	Sabine
Roberts, Zion	Walker	Robinson, Joel W.	Fayette
Robertson, A. B.	Austin	Robinson, John H.	Grimes
Robertson, Andrew	Washington	Robinson, Joseph	Fayette
Robertson, Arthur	Rusk	Robinson, Joseph	Goliad
Robertson, Asa	Rusk	Robinson, Joseph T.	Brazos
Robertson, F. W.	Galveston		
Robertson, H. M.	Upshur	Robinson, M. C.	Harris
Robertson, H. V.	Washington	Robinson, N. T.	Shelby
Robertson, Hays	Robertson	Robinson, Neil	Fayette
Robertson, Henry A.	Fayette	Robinson, R. O.	San Augustine
		Robinson, S. S.	Galveston
Robertson, J. B.	Washington	Robinson, Sarah A.	Fayette
Robertson, J. M.	Shelby	Robinson, Seborn J.	Harrison
Robertson, J. N.	Upshur		
Robertson, J. W.	Titus	Robinson, Smith	Henderson
Robertson, J. W.	Travis	Robinson, Tate	San Augustine
Robertson, James	Rusk	Robinson, Thomas	Fayette
Robertson, James P.	Rusk	Robinson, Thomas G.	Harris
Robertson, John	Galveston	Robinson, Thompson	Bexar
Robertson, Joseph R.	Robertson	Robinson, Tod	Brazoria
Robertson, Moses	Rusk	Robinson, William	Fort Bend
Robertson, R. G.	Rusk	Robinson, William	Victoria
Robertson, S. B.	Bowie	Robinson, William M.	Fayette
Robertson, S. C.	Robertson	Robison, Asa	Austin
Robertson, Samuel	Rusk	Robison, Ben	Walker
Robertson, Thomas	Bexar	Robison, Charles	Houston
Robertson, Thomas H.	Bowie	Robison, China M.	Cass
		Robison, G. W.	Walker
Robertson, Thomas H.	Harrison	Robison, Jack	Red River
		Robison, John	Washington
Robertson, W. L.	Rusk	Robison, Samuel	Victoria
Robertson, William	Upshur	Robison, William	Austin
Robinett, J. J.	Red River	Robison, William	Houston
Robinett, John	Harris	Robison, William	Walker
Robins, G. M.	Houston	Robson, Robert	Colorado

NAME	COUNTY	NAME	COUNTY
Rockwell, J. T.	Harris	Rogers, James M.	Grimes
Rodden, David B.	Shelby	Rogers, John	Harrison
Rodden, J. C.	Shelby	Rogers, John	Walker
Rodden, John	Shelby	Rogers, John A.	Jackson
Roddy, Ephriam	Washington	Rogers, John H.	Cass
Rodes, E.	Travis	Rogers, Jonathan	Bastrop
Rodes, Henry	Travis	Rogers, Joseph	Fannin
Rode, James	Red River	Rogers, Joseph	Grimes
Rodes, Lee	Red River	Rogers, Joseph E.	Polk
Rodes, Susan	Tyler	Rogers, Joseph H.	Jackson
Rodgers, A. G.	Leon	Rogers, Joseph N.	Nacogdoches
Rodgers, Bethany	Leon	Rogers, L. H.	Henderson
Rodgers, James	Liberty	Rogers, M. C.	Walker
Rodgers, M. T.	Harris	Rogers, M. E.	Grimes
Rodgers, Mary Ann	Liberty	Rogers, Moses	Brazoria
Rodgers, R. C.	Harris	Rogers, Nancy	Bastrop
Rodgers, Robert	Leon	Rogers, P. J.	Cherokee
Rodgers, Robert,		Rogers, R.	Anderson
Sr.	Leon	Rogers, Rolly	Montgomery
Rodgers, William		Rogers, S. B.	Cass
S.	Fayette	Rogers, S. C. A.	Jackson
Rodnjny, Ferdinand	Bexar	Rogers, Samuel	Liberty
Rodnjny(?), Gib	Bexar	Rogers, Samuel C.	Goliad
Rodnjny, Ramon	Bexar	Rogers, Sela	Grimes
Rodriguez, Antonio	Bexar	Rogers, Simeon	Cass
Rodriguez, Juan	Bexar	Rogers, Simeon	Victoria
Rodriguez, Manuel	Bexar	Rogers, Steven	Grimes
Rodriguez, Syl.	Bexar	Rogers, T. H. M.	Grimes
Roe, J. W.	Navarro	Rogers, T. J.	Titus
Roe, W. C.	Grimes	Rogers, Thomas H.	Nacogdoches
Roeark, J.	Henderson	Rogers, W. S.	Robertson
Roge, Henry	Comal	Rogers, Wiley	San Augustine
Rogers, Armsted	Grimes	Rohda, Hervey	Fayette
Rogers, Cossan	Fannin	Roher, Henry L.	San Augustine
Rogers, Daniel	Anderson	Roher, Jacob	San Augustine
Rogers, E. C.	Fannin	Roice, Wait F.	Grimes
Rogers, E. E.	Grimes	Roland, J. S.	Grimes
Rogers, E. G.	Titus	Roland, John	Lamar
Rogers, E. S.	Grimes	Roland, Sherwood	Lamar
Rogers, Elias	Navarro	Roland, T. M.	Collin
Rogers, Elias	Panola	Rolf, Calvin H.	Panola
Rogers, F. A.	Jackson	Rolin, Francisco	Bexar
Rogers, G. F.	Victoria	Rolin, J. S.	Walker
Rogers, George	Walker	Rolison, Ridley	Lamar
Rogers, Henry	Jackson	Rollins, E.	Cass
Rogers, Henry	Nacogdoches	Rollins, James	Fannin
Rogers, James	Anderson	Rollins, Mark	Walker
Rogers, James	Bastrop	Rolls, Elliott	Cherokee
Rogers, James	Hopkins	Rolls, Samuel	Cherokee
Rogers, James C.	Nacogdoches	Romaine, William	

NAME	COUNTY	NAME	COUNTY
C.	Grayson	Rousseau, L.	Harris
Roof, John E.	Henderson	Routhe, Michael	Goliad
Rooker, Isaac W.	Newton	Rowan, Milton	Angelina
Rooks, F.	Houston	Rowe, Francis M.	Galveston
Rooks, Henry	Nacogdoches	Rowe, J. R.	Smith
Rosa, Francisco	Bexar	Rowe, J. T.	Travis
Rosa, Lorenzo	Bexar	Rowe, Robert	Travis
Rosales, Francisco	Henderson	Rowe, Samuel	Polk
Rose, Francis	Cherokee	Rowe, T. M.	Jefferson
Rose, Henry	Cherokee	Rowe, Thomas E.	Travis
Rose, Hiram	Victoria	Rowell, James	Goliad
Rose, Horatio	Sabine	Rowland, John	Harrison
Rose, J.	Henderson	Rowland, Joseph	Burleson
Rose, J. W.	Victoria	Rowland, Riley H.	Limestone
Rose, Lewis	Henderson	Rowland, Susan J.	Harrison
Rose, Mrs. Mary	Cass	Rowlett, Daniel	Fannin
Rose, Preston	Victoria	Roxa, Jose	Bexar
Rose, R. R.	Cass	Royl, Peter	Walker
Rose, Thomas	Fannin	Royster, Thomas	Jackson
Rose, William	Cherokee	Rozell, James	Cherokee
Roseborough, J. P.	Harrison	Rozell, James, Jr.	Cherokee
Rosell, J.	Victoria	Rozier, John L.	Jackson
Roser, Henry	Comal	Rubio, Christoval	Goliad
Rosia, Diego	Victoria	Ruble, Fielding	Grimes
Rosin, Hiram	Walker	Rucker, Benjamin	
Ross, A. E.	Rusk	F.	Washington
Ross, D. K.	San Augustine	Rucker, Calvin	Anderson
Ross, David	Cass	Rucker, L. P.	Washington
Ross, Eli P.	Fort Bend	Rucker, Thomas J.	
Ross, Elizabeth	Robertson	R.	Washington
Ross, Francis W.	Lamar	Ruckman, John	Cherokee
Ross, George	Harris	Ruddell, Abraham	Cherokee
Ross, James	Fayette	Ruddell, John	Sabine
Ross, James	Rusk	Rudder, E. H.	Bastrop
Ross, John	San Patricio	Rudder, Nathaniel	Brazoria
Ross, Margaret M.	Fayette	Rue, R. J. W.	Brazoria
Ross, Robert	Rusk	Rugeley, Alexander	Matagorda
Ross, Robert C.	DeWitt	Rugeley, J.	Matagorda
Ross, S. B.	Walker	Ruise, F.	Robertson
Ross, Thomas	Calhoun	Ruiz, Antonio	Bexar
Ross, W.	Grayson	Ruiz, Francisco	Bexar
Ross, W. H.	Shelby	Ruiz, Jose	Bexar
Ross, William	Cherokee	Rump, J. E.	Galveston
Ross, William W.	Lamar	Rumphfield, S.	Montgomery
Rotan, Joseph A.	Tyler	Rundell, John	Harris
Rotthass, F. Jacob	Harris	Rundell, Joseph	Harris
Rounds, George	Brazoria	Runnels, Dudley	Brazoria
Rountree, James L.	Travis	Runnels, E. S.	Bowie
Rountree, Wm. A.	Travis	Runnels, H. A.	Bowie
Rouse, Daniel	Harrison	Runnels, H. R.	Bowie

NAME	COUNTY	NAME	COUNTY
Runnels, H. W.	Bowie	Ruth, H.	Collin
Runnels, Hal G.	Brazoria	Ruth, John	Fannin
Runnels, James	San Augustine	Ruth, L.	Collin
Runnels, Martha B.	Bowie	Rutherford, C. D.	Newton
Ruse, Moses	Cass	Rutherford,	
Rush, D. J.	Cass	Harriet	Austin
Rush, J. W.	Henderson	Rutherford, James	Titus
Rush, William	Rusk	Rutherford, John	
Rushing, A. B.	Lamar	A.	Lamar
Rushing, Allen	Rusk	Rutherford, R. A.	Bastrop
Rushing, Andrew J.	DeWitt	Rutherford, R. D.	Cherokee
Rushing, Ann	Rusk	Rutherford, Samuel	Cherokee
Rusk, David	Nacogdoches	Rutledge, Charles	Panola
Rusk, T. J.	Henderson	Rutledge, J. S.	Titus
Rusk, Thomas J.	Houston	Rutledge, John	Newton
Rusk, Thomas J.	Nacogdoches	Rutledge, Mary	Panola
Russell, A. C.	Bastrop	Rutledge, R.	Grimes
Russell, A. J.	Bowie	Rutledge, Richard	Harris
Russell, Alexander	Brazoria	Rutledge, Thomas	Grayson
Russell, Allen A.	Anderson	Rutledge, Thomas	Washington
Russell, David	Harris	Rutledge, Thomas	
Russell, Mrs. E.		P.	Gonzales
H.	Brazoria	Rutledge, William	
Russell, Eli H.	Nacogdoches	P.	Harrison
Russell, Gibson	Nacogdoches	Rutledge, Wm. P.	Washington
Russell, Hiram	Lamar	Rutza, Ambrose	Bexar
Russell, J.	Collin	Royle, Solomon	San Augustine
Russell, J.	Henderson	Ryan, David	Burleson
Russell, James	Lamar	Ryan, Henry	Lavaca
Russell, James	San Augustine	Ryan, James	Lavaca
Russell, James	Tyler	Ryan, James H.	Burleson
Russell, Jesse,		Ryan, John	Fort Bend
Jr.	Panola	Ryan, John	San Patricio
Russell, Jesse,		Ryan, Matthew	San Patricio
Sr.	Panola	Ryan, N.	Lavaca
Russell, John, Jr.	Lamar	Ryan, Richard	Shelby
Russell, John, Sr.	Lamar	Ryan, William	Burleson
Russell, L. M.	Anderson	Ryan, William	Goliad
Russell, Lurelia	San Augustine	Ryan, William R.	
Russell, N. G.	Henderson	P.	Lavaca
Russell, R. B.	San Augustine	Ryburn, H. W.	Grayson
Russell, R. R.	Houston	Ryder, Mary	Red River
Russell, Ross	Rusk	Rylie, James R.	Dallas
Russell, T. H.	Anderson	Ryneky, John	Grayson
Russell, Thomas	Colorado		
Russell, W.	Matagorda		
Russell, William	Cass	Sabinas, M.	Victoria
Russell, William	Goliad	Sadler, Frances	Grimes
Russell, William	Lamar	Sadler, Hiram	Lamar
Russell, Wm. J.	Brazoria	Sadler, James C.	Lamar

NAME	COUNTY	NAME	COUNTY
Sadler, James M.	Lamar	Sanders, Drury	Leon
Sadler, John	Lamar	Sanders, J.	Matagorda
Sadler, John W.	Walker	Sanders, J. F.	Tyler
Sadler, Thomas N.	Lamar	Sanders, J. H. T.	Bowie
Sadler, W. D.	Anderson	Sanders, J. T.	Liberty
Sadler, William S.	Lamar	Sanders, Jack	Red River
Saffle, John	Colorado	Sanders, James T.	Lamar
Saiherer, Gabriel	Comal	Sanders, John	San Augustine
St. Clair, D.	Jefferson	Sanders, John	Shelby
St. Clair, Daniel	Lamar	Sanders, Lemuel D.	Newton
St. Clair, Duncan	Liberty	Sanders, S. B.	Henderson
St. Clair, Samuel	Lamar	Sanders, S. H.	Shelby
St. Clair, Wm. H.	Shelby	Sanders, Thomas	Harrison
St. John, William	Refugio	Sanders, U.	Grimes
St. Martin, August	Bexar	Sanders, William	Fannin
St. Mary, E.	Travis	Sanderson, C. R.,	
St. Stephen,		Jr.	Henderson
Duncan	Jackson	Sanderson, C. R.,	
Salazar, Julian	Bexar	Sr.	Henderson
Salazar, Madera	Bexar	Sanderson, Polly	Galveston
Salazar, Tomas	Bexar	Sanderson, William	
Sales, Rebeca	Travis	A.	Shelby
Saligna, J.	Henderson	Sandford, A.	Shelby
Saligney, A.	Galveston	Sandford, E.	Shelby
Salinas, Antonio	Bexar	Sandford, George	Shelby
Salinas, Pablo	Bexar	Sandford, James	Navarro
Salmons, James	Lamar	Sandford, S. Z.	Shelby
Salziger,		Sandford, Samuel	Shelby
Gottfried	Comas	Sandford, Snider	Shelby
Sample, John	Brazoria	Sandford, Stephen	Navarro
Sample, John	Shelby	Sandford, William	Shelby
Sample, William M.	Brazoria	Sandidge, John M.	Grimes
Sampson, Allen	Harris	Sandman, Joseph	Harris
Sampson, Henry	Harris	Sandoval, Carlos	Bexar
Sampson, Hugh	Grayson	Sandoval, Fernando	Bexar
Sampson, J. L.	Henderson	Sandusky, J. M.	Galveston
Sampson, James	Red River	Sandusky, William	
Sampson, W.	Hunt	H.	Galveston
Samuel, A. L.	Walker	San Meguil, Padro	Bexar
Sanborn, William		Sanpier, James M.	Burleson
P.	Tyler	Sansbury, James W.	Fort Bend
Sanchez, David	Nacogdoches	Sansom, John W.	Polk
Sanchez, Jose	Henderson	Sansom, William	Fayette
Sanchez, Julian	Leon	Santos, Cornalo	Nacogdoches
Sanchez, Luis	Leon	Santos, Cos	Bexar
Sanchez, M.	Henderson	Santos, Nicholas	Bexar
Sanchez, Pedro	Bexar	Santos Coy, Benino	Nacogdoches
Sanchez, Ygnaclas	Leon	Santtoy, Antonio	Nacogdoches
Sanday, R. H.	San Augustine	Santy, W. A.	Grimes
Sanders, C. A.	Henderson	Sapp, A.	Tyler

NAME	COUNTY	NAME	COUNTY
Sapp, A. J. D.	Tyler	Scarborough, M. R.	Limestone
Sapp, B.	Tyler	Scarborough, Paul	Fayette
Sapp, S. H.	Shelby	Scarborough, Winey	Red River
Sargent, G.	Matagorda	Scates, William B.	Fayette
Sargent,		Schafer, Henry	Comal
Washington	Washington	Scheidemantel, D.	Galveston
Sasse, Jacob	Galveston	Schertz, Josef	Comal
Sattler, William	Comal	Schertz, S.	Comal
Sauerborn, widow	Comal	Schevallin, D.	Galveston
Saul, Charles	Walker	Schierman, Fred	Harris
Saul, John	Walker	Schlecht, Charles	Brazoria
Saul, Nimmo	Bexar	Schmidt, Adolph	Bexar
Saunders,		Schmidt, Edward	Comal
Alexander	Harrison	Schmidt, Ernst	Comal
Saunders, F. W.	San Augustine	Schmidt, F.	Galveston
Saunders, J. M.	Harrison	Schmidt, G.	Galveston
Saunders, J. S.	Bexar	Schmidt, Martin	Bexar
Saunders, John	San Augustine	Schmidt, Sconted	Comal
Saunders, John P.	Houston	Schmitz, Fokol	Comal
Saunders, Mary A.	Harrison	Schmottling,	
Saunders, Richard	Harrison	Catharine	Bexar
Saunders, Robert,		Schneider,	
Sr.	Shelby	Catherine	Bastrop
Saunders, Stephen		Schneider, F.	Liberty
N.	Smith	Schneider, John	Comal
Saunders, T. C.	Harrison	Schoonover,	
Saunders, Thomas		Benjamin	Lamar
C.	Harrison	Schrier, Nick	Bexar
Saunders, W. S.	Henderson	Schrimfer, John W.	Harris
Saunders, William	Harrison	Schrimfer, Johann	Comal
Sauters, John A.	Galveston	Schulze, J. H.	Comal
Savage, B. F.	Collin	Schumacher,	
Savage, J.	Collin	William	Comal
Savage, J. S.	Galveston	Schuman, T. M.	Galveston
Savage, James	Grayson	Schumm, B.	Bexar
Savage, N.	Matagorda	Schwab, Francis	Galveston
Sawey, James	DeWitt	Schwab, Thomas	Comal
Sawyer, William L.	Harris	Scoby, Andrew A.	Brazoria
Sayles, John	Washington	Scoby, Mary	Brazoria
Sayre, Charles D.	Bexar	Scoby, Matthew	Brazoria
Sayre, Charles D.	Brazoria	Scoby, Robert	Brazoria
Scagg, R.	Collin	Scoby, S.	Brazoria
Scales, Abraham	Liberty	Scofield, John	Polk
Scallern, Newton	Fayette	Scofield, William	Polk
Scallern, William	Fayette	Scott, Abner	Travis
Scallorn, Stephen	Fayette	Scott, Abram H.	Cass
Scallorn, T. J.	Fayette	Scott, Benjamin	Bowie
Scarborough, D. B.	Limestone	Scott, C.	Harrison
Scarborough, F. G.	Red River	Scott, Charles P.	Lamar
Scarborough, James	Wharton	Scott, Cyrus	Travis

NAME	COUNTY	NAME	COUNTY
Scott, David	Bastrop	Scott, Z.	Harrison
Scott, David	Jefferson	Scranton, Fred	Harris
Scott, F. B.	Harrison	Screws, Allen	Rusk
Scott, F. M.	Harrison	Screws, Nathan	Rusk
Scott, G. D.	Red River	Scrier, James	Walker
Scott, George W.	Harris	Scrimsher, J. W.	Fannin
Scott, George W.	Travis	Scroggins, William	
Scott, Henry	Refugio	V.	Rusk
Scott, Isaac	San Augustine	Scruggs, C. S.	Panola
Scott, J.	Brazos	Scruggs, E. H.	Houston
Scott, J. T.	Bastrop	Scruggs, Jesse T.	Sabine
Scott, J. W.	Brazos	Scrutchfield, L.	Milam
Scott, J. W.	Grimes	Scull, W. D.	Liberty
Scott, J. W.	Harris	Scurlock, John	Dallas
Scott, James	Grimes	Scurlock, William	Red River
Scott, James	Harris	Scurlock, William	Sabine
Scott, James	Harrison	Scurry, Richardson	Washington
Scott, James W.	Burleson	Seaborn, Henry	Brazoria
Scott, John	Burleson	Seabough, Conrad	Comal
Scott, John	Shelby	Seal, C. C.	Brazos
Scott, John M.	Sabine	Seal, Eli	Brazos
Scott, John W.	Cass	Seal, Joseph A.	Brazos
Scott, Jonathan	Brazoria	Seal, Joshua	Brazos
Scott, Jonathan	DeWitt	Seals, James	Tyler
Scott, Joseph	Travis	Seals, Solomon	Sabine
Scott, Joseph E.	Burleson	Sealey, James B.	Jackson
Scott, L. B.	Burleson	Sealey, Mrs. N. W.	Jackson
Scott, Levi P.	Fort Bend	Seals, C.	Fannin
Scott, Lyford	Grayson	Seals, Littleton	Walker
Scott, M. J.	Brazoria	Seaper, W. J.	Austin
Scott, Moses	Brazos	Searcy, C.	Collin
Scott, Moses	Fort Bend	Searcy, L. C.	Collin
Scott, Noah	Austin	Searcy, S. B.	Collin
Scott, P. B.	Burleson	Seaton, G. W.	Grimes
Scott, Phebe	Austin	Seawell, Maria	Galveston
Scott, R. J.	Bexar	Seawright, John	Lamar
Scott, Randolph	Lamar	Seay, David	Cass
Scott, Robert W.	Burleson	Secrest, Felix G.	Fort Bend
Scott, S.	Grimes	Secrest,	
Scott, Samuel A.	Burleson	Washington	Fayette
Scott, Sarah T.	Harrison	Secundo, Ramon	Bexar
Scott, Thomas	Leon	Seele, Hermann	Comal
Scott, Thomas L.	Washington	Seele, Thomas T.	Liberty
Scott, Timothy	Fort Bend	Seeley, David	Limestone
Scott, W. J.	Burleson	Seeligson, A.	Galveston
Scott, William	Lamar	Seeligson, Michael	Galveston
Scott, William	San Augustine	Seguin, Antonio	Bexar
Scott, William H.	Brazoria	Seguin, Cantetos	Bexar
Scott, William M.	Brazoria	Seguin, Erasmus	Bexar
Scott, William T.	Harrison	Seguin, Josefa	Bexar

NAME	COUNTY	NAME	COUNTY
Seguin, Ysabel	Bexar	Shaffer, John	Fannin
Seideman, Peter	Comal	Shafles, C. R.	Bowie
Seiders, E.	Travis	Shahan, David	Dallas
Seiter, Jacob	Comal	Shahan, Patrick	Panola
Seivis, George	Leon	Shaler, David	Shelby
Self, Thomas M.	Shelby	Shamblee, G. W.	Robertson
Salkirk, ----	Matagorda	Shandle, B.	Henderson
Sellers, Achilles	Harris	Shandon, Jackson	Henderson
Sellers, B. F.	Brazoria	Shanklin, D. J.	Collin
Sellers, Robert	Fayette	Shanks, ----	Henderson
Sellers, William	Brazoria	Shanks, J. T.	San Augustine
Sellkriggs, David	Wharton	Shanley, Jea.	Henderson
Sells, B. F.	Cherokee	Shannahan, J. B.	Red River
Selman, James W.	Cherokee	Shannon, A.	Grimes
Selman, P. F.	Washington	Shannon, Benjamin	Anderson
Selman, Stafford	Cherokee	Shannon, E. D.	Brazoria
Selman, Wesley	Cherokee	Shannon, J. K.	Limestone
Selvage, M. K.	Shelby	Shannon, Jacob	Montgomery
Semigo, Jose	Bexar	Shannon, James B.	Grayson
Semigo, Pedro	Bexar	Shannon, Jesse	Liberty
Senechal, A.	Harris	Shannon, John M.	Colorado
Sensaboy, G. A.	Washington	Shannon, M. W.	Montgomery
Sepolt, F.	Austin	Shannon, Margaret	Montgomery
Sergeant, William		Shannon, Owen	Montgomery
M.	Galveston	Shannon, S. J.	Grayson
Sessern, Rodden	Shelby	Shannon, T. J.	Red River
Sessions, B. N.	Harris	Shannon, V.	Victoria
Sessum, Jacob	Panola	Shannon, William	Montgomery
Sessum, Reuben	Panola	Shaver, John	Anderson
Sessum, Solomon	Panola	Shapard, J. T.	Washington
Settle, John A.	Galveston	Shapard, L. J.	Washington
Setzer, Martin	Red River	Shapard, Thomas P.	Washington
Sevier, E. G.	Victoria	Sharkey, John	Shelby
Sevier, E. J.	Henderson	Sharo, Dushee	Harrison
Sevier, George	Navarro	Sharo, Hugh B.	Red River
Sevier, John	Walker	Sharock, James	Dallas
Seward, J. A.	Wharton	Sharron, James	Walker
Seward, John	Washington	Sharp, A. V.	Brazoria
Seward, Lem	Washington	Sharp, Daniel	Refugio
Sewarts, J. H.	Collin	Sharp, J. M.	Henderson
Sexton, Emily	San Augustine	Sharp, James	Henderson
Sexton, Emily H.	Henderson	Sharp, James M.	Nacogdoches
Sexton, M.	Matagorda	Sharp, John	Burleson
Seybold, William	Newton	Sharp, John	Grimes
Shaben, Henry	Montgomery	Sharp, John D.	Cass
Shaben, Mary	Montgomery	Sharp, Joseph D.	Henderson
Shackelford, John,		Sharp, Joseph D.	Nacogdoches
Jr.	Harris	Sharp, Mahala L.	San Augustine
Shackelford, M. B.	Grayson	Sharp, William A.	Sabine
Shadown, James	Panola	Shattock, Horace	Brazoria

NAME	COUNTY	NAME	COUNTY
Shattock, V. P.	Galveston	Shelman, Joseph	Henderson
Shaver, P. J.	Fayette	Shelp, D. C.	Travis
Shaw, Amanda	Galveston	Sheltman, W.	Henderson
Shaw, B. A.	Washington	Shelton, A. H.	Milam
Shaw, D. W.	Harrison	Shelton, Eli	Lamar
Shaw, Ellis B.	Lavaca	Shelton, Francis	Smith
Shaw, J. C.	Walker	Shelton, G. W.	Liberty
Shaw, James	Burleson	Shelton, George A.	Anderson
Shaw, James	Cherokee	Shelton, James	Austin
Shaw, John	Grimes	Shelton, Jesse	Lamar
Shaw, Joseph	Fayette	Shelton, John	Hopkins
Shaw, Joshua C.	Galveston	Shelton, Johnson	Anderson
Shaw, Joshia	Colorado	Shelton, S. B.	Austin
Shaw, Josiah	Panola	Shelton, S. H.	Bastrop
Shaw, L.	Grimes	Shelton, W. H.	Dallas
Shaw, Peter V.	Fayette	Shelton, William	
Shaw, Robert	Cass	C.	Dallas
Shaw, William	Lavaca	Shelton, Willis H.	Dallas
Shaw, William N.	Newton	Shepherd, B. A.	Harris
Shea, John	Harris	Shepherd,	
Shearer, Benard	Fayette	Christopher	Hopkins
Shearer, H. R.	Henderson	Shepherd, David	Hopkins
Shearer, S. M.	Upshur	Shepherd, Hugh	Panola
Shearer, Spencer	Titus	Shepherd, J. R.	Polk
Shearn, Charley	Harris	Shepherd, John	Nacogdoches
Sheerwood, J.	Jackson	Shepherd, L. T.	Jackson
Sheerwood, William	San Augustine	Shepherd, M. H.	Harris
Sheets, Henry	Walker	Shepherd, Richard	Nacogdoches
Sheffield, James		Shepherd, S. D.	Cherokee
R.	Gonzales	Shepherd, Simpson	Nacogdoches
Sheffield, John C.	Guadalupe	Shepherd, Thomas	Liberty
Shelborne, Mrs.		Shepherd, William	
Margaret	Harrison	A.	Colorado
Shelburn, J. B.	Austin	Shepherd, Wm. D.	Hopkins
Shelburn, S. A.	Austin	Sheppard, A.	Matagorda
Shelburn, T. K.	Austin	Sheppard, C. B.	Washington
Shelby, A. B.	Galveston	Sheppard, D. J.	Matagorda
Shelby, A. J.	Jasper	Sheppard, J.	Victoria
Shelby, David	Austin	Sheppard, J. G.	Matagorda
Shelby, E.	Collin	Sheppard, John E.	Galveston
Shelby, John	Refugio	Sheppard, Jonas	Rusk
Shelby, Malinda	Jasper	Sheppard, S. A.	Montgomery
Shelby, Patrick	Refugio	Sheppard, William	
Shelland, William	Fayette	W.	Montgomery
Shellentrager, ---	Victoria	Sherban, Joseph A.	Calhoun
Shelly, Abram	Hopkins	Sheriden, J. F.	Grayson
Shelly, George	Fannin	Sherly, Felix	Jasper
Shelly, Hyram	Hopkins	Sherman, Humphrey	Harris
Shelly, James	Dallas	Sherman, J.	Henderson
Shelly, James	Gonzales	Sherman, Robert	Liberty

NAME	COUNTY	NAME	COUNTY
Sherman, Sidney	Harris	Short, Jesse	Lamar
Sherman, Silas	Fayette	Short, John	Fayette
Sherrill, Arthur	Colorado	Short, John	Grayson
Sherrod, J. E.	Austin	Short, M. H.	Harris
Sherrod, J. L.	Harrison	Short, William	Fayette
Sherrod, Mrs.		Shragley, C. M.	Henderson
Lucynda	Harrison	Shrock, H. G.	Matagorda
Sherrod, William	Austin	Shropshire, James	Harrison
Sherwood, A. B.	Bowie	Shrum, Isaac	Lamar
Sherwood, George	Polk	Shryock, M. H.	San Augustine
Sherwood, J. W.	Bowie	Shuburk, William	Austin
Sherwood, James P.	Galveston	Shudon, John	Houston
Shewitt, George	Victoria	Shuk, Adam	Titus
Shields, Jackson	Nacogdoches	Shuk, Joseph	Titus
Shields, Nathaniel	Burleson	Shults, V.	Shelby
Shields, Nathaniel	Milam	Shumate, S. L.	Hunt
Shields, William		Shupe, Samuel	Jackson
C.	Cherokee	Shurod(?), Wm.	Brazoria
Shimmer, B.	Colorado	Shuttles, C. W.	Fayette
Shimmer, B. G.	Colorado	Shuttles, John	Fayette
Shiner, Peter	Victoria	Shuw, Joseph B.	Travis
Shinn, Franklin	Harris	Sides, George	Fayette
Ship, James	San Augustine	Sidex, A.	Victoria
Ship, John	San Augustine	Siedikum, F.	Bowie
Ship, Joseph	San Augustine	Siegismund, August	Austin
Shipman, Calvin	Anderson	Siekenburger, Otto	Angelina
Shipman, Daniel	Washington	Sierra, Jose	Bexar
Shipman, Hunt	Hunt	Sierra, Norberto	Bexar
Shipman, J. L.	Upshur	Sigler, William N.	Sabine
Shipman, James R.	Fort Bend	Sikes, James H.	DeWitt
Shipman, L.	Fort Bend	Sikes, N. N.	Henderson
Shipman, Moses	Burleson	Sillard, W.	Navarro
Shirley, Edmund	Fannin	Silman, Wm. P.	Nacogdoches
Shirley, Nathaniel	Houston	Silvers, Hiram	Fannin
Shirley, T. P.	Bastrop	Silvey, James E.	Colorado
Shirley, Tyler	Tyler	Simler, E.	Harris
Shoat, Champion	Rusk	Simmons, Abner	Harris
Shocky, Henry	Lamar	Simmons, D. H.	Jefferson
Shoemaker, Calvin	Cherokee	Simmons, David P.	Grayson
Shoemaker, E.	Titus	Simmons, E. C.	Titus
Shoemaker, John	Cherokee	Simmons, Isaac	Grayson
Shofner, Acton	San Augustine	Simmons, J. W.	Fort Bend
Shofner, J. N.	San Augustine	Simmons, James	Limestone
Shofner, R. L.	Angelina	Simmons, James	Nacogdoches
Shook, J. W.	Harris	Simmons, James	Shelby
Shoop, Nathaniel	Cass	Simmons, James,	
Short, D. M.	Shelby	Jr.	Harris
Short, Eli S.	Grayson	Simmons, James,	
Short, Hubbard	Fannin	Sr.	Harris
Short, James	Lavaca	Simmons, John	Harris

NAME	COUNTY	NAME	COUNTY
Simmons, John B.	Lamar	Sims, E.	Grimes
Simmons, Joseph	Lamar	Sims, Isham	Fayette
Simmons, Joseph W.	Harris	Sims, J.	Fayette
Simmons, M.	Cass	Sims, J. T.	Walker
Simmons, Obediah	Hopkins	Sims, J. W.	Red River
Simmons, Richard	Newton	Sims, James	Panola
Simmons, Solomon	DeWitt	Sims, John	Anderson
Simmons, Stephen	Harris	Sims, John	Tyler
Simmons, Thomas	Titus	Sims, M. F.	Henderson
Simmons, W.	Bastrop	Sims, Mathew	Hopkins
Simmons, W. T.	Bowie	Sims, R. H.	San Augustine
Simmons, William		Sims, R. J.	Red River
M.	Tyler	Sims, Robert	Victoria
Simms, Michael	Brazos	Sims, Samuel H.	Red River
Simons, Barnes	Jackson	Sims, T. M.	Red River
Simons, Ferdinand	Comal	Sims, William	Red River
Simons, S. D.	Burleson	Sinclair, James	Grayson
Simons, Silvester	Comal	Sinclair, John	Grayson
Simons, Thomas	Jackson	Sinclair, Joseph	Lamar
Simons, William	Austin	Sinclair, Paschal	Titus
Simpson, B. H.	Nacogdoches	Singleton, A. J.	Red River
Simpson, Bartlet	Harrison	Singleton, Amos	Harris
Simpson, G. W.	Limestone	Singleton, John W.	Harris
Simpson, G. W.	Nacogdoches	Singleton, R.	Robertson
Simpson, Green J.	Cherokee	Singleton, S.	Harris
Simpson, Isaac	Henderson	Singleton, T.	Robertson
Simpson, J. H.	Red River	Sinks, George W.	Fayette
Simpson, James	Rusk	Sirkel, John	Lamar
Simpson, John	Montgomery	Sirles, Doss	Rusk
Simpson, John	Nacogdoches	Sisco, John	Bastrop
Simpson, John J.	Henderson	Sise, J.	Travis
Simpson, John J.	Nacogdoches	Sites, Benjamin	Cass
Simpson, John J.	Panola	Skidmore, Abraham	Lamar
Simpson, John R.	Fannin	Skidmore, C. D.	Houston
Simpson, John W.	Panola	Skidmore, John	Lamar
Simpson, Joshua	Rusk	Skidmore, S. B.	Lamar
Simpson, Lackey	Panola	Skidmore, Thomas	Lamar
Simpson, Miles	Refugio	Skidmore, William	Lamar
Simpson, Samuel B.	Harrison	Skiles, Harvey	Lamar
Simpson, Thomas	Fayette	Skillern, Isaac C.	Nacogdoches
Simpson, W. M.	Henderson	Skillern, James	Nacogdoches
Simpson, W. P.	Bexar	Skinner, J. W.	Cass
Simpson, Wilson	Fayette	Skinner, James	Bexar
Simpson, Wm.	Travis	Skinner, James	Walker
Simpson, Wm. M.	Nacogdoches	Skinner, Joseph	Nacogdoches
Sims, Augustus	Tyler	Skinner,	
Sims, B. G.	Henderson	Livingston	Titus
Sims, Charles H.	Henderson	Skinner, Lorenzo	Titus
Sims, Charles H.	Hopkins	Skinner, Mary	Walker
Sims, E.	Grimes	Skipper, B.	San Augustine

NAME	COUNTY	NAME	COUNTY
Slack, Daniel	Fannin	Smelyzer, John	Brazoria
Slack, John H.	Fort Bend	Smeltzer, Abram	Brazoria
Slack, Thomas	Washington	Smeltzer, Stephen	Brazoria
Slade, Clinton	Wharton	Smilley, E.	Fannin
Slade, William	Harris	Smilley, Everett	Polk
Sladen, Samuel H.	Denton	Smilley, F. P. C.	Washington
Slater, J.	Collin	Smith, Mrs.	Grimes
Slater, Stephen T.	Montgomery	Smith, A.	Bastrop
Slater, William	Austin	Smith, A. W.	Austin
Slaton, G. W.	Red River	Smith, A. W.	Upshur
Slaton, H.	Red River	Smith, A. W., Sr.	Liberty
Slatter, J. E.	Harrison	Smith, Absolom	Fannin
Slaughter, Ben	Sabine	Smith, Adam J.	San Augustine
Slaughter, G. W.	Sabine	Smith, Albert	Comal
Slaughter, Gabriel	Wharton	Smith, Alexander	Hunt
Slaughter, James		Smith, Alfred	Travis
W.	Panola	Smith, Amassa	Leon
Slaughter, John	Shelby	Smith, Anderson	Harris
Slaughter, Owen	Sabine	Smith, Anderson	Liberty
Slaughter, Samuel		Smith, Andrew F.	Jasper
M.	Sabine	Smith, Ann	Fannin
Slaughter, Solomon	Sabine	Smith, Ashbel	Galveston
Slaughter,		Smith, B.	Henderson
Virgilla	Colorado	Smith, B.	Upshur
Slaughter, W. H.	San Augustine	Smith, B. B.	Burleson
Slaughter, Wm. R.	Sabine	Smith, B. F.	Grimes
Slauter, F. M.	Robertson	Smith, B. P.	Red River
Slaven, Robert	Bowie	Smith, B. R.	Lemar
Slay, Sarah	Houston	Smith, Bartholomew	Fayette
Slay, W. W.	Houston	Smith, Benjamin P.	Fayette
Slayton, S. G.	Cass	Smith, Bennet	Rusk
Sleight, C. A.	Galveston	Smith, Berry	Rusk
Sleight, J. L.	Galveston	Smith, Bolin	Brazoria
Sleight, J. L.	Grimes	Smith, Bridget	Cass
Sleight, M. J.	Grimes	Smith, Bryant	Liberty
Slevin, Barney	Galveston	Smith, C.	Brazoria
Sloan, Benjamin S.	Lamar	Smith, C.	Cass
Sloan, D.	Navarro	Smith, C. A.	Guadalupe
Sloan, Love	Grayson	Smith, C. J.	San Augustine
Sloan, William	Harris	Smith, C. M.	Lamar
Slocumb, J. R.	Harris	Smith, C. R.	Leon
Sloson, John	Harris	Smith, Catlitia	DeWitt
Sluter, F. A.	Cass	Smith, Charles	Fannin
Small, John	Anderson	Smith, Charles	Guadalupe
Small, John	Bexar	Smith, Charles	Limestone
Small, William	Bexar	Smith, Charles	Rusk
Smalley, A.	Matagorda	Smith, Charles R.	Harris
Smalley, Harrison	Panola	Smith, Christian	Harris
Smart, James, Jr.	Galveston	Smith, D. D.	San Augustine
Smelson, Josiah	Henderson	Smith, D. E.	Harris

NAME	COUNTY	NAME	COUNTY
Smith, Daniel	Bastrop	Smith, J. C.	Fayette
Smith, Daniel R.	San Augustine	Smith, J. C.	Fayette
Smith, David	Austin	Smith, J. C.	Grimes
Smith, David	DeWitt	Smith, J. C.	Henderson
Smith, Drury	Nacogdoches	Smith, J. C.	Leon
Smith, E. A.	Harrison	Smith, J. D.	Nacogdoches
Smith, E. A.	Rusk	Smith, J. E.	Red River
Smith, E. B.	Titus	Smith, J. H.	Panola
Smith, E. B.	Travis	Smith, J. H.	Walker
Smith, E. C.	Shelby	Smith, J. J.	Harrison
Smith, E. F.	Shelby	Smith, J. L.	Bastrop
Smith, E. M.	Red River	Smith, J. L.	Victoria
Smith, E. N.	Sabine	Smith, J. M.	Lamar
Smith, E. S.	Leons	Smith, J. N. O.	Harris
Smith, Edward	Nacogdoches	Smith, J. R.	Grimes
Smith, Edwin	San Augustine	Smith, J. R.	Liberty
Smith, Elijah	Travis	Smith, J. R.	Red River
Smith, Elisha	Denton	Smith, J. S.	Cass
Smith, Elizabeth	Brazoria	Smith, J. T.	Cass
Smith, Elizabeth	Limestone	Smith, J. W.	Brazoria
Smith, Elizabeth		Smith, J. W.	Montgomery
B.	Travis	Smith, J. W.	Walker
Smith, F.	Cass	Smith, Jackson	Walker
Smith, F. W.	Brazoria	Smith, Jacob	Galveston
Smith, F. W.	Harris	Smith, James	Bastrop
Smith, Francis	Fayette	Smith, James	Cass
Smith, Francis	Lavaca	Smith, James	Fayette
Smith, Franklin	Titus	Smith, James	Fayette
Smith, French	Guadalupe	Smith, James	Liberty
Smith, G.	Hunt	Smith, James	Rusk
Smith, G. M.	Fannin	Smith, James	San Augustine
Smith, G. W.	Fannin	Smith, James	Shelby
Smith, G. W.	Jasper	Smith, James	Titus
Smith, Gabriel	Washington	Smith, James A.	Hopkins
Smith, George	Cass	Smith, James A.	Nacogdoches
Smith, George W.	Calhoun	Smith, James A. J.	Fayette
Smith, Green L.	Limestone	Smith, James E.	Brazoria
Smith, Guadalupe	Bexar	Smith, James M.	Montgomery
Smith, H. H.	Collin	Smith, James N.	Bowie
Smith, H. H.	Walker	Smith, James N.	DeWitt
Smith, H. M.	Galveston	Smith, James	
Smith, H. M.	Rusk	Richard	Bowie
Smith, Hancock	Panola	Smith, James W.	Nacogdoches
Smith, Harvey	Brazoria	Smith, Jeremiah,	
Smith, Henry	Austin	Jr.	Galveston
Smith, Henry	Refugio	Smith, Jesse	Titus
Smith, Henry C.	Grayson	Smith, Jesus C.	Bexar
Smith, Henry E.	Grimes	Smith, John	Anderson
Smith, Ishan	Fayette	Smith, John	Bastrop
Smith, J.	Matagorda	Smith, John	DeWitt

NAME	COUNTY	NAME	COUNTY
Smith, John	Fort Bend	Smith, R. W.	Grimes
Smith, John	Grimes	Smith, Rachel	Shelby
Smith, John	Harris	Smith, Richard	Liberty
Smith, John	Houston	Smith, Richard	Montgomery
Smith, John	Liberty	Smith, Robert	Cass
Smith, John	Montgomery	Smith, Robert	Colorado
Smith, John	Shelby	Smith, Robert A.	Polk
Smith, John C.	Montgomery	Smith, Robert H.	Sabine
Smith, John D.	Limestone	Smith, Robert W.	Rusk
Smith, John G.	Brazoria	Smith, S. C.	Red River
Smith, John L.	Fayette	Smith, S. G.	Titus
Smith, John N.	Gonzales	Smith, Mrs. S. M.	Harrison
Smith, John W.	Bexar	Smith, Sampson	Red River
Smith, Jonas	San Augustine	Smith, Samuel	Bexar
Smith, Jordan	Harris	Smith, Samuel	San Augustine
Smith, Jordan	Henderson	Smith, Samuel H.	Newton
Smith, Joseph	Matagorda	Smith, Samuel K.	Denton
Smith, Joseph	Rusk	Smith, Silas	Liberty
Smith, Joseph G.	Fayette	Smith, Spencer	Travis
Smith, Joseph M.	DeWitt	Smith, Stephen	Fayette
Smith, Josiah	Hopkins	Smith, Stephen	Hopkins
Smith, L.	Upshur	Smith, Stephen	Shelby
Smith, L. L.	Shelby	Smith, Sterrett D.	Burleson
Smith, Leander	Henderson	Smith, Sterling	Bowie
Smith, Lemuel	Houston	Smith, T. C.	Walker
Smith, Lemuel	Montgomery	Smith, T. J.	Fort Bend
Smith, Lily	Burleson	Smith, T. L.	Jefferson
Smith, M. C.	Bastrop	Smith, T. S.	Walker
Smith, Major	Sabine	Smith, Taylor	Bastrop
Smith, Malinda	Shelby	Smith, Temperence	Henderson
Smith, Mary	Walker	Smith, Thomas	Matagorda
Smith, Menean	Houston	Smith, Thomas B.	Fannin
Smith, Mitchell	Panola	Smith, Thomas J.	Navarro
Smith, Mitchell	Red River	Smith, Thomas J.	Washington
Smith, Morgan L.	Brazoria	Smith, Thomas S.	Fannin
Smith, N. A.	Brazoria	Smith, Tilmon	Red River
Smith, N. F.	Jefferson	Smith, W. A., Jr.	Liberty
Smith, Nael	Liberty	Smith, W. B. D.	Montgomery
Smith, Nathan	Galveston	Smith, W. P.	Fayette
Smith, Niles	Jasper	Smith, W. S.	Colorado
Smith, P. B.	Washington	Smith, Wager S.	Fayette
Smith, Patrick	Gonzales	Smith, Wiley	Harris
Smith, Pavir	Guadalupe	Smith, William	Anderson
Smith, Peter	Colorado	Smith, William	Cass
Smith, Peter	Guadalupe	Smith, William	Grimes
Smith, Peyton	Walker	Smith, William	Nacogdoches
Smith, Philip	Fannin	Smith, William	Newton
Smith, Pinkney	Anderson	Smith, William	Panola
Smith, R.	Henderson	Smith, William	San Augustine
Smith, R. F.	Sabine	Smith, William D.	Sabine

NAME	COUNTY	NAME	COUNTY
Smith, Wm. B.	Brazos	Sorelle, T. B.	Harrison
Smith, Wm. B.	Cass	Soresby, W. A.	Washington
Smith, Wm. D.	Harris	Sorrells, Alex.	Dallas
Smith, Wm. H.	Grimes	Sorrells, James	Gonzales
Smith, Wm. J.	Nacogdoches	Sory, John	Rusk
Smith, Wm. R.	Brazoria	Sossaman, C. R.	San Augustine
Smith, Wm. T.	Rusk	Sosserman, H. C.	San Augustine
Smithers, Ben	Rusk	Sosserman, Jacob	San Augustine
Smithers, J. H.	Bowie	Sotels, Matios	Bexar
Smithers, L.	Bexar	Soto, Maria D.	Henderson
Smithers, R.	Walker	Soulle, Wm. J.	Harrison
Smithson, H. C.	Brazoria	Sour, William	Travis
Smithson, Martha	Liberty	South, Elijah	Grayson
Smithson, R. F.	Bastrop	South, Samuel	Hunt
Smithson, Sarah	Bastrop	Southerland, B.	Wharton
Smock, Henry	Grimes	Southerland, E. C.	Henderson
Snailum, T. C.	Grimes	Southerland, John	Wharton
Snead, Fleming	Brazoria	Southmayd, J. A.	Harris
Snediker, William	Harrison	Southwick, S.	Galveston
Snee, James	Travis	Southwood, Iredell	Fannin
Sneed, Israel	Tyler	Southwood, William	Fannin
Sneed, J. P.	Washington	Sowders, A. L.	Harris
Sneed, John H.	Harris	Sowell, A. J.	Guadalupe
Sneed, William J.	San Augustine	Sowell, Asa J. L.	Guadalupe
Snell, John W.	Shelby	Sowell, John W.	Guadalupe
Snell, M. R.	Harris	Sowell, Ransom	San Augustine
Snider, E.	Victoria	Spain, Benjamin D.	Hopkins
Snider, Jesse	Panola	Spain, John D.	Titus
Snider, Joel	Shelby	Spain, Lewis B.	Hopkins
Snider, John	Red River	Spalding, Charles	Bastrop
Snider, Samuel	Panola	Sparks, Ab.	Hopkins
Snider, Sanford	Panola	Sparks, Elizabeth	Nacogdoches
Snider, V.	Grimes	Sparks, James H.	Nacogdoches
Snider, W.	Collin	Sparks, John	Jefferson
Snow, S.	Matagorda	Sparks, L.	Rusk
Snow, S. M.	Lamar	Sparks, Levi	Limestone
Snow, W. J.	Dallas	Sparks, Moses	Dallas
Snowden, L. H.	Harrison	Sparks, Richard	Nacogdoches
Snowden, Samuel	Lamar	Sparks, Stephen T.	Nacogdoches
Snyder, A.	Cass	Sparks, William	Nacogdoches
Snyder, J.	Cass	Sparks, William	Titus
Sofer, J. C.	Bastrop	Sparks, William C.	Brazos
Sohafer, Charles	Comal	Speaks, John	Cass
Sohlithting,		Spear, Abner B.	Shelby
Ferdinand	Comal	Spear, Herrison M.	Henderson
Solms, Jacob	Bexar	Spear, Jacob	Cass
Somervill, A.	Matagorda	Spears, Andrew	San Augustine
Somervill, J.	Matagorda	Spears, D.	Henderson
Sorelle, Mrs.		Spears, David	Houston
Barbara A. G.	Harrison	Spears, J.	Henderson

NAME	COUNTY	NAME	COUNTY
Spears, James	San Augustine	Splawn, Hansford	Smith
Spears, John	San Augustine	Splawn, Thomas	Smith
Spears, John	Victoria	Splawn, Z.	Brazos
Spears, T.	Henderson	Spoon, John	Fannin
Spell, John	Victoria	Spoonemon, S. J.	Fannin
Spell, Marshall	Harrison	Spotts, William	Washington
Spellenburger, A.		Sprague, M. S.	Harris
E.	Fort Bend	Sprague, Nathaniel	
Spelling, Benjamin	Cass	G.	Galveston
Spelling, F. M.	Cass	Spreacher, Andrew	Galveston
Spence, Absolum	Brazos	Spricker, Andrew	Harris
Spence, J. C.	Brazos	Springer, A. E.	Montgomery
Spence, J. P.	Fannin	Springer, A. N. U.	Montgomery
Spencer, A. H. C.	Brazos	Springer, A. U.	Grimes
Spencer, D.	Henderson	Springer, J. M.	Montgomery
Spencer, Elijah	Harrison	Springfield, James	
Spencer, Harband	Harrison	M.	Limestone
Spencer, Joel	Brazoria	Springston, James	Liberty
Spencer, Oliver	Red River	Sprouce, John	Grimes
Spencer, Thomas C.	Nacogdoches	Spurlock, Eliza	Wharton
Spencer, W. M.	Liberty	Spurlock, J. D.	Wharton
Spencer, W. R.	Fannin	Staats, N.	Red River
Spencer, William	Fannin	Staats, Nancy W.	Red River
Spencer, William		Staats, S. D.	Harris
R.	Harrison	Stacy, Frank	Red River
Spencer, Winfield	Brazoria	Stacy, William	Liberty
Spidle, Jacob	Nacogdoches	Stafford, J. S.	Harris
Spier, Thomas	Cherokee	Stafford, J. T.	Fort Bend
Spights, Asa	Liberty	Stafford, Samuel	Cherokee
Spights, C. A.	Liberty	Stafford, W. J.	Fort Bend
Spights, Joshua H.	Sabine	Stagner, William	Colorado
Spights, Nancy	Liberty	Stahl, A.	Montgomery
Spights, William		Stallcup, T.	Collin
M.	Sabine	Stallcup, Wm.	Cass
Spille, John	Colorado	Stallings, Abraham	Red River
Spiller, Daniel	Jefferson	Stallings, Henry	Cass
Spiller, J. W.	Walker	Stallings, Jacob	Harrison
Spiller, James	Jefferson	Stallings, Jacob	Red River
Spiller, Jeremiah	Jefferson	Stamps, James	Harris
Spiller, John	Montgomery	Stamps, John	Grayson
Spiller, William		Stanback, Mrs. M.	Jackson
H.	Montgomery	Stanbury, R. N.	Austin
Spillman, Joseph		Stanbury, T. J.	Henderson
H.	Harris	Stancil, B. B.	Walker
Spink, Henry	Colorado	Standefer, B.	Panola
Spink, John	Liberty	Standefer, Isaac	Milam
Spiva, Andrew	Lamar	Standefer, Israel	Burleson
Spivy, Enoch	Rusk	Standefer, M. R.	Panola
Spivy, Jethro	Wharton	Standefer, W. R.	Panola
Spivy, Templeton	Rusk	Standerford,	

159

NAME	COUNTY	NAME	COUNTY
Harrison	Fannin	Staunchfield, B.	Wharton
Standerford, Jacob	Bastrop	Steadham, Z.	Houston
Standerford, James	Bastrop	Steel, Alfonzo	Limestone
Standerford, John	Fannin	Steel, Henry	Walker
Standerford, William	Bastrop	Steel, J. D.	Tyler
Stanfield, W. W. O.	Harrison	Steel, L. G. A.	Harrison
		Steel, Robert	Leon
Stanley, C. M.	Cass	Steel, Wilis	Hunt
Stanley, Elizabeth	Angelina	Steel, William	Harrison
Stanley, F.	Red River	Steel & Colquhoun	Henderson
Stanley, Green	Angelina	Steen, D. L.	Harrison
Stanley, John D.	Red River	Steen, J.	Cass
Stanley, L. C.	Harris	Steen, James	Smith
Stannard, Thomas A.	Liberty	Steen, Mary Ann	Smith
		Steen, Richard	Fannin
Stansbury, George W.	Harris	Steen, Stephen	Bexar
		Steen, Thomas	Smith
Stansbury, Thomas	Harris	Steen, Thomas C.	Smith
Stansbury, W. L.	Harris	Steffner, Zarial	Panola
Stanton, ----	Jackson	Steger, Mrs. Lucy	Harrison
Stanton, Richardson	Lavaca	Stein, John	Harris
		Stell, G. W.	Lamar
Stapler, John A.	Polk	Stell, G. W., Jr.	Lamar
Stapleton, Wm.	Colorado	Stephens, A.	Nacogdoches
Stapp, A.	Collin	Stephens, C. R.	Shelby
Stapp, Akillis	Victoria	Stephens, Catherine	Bastrop
Stapp, D. M.	Victoria	Stephens, E. H.	Brazoria
Stapp, Hugh	Victoria	Stephens, E. P.	Shelby
Stapp, John D.	Angelina	Stephens, Edward	Lamar
Stapp, O. H.	Victoria	Stephens, George	Fannin
Stapp, Solomon	Angelina	Stephens, Henry	Washington
Stark, Asa L.	Newton	Stephens, Isaac	Harrison
Stark, J. T.	San Augustine	Stephens, J. C.	Liberty
Stark, Jeremiah	San Augustine	Stephens, J. F.	Bexar
Stark, Robert	Grayson	Stephens, James	Washington
Stark, Wm. H.	Newton	Stephens, John	Nacogdoches
Starkey, Jesse	Hopkins	Stephens, Julia	Liberty
Starkey, William	Harrison	Stephens, Lewis	Fannin
Starley, S. F.	Cherokee	Stephens, Miles G.	Polk
Starnes, A.	Titus	Stephens, Obid	Red River
Starnes, N. L.	Galveston	Stephens, Thomas	Washington
Starnes, Rebecca	Titus	Stephens, Thomas A.	Polk
Starnes, T. R.	Titus	Stephens, Thomas B.	Grimes
Starnes, W. A.	Harrison	Stephens, Wm.	Hopkins
Starr, J. F.	Cass	Stephenson, Charles	Harris
Starr, James H.	Nacogdoches	Stephenson, Dobson	Hopkins
Starr, Thomas	Shelby		
Starrett, James	Navarro		
Statler, Samuel	Burleson		

NAME	COUNTY	NAME	COUNTY
Stephenson, Elisha	Liberty	Eliz.	Cass
Stephenson, Ira	Newton	Stevenson, Gilbert	Jefferson
Stephenson, J. B.	Grimes	Stevenson, H. H.	Walker
Stephenson, J. W.	Harrison	Stevenson, James	
Stephenson, James	Grimes	B.	Austin
Stephenson, James	Harrison	Stevenson, John	Jefferson
Stephenson, James	Liberty	Stevenson, Josiah	Newton
Stephenson, James		Stevenson, Lydia	Jefferson
A.	Panola	Stevenson, Susan	
Stephenson, Jared		A.	Colorado
J.	Newton	Steward, Charles	Titus
Stephenson, John	Fannin	Steward, Daniel	Nacogdoches
Stephenson, John	Newton	Steward, James	Bastrop
Stephenson,		Steward, John	Bastrop
Jonathan	Harrison	Steward, Joshua	Bastrop
Stephenson, Josiah	Newton	Steward, R.	Upshur
Stephenson, R.	Navarro	Steward, Samuel	Titus
Stephenson, Sarah	Panola	Steward, T. D.	Bastrop
Sterick, William	Tyler	Steward, Thomas G.	Washington
Sterling, J.	Matagorda	Steward, Virgil A.	Wharton
Sterling, Lorenzo	Washington	Stewart, Adam S.	Newton
Sterman, William	Lamar	Stewart, B.	Bowie
Sterman, William,		Stewart, C. B.	Brazoria
Jr.	Lamar	Stewart, C. B.	Harris
Sterne, A.	Henderson	Stewart, C. B.	Montgomery
Sterne, A.	Nacogdoches	Stewart, Charles	Galveston
Sterne, John E.	Jackson	Stewart, Charles	Rusk
Sterne, Thomas	Victoria	Stewart, Charles	San Augustine
Sterne, William T.	Nacogdoches	Stewart, David	Montgomery
Stertzing,		Stewart, Isabella	Bowie
Theodore	Comal	Stewart, J. N.	Bowie
Stetson, Pat	Cass	Stewart, J. R.	Washington
Stevehr,		Stewart, J. T.	Montgomery
Constantine	Austin	Stewart, J. Y.	Nacogdoches
Stevender, A. W.	Newton	Stewart, John	Fayette
Stevens, A. T.	Walker	Stewart, John	Hunt
Stevens, George	Harris	Stewart, John	Titus
Stevens, Hiram B.	Cherokee	Stewart, John, Jr.	Titus
Stevens, Hugh R.	Fannin	Stewart, John V.	Bexar
Stevens, Isom	Titus	Stewart, Julia T.	Grimes
Stevens, J. M.	Grimes	Stewart, Mrs.	
Stevens, James	Colorado	Martha	Brazoria
Stevens, James H.	Harris	Stewart, Samuel	Dallas
Stevens, Jane A.	Polk	Stewart, Thomas	Lamar
Stevens, M.	Upshur	Stewart, W. T.	Dallas
Stevens, Wesley	Colorado	Stewart, W. W.	Matagorda
Stevenson,		Stewart, William	Grimes
Alexander	Lamar	Stewart, William	Titus
Stevenson, Elijah	Jefferson	Stibone, Charles	Anderson
Stevenson, Mrs.		Stiff, J.	Collin

NAME	COUNTY	NAME	COUNTY
Stiles, John	Cass	Stone, R. C.	Cass
Stiles, John	Red River	Stone, R. T.	Walker
Stiles, John B.	Red River	Stone, W. H.	Rusk
Stiles, Richard	Shelby	Stone, William	Fannin
Still, David	Cherokee	Stone, William	Hunt
Still, James	Anderson	Stone, Willie B.	Nacogdoches
Stillwell, Green	Walker	Stoneham, Erastus	Grimes
Stillwell, H. J.	Shelby	Stoneham, George	Montgomery
Stillwell, John	Walker	Stoneham, James	Lamar
Stimson, J. C.	Walker	Stonum, Bryant	Grimes
Stimson, S. R.	Walker	Stonum, George	Grimes
Stinson, David	Grimes	Stonum, George,	
STinson, David	Harrison	Jr.	Grimes
Stinson, Joel	Milam	Stonum, John D.	Grimes
Stinson, John	Cherokee	Storm, Leonard	Nacogdoches
Stith, Fabius	Harrison	Storm, Pleasant	Burleson
Stith, James	Henderson	Stork, Charles	Comal
Stith, Macklin	Wharton	Storrs, A.	Matagorda
Stockbridge, Elam	Harris	Storts, John	Comal
Stockbridge, John	Fort Bend	Story, C. L.	Gonzales
Stockbridge, M.	Wharton	Story, Henry	Cass
Stocking, Keziah	Harris	Story, J. T. S.	Gonzales
Stockman, Henry J.	Rusk	Story, J. W. C.	Cass
Stockman, Nancy	Rusk	Story, Joseph	Panola
Stockman, Peter	Shelby	Story, Mrs. Nancy	Cass
Stocksliger, P. A.	Fannin	Story, Napoleon	Houston
Stockton, B. F.	Colorado	STory, Samuel	Cass
Stockton, Elias	Red River	Story, Solomon	Houston
Stockton, John F.	Polk	Stotts, G. L.	Montgomery
Stockton, M. D.	Washington	Stout, David R.	Fayette
Stockton, S. A.	Nacogdoches	Stout, Henry	Upshur
Stoddard, J. W.	Grimes	Stout, James S.	Hopkins
Stokeley, J.	Grimes	Stout, John	Panola
Stokeley, John	Harrison	Stout, Mary	Hopkins
Stokeley, Thomas	Henderson	Stout, Peter B.	Dallas
Stokes, A. K.	Henderson	Stout, W. B.	Red River
Stokes, Andrew	Burleson	Stovall, E.	Titus
Stokes, Samuel	Grimes	Stovall, G.	Walker
Stokes, William	Navarro	Stovall, George H.	San Augustine
Stolge, Renki	Colorado	Stovall, James B.	Cherokee
Stolge, Runhard	Colorado	Stovall, John	Cherokee
Stone, A. T.	Cass	Stovall, John M.	Angelina
Stone, Elias	Jefferson	Stovall, T. J.	San Augustine
Stone, G. W.	Rusk	Stovall, Thomas H.	Nacogdoches
Stone, J.	Collin	Stover, C. D.	Anderson
Stone, James	Rusk	Stowe, Joel W.	Houston
Stone, James H.	Rusk	Stowe, Joseph	Galveston
Stone, John	Rusk	Stowel, Willard	Lamar
Stone, Martin	Rusk	Stracener,	
Stone, Nancy	Nacogdoches	Benjamin	Smith

NAME	COUNTY	NAME	COUNTY
Strahan, Matthew	Nacogdoches	Stuart, B.	Cass
Strahan, Thomas	Nacogdoches	Stuart, C. B.	Colorado
Strahan, Wm. H.	Colorado	Stuart, H.	Galveston
Strain, J. M.	Travis	Stuart, J. W.	Brazos
Strange, James	Liberty	Stuart, John	Fannin
Strattan, Mary	Brazoria	Stuart, Robert	Travis
Straughn, B.	Cass	Stubblefield,	
Straughn, Benjamin	Cass	Dickson	Rusk
Straw, L.	Shelby	Stubblefield, J.	Upshur
Strawhorn, Noah	Anderson	Stubblefield, J.	Walker
Strawn, William G.	Travis	Stubblefield, J.	
Street, J.	Grimes	J.	Polk
Street, Sarah	Bowie	Stubblefield,	
Streetmeter,		Robert	Rusk
Joseph	Grimes	Stubblefield,	
Strickland, Amos	Panola	Stephen	Rusk
Strickland, David	Shelby	Stubblefield,	
Strickland, Harty	Harrison	Thomas J.	Polk
Strickland, Isaac		Stubblefield, Wm.	Cherokee
O.	Shelby	Stubblefield, Wm.	Rusk
Strickland, Thomas	Hunt	Stubblefield, Wm.	
Stricklin, Amos	Henderson	H.	Austin
Stride, Thomas S.	Harris	Stubbs, G. W.	Liberty
Stringer, E.	Jackson	Stucky, Benjamin	Grimes
Stringer, Leonard	Fort Bend	Stucky, Christian	Fayette
Stringfellow,		Stuff, Charles	Bastrop
Chesley	Brazoria	Stugner, Henry	Jasper
Strintzel, Henry	Lamar	Stukenborg, H.	Galveston
Strode, Henry M.	Henderson	Stump, John S.	Gonzales
Strode, James	Lamar	Stuteville, James	
Strode, Jeremiah	Nacogdoches	C.	Brazos
Strode, L. P.	Grayson	Styles, A.	Upshur
Strode, Thomas V.		Styles, J. N.	Upshur
S.	Travis	Styles, William	Fort Bend
Strong, Asham	Shelby	Sublett, H. W.	San Augustine
Strong, Lorin	Cass	Suddeth, Henry W.	Newton
Strong, Samuel	Liberty	Suell, J. A.	Henderson
Stroop, George M.	Shelby	Suggs, John	Fayette
Strother, C. J.	Travis	Sullaven, A. W.	Milam
Strother, James	Victoria	Sullivan, A. W.	Anderson
Strother, John L.	Robertson	Sullivan, James S.	Fort Bend
Strother, Walter	Sabine	Sullivan, John	Cherokee
Stroud, A.	Titus	Sullivan, L. P.	Bastrop
Stroud, Charles	Travis	Sullivan, Pat	Hopkins
Stroud, Ethan	Limestone	Sullivan, Patric	Austin
Stroud, J. B.	Harrison	Sullivan, W. W.	Fort Bend
Stroud, Mandred	Limestone	Sullivent, William	Harrison
Stroud, Mark	Rusk	Summers, H. C. G.	Tyler
Stroud, Memory	Limestone	Summers, R. B.	Cass
Stroud, O.	Cass	Summers, William	Nacogdoches

163

NAME	COUNTY	NAME	COUNTY
Summerville, M. B.	Robertson	Swigley, Joseph	Red River
Sumner, Charles W.	Harris	Swingle, Alfred	Galveston
Sundberg, L. P.	Galveston	Swinney, Milton	Liberty
Super, Daniel	Harris	Swinney, W. R.	Liberty
Superiele, A.	Harris	Swisher, James G.	Travis
Sussey, Asa	Liberty	Swisher, James M.	Travis
Sutherland, George	Jackson	Swisher, John M.	Travis
Sutherland, N. T.	Red River	Swoop, Franklin	Burleson
Sutherland, T. S.	Jackson	Sydnor, John S.	Galveston
Suttle, James F.	Fannin	Sylvester, J. H.	Galveston
Sutton, Isaac	Walker	Sypert, Thomas	Washington
Sutton, John	Fayette	Syrus, Jesse	Bastrop
Sutton, R. E.	Victoria		
Sutton, Wesley	Fayette		
Sutton, William	Fayette	Tabor, George T.	Harrison
Swain, R.	Matagorda	Tabor, H.	Henderson
Swain, R. W.	Navarro	Tabor, Hudson	Montgomery
Swain, William W.	Harris	Tabor, James	Henderson
Swanson, James M.	Harrison	Tabor, Mrs. Susan	Harrison
Swanson, Peter	Harrison	Tackett, Hilyard	Fannin
Swanson, S. M.	Fort Bend	Tadlock, Severe	Fayette
Swarte, John	Colorado	Tafirevino, M.	Victoria
Swearingen, A. C.	Newton	Tailor, Hezekiah	Anderson
Swearingen, E.	Austin	Tailor, J. F.	Anderson
Swearingen, Henry	Panola	Tailor, Perry C.	Hopkins
Swearingen, Mary		Tait, C. W.	Fayette
E.	Newton	Talbot, Mrs. H. S.	Matagorda
Swearingen, R. J.	Washington	Talbot, J. A.	Bowie
Swearingen, S. S.	Newton	Talbot, James	Tyler
Swearingen, Samuel	Austin	Talbot, John	Brazoria
Swearingen, V. W.	Austin	Talbot, Thomas	Jackson
Sweatt, Edward	Panola	Taliaferro,	
Sweatt, George W.	Panola	Charles E.	Nacogdoches
Sweatt, Shadric	Tyler	Taliaferro, Lewis	
Sweeney, John, Jr.	Brazoria	B.	Nacogdoches
Sweeney, John, Sr.	Brazoria	Taliaferro, Martha	
Sweeney, Jordan	Brazoria	A.	Nacogdoches
Sweeney, Thomas J.	Brazoria	Tam, James	Cass
Swenson, Peter	Cass	Tammy, John	Bastrop
Swett, Joseph A.	Galveston	Tamplin, Henry H.	Shelby
Swift, A.	Guadalupe	Tandy, R. H.	Washington
Swift, Arthur	Gonzales	Tankersly, B. F.	Harris
Swift, Mrs. H.	Nacogdoches	Tankersly, J. H.	Milam
Swift, H. M.	Guadalupe	Tankersly, J. M.	Milam
Swift, J. A.	Guadalupe	Tankersly, R.	Milam
Swift, Jefferson	Newton	Tanner, Daniel	San Augustine
Swift, Lydia G.	Newton	Tanner, E. M.	Liberty
Swift, Paul	Newton	Tanner, Edward	Cass
Swift, Seth	Newton	Tanner, James	Liberty
Swift, Willis J.	Nacogdoches	Tanner, John A.	Burleson

NAME	COUNTY	NAME	COUNTY
Tanner, Joseph	Liberty	Taylor, Joseph	Robertson
Tanner, Joseph R.	Harrison	Taylor, Joseph P.	Red River
Tanner, T. W.	Bastrop	Taylor, Joshua	Galveston
Tanner, William F.	Newton	Taylor, Josiah	DeWitt
Tannihill, J. C.	Travis	Taylor, Lemuel	Travis
Tapp, William S.	Bowie	Taylor, M.	Henderson
Tardif, John	Harris	Taylof, M.	Upshur
Targinton, B.	Liberty	Taylor, M. D.	Leon
Targinton, J. H.	Liberty	Taylor, M. N.	Grimes
Tarrant, ---	Navarro	Taylor, Margaret	Milam
Tarver, B. E.	Washington	Taylor, Nancy	Fayette
Tarver, E. D.	Washington	Taylor, Owen	Newton
Tate, G. W.	Leon	Taylor, P. P.	Cass
Tate, James	Red River	Taylor, Parson	Cass
Tatam, A. G.	Shelby	Taylor, Pitkin B.	DeWitt
Tatam, J. C.	Shelby	Taylor, Pleasant	Dallas
Tatman, Ira	Fannin	Taylor, Robert	Rusk
Tatman, S. R.	Liberty	Taylor, Robert H.	Fannin
Tausch, Frederick	Comal	Taylor, Robert P.	Harrison
Tavener, William	Navarro	Taylor, Rufus	DeWitt
Taylor, A. B.	Walker	Taylor, Samuel J.	Harrison
Taylor, C. C.	Robertson	Taylor, Sarah Ann	Fayette
Taylor, C. H.	Fayette	Taylor, T. B.	Henderson
Taylor, C. R.	Henderson	Taylor, T. W.	Leon
Taylor, C. S.	Henderson	Taylor, Thomas	Henderson
Taylor, Camel	Bastrop	Taylor, Thomas B.	Upshur
Taylor, Charles	Leon	Taylor, W. B.	Titus
Taylor, Charles	Polk	Taylor, William	Harris
Taylor, Charles S.	Nacogdoches	Taylor, William	Nacogdoches
Taylor, D. P.	Cass	Taylor, William S.	Montgomery
Taylor, E. W.	Washington	Taylor, Wm.	Dallas
Taylor, Felix	Fayette	Taylor, Wm. H.	Panola
Taylor, Gary J.	DeWitt	Taylor, Wm. R.	Calhoun
Taylor, George	Fayette	Taylor, Wm. R.	DeWitt
Taylor, Hugh A.	Panola	Taylor, Wm. S.	Grimes
Taylor, Irs	Tyler	Teal, C. A.	Upshur
Taylor, J. D.	Henderson	Teal, Edward	San Augustine
Taylor, J. D.	Montgomery	Teal, George	San Augustine
Taylor, J. M.	Tyler	Teal, John	Burleson
Taylor, J. P.	Harrison	Teal, P.	Upshur
Taylor, Jacob	Rusk	Teal, P.	Victoria
Taylor, James	Jefferson	Teal, R. S.	Burleson
Taylor, James	Liberty	Teal, Thomas W.	Burleson
Taylor, James F.	Harrison	Teas, A. G.	Houston
Taylor, James H.	DeWitt	Teas, Samuel	Walker
Taylor, John	Grimes	Tejada, Clemente	Bexar
Taylor, John	Harrison	Tejada, Jose	Bexar
Taylor, John	Jefferson	Tejada, Pedro	Bexar
Taylor, John	Travis	Tejada, Yg.	Bexar
Taylor, John R.	Upshur	Temple, C. A.	Henderson

NAME	COUNTY	NAME	COUNTY
Temple, THomas G.	Guadalupe	Thomas, A. A.	Dallas
Temple, William	Austin	Thomas, A. J.	Bexar
Tenney, John	Bexar	Thomas, A. T.	San Augustine
Terheun, Eliza	Galveston	Thomas, Andrew	Fannin
Terrell, Betsy A.	Cass	Thomas, B.	San Augustine
Terrell, Charles		Thomas, Benjamin	Bexar
M.	Tyler	Thomas, Benjamin	San Augustine
Terrell, E. S.	Fannin	Thomas, Benjamin	
Terrell, Henry	Colorado	R.	Washington
Terrell, James	Cass	Thomas, C. W.	Comal
Terrell, John	Lamar	Thomas, C. W.	Fayette
Terrell, Julius	Cass	Thomas, Claburn	Austin
Terrell, M. B.	Washington	Thomas, David	Travis
Terry, Andrew	Fannin	Thomas, E.	Titus
Terry, Anselm	Fannin	Thomas, E. B.	Jefferson
Terry, B. J.	Harrison	Thomas, E. C.	Dallas
Terry, Benjamin F.	Brazoria	Thomas, E. C.	Shelby
Terry, David S.	Brazoria	Thomas, E. M.	Brazoria
Terry, Ephriam	Nacogdoches	Thomas, F. M.	Red River
Terry, J. H.	Henderson	Thomas, G. S.	Liberty
Terry, James	Fannin	Thomas, George	Harrison
Terry, John	Fayette	Thomas, George	Titus
Terry, John	Red River	Thomas, Isaac P.	Dallas
Terry, John	Smith	Thomas, J.	Henderson
Terry, John L.	Fannin	Thomas, J. D.	San Augustine
Terry, Joseph A.	Bexar	Thomas, J. M.	Grayson
Terry, M.	Austin	Thomas, J. W.	Walker
Terry, Matthew	Nacogdoches	Thomas, Jacob	Galveston
Terry, R.	Brazos	Thomas, Jacob	Refugio
Terry, S. D.	Brazoria	Thomas, James	Grimes
Terry, Stephen	Harrison	Thomas, James	Rusk
Terry, William	Brazoria	Thomas, James J.	Rusk
Terry, William J.		Thomas, James N.	Nacogdoches
T.	Austin	Thomas, Janis H.	Shelby
Testard, A.	Washington	Thomas, Jefferson	Rusk
Thackara, J. H.	Brazoria	Thomas, Jeremiah	
Thacker, A. G.	Walker	W.	Burleson
Thacker, Henry	Walker	Thomas, Jesse F.	Fannin
Thacker, Hiram	Walker	Thomas, Jesse G.	Burleson
Thacker, Isaac H.	Henderson	Thomas, Jessey G.	Anderson
Thacker, J. B.	San Augustine	Thomas, John	Dallas
Thacker, J. H.	San Augustine	Thomas, John	Harrison
Thacker, J. R.	San Augustine	Thomas, John	Houston
Thacker, S. J.	San Augustine	Thomas, John	Montgomery
Thatcher, G. W.	Colorado	Thomas, John	Refugio
Thatcher, Thomas	Wharton	Thomas, John C.	Grimes
Thatcher, Thornton	Wharton	Thomas, John D.	Colorado
Theltmon, G.	Henderson	Thomas, John D.	Lamar
Theron, Benjamin	Galveston	Thomas, John W.	Newton
Thielepape, G.	Comal	Thomas, Jonathan	

NAME	COUNTY	NAME	COUNTY
G.	Fannin	Thompson, E. A.	Matagorda
Thomas, Josiah	Smith	Thompson, E. J.	Panola
Thomas, L. R.	Jefferson	Thompson, E. R.	Liberty
Thomas, Martha	Harrison	Thompson, Edward	Lamar
Thomas, N. B.	Burleson	Thompson, Franklin	Rusk
Thomas, Nathan	Austin	Thompson, G. B.	Harrison
Thomas, Pleasant	Rusk	Thompson, George	Newton
Thomas, S. A. J.	Montgomery	Thompson, Giles	Grayson
Thomas, S. D.	San Augustine	Thompson, H. M.	Smith
Thomas, Samuel	Wharton	Thompson, Henry	Panola
Thomas, Theo	San Augustine	Thompson, Henry D.	Polk
Thomas, W.	Upshur	Thompson, Isham	Wharton
Thomas, W. L.	Bexar	Thompson, J.	Cass
Thomas, William	Burleson	Thompson, J. J.	Galveston
Thomas, William	Harrison	Thompson, J. M.	Walker
Thomas, William	Houston	Thompson, J. S.	Henderson
Thomas, William	Leon	Thompson, Jackson	Travis
Thomas, William	Shelby	Thompson, James	Jackson
Thomas, William D.	Travis	Thompson, James G.	Grayson
Thomas, William E.	Harris	Thompson, James H.	Anderson
Thomas, William J.	Shelby	Thompson, James W.	Polk
Thomas, William M.	Montgomery	Thompson, Jessa G.	Lavaca
Thomason, David	Nacogdoches	Thompson, John	Panola
Thomason, Eli M.	Cherokee	Thompson, John	Washington
Thomason, G.	Cherokee	Thomspon, John,	
Thomason, James	Cherokee	Sr.	Harris
Thomason, James	Fort Bend	Thompson, John P.	Panola
Thomason, Jesse	Fort Bend	Thompson, John S.	Cherokee
Thomason, John	Fort Bend	Thompson, Joseph	Newton
Thomason, Joseph		Thompson, Joseph	
B.	Fort Bend	B.	Travis
Thomason, Tailor	Cherokee	THompson, Josiah	Hopkins
Thomason, Victor	Cherokee	Thompson, Miss. K.	Jackson
Thomason, Wiley	Cherokee	Thompson, Martin	Travis
Thomason, William	Fort Bend	Thompson, N. B.	Jackson
Thompson, A.	Grayson	Thompson, N. L.	Liberty
Thompson, A. P.	Harris	Thompson, Philip	Harris
Thompson, A. T.	Harrison	Thompson, R. H.	Galveston
Thompson, Amos	Panola	Thompson, Samuel	Henderson
Thompson,		Thompson, Sary	Walker
Archibald	Harrison	Thompson, T. J.	Washington
Thompson, B. C.	Anderson	Thompson, W. A.	Henderson
Thompson, B. J.	San Augustine	Thompson, W. D.	Milam
Thompson, B. R.	Milam	Thompson, Wiley	Bowie
Thompson, Bart T.	Nacogdoches	Thompson, William	Bowie
Thompson, C. W.	Liberty	Thompson, William	Grayson
Thompson, Charles	Wharton	Thompson, William	Harris
Thompson, David	Polk	Thompson, William	Polk
Thompson, David	Walker	Thompson, William	
Thompson, Dickson	Panola	A.	Cherokee

NAME	COUNTY	NAME	COUNTY
Thompson, William B.	Smith	Thweatt, James	Hunt
Thompson, William T.	Sabine	Thweatt, L.	Hunt
Thomson, A. J. R.	Burleson	Thweatt, S.	Henderson
Thomson, Alex.	Burleson	Tibbet, B.	Victoria
Thomson, F. A.	Burleson	Tibbet, Milton	Victoria
Thomson, H. C.	Henderson	Tibble, John	Milam
Thomson, J. F.	Burleson	Tichenor, V. W.	Galveston
Thomson, John S.	Burleson	Tidwell, Peter	Panola
Thomson, Napoleon B.	Henderson	Tidwell, S. M.	Panola
Thomson, Robert	Navarro	Tier, Thomas	Hopkins
Thomson, Thomas C.	Burleson	Tierwester, Ann	Harris
Thorn, D. K.	Lamar	Tiller, G. W.	Bowie
Thorn, Frost	Henderson	Tiller, William	Harrison
Thorn, Frost	Nacogdoches	Tilley, Jafferson	Dallas
Thorn, John S.	Henderson	Tillis, James M.	Polk
Thorn, John S.	Nacogdoches	Tilles, Richard	Polk
Thorn, Joseph G.	Lamar	Tillis, Willoby	Polk
Thorn, L. M.	Henderson	Tilton, C.	Matagorda
Thorn, Thomas	Leon	Tilly, G. W.	Matagorda
Thornhill, Achilles	Fannin	Tilly, John	Lavaca
Thornhill, William	Fannin	Timmens, Barbara C.	Harrison
Thornton, F.	Walker	Timmens, James F.	Harrison
Thornton, W. S.	Bastrop	Timmens, Mary B.	Harrison
Thorp, G. H.	Burleson	Timmens, T. G.	Henderson
Thorp, H.	Milam	Timmens, Thomas	Rusk
Thorp, J. S.	Matagorda	Tims, U. B.	Red River
Thorp, Pleasant	Burleson	Tindall, Henry W.	Grimes
Thorp, T.	Henderson	Tindall, William	Nacogdoches
Thorp, Tyre	Lamar	Tinery, James	Navarro
Thorp, William	Galveston	Tinin, J. G.	Lamar
Thorp, William	Travis	Tinin, William	Lamar
Thrash, J. B.	Austin	Tinkler, Joseph	Colorado
Thrawl, Homer S.	Travis	Tinnelle, George	Bastrop
Threlkeld, Timothy	Calhoun	Tinney, Margaret	Gonzales
Throckmorton, W. E.	Collin	Tinsley, Isaac T.	Brazoria
Thurmana, A. T.	Victoria	Tinsley, Susan	Walker
Thurmond, Mark J.	Austin	Tippet, Andrew	Panola
Thurmond, T. R.	Leon	Tippet, B. E.	Austin
Thuner, Lewis	Polk	Tippet, Robert	Panola
Thweatt, B. G.	Henderson	Tippet, Stephen	Austin
Thweatt, B. T.	Hunt	Tippet, William	Panola
Thweatt, Federic	Henderson	Tipps, Leander	Rusk
Thweatt, J. W.	Henderson	Tipps, Peter	Rusk
Thweatt, J. W.	Hunt	Tipton, Eli	Polk
Thweatt, James	Henderson	Tisdell, John	Bowie
		Tittle, G. W.	Henderson
		Tittle, W.	Henderson
		Titus, A. J.	Red River
		Titus, James, Jr.	Red River

NAME	COUNTY	NAME	COUNTY
Titus, M.	Hunt	Tongate, L.	Grimes
Titus, P. W.	Fannin	Tooke, Isam	Colorado
Titus, T. J.	Red River	Tool, Martin O.	Victoria
Tivis, G. W.	Jefferson	Toomey, William	Bexar
Tivis, Jackson	Jefferson	Toops, John	Washington
Tivis, Nancy	Jefferson	Torn, William C.	Washington
Tobin, Robert H.	Colorado	Torr, Margareta	Bexar
Toby, George	Leon	Torres, Miguil	Nacogdoches
Todd, C. J.	Cass	Torrey & Bros.	Harris
Todd, Jackson	Henderson	Touchstone, John	Robertson
Todd, Jackson	Nacogdoches	Towns, David	Bexar
Todd, James D.	Harrison	Towns, David	Henderson
Todd, William, Jr.	Shelby	Towns, David	Nacogdoches
Todd, William, Sr.	Shelby	Towns, Louisa	Nacogdoches
Tolbatt, Joseph	Titus	Towns, Peter	Nacogdoches
Toler, Daniel J.	Galveston	Towns, Robert S.	Brazoria
Tolle, George F.	Comal	Townsend, Asa	Colorado
Tollett, E.	Henderson	Townsend, B.	Harris
Tollett, Elija	Hopkins	Townsend, Elvira	Colorado
Tollett, J.	Henderson	Townsend, Jeshua	Limestone
Tollett, W.	Henderson	Townsend, John	Fayette
Tollett, Wesley	Henderson	Townsend, Morris	Colorado
Tolison, H.	Liberty	Townsend, Moses	Colorado
Toliver, B.	Lavaca	Townsend, Richard	Bastrop
Toliver, G. W.	Harris	Townsend, Stephen	Colorado
Toliver, John	Colorado	Townsend, Stephen	Fayette
Tom, James H.	Washington	Townsend, T. R.	Houston
Tom, John F.	Guadalupe	Townsend, W. S.	Fayette
Tom, William	Guadalupe	Townsend, William	Grimes
Tom, William C.	Washington	Townsend, William	Limestone
Tomkins, John S.	Newton	Townsend, William	
Tomkins, S. S.	Harris	T.	Colorado
Tomkins, T. D.	Houston	Townsley, Witt	Cass
Tomkins, Thomas	Newton	Towsey, Samuel A.	Brazoria
Tomlin, James	Red River	Traber, Joseph	Jackson
Tomlinson, Aaron	Jasper	Tracy, Herman	Harris
Tomlinson, J. W.	Red River	Tracy, Moses C.	Polk
Tomlinson, John C.	Nacogdoches	Trahern, G. W.	Calhoun
Tomlinson, Leonard	Rusk	Trainer, David S.	Gonzales
Tomlinson,		Travieso, Justo	Bexar
Margaret A.	Nacogdoches	Travino, By.	Bexar
Tomlinson, Richard	Red River	Travino, Jose	Henderson
Tomlinson, William	Fannin	Travino, Juan	Bexar
Tompkins, A. B.	Tyler	Travis, Conrad	Fannin
Tompson, James	Tyler	Travis, Mathew	Navarro
Tondre, Nicholas	Bexar	Travis, Mathias	Navarro
Toner, Daniel	Grimes	Travis, Sandford	Fannin
Toney, Edward	Fayette	Traylor, Winn	Victoria
Toney, James C.	Fayette	Treadwell, John	Navarro
Toney, Seth	Fayette	Treat, George H.	Galveston

NAME	COUNTY	NAME	COUNTY
Trebotham, Thomas	Houston	Tucker, W. B.	Collin
Tribble, James	Houston	Tucker, William H.	Shelby
Tribblehorn, Jacob	Guadalupe	Tuder, Kinzy L.	Lamar
Trimble, Henry	Lamar	Tuder, S. B.	Lamar
Trimble, Jane	Galveston	Tuggle, A. J.	Red River
Trimble, John S.	Cherokee	Tuggle, G. W.	Anderson
Trimble, Joseph W.	Cherokee	Tullock, James	Galveston
Trimble, Philip	Cherokee	Tumblinson, David	Dherokee
Trimble, Robert C.	Brazoria	Tumblinson, H.	Grimes
Trimmer, Thomas	Washington	Tumblinson, James	Cherokee
Trino, J. J.	Tyler	Tumblinson, John	Victoria
Tronson, John	Galveston	Tumblinson, Joseph	DeWitt
Trotti, James F.	Newton	Tumblinson, Peter	Grimes
Troy, John	DeWitt	Tumblinson, Wert.	Walker
Truax, A. M.	Shelby	Tunderworth, John	Austin
Truce, Crawford	Dallas	Tunnelle, Marcus	Bexar
Trueheart, J. O.	Galveston	Turberville,	
Trueheart, James		William	Walker
L.	Bexar	Turley, James M.	Rusk
Truett, J. M.	Shelby	Turley, William	Titus
Truett, James	Shelby	Turnelly, A. J.	Harris
Truett, Leander	Shelby	Turner, Mrs.	Harris
Truett, Mary	Shelby	Turner, Amasa	Harris
Truett, S. J.	Shelby	Turner, Bird	Tyler
Truett, Susan	Shelby	Turner, Charles	Shelby
Truett, Wingate	Titus	Turner, Edmund	Tyler
Trussell, John	Brazoria	Turner, Elisha	San Augustine
Tryon, Selden	Houston	Turner, Fielding	
Tryon, William M.	Harris	B.	DeWitt
Tschudy, C.	Galveston	Turner, George L.	Harris
Tubb, E.	Henderson	Turner, George S.	Colorado
Tubb, Elisha	Cherokee	Turner, H. B.	Nacogdoches
Tubb, George	Jackson	Turner, H. M.	Bastrop
Tubb, John	Bexar	Turner, J. H.	Guadalupe
Tubb, Stafford	Cherokee	Turner, J. S.	Anderson
Tubb, Thomas	Cherokee	Turner, John	Grayson
Tucker, Abben	Walker	Turner, John	Jefferson
Tucker, Alexis	Lavaca	Turner, John	Lamar
Tucker, H. H.	Collin	Turner, John	Rusk
Tucker, Henry	Rusk	Turner, John W.	Brazoria
Tucker, J. L.	Liberty	Turner, Joseph	Cass
Tucker, James	Shelby	Turner, Joseph T.	Denton
Tucker, Jefferson	Red River	Turner, Panola	Panola
Tucker, John	Robinson	Turner, R. A.	Red River
Tucker, John T.	Walker	Turner, R. H.	Henderson
Tucker, Joseph R.	Anderson	Turner, Robert	Shelby
Tucker, L. J.	Walker	Turner, Robert	Victoria
Tucker, Robert R.	Fannin	Turner, Ruffin	Jasper
Tucker, Samuel	Dallas	Turner, S. S.	Red River
Tucker, Thomas F.	Shelby	Turner, Samuel	Brazoria

NAME	COUNTY	NAME	COUNTY
Turner, Samuel	Guadalupe	Underton, Charles	Galveston
Turner, Samuel	Jasper	Underwood, Ammon	Brazoria
Turner, Stephen	Jackson	Underwood,	
Turner, W. R.	Colorado	Benjamin	Brazoria
Turner, William J.	Guadalupe	Underwood, Edmund	Fannin
Turner, William R.	Guadalupe	Upchurch,	
Turner, Winslow	Gonzales	Henderson	Travis
Turner, Zachariah	San Augustine	Upshur, H. L.	Bexar
Turney, A. G.	Panola	Urban, A.	Walker
Turney, R.	Grayson	Urban, Joseph	Grimes
Turnham, J. J.	Milam	Urrigas, Juan	Bexar
Turpin, William	Shelby	Urritria, Juan	Bexar
Tuton, Charles	Austin	Urritria, Victoria	Bexar
Tutt, Clement C.	Rusk	Urquehart, Allen	Cass
Tutt, H. G.	Rusk	Urquehart, Norman	Liberty
Tutt, Merina	Rusk	Ury, Amos	Cass
Tutt, Richard	Rusk	Ury, Eunis	Cass
Tutt, W. G.	Rusk	Usener, Fred	Harris
Tuttle, Daniel	Nacogdoches	Ussery, B. B.	Cass
Tuttle, Daniel	Panola	Ussery, Benjamin	Liberty
Tuttle, Elizabeth	Panola	Ussery, David	Liberty
Tuttle, George	Fayette	Ussery, James	Liberty
Tuttle, Mary	Panola	Ussery, Lucynda	Harrison
Tweedy, Thompson	Lamar	Ussery, M. S.	Harrison
Twitty, W. C.	Fannin	Utley, Fred	Walker
Twohig, John	Bexar	Uzzell, E.	Montgomery
Twomey, Hastin	Panola	Uzzell, T. M.	Montgomery
Twomey, William	Panola		
Tyler, Edward	Walker		
Tyler, Jordan	Brazoria	Vaca, Antonio	Bexar
Tyler, O. T.	Galveston	Vaganfaus, John	Colorado
Tyler, Oscar	Austin	Vail, A. L.	Fayette
Tyler, Reuben	Travis	Vail, C. H.	Fayette
Tyler, William	Harrison	Vail, D. H.	Henderson
Tyman, D. C.	Bexar	Vail, Daniel H.	Nacogdoches
Tyner, Anson	Seon	Valdez, Fern.	Bexar
Tyra, E. H.	Collin	Valdez, Juan	Bexar
Tyrrell, Timothy	Jackson	Valdez, Julian	Bexar
Tyrrell, Wm. J. T.	Jackson	Valdez, Manuel	Victoria
Tyson, Eson	Austin	Vale, Hiram	Dallas
Tyson, Isaac	Bowie	Valentine, F.	Galveston
Tyus, R. M.	Robertson	Vallo, F.	Matagorda
		Van, George	Bexar
		Van, James S.	Walker
Ufford, W. L.	Galveston	Van, John F.	Walker
Ullrich, George	Comal	Van Alstyne, W. A.	Harris
Umminger, J. W.	Liberty	Van Bibber, John	Victoria
Umphries, Bryan	Nacogdoches	Van Blucher, F. A.	Comal
Underhill, C. B.	Galveston	VanBuren, Henry	Harris
Underhill, D. M.	Washington	Vance, Bailey	Polk

171

NAME	COUNTY	NAME	COUNTY
Vance, Charles K.	Dallas	Varner, W.	Henderson
Vance, D.	Titus	Varney, B.	Fort Bend
Vance, John	Washington	Varney, M. J.	Fort Bend
Vance, John S.	Polk	Vary, D. W. C.	Limestone
Vance, John W.	Dallas	Vass, Edward	Brazoria
Vance, L. D.	Shelby	Vaughn, D. D.	Limestone
Vance, Mary	Walker	Vaughn, Eldridge	Rusk
Vance, Thomas	Dallas	Vaughn, Willis	Panola
Vance, William	Bexar	Vaught, A.	Titus
Vance, William S.	Polk	Vaught, J. B.	Nacogdoches
Vancil, Peter	Washington	Vaught, N.	Cass
Vancleave, S.	Bastrop	Vaught, William	Cass
Vancleck, G. W.	Tyler	Vaughter, Lewis	Panola
Vandam, W.	Polk	Vaughter, Lucinda	Panola
Vandergrift,		Veach, J. M.	Austin
William	Fannin	Veach, T. S.	Bastrop
Vanderlip, D. C.	Bexar	Veasey, Wiley G.	Washington
Vanderipper, John	Shelby	Veatch, John B.	Guadalupe
Vanderpool, James	Brazoria	Veham, Henry	Austin
Vandervant, John	Fannin	Veick, Casper	Comal
Vandeveer, C. H.	Matagorda	Veil, Richard	Lavaca
Vandeveer,		Vela, Christiana	Bexar
Elizabeth	Fannin	Venabore, John	Victoria
Vandeveer, Logan	Bastrop	Vanibles, P.	Henderson
Vandeveer, Moses	Fannin	Venohr, F. R.	Henderson
Vandorn, J.	Matagorda	Ventura, Paro	Victoria
Vandyke, L. D.	Bowie	Veramendi, M. A.	Bexar
Vandyke, R. F.	Matagorda	Vernoy, C.	Red River
Vandyne, John	Grimes	Vesey, Samuel	Brazoria
Van Hearne, N. A.	Gonzales	Vess, Mrs. E.	Jackson
Vankerchehain, H.		Vess, Minerva	Brazos
J.	Anderson	Vestal, William B.	Tyler
Van Norman, T. W.	Victoria	Vestal, Zimel	Lamar
Vannoy, Andrew	Rusk	Vice, Nathaniel	Red River
Vannoy, Isaac R.	Rusk	Vick, Isaiah	Montgomery
Vannoy, Richard	Rusk	Vick, J. J.	Shelby
Van Pradellis, A.		Vickers, Harris	Polk
G.	Liberty	Vickers, James	Sabine
Vansent, Wm. A.	Grimes	Vickers, James R.	Grimes
Vansickle, B. A.	Rusk	Vickery, C. W.	Victoria
Vansickle, Elija	Rusk	Vickery, Elisha	Polk
Vansickle, Ephriam	Henderson	Victor, Prichard	Galveston
Vansickle, Stephen	Galveston	Vidal, George	Bexar
Vantevner, James	Fannin	Vidle, Jacob	Anderson
Van Vechten, D. H.	Comal	Vietch, Eliza	Nacogdoches
Van Zandt, Isaac	Harrison	Villagrand,	
Vardeman, William	Rusk	Gabriel	Bexar
Varnell, M. M.	Gonzales	Villareal, Juan	Bexar
Varner, C. S.	Montgomery	Villareal, Rafael	Bexar
Varner, Martin	Henderson	Villareal, Val	Bexar

NAME	COUNTY	NAME	COUNTY
Villeneve, G.	Galveston	Wadkins, Wiley B.	Harrison
Villenger, Leon	Galveston	Wadlington,	
Villmare, -----	Victoria	Spencer	Harrison
Vincent, Adam	Grimes	Wadsworth, A.	Matagorda
Vincent, Archibald	Angelina	Wadsworth, George	Refugio
Vincent, E.	Galveston	Wafer, Mrs.	
Vincent, S. H.	Grimes	Elizabeth	Lamar
Vincent, Thomas C.	Lamar	Wafer, Joel	Henderson
Vining, Cosby	Cherokee	Wafer, Joel	Lamar
Vining, Lewis M.	Cherokee	Wafford, Rollin B.	DeWitt
Vining, Wade H.	Wharton	Waggoner, David	Lamar
Vinzent, Charles	Rusk	Waggoner, J.	Upshur
Vinzent, Edward	Rusk	Waggoner, Solomon	Red River
Vires, W. T.	Walker	Wagley, S.	Upshur
Vires, William	Walker	Wagner, George W.	Cherokee
Viveon, B. S.	Harrison	Wagner, H. W.	Galveston
Viveon, James	Henderson	Wagner, John	Denton
Viveon, V. H.	Harrison	Wagner, Lewis	Cherokee
Viveon, Walker	Henderson	Wagner, Newton	Cherokee
Vivien, John	Harris	Wagstaff, James	Shelby
Voelker, Julius	Comal	Waid, R. W.	Henderson
Vogel, Ludwig	Comal	Waikand, S.	Leon
Voges, J. H.	Comal	Waikand, Sarah	Leon
Vogle, Frederick	Brazoria	Waites, A. J.	Sabine
Vogt, Adam	Comal	Waites, James	Cass
Vogt, Ludwig	Comal	Wakefield, Uzziel	Brazoria
Voiles, J.	Harrison	Wakeland, Wm. C.	Harrison
Volentine, Henry	Lavaca	Wakeman, M. B.	Harris
Volk, Fred	Bexar	Walbridge, E.	Galveston
Voshary, John	San Augustine	Walden, Charles S.	Burleson
Voss, Charles	Harris	Walden, David	Grayson
Votaw, Elijah	Gonzales	Walden, Hendrick	Grayson
Votaw, Isaac	Grimes	Waldmann, ----	Matagorda
		Waldrip, W.	Henderson
		Wales, Prosper	Fayette
Waddell, F. B.	Austin	Waley, James	Jefferson
Waddell, R. H.	Colorado	Walker, A. M.	Grimes
Waddle, A. C.	Bowie	Walker, Alfred M.	DeWitt
Waddle, C. M.	Bowie	Walker, B. M.	Nacogdoches
Waddle, Isaac	Henderson	Walker, Benjamin	Fannin
Wade, David	Fayette	Walker, Benjamin	
Wade, Huldy E.	Austin	L.	Fannin
Wade, Isaac E.	Harris	Walker, C. C.	Grimes
Wade, J. M.	Walker	Walker, C. P.	Upshur
Wade, John	Panola	Walker, Charles	Travis
Wade, N.	Henderson	Walker, E. L.	Wharton
Wade, Nathan	Nacogdoches	Walker, Edward	Harris
Wade, William	Austin	Walker, Elizabeth	Robertson
Wadham, W.	Colorado	Walker, Gideon	Limestone
Wadkins, W. B.	Collin	Walker, Hiram	Rusk

173

NAME	COUNTY	NAME	COUNTY
Walker, J. C.	Wharton	Walker, William	Robertson
Walker, J. H.	Upshur	Walker, William	Walker
Walker, J. K. T.	Washington	Walker, William	Washington
Walker, J. N.	Fannin	Walker, Wm. A.	Nacogdoches
Walker, James	Cass	Walker, Wm. B.	Harris
Walker, James	Robertson	Walker, Wm. C.	Brazos
Walker, James	Washington	Walker, Wm. C.	Panola
Walker, James M.	Polk	Walker, Wm. H.	Grimes
Walker, Jeremiah	Bowie	Walker, Z. C.	Shelby
Walker, Jesse	Walker	Wall, Albert G.	Panola
Walker, Joel	Dallas	Wall, Benjamin	Brazoria
Walker, Joel	Grimes	Wall, C. L.	Harrison
Walker, John	Fayette	Wall, H. H.	Harrison
Walker, John	Henderson	Wall, J. F.	Titus
Walker, John	Nacogdoches	Wall, Samuel	Fannin
Walker, John	Robertson	Wall, William T.	Panola
Walker, John C.	Harrison	Wallace, B. R.	San Augustine
Walker, John M.	Washington	Wallace, E. P.	Red River
Walker, Joseph	Walker	Wallace, G. W.	Wharton
Walker, Kidder	Colorado	Wallace, Green	Cherokee
Walker, L. H.	Cass	Wallace, H. B.	Sabine
Walker, Landon	Limestone	Wallace, J. W. E.	Colorado
Walker, Lewis	Grimes	Wallace, James	Grimes
Walker, Lewis H.	Bowie	Wallace, James T.	Bastrop
Walker, M. A.	Houston	Wallace, Jefferson	Cherokee
Walker, Martha A.	Gonzales	Wallace, John	Hunt
Walker, Martin	Bastrop	Wallace, R. B.	Houston
Walker, Mary	Angelina	Wallace, S. G.	Matagorda
Walker, Matthias	Polk	Wallace, Thomas J.	Cass
Walker, O. H. T.	Walker	Wallace, W. A.	Bexar
Walker, P. L.	Fort Bend	Wallace, W. N.	Bowie
Walker, Philip	Shelby	Wallace, Wm. S.	Travis
Walker, R. J.	Walker	Waller, Anderson	Houston
Walker, R. S.	San Augustine	Waller, Edwin, Jr.	Austin
Walker, Richard H.	Henderson	Waller, Edwin, Sr.	Austin
Walker, Robert	Lamar	Waller, H.	Houston
Walker, S.	Matagorda	Waller, Hiram B.	Austin
Walker, S. A.	Robertson	Waller, Juliet	Austin
Walker, Samuel	Bowie	Waller, Robert	Angelina
Walker, Sanders	Limestone	Walley, F. A.	Galveston
Walker, T. C.	San Augustine	Walling, Alfred	Rusk
Walker, Tandy H.	Grimes	Walling, Elisha	Houston
Walker, Theo.	Brazos	Walling, H. L.	Houston
Walker, Thomas	Angelina	Walling, James	Houston
Walker, Thomas	Liberty	Walling, James	Nacogdoches
Walker, Thomas	Limestone	Walling, Jefferson	Rusk
Walker, W. C.	Red River	Walling, Jesse	Houston
Walker, W. L.	Wharton	Walling, Jesse	Rusk
Walker, William	Bastrop	Walling, John	Henderson
Walker, William	Grimes	Walling, John	Rusk

NAME	COUNTY	NAME	COUNTY
Walling, John, Sr.	Rusk	Wampler, Martin J.	Dallas
Walling, N. D.	Henderson	Wampler, Valentine	Dallas
Walling, N. D.	Shelby	Wan, Henry	Colorado
Walling, Preston	Rusk	Wandlirt, D. J.	Fort Bend
Walling, V.	Henderson	Wanest, John B.	Bexar
Walling, Vance	Nacogdoches	Wantland, Marshall	Fannin
Wallis, Alfred	Fort Bend	War, John R.	Washington
Wallis, D.	Liberty	Warbington, W. B.	Harrison
Wallis, E. H.	Liberty	Ward, A. J.	Henderson
Wallis, E. W.	Liberty	Ward, Abner	Austin
Wallis, Jacob	Hopkins	Ward, Andrew	Titus
Wallis, Jeremiah	Lamar	Ward, B. F.	Houston
Wallis, Robert	Lamar	Ward, C. G.	Wharton
Wallis, S.	Liberty	Ward, H. W.	Houston
Wallis, William	Liberty	Ward, Henry	Fannin
Wallis, Wm. S.	Leon	Ward, Herman	Brazoria
Walsh, D.	Travis	Ward, J. J.	Cass
Walson, L.	Henderson	Ward, J. N.	Brazoria
Walters, B. C.	Cherokee	Ward, Jacob	Walker
Walters, B. C.	Nacogdoches	Ward, James	Hopkins
Walters, Baly C.	Henderson	Ward, James	Red River
Walters, C. M.	Henderson	Ward, James J.	Red River
Walters, C. W.	Montgomery	Ward, Jeremiah	Fannin
Walters, Charles		Ward, Jeremiah	Hopkins
M.	Nacogdoches	Ward, Jesse	Austin
Walters, Ezekiah	Harrison	Ward, John	Austin
Walters, F. B.	Bastrop	Ward, John	Harrison
Walters, George	Panola	Ward, John	Limestone
Walters, George,		Ward, John	Navarro
Jr.	Panola	Ward, Lafayette	Jackson
Walters, George T.	Henderson	Ward, Lemual W.	Red River
Walters, George T.	Smith	Ward, M.	Cass
Walters, Henry	Colorado	Ward, M.	Red River
Walters, Isaac	Harrison	Ward, Morris	Cass
Walters, J. N.	Panola	Ward, R. M.	Lamar
Walters, James H.	Fannin	Ward, Russell	Jackson
Walters, John H.	Harris	Ward, Solomon	Austin
Walters, Josiah	DeWitt	Ward, Stephen	Limestone
Walters, Killis	Panola	Ward, Thomas	Travis
Walters, L. S.	Cherokee	Ward, Thomas W.	Travis
Walters, L. S.	Jasper	Ward, Trobridge	Matagorda
Walters, Moses	Cherokee	Ward, W. C.	Cass
Walters, Robert	Austin	Ward, W. H.	San Augustine
Walters, Robert	Bastrop	Ward, W. J.	Matagorda
Walters, Robert	Smith	Ward, W. R. D.	Harrison
Walters, Stephen	Fayette	Ward, William	Liberty
Walters, Tilman	Smith	Ward, William	Navarro
Walters, Wade H.	Cherokee	Ward, William	Red River
Walters, William	Washington	Ware, Hardy	Houston
Wamble, J. W.	Bowie	Ware, J. L.	Leon

NAME	COUNTY	NAME	COUNTY
Ware, James	Cherokee	Watkins, Lewis	Shelby
Ware, James R.	Robertson	Watkins, R. M.	Nacogdoches
Ware, John	Red River	Watkins, R. O.	Nacogdoches
Ware, M. L.	Houston	Watkins, S.	Milam
Ware, Thomas	Colorado	Watkins, Thomas	Cass
Ware, William	Henderson	Watkins, William	Cass
Warfield, C. A.	Lamar	Watkins, William	Limestone
Waring, B. T.	Liberty	Watson, Abraham	Hunt
Waring, E. G.	Liberty	Watson, Benjamin	Hunt
Waring, F. G.	Liberty	Watson, Cary	Bowie
Waring, J. E.	Liberty	Watson, Coleman	Bowie
Waring, Kitty	Liberty	Watson, Dexter	San Augustine
Warren, D. O.	San Augustine	Watson, E. T.	Bowie
Warren, Eli	Rusk	Watson, Evan	Cass
Warren, G.	Upshur	Watson, George W.	Panola
Warren, Henry	Henderson	Watson, H. E.	San Augustine
Warren, James	Sabine	Watson, Mrs.	
Warren, James C.	Lamar	Harriet	Washington
Warren, John	Galveston	Watson, I.	Grayson
Warren, John W.	San Augustine	Watson, J. M.	Titus
Warren, R.	Upshur	Watson, J. W.	Cass
Warren, William	Anderson	Watson, James	Fannin
Warren, William G.	Brazoria	Watson, John	Bowie
Warrenberger, John	Travis	Watson, John	Cherokee
Warrican, J.	Shelby	Watson, John	Colorado
Warnock, B. F.	Travis	Watson, Julius	Newton
Wartman, Henry E.	Grayson	Watson, Martin	Cass
Warton, James	Titus	Watson, Martin	Grayson
Washburn, James	Cherokee	Watson, Michael	San Augustine
Washburn, Josiah		Watson, Ordera	Burleson
M.	Fannin	Watson, Orrin D.	Bowie
Washburn, L. L.	Harrison	Watson, Paul	Fannin
Washing, R. G.	Walker	Watson, Rhoda	Bowie
Washington,		Watson, S. C.	San Augustine
Darlington	Rusk	Watson, S. E.	San Augustine
Washington, Lewis		Watson, Samson	Newton
M. H.	Travis	Watson, Thomas	Cass
Washington, M. H.	Travis	Watson, W.	Henderson
Washington, Thomas		Watson, William	Houston
P.	Travis	Watson, William	Panola
Waterman, Joseph	Galveston	Watts, Absylom	Smith
Waters, Clement	Grimes	Watts, B. T.	Smith
Waters, Jacob	Austin	Watts, Hyram	Tyler
Waters, John D.	Fort Bend	Watts, James	Jackson
Watkins, B. R.	Shelby	Watts, James	Lavaca
Watkins, Daniel	Fannin	Watts, John	Polk
Watkins, G. B.	Sabine	Watts, Richard	Lavaca
Watkins, J. T.	Montgomery	Watts, Susan	Jasper
Watkins, John M.	Nacogdoches	Watts, Thomas	Smith
Watkins, Joseph	Fannin	Watts, Thomas, Jr.	Jasper

176

NAME	COUNTY	NAME	COUNTY
Watts, W. G.	Harris	Webb, Joel D.	Lamar
Waugh, John	Burleson	Webb, John J.	Jasper
Wauhoss, J. W.	Red River	Webb, John W.	Harrison
Weaks, Albert	San Augustine	Webb, Joseph	Robertson
Weaks, James	San Augustine	Webb, Joseph N.	Robertson
Wear, Joseph	Jackson	Webb, Meredith	Shelby
Weatherby, Thomas		Webb, Morris	Robertson
H.	Cherokee	Webb, Nancy	Lamar
Weatherby, William		Webb, Reuben	Cherokee
F.	Harrison	Webb, T. F.	Henderson
Weathered, Ben F.	Sabine	Webb, Thomas	Robertson
Weathered, F. M.,		Webb, Thomas H.	Walker
Jr.	Sabine	Webb, Thomas R.	Robertson
Weathered, F. M.,		Webb, Thomas W.	Smith
Sr.	Sabine	Webb, Wesley	Robertson
Weathered, James		Webb, William D.	Cherokee
H.	Sabine	Webb, William M.	Robertson
Weathered, R.	Red River	Webb, William S.	Jasper
Weathered, Wm. C.	Sabine	Webber, Henry	Comal
Weatherford, Money	Lamar	Webber, John F.	Travis
Weathers, Alex.	Polk	Webber, Mark	Bastrop
Weatherspoon, M.	Lamar	Webberlene, F.	Austin
Weatherspoon,		Weber, Pedro	Bexar
Wiley	Lamar	Webster, Jane	Galveston
Weaver, Daniel	Navarro	Webster, E. D.	Grayson
Weaver, Ezekiel	Shelby	Webster, J. J.	Harrison
Weaver, Green	Hopkins	Webster, Jane	Galveston
Weaver, John	Hopkins	Wedemier, A. F.	Comal
Weaver, John	Liberty	Weed, Benjamin	Liberty
Weaver, Julia	Liberty	Weed, Solomon	Liberty
Weaver, L. G.	Montgomery	Weedin, J. M.	Nacogdoches
Weaver, P. J. or		Weekley, Edmund	Brazoria
G.	Matagorda	Weekley, George M.	Grimes
Weaver, S. W.	Upshur	Weeks, Benjamin	Brazoria
Weaver, Tillman	Fayette	Weeks, Daniel	Nacogdoches
Weaver, Tinsley	Hopkins	Weeks, F. G.	Fannin
Weaver, W. H.	Nacogdoches	Weeks, James	Newton
Webb, Anderson	Nacogdoches	Weeks, Wm. F.	Harris
Webb, Arena	Burleson	Weems, M. D.	Wharton
Webb, Benjamin	Hopkins	Wehrly, John	Galveston
Webb, D. F.	San Augustine	Weigle, John	Colorado
Webb, Edmond	Robertson	Weihl, Joseph	Galveston
Webb, F. B.	Victoria	Weil, Jacob	Comal
Webb, G. H.	Fayette	Weil, widow	Comal
Webb, George W.	Hopkins	Weinert, Wm.	Fayette
Webb, Isaac B.	Dallas	Weir, Isaac H.	Montgomery
Webb, James	Travis	Weir, James	Bexar
Webb, James M.	Robertson	Weir, John	Bowie
Webb, Jesse	Jasper	Weir, Reuben L.	Brazoria
Webb, Jesse	Robertson	Weir, Wm. R.	Washington

NAME	COUNTY	NAME	COUNTY
Weirkman, Earas	Colorado	West, B. L.	Harrison
Welborn, W.	Upshur	West, Benjamin B.	Harris
Welch, C. C.	Liberty	West, Berry	Newton
Welch, Charles	Limestone	West, Claiborne	Montgomery
Welch, David	Sabine	West, Edward	Red River
Welch, Henry	Walker	West, Ellis H.	Rusk
Welch, John	Anderson	West, Francis, Jr.	Harrison
Welch, John	Henderson	West, Francis, Sr.	Harrison
Welch, John	Navarro	West, George	San Augustine
Welch, John	Smith	West, Gilford	Harris
Welch, Robert G.	Washington	West, Hampton	Panola
Welch, Sarah	Robertson	West, Isaac	Washington
Welch, Thomas	Hopkins	West, Jacob	Harrison
Welch, W. W.	Red River	West, James	Harris
Welch, William	Limestone	West, James	Newton
Welch, William	Navarro	West, James	Panola
Welch, William	Titus	West, Mrs. Jane	Limestone
Weldon, Isaac	Gonzales	West, John	Limestone
Weldon, James S.	Denton	West, John H.	Newton
Weldon, Wm. B.	Denton	West, John W.	Red River
Wells, Albert	Smith	West, Joshua	Grayson
Wells, Benjamin	Panola	West, Martin	Grimes
Wells, Calvin	Smith	West, Michael	Limestone
Wells, Felix	Smith	West, R. J.	Dallas
Wells, Francis F.	Jackson	West, Sarah	Newton
Wells, Hiram	Fannin	West, W. W.	Harrison
Wells, J. A.	Fayette	West, William	Liberty
Wells, J. F. M.	Panola	Westall, Andrew E.	Brazoria
Wells, J. G.	Harrison	Westall, H. G.	Brazoria
Wells, James	Fannin	Westall, Thomas	Brazoria
Wells, James	Harris	Westbrook, Joshua	Newton
Wells, James	Harrison	Westbrook, Stephen	Panola
Wells, John	Walker	Westbrook, T. B.	Newton
Wells, Lewis	Washington	Westbrook, T. S.	Polk
Wells, M.	Bastrop	Westcott, Mrs.	
Wells, Moses	Limestone	Catherine	Galveston
Wells, Rezin	Fannin	Westcott, Leander	Galveston
Wells, Rice	Smith	Westcott, R. D.	Montgomery
Wells, T.	Walker	Westervelt	Brazoria
Welty, John	Harrison	Westfall,	
Wensett, Valentine	Liberty	Zachariah	Fayette
Wentzel, George	Comal	Westmoreland,	
Wepler, Phillip	Robertson	Joseph	Panola
Werdner, Frank	Washington	Westmoreland, R.	
Wernell, N. G.	Bowie	S.	Houston
Wersdoerfer,		Westmoreland, S.	
Joseph	Comal	J.	Houston
Wessen, Thomas E.	Lamar	Weston, Thomas	Bexar
West, Aaron	Dallas	Westroop, H. G.	Galveston
West, Abraham	Harrison	Wethers, Stephen	

NAME	COUNTY	NAME	COUNTY
T.	Hopkins	Whitaker, G. W. B.	Houston
Wethersby, Reuben	Fannin	Whitaker, Isaac	Nacogdoches
Wethertz, James	Rusk	Whitaker, John H.	Nacogdoches
Wetzel, Wm.	Comal	Whitaker, Jno.	Washington
Wever, J. W.	Bowie	Whitaker, L. W.	Houston
Weyers, Henry	Galveston	Whitaker, M.	Houston
Whaley, W. D.	Cherokee	Whitaker, M. G.	Nacogdoches
Wharton, J. A.	Brazoria	Whitaker, P. C.	Limestone
Whatley, G. W.	Liberty	Whitaker, T. M.	Austin
Whealey, George	Henderson	Whitaker, W. G.	Henderson
Wheat, A. L.	Walker	Whitaker, Willis	Bowie
Wheat, B. M.	Tyler	Whitaker, Willis	Cass
Wheat, Bazel	Fort Bend	Whitaker, Wm.	Nacogdoches
Wheat, J. W.	Cass	White, A. H.	Montgomery
Wheat, James	Lamar	White, A. J.	Montgomery
Wheat, James	Tyler	White, Alexander	Cherokee
Wheat, John	Lamar	White, Alfred	Harris
Wheat, John	Tyler	White, Anderson	Washington
Wheat, Joseph	Tyler	White, B.	Lamar
Wheat, Robert	Red River	White, Ben	Bowie
Wheat, Samuel	Red River	White, Benjamin	Cherokee
Wheat, W.	Grayson	White, Benjamin	Fayette
Wheat, William	Lamar	White, Benjamin J.	Jackson
Wheat, William	Red River	White, Bigham	DeWitt
Wheaton, Elizabeth	Harris	White, Bigham	Grimes
Wheeler, D. M.	Matagorda	White, Carey	Washington
Wheeler, Daniel G.	Harris	White, Charles	Nacogdoches
Wheeler, H. H.	Grimes	White, David	Matagorda
Wheeler, J.	Matagorda	White, David, Jr.	Navarro
Wheeler, J. E.	Matagorda	White, David, Sr.	Navarro
Wheeler, J. O.	Victoria	White, Dudley J.	Grimes
Wheeler, R. T.	Galveston	White, E. P.	Liberty
Wheeler, R. T.	Henderson	White, Elijah	Leon
Wheeler, Ramon	Shelby	White, F.	Liberty
Wheeler, T. G.	Fayette	White, Francis	Galveston
Wheeler, Thomas	Fannin	White, Francis M.	Jackson
Wheeler, William	Washington	White, George	Harris
Wheelock, G. R.	Robertson	White, H. A.	Leon
Wheelock, Mary	Robertson	White, H. H.	Nacogdoches
Wheelock, Robert	Grayson	White, H. M.	Bastrop
Whelan, Michael	Refugio	White, Harden	Washington
Whetstone, A.	Houston	White, Hardy H.	Nacogdoches
Whetstone, M.	Houston	White, Henry	Harris
Whim, A. G.	Leon	White, Henry	Walker
Whipple, Josiah	Bastrop	White, Henry, 1st	Harris
Whipple, Sarah	Bastrop	White, Hugh	Bastrop
Whisenant, R. C.	Collin	White, Isaac B.	Polk
Whitacre, Peter	Grimes	White, Isham	Fayette
Whitacre, William	Grimes	White, J. B.	Liberty
Whitaker, B. F.	Nacogdoches	White, J. B.	Titus

NAME	COUNTY	NAME	COUNTY
White, J. E.	Nacogdoches	White, Stephen	Houston
White, J. T.	Shelby	White, T. B.	Houston
White, Jackson	Shelby	White, T. J.	Hunt
White, James	Grimes	White, Thomas B.	Austin
White, James F.	Tyler	White, Thomas J.	Cass
White, James G.	Jackson	White, Thomas M.	Grimes
White, James T.	Liberty	White, Timothy	Harris
White, James T.	Sabine	White, W. M.	Liberty
White, Jeremiah	Montgomery	White, W. T.	Henderson
White, Jeremiah L.	Panola	White, Wesley	Cass
White, Jesse	Harris	White, Wiley B.	Polk
White, Joel	Panola	White, Wiley G.	Nacogdoches
White, John	Grimes	White, William	Burleson
White, John	Liberty	White, William	Grimes
White, John	Milam	White, William	Grimes
White, John A.	DeWitt	White, William	Harris
White, John C.	Grimes	White, William H.	Shelby
White, John S.	Jackson	White, William T.	San Augustine
White, John S.	Panola	White, Zachariah	Grimes
White, John W.	Harris	Whitehead, Richard	Grimes
White, John W.	Jackson	Whitehead, Thomas	Bexar
White, Joseph	Leon	Whitehorn, John M.	Harrison
White, Josiah	Shelby	Whitehurst,	
White, L. B.	Nacogdoches	Benjamin	Brazoria
White, L. C.	Cherokee	Whiteside, G. W.	Harris
White, Leonard	Harris	Whiteside, John J.	Grimes
White, Levi	Houston	Whiteside, Q. B.	Polk
White, M. G.	Liberty	Whiteside, R. M.	Titus
White, M. H.	San Augustine	Whiteside, W. N.	Titus
White, M. L.	Liberty	Whitfield, John O.	Austin
White, M. L., Jr.	Liberty	Whitfield, W. B.	Austin
White, Mary	Jackson	Whitfield, William	Gonzales
White, Mary	Panola	Whitford, S. G.	Cass
White, Maston	Navarro	Whitford, Samuel	
White, N. L.	Travis	G.	Red River
White, Nancy	Leon	Whiting, G. R. A.	Grimes
White, Nancy	Sabine	Whiting, Henry	Harris
White, Peter	Jackson	Whiting, Jesse	Harris
White, Reuben	Harris	Whiting, Lewis P.	Harris
White, Reuben B.	Shelby	Whitler, Louis	Austin
White, Robert	Leon	Whitley, Archibald	Austin
White, Robert	Liberty	Whitley, Hopson	Austin
White, Robert N.	Navarro	Whitley, John	Walker
White, S.	Collin	Whitley, Mills	Walker
White, S. A.	Robertson	Whitley, Sharp	Henderson
White, S. G.	Liberty	Whitley, Sharp	Walker
White, S. L.	Bowie	Whitley, Thomas	Austin
White, Sarah	Sabine	Whitley, William	Walker
White, Sidney B.	Polk	Whitlock, B.	Liberty
White, Sofira	Panola	Whitlock, Mary	Liberty

NAME	COUNTY	NAME	COUNTY
Whitlock, Robert	Liberty	Wilborne, K. A.	Cass
Whitmer, Elias	Polk	Wilborne, Kentch	Cass
Whitmer, Elija	Polk	Wilborne, L. T.	Shelby
Whitmer, Stephen	Polk	Wilborne, R. W.	Liberty
Whitmore, J. L.	Sabine	Wilborne, Wm.	Liberty
Whitmore, William	Houston	Wilcox, A. D.	Fannin
Whitney, Mrs. A.		Wilcox, C.	Liberty
H.	Lamar	Wilcox, Henry	Galveston
Whitt, Mrs. A.	Montgomery	Wilcox, Henry C.	Brazoria
Whittenberg,		Wilcox, J. H.	Collin
Iremus	Fannin	Wilcox, Jacob	Lamar
Whittenberg, John	Fannin	Wilcox, John	Brazoria
Whittenberg, M. W.	Fannin	Wilcox, O.	Travis
Whittlesey, E. A.	Sabine	Wilder, E. M.	Harrison
Whitton, E. H.	Leon	Wilder, J. W.	Montgomery
Wice, J. Booth	Henderson	Wildman, A. B.	Liberty
Wick, John	Shelby	Wiles, John P.	Jefferson
Wickson, Asa	Brazos	Wiles, William	Panola
Wickson, D.	Brazos	Wiley, W. E.	Fannin
Wickson, Eli	Brazos	Wilhelm, Sarah	Washington
Wickson, Franklin	Brazos	Wilhite, John	Gonzales
Wickware, Alpheus	Matagorda	Wilhite, W.	Collin
Wideman, Edward	Lamar	Wilkerson, D.	Henderson
Wideman, Samuel	Lamar	Wilkerson, John E.	Shelby
Wideman, Thomas	Lamar	Wilkes, Albert	Harris
Wiess, Margaret	Jasper	Wilkes, C. B.	Red River
Wiess, S.	Jasper	Wilkes, William	Travis
Wiggington, A. M.	Victoria	Wilkie, J. W.	Cass
Wiggins, C. A.	Liberty	Wilkins, A. G.	Houston
Wiggins, C. A.	Jefferson	Wilkins, B.	Cass
Wiggins, D. D.	Jefferson	Wilkins, B. L.	Cass
Wiggins, D. P.	Liberty	Wilkins, George	Hopkins
Wiggins, H. L.	Leon	Wilkins, Hamilton	Cass
Wiggins, M. W.	Liberty	Wilkins, Isaac	Smith
Wiggins, R. R.	Shelby	Wilkins, John	Bowie
Wiggins, Thomas S.	Shelby	Wilkins, John B.	Washington
Wight, Lyman	Travis	Wilkins, Jonathan	Smith
Wight, O. L.	Travis	Wilkins, Joseph	Cass
Wightman, M.	Montgomery	Wilkins, Mary	Gonzales
Wilbanks, Garner	Rusk	Wilkins, Matthew	Hopkins
Wilbanks, Hiram	Lamar	Wilkins, W.	Walker
Wilbanks, Jesse	Lamar	Wilkins, William	Hopkins
Wilbarger, John W.	Bastrop	Wilkinson, J. A.	Upshur
Wilbarger, Mathias	Bastrop	Wilkinson, James	
Wilborne, C.	Liberty	G.	Burleson
Wilborne, Caleb	DeWitt	Wilkinson, Joel	Burleson
Wilborne,		Wilkinson, John	Newton
Elizabeth	Nacogdoches	Wilkinson, John	Shelby
Wilborne, James J.	Washington	Wilkinson,	
Wilborne, Joel	Nacogdoches	Livingston	Washington

NAME	COUNTY	NAME	COUNTY
Wilkinson, Mellville	Washington	Williams, Eliza	Burleson
Wilkinson, W. G.	Washington	Williams, Eliza	Jasper
Wilkinson, Warren	Washington	Williams, Ephriam	Lamar
Wilkinson, Willie Mc.	Harris	Williams, Erasmus	Jasper
		Williams, F. E.	Fannin
Wilkinson, Wm.	Burleson	Williams, F. Wm.	Rusk
Wilkison, James	Dallas	Williams, Francis	Cass
Willard, J. C.	Cass	Williams, G.	Cass
Willborne, C. C.	Red River	Williams, G. G.	Wharton
Willborne, Edward	Dallas	Williams, G. S.	Sabine
Willborne, Hiram	Dallas	Williams, George	Hunt
Willborne, Robert	Dallas	Williams, George R.	Polk
Willdy, Samuel	Jackson	Williams, George W.	Panola
Willett, R. W.	Anderson		
Willey, Barzillair	Nacogdoches	Williams, Greenberry	Jasper
Willey, M. M.	Tyler	Williams, H.	Henderson
Williams, A.	Brazos	Williams, H.	Liberty
Williams, A. B., Jr.	Washington	Williams, H.	Nacogdoches
Williams, A. B., Sr.	Washington	Williams, H. G.	Houston
Williams, A. C.	Galveston	Williams, H. H.	Galveston
Williams, A. G.	Navarro	Williams, H. L.	Lamar
Williams, A. G.	Washington	Williams, H. L.	Lamar
Williams, A. M.	Lamar	Williams, Hansford	Fannin
Williams, Abraham	**Jefferson**	Williams, Henderson	Newton
Williams, Allen	Navarro	Williams, Henry	Jasper
Williams, Allison	Bastrop	Williams, Henry	Washington
Williams, Bazil	Hunt	Williams, Hezekiah	Jefferson
Williams, Benjamin	Jackson	Williams, Hiram	Lamar
Williams, Benjamin	Jasper	Williams, Hiram	Walker
Williams, Benjamin	Rusk	Williams, Isom	Upshur
Williams, C. W.	Lavaca	Williams, J.	Matagorda
Williams, Charles	Jefferson	Williams, J. A.	Liberty
Williams, D. O.	Henderson	Williams, J. J.	Cass
Williams, D. W.	Collin	Williams, J. J.	Lamar
Williams, David	Galveston	Williams, J. R.	Newton
Williams, David	Henderson	Williams, J. S.	Cass
Williams, E.	Henderson	Williams, J. T.	Cass
Williams, E.	Matagorda	Williams, J. T.	Sabine
Williams, E.	Nacogdoches	Williams, J. W.	Cass
Williams, E. A.	Fayette	Williams, J. W.	Jasper
Williams, E. H.	Galveston	Williams, J. W.	Montgomery
Williams, Elbert	Cherokee	Williams, Jackson	San Augustine
Williams, Eli	Harris	Williams, James	Henderson
Williams, Elijah	Nacogdoches	Williams, James	Panola
Williams, Elijah	Panola	Williams, James	Washington
Williams, Elisha	Harrison	Williams, James C.	Fannin
Williams, Elisha	Wharton	Williams, James H.	Lamar

NAME	COUNTY	NAME	COUNTY
Williams, James		Sylvester	Red River
W., Jr.	Sabine	Williams, T. H.	Fannin
Williams, James		Williams, Theodore	Galveston
W., Sr.	Sabine	Williams, Thomas	Cass
Williams, Jeremiah	San Augustine	Williams, Thomas	Fannin
Williams, Jessa	San Augustine	Williams, Thomas	Houston
Williams, Jesse	Brazoria	Williams, Thomas	Navarro
Williams, Jesse	Cass	Williams, Thomas	Polk
Williams, Job	Jackson	Williams, Thomas	Robertson
Williams, John	Fayette	Williams, Thomas	Rusk
Williams, John	Nacogdoches	Williams, Thomas	
Williams, John C.	Fannin	C.	Jasper
Williams, John D.	Hunt	Williams, Thomas	
Williams, John M.	Fannin	J.	Fayette
Williams, John S.	Cherokee	Williams, Thomas	
Williams, John V.	Polk	N.	Navarro
Williams, John W.	Lamar	Williams, W.	Cass
Williams, John W.	Panola	Williams, W.	Henderson
Williams, Jonathan	Milam	Williams, W.	Liberty
Williams, Joseph	Fannin	Williams, W. B.	Bowie
Williams, Josephus	Henderson	Williams, W. C.	Lamar
Williams, Josephus	Limestone	Williams, W. W.	Brazoria
Williams, Keeler	Fannin	Williams, W. W.	Montgomery
Williams, L. R.	Sabine	Williams, Wade H.	Fannin
Williams, Levy	Jackson	Williams, Warnell	Rusk
Williams, Lucinda	Rusk	Williams,	
Williams, M.	Wharton	Washington	Navarro
Williams, Malkyat	Jackson	Williams, William	Bastrop
Williams, Matthew	Galveston	Williams, William	Cass
Williams, Nancy	Wharton	Williams, William	Harrison
Williams, Oliver	Liberty	Williams, William	Lamar
Williams, P. G.	Fannin	Williams, William	Rusk
Williams, Parker	Brazoria	Williams, William	Rusk
Williams, Pat	Anderson	Williams, William	Sabine
Williams, Purvince	Panola	Williams, William	
Williams, R.	Montgomery	H.	Polk
Williams, R.	Upshur	Williams, Willis	Houston
Williams, R. H.	Matagorda	Williams, Wm.	Jasper
Williams, Reuben	Lamar	Williams, Wm. M.	Lamar
Williams, Richard	Newton	Williams, Wm. N.	Jasper
Williams, Robert		Williams, Young	Walker
L.	Newton	Williamson, C. J.	Jasper
Williams, Roderick	Navarro	Williamson, George	
Williams, Russell	Rusk	T.	DeWitt
Williams, S.	Fayette	Williamson, H.	Henderson
Williams, S. A.	San Augustine	Williamson, J. S.	Bexar
Williams, S. E.	Lamar	Williamson, Joseph	Rusk
Williams, S. M.	Galveston	Williamson, M. B.	Brazoria
Williams, Stephen	Jasper	Williamson, R. M.	Washington
Williams,		Williamson,	

NAME	COUNTY	NAME	COUNTY
Stephen Williamson,	Rusk	Wilson, Alex	Newton
		Wilson, Alph	Cass
William	Grayson	Wilson, Ann Eliza	Brazoria
Williamson, Wm. B.	Polk	Wilson, B. S.	Montgomery
Willingham, Alfred	Washington	Wilson, E. N.	Bastrop
Willingham,		Wilson, Ewing	San Augustine
Archibald	Washington	Wilson, Ezra	Rusk
Willingham, E.	San Augustine	Wilson, F.	San Augustine
Willingham, Edward	Henderson	Wilson, G. W.	Houston
Willingham, F. M.	Washington	Wilson, George	Lamar
Willie, James	Washington	Wilson, H. A.	Henderson
Willie, Thomas	Fayette	Wilson, H. A.	San Augustine
Willis, D.	Henderson	Wilson, Henriette	Red River
Willis, George	Calhoun	Wilson, Hugh	Washington
Willis, P. J.	Montgomery	Wilson, Ira L.	Washington
Willis, R. S.	Grimes	Wilson, J.	Collin
Willis, R. S.	Montgomery	Wilson, J. B.	Harrison
Willis, T. J.	Grimes	Wilson, J. E.	Robertson
Willke, H. H.	Comal	Wilson, J. H.	Collin
Willoughby, R.	Victoria	Wilson, J. S.	Bastrop
Willoughby,		Wilson, J. W.	Walker
Weipper	Fayette	Wilson, Jacob	Henderson
Wills, D. A.	Bastrop	Wilson, James	Collin
Wills, G. J.	Grimes	Wilson, James	Lamar
Wills, J. B.	Washington	Wilson, James	Walker
Wills, J. M.	Bastrop	Wilson, James C.	Brazoria
Wills, James A.	Rusk	Wilson, James T.	
Wills, James B.	Refugio	D.	Harris
Wills, John S.	Rusk	Wilson, Jason	Lamar
Wills, Peter	Rusk	Wilson, Jeremiah	Navarro
Wills, R. B.	Washington	Wilson, John	Cass
Wills, Reuben	Washington	Wilson, John	Cass
Wills, Sarah	Bastrop	Wilson, John	Lamar
Wills, W. F.	Bastrop	Wilson, John H.	San Augustine
Wills, William	Polk	Wilson, John R.	Harris
Willshire, Thomas		Wilson, John S.	Harrison
L.	Smith	Wilson, Joseph	Grayson
Willson, Andrew	Dallas	Wilson, Joseph E.	Brazoria
Willson, H.	Henderson	Wilson, L.	Grimes
Willson, J.	Hunt	Wilson, M.	Collin
Willson, Joseph L.	Fayette	Wilson, Mrs.	
Willson, Moses T.	Fayette	Martha	Harrison
Willson, Richard	Dallas	Wilson, Mary	Houston
Willson, Robert	Grayson	Wilson, Nathan B.	Burleson
Willson, Thomas	Titus	Wilson, P.	Collin
Wilmeth, H. C.	Collin	Wilson, Peter	Harris
Wilmeth, J. B.	Collin	Wilson, R. H.	Harrison
Wilson, A. Y.	Cherokee	Wilson, R. P.	Nacogdoches
Wilson, Aaron B.	Dallas	Wilson, Robert	Harris
Wilson, Alec	Tyler	Wilson, Robert	Tyler

NAME	COUNTY	NAME	COUNTY
Wilson, Robert F.	Nacogdoches	Johannes	Guadalupe
Wilson, S. P.	San Augustine	Wingfield, W. W.	Nacogdoches
Wilson, Samuel	Cass	Wingfield, Wm. W.	Henderson
Wilson, Samuel	Limestone	Wingo, J.	Navarro
Wilson, T. A.	Collin	Wink, Jesse	Anderson
Wilson, Thomas	Calhoun	Wink, Louis	Colorado
Wilson, Thomas	Cherokee	Winkler, David T.	Limestone
Wilson, Thomas D.	Harrison	Winkler, Jakol	Comal
Wilson, Thomas R.	Cass	Winkler, Thomas L.	Limestone
Wilson, Thomas R.	Titus	Winn, G. W.	Leon
Wilson, W.	Cass	Winn, James	Polk
Wilson, W.	Grayson	Winn, James	Rusk
Wilson, W. K.	Henderson	Winn, John A.	San Augustine
Wilson, W. L.	Nacogdoches	Winn, Peter	San Augustine
Wilson, W. S. G.	Milam	Winn & Mhoon	San Augustine
Wilson, Walker	Harrison	Winnie, Gilbert	Galveston
Wilson, William	Henderson	Winsor, Marstin	Harrison
Wilson, William	Jasper	Winters, Agabus	Brazoria
Wilson, William	Wharton	Winters, Andrew	Grayson
Wilson, William C.	Limestone	Winters, B. L.	Cass
Wilson, William F.	Colorado	Winters, James	Walker
Wilson, William J.	Grimes	Winters, John	Walker
Wilson, William K.	Harris	Winters, Mrs.	
Wilson, William L.	Harrison	Lavinia	Cass
Wilson, William N.	Harris	Winters, Orin	Walker
Wilson, William S.	Newton	Winters, W. B.	Cass
Wilson, Wm. C.	Washington	Winters, Wm.	Walker
Wiltshire, Ben	Sabine	Wirtzner,	
Wilver, Jasper	Henderson	Christian	Fayette
Wimberly, Warren	Washington	Wise, Carlos	Dallas
Wimley, James	Hunt	Wise, Henderson	Henderson
Winans, Francis	Bastrop	Wiseman, G. C.	Liberty
Windall, John A.	Rusk	Wiseman, Robert	Liberty
Windr, Christopher	Panola	Wisner, Wm.	Nacogdoches
Winburn, J. D.	Wharton	Witham, W. H. B.	Harris
Winburn, McHenry	Fayette	Withers, Charles	Shelby
Windham, J.	Angelina	Withers, Horace	Shelby
Windham, John	Angelina	Withers, James W.	Denton
Windham, Thomas	Angelina	Withers, Matthew	
Winfer, Amanda	Liberty	K.	Shelby
Winfer, J. F.	Liberty	Withers, V. J.	Shelby
Winfer, Julia A.	Liberty	Witherspoon,	
Winfer, T. B.	Liberty	Alexander	Panola
Winfer, T. G.	Liberty	Withery, William	
Winfield, Charles	Wharton	H.	Cass
Winfield, E. H.	Galveston	Withie, J. W.	Cass
Winfree, Abraham	Jefferson	Witt, A. J.	Lamar
Wingate, S. W.	Houston	Witt, H.	Collin
Wingate, William	Jefferson	Witt, John	Dallas
Wingeworth,		Witt, P.	Collin

NAME	COUNTY	NAME	COUNTY
Witt, Preston	Dallas	Wood, James H.	Fannin
Witt, W. H.	Dallas	Wood, John	San Patricio
Wittenton, W. M.	Victoria	Wood, John W.	Nacogdoches
Witter, M.	Henderson	Wood, L.	Henderson
Wittey, David	Fannin	Wood, L. L.	Montgomery
Wixon, Byrum	Grimes	Wood, Madison	Gonzales
Wofford, Daniel	Polk	Wood, Matthew	Rusk
Wofford, Elizabeth	Polk	Wood, Oliver H. P.	Grimes
Wofford, J. B.	San Augustine	Wood, Reuben D.	San Augustine
Wofford, J. C.	San Augustine	Wood, Robert	Grimes
Wofford, John	Grimes	Wood, Thomas	Cherokee
Wofford, William	San Augustine	Wood, Tilletson	Grimes
Woldert, George	San Augustine	Wood, Wm. H.	Montgomery
Wolff, Solomon	Angelina	Woodall, Thomas	Panola
Wolfe, Lewis	Sabine	Woodall, William	Panola
Wolfe, Theresa	Harris	Woodard, Felix G.	DeWitt
Wolfenbarger,		Woodard, Felix G.	Refugio
Samuel	Bastrop	Woodard, Jacob	Lavaca
Wolfin, John L.	Polk	Woodard, R. J.	Fayette
Wollen, Gwin	Lamar	Woodburn, John	Burleson
Wolls, Samuel G.	Anderson	Woodfer, Elizabeth	Shelby
Wolverton, Berel	Anderson	Woodford, E.	Matagorda
Wolverton, John	Anderson	Woodford, Wm.	Washington
Wolverton, T. L.	Limestone	Woodlan, Daniel	Nacogdoches
Wolverton, Thomas	Anderson	Woodley, William	Harrison
Wolverton, W.	Cass	Woodlief, Thomas	
Womack, Abram M.	Grimes	C.	Washington
Womack, Ann	Harrison	Woodruff, J. W.	Grimes
Womack, E. P.	Harrison	Woods, A. G.	Harrison
Womack, F. H.	Montgomery	Woods, A. H.	Harrison
Womack, George L.	Nacogdoches	Woods, Augustus H.	Washington
Womack, J. P.	Harrison	Woods, Caleb	Hopkins
Womack, Jacob	Harrison	Woods, D. R.	Anderson
Womack, Jesse	Montgomery	Woods, G. B.	Harrison
Womack, John	Panola	Woods, G. H.	Fayette
Womack, John	Polk	Woods, J. W.	Walker
Womack, John F.	Harrison	Woods, James	DeWitt
Womack, Lockey Ann	Harrison	Woods, John	Brazos
Womack, W. G.	Cass	Woods, John	Newton
Womack, Wm. T.	Harrison	Woods, John	Refugio
Wood, Brazellae	Grimes	Woods, John H.	Hopkins
Wood, Charles	Nacogdoches	Woods, Mrs. L.	Harrison
Wood, D. L.	Fayette	Woods, Margaret	Liberty
Wood, David	Rusk	Woods, Montiville	Fayette
Wood, Elihu	Shelby	Woods, N.	Fayette
Wood, Franklin	Lamar	Woods, S. J. R.	Harris
Wood, J. H.	Montgomery	Woods, Sebern	Newton
Wood, J. P.	Shelby	Woods, T.	Hunt
Wood, James	Grimes	Woods, Thomas	Bowie
Wood, James A.	Fannin	Woods, W. C.	Harrison

NAME	COUNTY	NAME	COUNTY
Woodson, William	Walker	Wortham, John	Houston
Woodward, A. B.	Montgomery	Wortham, L. M.	Harrison
Woodward, Elbert	Bexar	Wortham, R. M.	Lamar
Woodward, Haz.	Nacogdoches	Worthington,	
Woodward, James	Navarro	Chesly	Lamar
Woodward, John G.	Bexar	Wotin, La Comte	Bexar
Woodward, Sandford	Washington	Wren, Craig	Smith
Woodworth, H. D.	Lamar	Wren, E. H.	Hopkins
Woodyard, Walter	Panola	Wren, Johnson	Hopkins
Wooldridge, John	Travis	Wren, Nicholas	Smith
Wooldridge, E.	Lamar	Wright, A. W.	Lamar
Wooldridge, Wm.	Lamar	Wright, Alexander,	
Woolf, G. H.	Panola	Jr.	Jasper
Woolley, E. S.	Fayette	Wright, Alfred	Lamar
Woolsey, Abner	Wharton	Wright, Asa	San Augustine
Woolsey, E. R.	Wharton	Wright, C.	Upshur
Woolsey, Virgilla	Wharton	Wright, C. J.	Galveston
Woolwine, William	Rusk	Wright, Calvin	Grimes
Wooton, E. B.	Matagorda	Wright, D. R.	Galveston
Wooton, G. T.	Brazos	Wright, D. S.	Victoria
Wooton, Gilbert H.	Red River	Wright, E. B.	Lamar
Wooton, J. B.	Red River	Wright, Edward D.	DeWitt
Wooton, Moses	Shelby	Wright, Elijah	Colorado
Wooton, T. A.	Liberty	Wright, F. A.	Fannin
Wooton, Thomas	Jefferson	Wright, G. W.	Rusk
Wooton, W. W.	Bowie	Wright, G. W.	Victoria
Wooton, William	Smith	Wright, George	San Augustine
Wooton, William J.	Walker	Wright, George W.	Lamar
Worden, J.	Collin	Wright, H. P.	Nacogdoches
Worden, John	Liberty	Wright, Hansel	Rusk
Worden, John	San Augustine	Wright, Harden	Shelby
Worden, T. M.	Anderson	Wright, Henry	Anderson
Working, Elijah	Colorado	Wright, J. P.	Bowie
Worland, C. R.	Wharton	Wright, J. V.	Galveston
Worldley, Z.	Houston	Wright, James	Cherokee
Worley, A.	Montgomery	Wright, James	Victoria
Wornall, N. G.	Cass	Wright, John	Jasper
Wornell, R. W.	Cass	Wright, John M.	Lamar
Worrall, John	Brazoria	Wright, John W.	Dallas
Worsham, A. R.	Liberty	Wright, Johnson V.	Polk
Worsham, Elizabeth	Henderson	Wright, Lewis L.	Rusk
Worsham, Israel	Montgomery	Wright, M. H.	Fannin
Worsham, J.	Montgomery	Wright, Mahala	Houston
Worsham, J. L.	Montgomery	Wright, Moirah	Navarro
Worth, A.	Fannin	Wright, P.	Upshur
Worth, Joseph	Grimes	Wright, Ralph	Wharton
Wortham, C.	Lamar	Wright, Rufus	Harris
Wortham, James B.		Wright, S. D.	Bowie
G.	Lamar	Wright, S. J.	San Augustine
Wortham, James W.	Harrison	Wright, Sherrod	Jasper

NAME	COUNTY	NAME	COUNTY
Wright Solomon	Jasper	Yarbrough, Asa	Nacogdoches
Wright, T. G.	Red River	Yarbrough, G.	San Augustine
Wright, T. J.	Cass	Yarbrough, M.	Montgomery
Wright, W.	Navarro	Yarbrough, Richard	Shelby
Wright, W. F.	Lamar	Yarbrough, S.	Houston
Wright, Washington	Rusk	Yarbrough, William	Shelby
Wright, William	Anderson	Yard, N. B.	Galveston
Wright, Wilson	Bowie	Yarnell, Jesse	Panola
Wright, Winfield	Angelina	Yates, Albert	Fannin
Wright, Wm.	Galveston	Yates, G. W.	Houston
Wrightman, E.	Collin	Yates, L. T.	Liberty
Wrigley, J. W.	Liberty	Yates, Lewis	Hopkins
Wrigley, James	Liberty	Yates, Lewis	Lamar
Wroutt, G. W.	Liberty	Yates, Milton	Galveston
Wurt, Adam	Comal	Yates, Stephen	Nacogdoches
Wutrich, Ulrich	Travis	Yates, Thomas	Lamar
Wyatt, A.	Upshur	Yates, W. G.	Lamar
Wyatt, E. P.	Harrison	Yates, William	Fannin
Wyatt, J. W.	Washington	Yates, William	Lamar
Wyatt, Jordan	Fannin	Ybarbo, Canata	Nacogdoches
Wyatt, Robert	Panola	Ybarbo, Magil	Nacogdoches
Wyatt, S.	Upshur	Ybarbo, Manuel	Henderson
Wyatt, William	Panola	Yeaman, D.	Matagorda
Wybrants, S. M.	Walker	Yeaman, H.	Matagorda
Wyche, William P.	Henderson	Yeaman, J.	Matagorda
Wynn, Archibald	Harris	Yeaman, James A.	Galveston
Wynn, Devereaux	Nacogdoches	Yeary, David	Fannin
Wynn, G. L.	Lamar	Yeary, James	DeWitt
Wynn, Harmon	Grayson	Yeary, John	Fannin
Wynn, Obie K.	Colorado	Yeary, W. G.	Upshur
Wynn, R. J.	Cass	Yeary, Walter	Fannin
Wynn, Robert E.	Nacogdoches	Yeeser, D. H.	Brazoria
Wynn, W. H.	Lamar	Yewers, Albert	Jackson
Wynn, William B.	Rusk	Yewers, John	Jackson
Wyres, E.	Angelina	Yndo, Manuel	Bexar
Wyres, John	Dallas	Yndo, Miguil	Bexar
Wyse, James	Bowie	Yokum, Adam	Fannin
Wyse, Patience C.	Bowie	Yokum, H.	Walker
		York, Aaron	San Augustine
		York, Harison	Robertson
Ximenez, Maria	Nacogdoches	York, J. A.	Austin
		York, John	DeWitt
		York, L.	Henderson
Yakney, John	Rusk	York, Thomas	Austin
Yancy, Archelous	Nacobdoches	York, Wesley	Cass
Yancy, J.	Henderson	Young, A.	Angelina
Yancy, John	Rusk	Young, A. S.	Hopkins
Yancy, N. B.	Bastrop	Young, Alfred	Fayette
Yancy, S. M.	Upshur	Young, Caleb	Polk
Yandal, M.	Nacogdoches	Young, Charles	Austin

NAME	COUNTY	NAME	COUNTY
Young, Daniel	Harris	Youngblood, Isaac	Panola
Young, E.	Cass	Youngblood, J.	Victoria
Young, G. S.	Red River	Youngblood, J. J.	
Young, G. W.	Harrison	B.	Newton
Young, George	Montgomery	Youngblood, Polly	Newton
Young, George	Navarro	Youngblood,	
Young, Habin	Bexar	Richard	Newton
Young, Henry	Navarro	Youngblood, S. K.	Harrison
Young, Hu F.	Red River	Youree, James	Navarro
Young, Hugh B.	DeWitt	Yost, John	Panola
Young, James	Fayette	Yowell, Lindsey T.	Guadalupe
Young, James	Titus		
Young, James	Travis		
Young, James A.	Harris	Zachary, B. H.	Newton
Young, John	Dallas	Zasthtag, W. R.	Comal
Young, John L.	Washington	Zavalla, Francisco	Bexar
Young, Joseph	Bastrop	Zelinor, Francis	Jefferson
Young, Levi W.	Bastrop	Zepada, Juan	Bexar
Young, Mary	Red River	Zepada, Manuel	Bexar
Young, Mary	Walker	Zerda, Nemacio	Bexar
Young, Mary M.	Harrison	Zilla, M.	Travis
Young, Michael	Bastrop	Zilphy, M.	Lavaca
Young, N. A.	Rusk	Zink, Nicholas	Comal
Young, P. S.	Leon	Zimmerman, E.	Anderson
Young, Peter	Houston	Zimmerman, J. M.	Washington
Young, Pleasant	Henderson	Zimmerman, James	Bexar
Young, Pleasant	Walker	Zimmerman, Joseph	Bexar
Young, Richard	Houston	Zimmerman,	
Young, Samuel	Fayette	Theobald	Bexar
Young, Samuel L.	Harrison	Zuber, Abram	Grimes
Young, W. C.	Red River	Zuber, William T.	Grimes
Young, William	Bowie	Zumwalt, Adam	Gonzales
Young, William	Fayette	Zumwalt, Adam	Lavaca
Young, William	Harrison	Zumwalt, Andrew	Lavaca
Young, William	Houston	Zumwalt, Gabriel	Lavaca
Young, William	Navarro	Zumwalt, Hancy	Lavaca
Young, William	Washington	Zumwalt, Jane C.	Gonzales
Young, William J.	Polk	Zurcher, Nicholas	Comal
Youngblood, A. J.	Polk	Zuschlag, Henry	Comal
Youngblood, D. H.	Newton